ANDREW SINCLAIR

War Like a Wasp

The Lost Decade of the 'Forties

Hamish Hamilton · London

HAMISH HAMILTON LTD

Published by the Penguin Group, 27 Wrights Lane,
London W8 5TZ, England
Viking Penguin Inc., 40 West 23rd Street, New York,
New York 10010, USA
Penguin Books Australia Ltd, Ringwood, Victoria, Australia
Penguin Books Canada Ltd, 2801 John Street, Markham, Ontario,
Canada L3R 1B4
Penguin Books (NZ) Ltd, 182–190 Wairau Road, Auckland 10,
New Zealand

Penguin Books Ltd, Registered Offices: Harmondsworth,
Middlesex, England

First published in Great Britain by Hamish Hamilton Ltd 1989

Copyright © Andrew Sinclair, 1989

Designed by Craig Dodd
Typeset in Ehrhardt by Wyvern Typesetting Ltd, Bristol

Printed in Great Britain by Butler and Tanner Ltd, Frome and
London

A CIP catalogue record for this book is available from the British
Library

ISBN 0-241-12531-6

To Sonia

And I say to you who have seen
war like a wasp under a warm apple
rise and sting the unwary,
that its breed shall multiply
and fill the air with wings, and dapple
disaster on the bright sky,
and worse things shall be than have been.

But there shall yet be better.

JOHN BAYLISS

From 'Epilogue: Testament and Prophecy'

CONTENTS

A Finch's The One Tun
B L'Étoile
C Schmidt's
D The Duke of York
E Bertorelli's
F Plumbing Supplies
G The Fitzroy Tavern
H Pogiolli's
I The Marquis of Granby
J Le Tour Eiffel
K Madame Buhler's First
L The Wheatsheaf
M The Bricklayer's Arms
N Winsor & Newton
O The Black Horse
P W. R. Loftus

FITZROVIA

PART OF SOHO

Q "The Two-thirty House"
R The Highlander
S The Pillars of Hercules
T The Shanghai
U Bakery
V All Night Café
W The Gargoyle Club
X The Mandrake Club
Y Patisserie Valerie
Z The Swiss
AA Madame Buhler's Second Café
BB F. Denny, outfitters for Chefs and Waiters
CC The York Minster
DD St. Anne's
EE Zwemmer's Bookshop
FF The Colony Club

Ruthven Todd's map of the haunts of the Fitzrovians.

PROLOGUE

The decade of the nineteen-forties led to a sea-change in the arts in Britain. Because of their war experience, established artists altered their perceptions and found new means of expression. Unknown artists from the armed forces and civil defence discovered fresh outlets during the only democratic and popular decade of modern British culture. The war years saw T. S. Eliot write the last three of his *Four Quartets*, Henry Moore produce his Shelter drawings, Joyce Cary publish his major trilogy ending with *The Horse's Mouth*; the post-war years saw Evelyn Waugh's first serious novels after *Brideshead Revisited*, Francis Bacon painting his three figures at the base of a Crucifixion, major compositions from Benjamin Britten, the theatrical language of John Gielgud and Laurence Olivier and Ralph Richardson, and the apogee of British cinema with its documentaries and Ealing comedies. The state aid that would transform the arts in Britain also began at this time. These were the *anni mirabiles* of a national culture.

This flowering of the arts coalesced round the pubs and drinking clubs of Fitzrovia and Soho and Chelsea. Owing to shortages of alcohol, the pub became the centre of social life. The Wheatsheaf and the Marquis of Granby, the Swiss and the French pubs saw the encounters of most of the leading writers and painters and actors and film-makers and musicians of their day. These were the Fitzrovians, brought together in a transient bohemia, encouraged and interrupted by the circumstances of the war. The many millions of the armed forces, both Allied and British, passed through London on leave before embarkation or demobilization. If they had things to express, they went to the places where they might meet their fellow artists. Bloomsbury committed suicide with Virginia Woolf in 1941. The Fitzrovians bloomed under the blitz and the black-out, conscription and rationing, the fear of sudden death and the snatch at urgent life. In the intellectual and alcoholic ferment of a London group which split and congealed nightly, some extraordinary poetry and painting, drama and cinema were created that still inform us all.

The Fitzrovians have not been considered as a literary group because they did not keep together. War conditions and drink restrictions forced them to meet in the clubs and the pubs; but when drink became available in the home and prices rose in London, they dispersed in the main in the early 'fifties. They were a loose coterie for a decade, not permanent as was the Bloomsbury group. Their chief editor undervalued them – Cyril Connolly in *Horizon* put his own failure as a writer of masterpieces on to his whole generation. This allowed the culture of the war decade to be trashed as neo-Romantic and of no importance. It sank without trace between the Scylla and Charybdis of modernism and post-modernism. These two arbitrary labels consigned a period of creative genius to the depths of irrelevant insignificance.

Actually, modernism does not exist except in the terminology of modern critics. It is merely a category attached to some pioneers in the arts experimenting in form and sensibility at the turning and toward the middle of this century. 'Just as every attempt to define modern poetry must be regarded as a blackboard exercise, to be erased as soon as completed,' T. S. Eliot wrote in 1941, 'so every attempt to appraise the value of modern poetry as a whole is meaningless.' To advise or disparage or label the work of a period was of no meaning. Every age got the art it deserved, and every age had to accept the art it got. To arraign a generation of writers was merely bad sociology. Eliot was correct. Experiments in language and music and painting and drama and cinema, in perception and in psychology have continued throughout the twentieth century, and the present convention that they should be called modern or post-modern or contemporary is arbitrary and meaningless. Most artists are modernists. Experiments continue. We go on living in modern times.

After walking through the glass-strewn streets of London during the blitz, the influential critic Herbert Read reflected that the war machine was absorbing the artists and the writers and the producers of culture. But the previous world war had accelerated and intensified in the arts a reckless spirit of experiment and adventure. This world war would also affect the arts in the same way or civilization would die. 'The modern movement has its roots far back in the nineteenth century; it is only modern in the sense that modern science is modern, or modern political theory.' Read was also correct. There was a reckless spirit of experiment and adventure in the arts of the nineteen-forties. The language of *The Horse's Mouth* was as insurrectionary as that of *Finnegans Wake*. The iconography of Francis Bacon's paintings exhibited at the Hanover Gallery in 1949 showed the most revolutionary and wrenching images of the century. War conditions fed a resistance to the present world, a sense of loss and alienation – this was the decade of the holocaust and the atomic bomb. The burden of revolt against a mechanical age was never halted. Technology more than human beings decided the outcome of the conflict, as nuclear fission demonstrated. There was no break in the continuity of modern culture in the nineteen-forties, only the acceleration of an artistic rebellion against a vocabulary and a perception that seemed inadequate to define society or to distance the self from the historical processes of the time.

Unfortunately, the important culture and experiments of the war decade fell into a trench between categories invented by critics of literature and art. The tendency of the champions of modernism and structuralism to discount the influence on literature of history and background made the texts of the period seem unworthy of study because they were so much influenced by war conditions. Their provenance was their nemesis. Their significance was discounted as a mere product of the time, itself held to be of little value. Modern studies condemn the nineteen-forties as 'a vacancy in recent cultural history'. The period has become a lost decade in critical perception. Yet these were the years of some fifty million deaths through global war, of the holocaust and the atomic bomb, and of the beginning of the age of computers. Were there really no experimental works capable of describing the period or the alienation from it? Were these ten years a wasteland of the arts, an arid decade? Was there, as Adorno said, no poetry after Auschwitz?

There was, as this book will seek to show. War and post-war conditions led to an extraordinary contact between all sorts of artists, to a rare period of democratic British culture, and to a radical change in the perceptions and work of both established and fresh creators. Poetry was particularly the language of the period – the poetry of a multitude of voices. It was popular, it was read, it was a true commentary on the time. The poets were the best witnesses. But the artists of the lost decade were the victims of convenient, although mistaken, categories and of the false reports written on them by their disillusioned editors and later critics. Their neo-Romantic works were as true in their descriptions as their realistic or laconic ones. These were statements of their experience, stimulated by war. These were different approaches to the truth, and by these creations, you shall know them. In my view, the anecdotal illustrates the critical and the analytical; I have tried to give full weight to all the evidence in an endeavour to describe the period as far as possible in the words and acts of those who were then and there.

Andrew Sinclair

Osbert Lancaster's cartoon of Fitzrovia for *Horizon*

ONE

When the War Came

Leonard Rosoman

'There is only one way of avoiding cliques,' Geoffrey Grigson wrote in the final issue of *New Verse*, '– to have your own cliques. Only you must make sure that your clique is a clique of the best and the truest and most lively writers of the time.' The London quarter of Bloomsbury gave its name to one important clique between the two world wars, but its members were hardly bohemians. They were upper middle-class with aristocratic and Cambridge University connections. They had private incomes and the advice of the economist John Maynard Keynes on their investments. They owned a small publishing house, the Hogarth Press, which printed the prose and illustrations of some of the group, notably of Virginia Woolf, the wife of the proprietor. They were influential in philosophy and economics, art and literary criticism. And they promoted and loved one another, bisexually and promiscuously. Their legend still grows, although by 1939 their influence was already on the wane.

To the west of Bloomsbury on the other side of Tottenham Court Road and to the east of Upper Regent Street and the British Broadcasting Corporation and the Ministry of Information lies northern Fitzrovia. It is a marginal area of hospitals, the rag trade, small businesses, good pubs and ethnic restaurants flanking Charlotte Street. Southern Fitzrovia lies below Oxford Street and carries the name of Soho after a hunting call 'So-ho' once shrieked to Jacobean hounds. In the nineteen-thirties, northern Fitzrovia became the bohemia of London, snatching the reputation from Chelsea and attracting to its pubs and restaurants many of the artists and writers and provincial aspirants of the time. The converging and swirling and splitting groups in the Fitzroy Tavern and the Marquis of Granby, the Wheatsheaf and the Bricklayer's Arms, the Eiffel and the White Towers, were the bohemians of the city and period. They were what the poet John Heath-Stubbs called them – the overspill from Bloomsbury.

The life of urban bohemians was first described by Henri Mürger, whose scenes of their life in Paris in the eighteen-thirties were used as the libretto for Puccini's *La Bohème*. In his introduction to his book, Mürger distinguished between amateur bohemians, who liked the style of life but were rich enough to avoid the consequences, and deluded bohemians, who were not dedicated to the arts but to their own self-destruction for a chimera. Their axiom was that Bohemia was not a way but a cul-de-sac. True bohemians were called or elected to the arts. They lived between two abysses – poverty and doubt. Their everyday survival was a work of genius, a daily problem that they managed always to resolve with the help of audacious mathematics. The American poet George Sterling agreed in his definition of the two elements essential to the true bohemian. 'The first is devotion or addiction to one or more of the Seven Arts; the other is poverty. I like to think of my Bohemians as young, as radical in their outlook on art and life, as unconventional.'

The kings and queens of pre-war Fitzrovia attracted the young and the radical and the unconventional, who provided their bed-fellows and beer-money. When he was not roistering in Chelsea, the ageing painter Augustus John often went to the Wheatsheaf, where he mesmerized the young Dylan Thomas up from Wales and introduced him to the ravishing Caitlin Macnamara, later the poet's wife, but immediately his passionate mistress at the Eiffel Tower hotel with the bill charged to John. The aged painter paid £43 for his next lunch at the Eiffel Tower. 'Little Welshman with curly hair,' the proprietor Stulik explained. 'He stay two weeks and eat. He says you pay.' And John did pay, swearing to settle the score with Dylan. But other Fitzrovians settled for him, displaying the envy current among the rival lords of the local pubs. 'John, a great fornicator,' the poet John Gawsworth wrote in his diary, 'is disgusted at the betrayal by Dylan Thomas who, he says, robs his £3-in-Post-Office mistresses of their honest earnings, drinks the cash, and leaves the c—t ... Sexually speaking and economically, I suspect A. J. in his early days went further than the absurd Thomas: i.e. spent the contents of the P. O. Book but, being far from impotent, presented a bastard in exchange ... A. J. is a God, D. T. is verbal D.Ts, anaemic diarrhoea, a Welsh slag-heap.'

There was competition and judgement between the *habitués* of Fitzrovia. One denizen, Philip O'Connor, declared that the uprooted artists were babies, prattling themselves into worlds of great achievements. Yet they never delivered anything except disasters, while they watched, sportingly, out for each other's blood. A queen of the Wheatsheaf, the painter Nina Hamnett, described the decline of the area before the outbreak of the Second World War. The news circulated that it was the only quarter in London where drinks were cheap and people amusing. The old inhabitants did not like being gazed at like so many wild animals, and Nina resented the competition of grubby medical and art students sketching the regular drinkers so that she could not.

The reputation of Fitzrovia, however, attracted wealthy young misfits from Oxford and Cambridge, and O'Connor remembered the regulars clustering round the undergraduates like wasps round a jam-pot, driving them away quickly with needs and stings. He thought there were two neighbouring bohemias with Bloomsbury representing the rich one, even though there was no true bohemia for the rich, only the illusion of playing the gypsy artist over a safety-net of privilege set firmly in place. Through love affairs and a marriage to a wealthy and demented woman, O'Connor himself had connections with Bloomsbury as well as Fitzrovia, but he admitted that contacts between them were infrequent. Income was the frontier. To him, 'Fitzrovia was a national social garbage centre. But its inhabitants had the sweetness as well as the gameness of humanity gone off. They lived a life of pretence among themselves, and the successful ones pretended also to become outsiders, leaving the district to slander it.'

Before the war, the artistic and radical political life of Britain was managed from a small part of Central London to the east of Fitzrovia. The left-leaning publishers and magazines and meeting-places ran down from Bloomsbury to Holborn and Covent Garden. There were Jonathan Cape's in Bedford Square and the Hogarth Press in Tavistock Square; the Workers' Bookshop and *Left Review* in Theobald's Road; the *New Statesman* in Great Turnstile Street and the Arts Café and publishers and bookshops in Red Lion Square and in Red Lion and Parton Streets. On the fringes of Fitzrovia were the Group Theatre in Great Newport Street and Collet's Bookshop in the Charing Cross Road, where the 'Bomb Shop' had been. In King and Henrietta Streets were located the Communist Party headquarters and Victor Gollancz and the Left Book Club. Although the documentary film-makers were grouped round Soho Square and the fund-raising events for the Republican cause during the Spanish war took place in the restaurants of Greek and Frith Streets in Soho, socialist politics and the arts centred on Bloomsbury and Holborn in the nineteen-thirties. Even John Gawsworth and his romantic literary group of adventurers and novelists and poets including T. E. Lawrence and Arthur Machen and Patrick Kavanagh and Dylan Thomas met in Henekey's in the 'Holborn Republic', as the traveller Tschiffely called it in his *Bohemia Junction*. But the disillusion of the fellow-travellers at the time of the Nazi-Soviet pact and the declaration of the Second World War finally shifted the bohemian frontier from the red dawn of eastern Central London westward across the Tottenham and Charing Cross Roads. Northern and southern Fitzrovia were to take in the burned idealists of the failed revolution.

The bohemians could not be independent. They had to scrounge. Even the most determined of the *enfants terribles* such as Dylan Thomas depended on powerful patronage to survive. He might complain to his fellow Fitzrovian Rayner Heppen-stall that he was tired of sleeping with pub women he didn't even like, but he was prepared to pay court to one necessary literary lady, the formidable Edith Sitwell. With her brothers Osbert and Sacheverell, she formed an alternative to Bloomsbury, based on Osbert's ornate home in Carlyle Square in Chelsea and on the sea-green melancholia of the dining-room at the ladies' Sesame, Lyceum and Imperial Pioneer Club. Before the war, Edith Sitwell took up the cudgels for Thomas's surreal and romantic early poetry, causing a rift with the acidulous critic, Geoffrey Grigson, whose magazine *New Verse* was a bardic barometer. A Sitwell dinner at the Sesame with Dylan and Robert Herring, the editor of *Life and Letters*, went almost too well. According to Edith, Dylan behaved beautifully, 'like a son with his mother'. It could not last; Fitzrovia and the other Bloomsbury of the Sitwells mixed like fire and ether. Soon Edith was giving Dylan 'an awful ticking-off' because he had been rude to Augustus John about Caitlin Macnamara – the aged painter ended by knocking down the young poet in a Carmarthen car park. And Dylan was read out of his patroness's patience. She could feel the tips of her fingers tingling to come into contact with the lobes of his ears. 'And it would do him a lot of good, for he was evidently insufficiently corrected as a child.'

Class barriers and expectations still divided rich and poor bohemians as well as the patrons of the arts. Two important salons at the time were run by the titled Emerald Cunard and Sibyl Colefax. Both had dreams of establishing an artistic English Versailles, which were dispelled by the abdication of King Edward the Eighth. Emerald felt personally abandoned, wailing, 'How could he do this to me?' while an anonymous couplet commented:

The Ladies Colefax and Cunard
Took it very, very hard.

Deprived of an artistic centre at court and bombed out of her house in Grosvenor Square, Lady Cunard was to supervise her gatherings of musicians (Sir Thomas Beecham was her permanent admirer) and politicians and writers from her suites in the wartime Ritz and Dorchester hotels. Lady Colefax operated from a *bijou* house in North Street, sending to current celebrities her indecipherable invitations to her passionless and ghastly functions, which she knew her guests in a way hated. Outside Fitzrovia, the two hostesses were the foci of those artists who wanted the accolade of London society and could survive its scrutiny.

One group knew each other from their schooldays and bridged the gap between a classical education and modern times, between the salons and the pubs, between the rich and the poor bohemians. These were the Old Etonian editors and novelists, who hid their origins under discarded old school ties. 'One in five of the major novelists of this century', Anthony Powell once said, 'was an Etonian.' The list was impressive. Osbert and Sacheverell Sitwell, indeed; Aldous Huxley and Anthony Powell himself; Henry Yorke alias Henry Green and Eric Blair alias George Orwell; and, in their way, Peter and Ian Fleming. The littérateurs and critics and occasional poets and editors were as impressive. Harold Acton and the epicene Brian Howard; Alan Pryce-Jones of *The Times Literary Supplement* and the publisher Rupert Hart-Davis and John Strachey; and the dominant magazine editors of the Second World War, John Lehmann at Penguin *New Writing* and Cyril Connolly at *Horizon*. When the philosopher Freddie Ayer, the theatrical afflatus George 'Dadie' Rylands, the designer Oliver Messel and the art patron Peter Watson were added to the list, Eton seemed a modern pantheon despite its reputation for playing-fields. Connolly's denunciation of the values of his old school in *Enemies of Promise* seemed to describe only his own indolence and self-despair, not the success of his colleagues in their artistic endeavours. This uncommon education was a picklock to every literary door and group in London. The Cambridge puritan critic F. R. Leavis's wife Queenie was not wrong when she wrote a review of *Enemies of Promise* in 1939 in *Scrutiny*: 'The odious spoilt little boys of Mr Connolly's and so many other writers' schooldays move in a body up to the universities to become pretentious young men, and, still essentially unchanged, from there move into the literary quarters vacated by the last batch of their kind.'

The cross-connections of those with a privileged education were illuminating and important for the culture of the war decade to come. John Lehmann worked with the Hogarth Press and knew the Bloomsbury group as well as the Sitwells, whom Cyril Connolly called 'an alternative Bloomsbury'. Edith Sitwell was particularly a champion of T. S. Eliot and promoted other new poets through him in the publishing house of Faber & Faber as well as in the magazine he edited, the *Criterion*, closed by him in 1939 with the comment that a very small number of people indeed might have to maintain the continuity of culture. Anthony Powell worked at Duckworth's and tried to arrange to publish Evelyn Waugh, a friend 17 from Oxford, which formed with Cambridge the privileged university background for most of the radical poets and writers of the nineteen-thirties – as the fading Virginia Woolf commented, the young Oxbridge radical sat and judged society and Bloomsbury from a leaning tower 'built first on his parents' station, then upon his parents' gold'. After the failure of *Living*, Henry Green eventually sent another novel, *Party Going*, to John Lehmann, and the Hogarth Press duly published it in 1939. Even that mock proletarian, George Orwell, was frequently printed by *Horizon* and *New Writing* and lunched weekly in wartime with Anthony Powell on synthetic Victory Pie. His editor at Secker & Warburg was also Connolly's, Roger Senhouse, a fellow Etonian and a lover of Lytton Strachey. The literary evenings given by Lehmann or Connolly outshone the gatherings given by the two Ladies Cunard and Colefax during the hostilities, and Evelyn Waugh could congratulate Connolly for claiming that the civilians had the worst of the war and for 'making a delightful salon for men on leave, giving them a further choice than Emerald's oven or Sibyl's frigidaire'.

The London rendezvous of littérateurs and artists in the pre-war years were governed by the whims of the proprietors as well as the incomes of the guests. The Cavendish hotel in Jermyn Street was the most raffish and elegant of its time. It was run on double standards by King Edward the Seventh's mistress Rosa Lewis, who was the Robin Hood of the hotel trade – the rich paid the bills of the poor young men she fancied. 'Half an unashamed knocking-shop,' a contemporary writer described it, 'but parsons would come there.' Aristocratic families kept their own suites of rooms on the premises; Anthony Eden was born in the Cavendish. Everybody who was anybody, Lemuel Gulliver declared in *Lilliput*, went to be seen or unseen there. The hotel was run for men and the women the men wanted. Rosa Lewis thought little of modern girls, saying they only came in to have a pee and pick someone up. Evelyn Waugh caricatured the Cavendish in *Vile Bodies* and was never forgiven by Rosa Lewis, who preferred painters like Augustus John and William Orpen and Alfred Munnings to writers who might mock her aristocratic manner and pungent cockney vocabulary. Anthony Powell, however, was a welcome visitor. He commented that the difference between the Cavendish and the Eiffel Tower restaurant was that the former put the emphasis on the Brigade of Guards rather than artists, though both elements might merge in drifting scenes of a semi-smart, semi-bohemian world.

The large red brasserie of the Café Royal off Piccadilly Circus had been the traditional meeting-place of wealth and bohemia since the eighteen-nineties, when Oscar Wilde and Lord Alfred Douglas and their friends, both high and low, had ruled the floor of the café and the balcony above. The memory of that decadent decade attracted all those who wished to meet artists and had the money to pay for it. The painters were there many evenings, Matthew Smith and Paul Nash, Epstein and Bomberg, the composer Constant Lambert and Cyril Connolly and the gigantic poet Anna Wickham, who bit people's heads and tried to pull off the breasts of other women, when she was provoked. Her poetry, edited by John

18

Gawsworth, contained 'The Sick Assailant', with lines such as 'I hit her in the face because she loved me; it was her sticky, irritating patience moved me.' Or in 'Pugilist':

> My mind is dull with fullness, yet I know
> I have one utter need –
> To find a foe!
> I will strip off this fine constricting coat
> And grip Necessity by his thin throat.

European refugees liked the style of the Café Royal, and Kerensky and Arthur Koestler were often there. Geoffrey Grigson might meet his contributors to his influential *New Verse* in the brasserie, for he was an editor who knew the power of incestuous groups. They were, as one publisher thought, 'as permanent a feature of the place as the pillars and the marble-topped tables'. But the coming of the war added to their numbers. Hundreds of young strangers arrived, looking for a Saturday night spree. 'The great room seemed suspended under a pall of smoke. It floated like seaweed, swaying this way and that; it floated above the uncertainty about what was happening outside. So many fresh young faces, barometers for so many intelligent minds, but not one showed fear or dejection. Not one showed belligerency either, nor indifference: what they showed was life – keen, pulsing life.'

The Café Royal of the night-clubs was the Gargoyle located on the top floor of a Meard Street house off Dean Street in Soho. Two large murals by Matisse hung on the walls and access was by a coffin large enough for two, which was called the lift. Its members included princes and aristocrats, actors and rich painters and writers – King Carol of Romania and Adele Astaire, Lucian Freud and John Minton and Evelyn Waugh and even bohemians in the diplomatic and intelligence services, Donald Maclean and Guy Burgess and Brian Howard, who once told the heterosexual poet Ruthven Todd at the Gargoyle bar what was wrong with a book of his poems. 'The trouble, my dear, is that you're not one of *us*.' Recollections of drunken evenings clustered round the Gargoyle giving it almost Proustian reverberations – Remembrance of Time Pissed. There the wealthy Minton would sit looking like an El Greco and surrounded by sailors in uniform, complaining, 'I'm only liked because I'm rich,' and then adding, 'I can buy anyone I want.'

Later in the 'forties, beside the Gargoyle the Mandrake appeared, a basement club run by the unkempt Boris Watson, who had run the Coffee An' and now advertised London's Only Bohemian Rendezvous. It had tables for playing chess; but its self-consciousness was its nemesis. But the Cavendish of the night-clubs was the Café de Paris off Leicester Square, where the wealthy bohemians danced to the music of Ken 'Snakehips' Johnson and his black band, or sat in the high balcony looking down at the jigging packed floor below. The Café de Paris was the only night spot to suffer a direct hit in the blitz: its cavern became a bomb crater. But the other popular clubs, Murray's and the Embassy and the Orchid Room, the

Havana and the Coconut Grove, the Cosmo and the Cabaret, the 400 and the Paradise with its nightly 'Blitz Reunion Party', the Horseshoe and the Colony, the Jamboree and the Nest and the Suivi were spared destruction. In their dim and dense atmosphere, which writers like Peter Quennell found to be semi-solid towards the end of the night, weird and monotonous chants gave the impression of a barbaric tribal ceremony. At the Nut-house in Kingly Street in Soho, the packed revellers used to yell rhythmically the chorus of the proprietor's nightly doggerel:

> You push the damper in
> And you push the damper out
> And the smoke goes up the chimney
> All the same!

After two visits to the Nest, Anthony Powell's wife, Lady Violet, had to have her dress cleaned because it smelt so appalling from the thick atmosphere which spread itself on clothes. But 'Fats' Waller sometimes played piano there, and it was the only jazz club in London where blacks and whites mixed freely.

The Hungaria in Regent Street was the counter-attraction to the Café Royal. Its host Joseph Vecci had run restaurants in Berlin and St Petersburg and Kiev, and he knew his trade, attracting particularly the writers and artists who were to work in British intelligence during the war. He converted the basement grillroom into a restaurant shelter where the diners and dancers could sleep overnight on couches during air raids – Hatchett's and the Lansdowne, the Mayfair and Grosvenor House did the same, while the Savoy had shelters in the wine-cellars, although later, during the flying bomb raids, the Hungaria proved more popular than the Savoy, which was thought to be on the flight path of the V1's down the Thames. The fear of being bombed was temporarily to empty the clubs and dining-places early in the war, until Londoners grew used to the risk. At the Milroy, a trick was used to pretend the night-club was safely underground. The tiny lift was marked *Basement*, although it actually rose to the third floor as at the Gargoyle.

Yet the heart of bohemian London after the outbreak of the Second World War was to be Fitzrovia and its pubs. Because of the shortage of drink and the fear of dying alone during the air raids and the need of men on leave to meet their friends in recognized places, the pubs of central London were a magnet. The first literary discovery of the war, the short-story writer Julian Maclaren-Ross, is the guide to that territory in his *Memoirs of the Forties*. After his discharge from the army for psychiatric reasons, he was in the Swiss pub in Old Compton Street in Soho, where he was approached by the extraordinary Tamil poetry editor Tambimuttu, who had something of the snake-charmer, was dressed in a blue overcoat buttoned to the chin and was surrounded by acolytes. He had begun *Poetry London* in 1938 with an attack on the diseased and emasculated public-school mind of other poets and critics and editors. 'The man who decries the praise of beauty or love is a pervert, an intellectual, a more than dead rabbit. Bury him.' To Maclaren-Ross, his approach was different. 'You must meet people,' Tambimuttu declared, 'and it is better you meet them under my aegis ... Only beware of Fitzrovia. It's a dangerous place, you must be careful.'

'Fights with knives?'

'No, a worse danger. You might get Sohoitis you know.'

'No, I don't. What is it?'

'If you get Sohoitis, you will stay there always day and night and get no work done ever. You have been warned ... Now we will go to the Black Horse, the Burglar's Rest, the Marquis of Granby, the Wheatsheaf, then the Beer House and after 10.30 back to the Highlander which closes later at eleven and after this eat curries in St. Giles's High or steak at the Coffee An'.'

So Julian Maclaren-Ross was introduced to Fitzrovia. The coming of the war was creating new peers and arbiters in literary and artistic London. For paper was being restricted as well as drink, while conscription was thinning the ranks of those prepared to serve as well as scribble. Tambimuttu was backed by the publishing firm of Nicholson & Watson, which had access to paper supplies. He set up Editions Poetry London on the principle that 'there was no nonsense about regionalism or Liverpool or Salford being the centre of the arts, London was the centre and that was bloody well that.' He supplemented the occasional publishing of two other strange regulars of Fitzrovia, David Archer of the Parton Press, whose four books were to be the first poems of Dylan Thomas and George Barker and David Gascoyne and W. S. Graham, and also the spidery Caton of the Fortune Press, printers of erotica as well as excellent new poetry. The other new editor of the time was the introspective Charles Wrey Gardiner, a landlord who looked like a rent-collector, but who was convinced of his own genius, although fellow poets thought that his verses never deviated into sense. He seemed nebulous and was said to vanish if the observer took an aspirin, but he possessed a rare gargoyle wit. As the editor of *Poetry Quarterly* and publisher of the Grey Walls Press, staffed entirely by poets, Gardiner supported neo-Romantic or unknown poets with fine catholicity and disdain for the established. He declared the importance of the nineteen-forties, saying wrongly that it would live in history like Wilde's London of the 'nineties or Bloomsbury of the 'twenties. Yet his self-despair was stronger than his recognition of the period which he influenced. He wrote in his final auto-biography with his usual gnomic pronouncements:

The mania of decades is no more stupid than the passion of sailors for the exactitude of latitudes which only exist in the minds of the makers of maps. The French created a white painted board on one of the north-south tracks across the Sahara marked Tropic of Cancer. It didn't last long. The blinding wind or a few passing Tuareg uprooted it and now you are as many hours from an oasis or death as all the Capricorns and Cancers ever calculated in their armchairs in Paris or London.

Although Faber & Faber still had large quantities of paper available, due to their patriotic foresight in publishing sixteen books of covert propaganda for the Ministry of Information, their dominant editor T. S. Eliot was considered too   21 right-wing and reactionary for the times. Although he did his duty fire-watching from the roof of the publishing house in Russell Square, meeting the local cats which he had immortalized in his *Old Possum's Book* about them, his influence was in decline, even if he was personally to write superior poetry under war conditions, the later of the *Four Quartets*. His little magazine the *Criterion* had collapsed with eleven others including the venerable *Cornhill Magazine*, *New Stories*, *New Verse*, *Fact*, *Seven*, *London Mercury* and *Twentieth Century Verse*. Their places were being taken by a host of other small magazines and anthologies, which were favoured in their paper requirement by the civil servants because they printed many points of view rather than one. Although John Lehmann's *New Writing* and Penguin *New Writing* and Cyril Connolly's *Horizon* kept editorial power in privileged hands, John Waller's *Kingdom Come* and George Woodcock's *Now* and Keidrych Rhys's editions of poetry from the forces joined Tambimuttu and Wrey Gardiner in providing outlets for neo-Romantic and new writers, as did *Lilliput*, a popular success as much for its sketches and articles as for its surreal photographs and discreet nudes.

The neo-Romantic poets had an influence in the late 'thirties, particularly George Barker and David Gascoyne and the young Dylan Thomas. They were not only reacting from the pervasive influence of Wystan Auden's work – or so Stephen Spender said – but they were reacting to a time when it was no longer possible to imagine that by understanding events they could diagnose a disease and point to a cure. That had been the delusion of the dominant literary movement before the war, which Cyril Connolly thought was more ambitious, more organized and more popular than any since the Lake Poets. Two school friends, Auden and Christopher Isherwood, had formed a group with new friends at university, Cecil Day Lewis and Louis MacNeice and Stephen Spender at Oxford, and Rex Warner and John Lehmann at Cambridge. All of them shared beliefs in the Marxist class struggle and anti-fascism, which answered a deep public need. There was an extraordinary cohesion and collaboration among them. *New Verse* and *New Writing* published their poems, Benjamin Britten wrote their music, while they monopolized the Hogarth Press and the Group Theatre. Their output was a heavy industry, ended by the rise of Hitler. The defeat of the Republican Spanish government, the appeasement at Munich and the cynicism of the Nazi-Soviet pact which led to the outbreak of the Second World War and the partition of Poland destroyed a literary movement that believed in a brave new socialist world. The decision of Auden and Isherwood to emigrate like Aldous Huxley to the safety of the United States of America before the coming of the war which they had predicted, did untold harm to their cause in embattled Britain. Their commitment in the 'thirties now seemed a defection or a delusion. As Nicolas Bentley wrote:

> Auden and Isherwood went to sea
> In a beautiful pea-soup fog ...

22 Cyril Connolly considered that the whole output of this young movement had

delivered no single work of art. Perhaps the conditions of war in England would provoke better work from those who stayed like Spender or those who returned from America like MacNeice. Real conflict might inspire creation where the unreality of the pre-war group's seriousness had not. In one of his rare poems printed by Connolly, the Marxist gossip columnist and wit Tom Driberg wrote of the coming of war as clearing the confusion about the 'Party Line':

Reassembling on the border
We realise in reassembly.

Coming out of the dream, it is clear now
Clear to us again
Clear that there is a border.

See the dotted line. On the Ordnance Survey
It turns to and fro. A loop of it,
Red for the next county, misled us ...

The flight of Auden and Isherwood across the Atlantic and the Nazi and Soviet invasion of Poland did lead to a dark night of the soul for the socialist intellectuals who stayed in England. John Lehmann wrote of agonizing with Stephen Spender. 'Like prisoners tapping every corner of a cellar into which they have been flung in the hope of finding a loose stone, we went through every tiniest possibility of escape.' The declaration of war with Germany was almost a relief. 'War we dreaded, but war was better than giving in to Hitler if it came to that.' Lehmann felt a pang, however, for the many lovers he had in Germany and Austria, who would now become his enemies. In his autobiographical novel, *In the Purely Pagan Sense*, he described a last encounter with a *Luftwaffe* officer by the Danube. 'He flung off his airforce cap, and loosened his trousers as I loosened mine, and, with war between our two countries only a couple of months away, as our forebodings knew all too well, we made love.'

For very different reasons, Lehmann's schoolmate George Orwell felt relief when war was declared. Badly wounded in the throat in the Spanish Civil War, he found the nightmare of the coming of the conflict worse than the fact of it. The night before the signing of the Nazi-Soviet pact, he dreamed that the war had started. He found that he was relieved and patriotic at heart. He would support the war and fight if possible. Stephen Spender kept a journal, feeling that he could not write again. 'Words seem to break in my mind like sticks when I put them down on paper.' The facts in London were that aluminium balloons seemed nailed into the sky, the West End was full of shops to let, sandbags covered the glass pavements on the streets. He decided not to be a pacifist, but to help Cyril Connolly do something, because Connolly did not want to be 'only pink cannon-fodder by the time the days draw in – if we're all back at school one must be a prefect.'

Luckily for Connolly, whom Orwell accused of living in a state of permanent adolescence, the wealthy Peter Watson decided to finance a new magazine   23 suggested by Connolly to be called *Horizon*, which Spender would also edit. Connolly's daydream of the 'thirties had been to edit a monthly magazine with a harmless title and 'deleterious content'. Certainly, he did not wish to fight, an issue that split many of the writers and artists of the time, and led to guilt among those who did not serve. The young Marxist poet Roy Fuller dug a slit trench in his back garden at Blackheath and lay in it when the sirens sounded on Sunday after the declaration of war; then he joined up.

> The movements of people are directed by
> The officious finger of the gun and their
> Desires are sent like squadrons in the sky,
> > Uniform and bare.

Patric Dickinson also debated whether to conscientiously object, then drove to the nearest recruiting centre, while Phyllis Castle became an airwoman in the WAAF, commenting, 'Impossible to fiddle with a pencil while Albion burned.'

The coming of the war was a solace to all those who had found themselves inadequate to deal with the successive crises of the 'thirties. In his picaresque but acute book *William Medium*, Edward Hyams made his marginal hero greet the oubreak of the conflict with a sense of release. Hitler and his kind had exalted war, which was, all cant aside, preferable to an arid peace.

Here, at last, after years of the sultry oppression which precedes the storm, came the lightning, the thunder, the rain; and, like millions of others, while outwardly grave, I welcomed the storm. For what had the peace meant to so many? It had meant semi-starvation on a grudged dole. Or hard work, at uncongenial labour, for a bare living wage, without any security. These facts are notorious. But there are others: no young man or woman, of whatever class, could say that, when he or she left school, there would be interesting and remunerative work to do. But what would happen now that the war had come? There would be a sense of purpose and community of interest. The youth, leaving school, would face not misery, not boredom, but dangerous adventure, which is congenial to a young man, if he be sufficiently fed ... He could look forward to comradeship, to quick promotion, to authority ... The man who, hitherto, had found himself a public nuisance, would now be a public pet. The woman who had been bound to the terrible and unremitting grind of housekeeping and breeding children, on an inadequate income, would go into the factory, enjoy amusing and friendly company, high pay and regular hours, for the first time in her life.

Those poets and artists, whose agony was internal in the years before the war, also felt release when it came. David Gascoyne, who usually lived on the brink of sanity and homosexuality, was struck by the horror of actuality. With the German invasion of Poland, everyone knew the war was already come. 'At the same moment the mental and spiritual war which had been going on inside me for weeks and months – perhaps years? – beforehand, suddenly reached its final cataclysm, and I knew that it had to come to an end, had in fact already ended. *Zero is over.* Now I have some sort of assurance and strength which I never had before.' He had overcome the void, the suffering of uncertainty and suspense – because of the irrevocable decision to fight. He must find a job, create a truth, help in the inner change of people that was needed to build up a better order of things after the war. 'I believe that we must learn to *think with our hearts* and *feel with our minds*; and that we shall be forced to learn this lesson by the ultimately inescapable Anguish brought by the War.'

Moreover, many writers were in revolt from their fathers and previous standards. They blamed the new war on those who had fought the old one and had not learned its grim lessons. They had left their sons a scourge and another world war as their epitaph.

> They danced for twenty years. They danced
> to the hammering, same refrain,
> louder and louder as though they sought
> to drown the sound of pain ...

Yet in the end, there was little choice but to fight. The triumph of fascism was worse than any other conceivable solution. Anne Ridler, who was to become an important post-war poetry editor, married a man who served in the army, yet found all guilty – more or less – who went to war. Yet of two evils, England's victory would be the less. It was hard to blame fathers for setting their children's hands on bayonets. Roy Fuller recognized as much because his feelings and experiences were the same as the fathers of his own generation in their half-forgotten war. They should have consigned the world of weapons to the abyss or made it a mere emotion, but they had also sensed in their time the reality of gun and hunger and the coming of the end of the world.

The problem was to keep writing while faced with the horrors to come. Lawrence Durrell wrote a poem to David Gascoyne about the days before the declaration of hostilities. Monday escaped destruction; on Tuesday visibility was good; Wednesday had a little thunder and light showers; while Friday was already hazardous. Then on the Sabbath was heard the Prime Minister telling of war.

> And today, Sunday. The pit.
> The axe and the knot. Cannot write.
> The monster in its booth
> At a quarter to one the mask repeating:
> 'Truth is what is.
> Truth is what is Truth?'

The reason many accepted the coming of the war was that they felt obscurely that they were responsible for it. In his remarkable series of sonnets called *Crisis*, the religious Christopher Hassall made clear that men were at fault, not God, and that the manufacture of weapons had made the use of them inevitable. For ten years scientists had been sowing scrap-iron, manured with the lust of power. Never had such a dreadful reaping been so long postponed, and dead children would sing Harvest Home. Hassall himself dug gun-emplacements during the war, for he

25

knew where the blame lay. The fire in heaven was man-made, the war birds carried passengers with heavy fountain-pens.

> – What will they write?
>   Death-warrants.
>   Who must die?
> Since you demand an answer: You and I.
> My friend grew pale. Is this our Judgement Day?
> How have we sinned? How have these Things intruded
> On our sweet sleep? Who made them, anyway?
> Startled, we both replied together – YOU DID.

And they had, even the poets. The quintessential Fitzrovian, Ruthven Todd, fled to Edinburgh in September 1939, hoping some good might come out of all this evil. Even if he was sure of nothing and might not believe what he said today in the train tomorrow, the future was now certain to arrive. There was little chance of taking refuge in pacifist or Marxist niceties now. The choice might be a labour battalion on the land or a khaki battalion at the front, but serve one must, even if the system one served might appear far from the best. 'My truth is plighted,' a public school poet declared, 'with guilty classes sure to be defeated.'

The likelihood of regimentation was paradoxically a freedom from the intellectual indecision of the late 'thirties. In his epigram called *Prospect 1939*, Martin Bell complained of being left at twenty-one stranded on the station with heaps of luggage and nowhere to go. The war authorities would point everyone in some direction even if it was not where he or she wished to proceed. Still at Oxford, Henry Green found himself to his surprise agreeing to work as a docker during the national emergency of the summer before the war. He despaired at his acquiescence, yet he had accepted that he would fight and die for something which for the life of him he could not understand. Even those such as Ruthven Todd who sought to evade their duty knew that they would be called in the end:

> History will not weep for shattered Europe.
> At twenty now the boy falls smartly into step,
> To die or else to kill, while, outside, his world
> Runs like a crazy dog, baying for sweet Death ...

Not so Dylan Thomas and most of the Fitzrovians. Dylan refused to give his one and only body to the war, and joined all the shysters and half-poets in London grovelling about the Ministry of Information. In the end, working on documentary films kept him in Soho with Julian Maclaren-Ross, after he had failed his medical. The urban poet A. S. J. Tessimond thought he would be intensely miserable and a danger to others in the army, so he went underground from his job as a copywriter in advertising; but his effort to avoid the call-up was futile, for he failed his medical too. And in a hilarious part of his *True Confessions*, George Barker told of running away to Japan – not a far-sighted decision.

I sat one morning on the can
    That served us for a lavatory
Composing some laudatory
    Verses on the state of man:
My wife called from the kitchen dresser:
    'There's someone here from Japan.
He wants you out there. As Professor.
    Oh yes. The War just began.'

Laurence Olivier was already out in California on a yacht with Vivien Leigh and Douglas Fairbanks Jr; he proceeded to get as drunk as a hoot-owl and rowed round the other American yachts, announcing, 'This is the end! You're all washed up! Finished! Enjoy your last moments. You're done for ...'

Most people in England expected an instant obliteration by German bombers. They had seen the extravagant film of H. G. Wells's book, *The Shape of Things to Come*, and they thought they would soon be bombed or gassed or live in holes in the ground. Preparations for the expected blitzkrieg had been going on all year with silvery barrage balloons flying like monstrous kites over the royal parks, sticky paper criss-crossing the shop windows and discarded editorials blackening out the glass of Fleet Street. Nearly one and a half million women and children were evacuated from the cities by the government in the two days before the declaration of war, and another two million people left individually. An eerie gaiety filled the pubs and the Café Royal, where half London seemed drawn when Osbert Lancaster sat there, waiting for annihilation. The cartoonist had reported to his ARP post and was called to duty on the morrow. He spent the early morning before the war waking up in his empty house, 'expecting to hear the roar of vast aerial armadas heading straight for West Kensington'. Instead, nothing happened, no bombs fell. As a result, on his way to serve as an air raid warden, he changed directions and turned smartly into a public bar. He had to hear the news on the wireless before reporting to avert a catastrophe that was not occurring. In St James's Palace itself, where the occupants ran to the shelter on the banshee wails of the first sirens, they found all the Brigade of Guards already installed, sitting with their bearskins on their laps like giant tea-cosies to keep their knees warm.

The guardsmen were back guarding the King in Buckingham Palace that night, but no blitzkrieg fell to confirm the fears of the Londoners. They were little boys on the Fourth of July – a report went back to America – stuffing their fingers in their ears only to find the cannon cracker had not gone off. The immediate closure of all the theatres and cinemas was followed by their reopening, although Eros was taken off his plinth in Piccadilly Circus for the duration. Not all the publishers fled to the presumed safety of the countryside. Macmillan's issued an announcement drafted by Harold himself, that they proposed to carry on their business at St Martin's Street, London, WC2, until they were either taxed, insured, ARP'd, or bombed out of existence. But it simply did not happen, and Lovat Dickson, a Canadian publisher there, thought that they had all been led up the garden path by 27

Hitler. 'The British will stand anything except being made to look silly.'

The declaration of war led the Fitzrovians to personal decisions, some wise and some silly. The luckier ones were excused the moral choice of being combatants or conscientious objectors by physical disability. Of the neo-Romantic poets who went to Fitzrovia as their wartime university, John Heath-Stubbs was half-blind and the South African poet David Wright was deaf. Many tried to avoid call-up for as long as possible, including the editor Julian Symons and the alcoholic art historian Ruthven Todd, but above all they felt that the war had been declared against each man individually. Like Muslim fanatics, most of the Fitzrovians thought that a German bullet had their name on it, which gave them a good reason to avoid going near flying bullets. As Todd wrote:

Time may have answers but the map is here.
Now is the future that I never wished to see.
I was quite happy dreaming and had no fear:
But now, from the map, a gun is aimed at me.

The British and the Victoria and Albert museums evacuated their treasures to a quarry near Bath, the National Gallery sent three thousand of its best pictures to a quarry in North Wales. This clearance of space opened the way for remarkable experiments in musical appreciation and popular art. Six weeks after war broke out, Myra Hess began a series of piano recitals at lunchtime in the octagonal room of the empty National Gallery, soon packed with listeners shouldering their gas masks. The Queen herself often went to hear Myra Hess, who was to compete with the bells of St Martin's and an occasional lump of high explosive falling on the gallery, which was to be hit seven times during air raids. Once a time-bomb was to explode in the middle of Beethoven's F Major 'Rasoumovsky' Quartet, but the band played the very intricate scherzo without missing a beat.

The quiet desperation which afflicted England on the outbreak of the conflict threw nearly all the artists out of work. The orchestras had no bookings, and the queues of unemployed musicians lengthened outside their union headquarters in Archer Street at the back of the Windmill Theatre, that showcase of naked girls and comic turns which never closed for the duration of the war except in the dark opening weeks of it. The out-of-work actors congregated in the Duke of Wellington near the Globe Theatre and the White Horse near the Apollo and the Salisbury near the Coliseum, where they met the disparate group of poets published by Julian Symons in *Twentieth Century Verse*, Roy Fuller and Gavin Ewart, D. S. Savage and Ruthven Todd, Keidrych Rhys and Lynette Roberts, who later married each other. The little magazine's successor *Now* was edited by George Woodcock, who moved the regular drinking spots of its contributors to Soho and the Swiss Tavern and the York Minster, usually called the 'French pub', which Woodcock and Tambimuttu used as virtual offices. Up the Soho streets were the Highlander and the Crown and Two Chairmen, where the film-makers trained by the four luminaries of the pre-war documentary cinema, the ex-painter

Humphrey Jennings and the realistic John Grierson and Basil Wright and Cavalcanti, all had beer-money falling from their pockets because of the multitude of newsreels and propaganda shorts demanded by the Ministry of Information. Documentary films were to be a lifeline to many of the unemployed writers and actors and artists who mixed in Fitzrovia, where the theatres and casting agencies and film cutting-rooms and editorial offices and small publishers clustered round a hurly-burly of restaurants and cafés, clubs and pubs. Although the members of the various professions and trades used to stick together and talk shop, they were thrown into each other's company by the circumstances of the war, the shortage of drink, the loss of many of them to the armed forces, and the curious camaraderie which hardship and the blitz were to create among different groups and classes.

For young men waiting for call-up or on leave from the forces, Fitzrovia was a heady education. What drew the young poet Michael Hamburger there was not only his Oxford friends, John Heath-Stubbs and David Wright, but the feeling that the Soho pubs broke down class and nationality. Though predominantly upper middle-class or parasitical on it, 'that war-time and pre-war bohemia could accommodate the Welshness of Dylan Thomas, the Scottishness of W. S. Graham, of John Burns Singer and of the two (artist) Roberts, Colquhoun and MacBryde, the East End Jewishness of Willy Goldman. Paul Potts was a Canadian, Tambimuttu a Ceylonese. There was a very young Polish boy killed in an accident a year or two later. There were painters like John Banting already out of fashion; and others – like John Craxton, David Haughton, John Minton, Keith Vaughan, Lucian Freud or Francis Bacon – recently established or not yet at the height of their reputations. Among the rarer visitors Brian Howard – better known as a character than as a poet – was as affectedly and self-consciously elegant as Anna Wickham was negligent of her appearance, warm-hearted and bluff.' Hamburger was unaware of any professional envy or competition among these drifting configurations. He did not know what people did by day, if anything at all. There were quarrels, but nothing to do with the intrigues that beset most literary groups or magazines. The cult of success was considered vulgar, and Hamburger was too young yet to see the objections to the cult of failure.

The literary heir of John Gawsworth, who was reviewed favourably in comparison with T. S. Eliot before the war, knew the attraction of the cult of failure to Gawsworth and other Fitzrovian drinkers. Jon Wynne-Tyson was attracted to the Soho pubs, as most nascent writers were. 'The war came and gave them a form of camaraderie. They were potential victims of a holocaust which destroyed people, young minds trying to find their way and an identity. None of them had a real amount of output behind them. They talked about art and themselves rather than got on and did their own thing – only fragmented things without a background which was destroyed by the war. They were struggling for a background which they found difficult to realise. The war produced the bohemia which was the death of art and identity. It was a decade of fragmentation.'

Yet this very fragmentation created the opportunity for a democratic and real   29 culture within the bohemia of Fitzrovia and its outlying stamping-ground, Chelsea. Five categories of artists were bound to meet there during the war: the home Fitzrovians, who avoided conscription or worked for the government or the forces stationed near London; those escaping from provincial exile in training camps or on conscripted duties working on the land or in factories; those on leave from service overseas; the refugees from Europe or the voluntary exiles driven back to England by shame or the belated urge to serve their country; and, finally, the Commonwealth and American artists and journalists, shipped by the tides of war to London. 'Even if you steer clear of Piccadilly with its seething swarms of drunks and whores,' George Orwell wrote after the invasion of foreign allies, 'it is difficult to go anywhere in London without having the feeling that Britain is now Occupied Territory.'

Yet Fitzrovia was a territory that was occupied only by its few permanent residents, who were merely the lees in the wine barrel to its transient visitors, drawn from across the globe to this hangout of the intelligentsia, this hangover of bohemia, this crowded squalor of instant nostalgia. As David Wright put it:

> Now I would say that it is nine o'clock at the Wheatsheaf
> That it will not be long before the place is full.
>
> Who was it who said
> Friends are born, not made?
>
> I remember, as now
> You no longer do,
>
> The recognition
> Across a long room;
>
> After the eyes met
> Was articulate
>
> Before we had spoken
> What had always been.

TWO

The Waiting Time

That first year, waging war was waiting for something to happen. Loitering in uniform or fearing the call-up was a way of life – anticipating a convoy, solitary on night duty, watching the black-out for fires that never started, looking among the post for a buff envelope from the Ministry. In this time of preparation, pocket-books were needed such as Penguin *New Writing* or small magazines, *Horizon* or *Lilliput*, full of short articles or stories, sketches and poems, pictures or cartoons by Henry Moore or Osbert Lancaster, or even photographs of bombed buildings or shady nudes by Cecil Beaton and Everard and the painter Rose Pulham. These were the months of short attention and disappointed expectation, the time that was called the Bore War. In the words of Malcolm Muggeridge:

Every circumstance of war was present except warfare. Armies existed, apparently in battle-array; uniforms were worn, both at home and abroad; fortifications were dug, passwords were exchanged, trumpets were sounded, canteens were organised, songs were sung – washing to be hung on the Siegfried Line, rabbit to be made to run, run, run, or of the tenderer sort, 'Somewhere in France with you'. The champions were in the ring, proclaiming what they would do to one another, asserting their prowess, but carefully refraining from coming to grips ... So strange a situation has rarely existed. Clouds were dark and menacing; the wind had dropped, and there was the stillness which precedes a mighty storm, and still the first heavy drops of rain did not fall, still it seemed that, after all, no storm might come. Was it, perhaps, on the part of all concerned a sense of the awful consequences which would follow the explosion when at last it came?

The artists in London moved about in an intense hallucination. The young Joan Wyndham, wanting a life among artists, found herself trying to become a Chelsea Tart to please them and waiting for the bombs to fall, although these hardly entered the fringe of her consciousness. 'Bombs and death are real,' she wrote in her diary, 'and I and all the other artists around here are only concerned with unreality. We live in a dream, and it may be desperate but it's not dull.' The facts of the Bore War at home, however, did impinge on the lives of every person. Many writers and artists joined the Auxiliary and later the National Fire Service, Stephen Spender and Henry Green and William Samson and Maurice Richardson, and the painter Leonard Rosoman. An illustrated anthology, *Fire and Water*, of their poems and stories about their duties showed how their experiences as firemen would bring out the best in their work as individual artists. As Spender wrote:

> Burning, burning image
> Of self, projected in
> The years, as in a book,
> To-day has opened on the page
> That paints your soul reflected in
> The hell on which you look ...

Other writers became air raid wardens or worked in the control rooms of the fire services or joined anti-aircraft and barrage balloon units. There was a certain blitheness and lack of animosity in the early months of this strange war that was hardly a war yet. Woodrow Wyatt, who was to edit the annual collection *English*

Story from a succession of army huts and tents and barrack rooms across the world, remembered firing off antiquated guns in Kent at any aeroplane that looked like a Stuka and was often a Spitfire and giving cups of tea to any German parachutist who dropped down from an abandoned aircraft. The soft option for sybarite warriors was provided by Victor Cazalet's Anti-Aircraft Battery, which even Dylan Thomas tried to join. Like Lovat's Horse, the wealthy Cazalet treated the 16th Light AA Battery as a recruiting station for a private force, which happened to be chosen from his artist friends. They were Evelyn Waugh's monstrous regiment of gentlemen in *Men at Arms*. Entrance was hard to procure without a fellowship from a Royal Society or membership of Equity. The aesthete James Pope-Hennessy, who skipped about in grey pyjamas and scarlet slippers during air raids, acted as the librarian of its magnificent collection of books, suitable for browsing between calls to ack-ack duty. 'You can swing as much leave as you want,' the actor Dennis Price told Alec Guinness. 'All you have to do is say you have a dinner engagement at the Savoy which you simply can't get out of. I think we should sit out the war very comfortably.' Unfortunately, jealousy at the War Office caused the disbandment of the epicurean gunners who served with such delight. 'Imagine,' Pope-Hennessy wrote to Clarissa Churchill, 'no Cazalet, no-one to talk to, becoming an ordinary private in the real rough-and-tumble army. My despair and irritation proved how bogus my wish to do something "active" basically is!'

Outside the British Broadcasting Corporation and the Ministry of Information, efforts failed to employ writers as war artists or to exempt them from conscription. An informal committee was set up by Lord Esher aided by John Lehmann, but could not even preserve fifty leading artists from the call-up. An official Authors' Planning Committee had A. P. Herbert and Dorothy L. Sayers serving on it in order to produce plans for harnessing authors to the war effort. It was attacked by many; John Strachey wrote in *The Author*, 'The best thing that the government can do for authors in wartime is to leave them alone. The business of an author is to write.' Osbert Sitwell agreed. 'The writer can do more for his country by writing than by fighting.' So the Authors' Planning Committee was dissolved. All the arts seemed to be marking time. Mass-Observation wrote of a suffering culture in 1940 with publishers seeing no future, the closure of art galleries and museums, the cancellation of concerts, no boom in poetry reading as in the First World War, and the refusal of creative artists to do much more than linger and watch. The opening editorial of *Horizon* written by Cyril Connolly was quoted: 'At the moment civilization is on the operating table and we sit in the waiting-room.'

Stephen Spender was also editing *Horizon* with its backer, the wealthy and enigmatic Peter Watson, who thought Connolly a brilliant editor because he was 'like a brothel-keeper, offering his writers to the public as though they were girls'. Spender liked Connolly's kind of defiance, the aesthete in the last ditch with his highbrow worm's-eye view. Connolly wrote for the *New Statesman* a piece called 'The Ivory Shelter'; artists were now locked up in their island; war was 'a tin-can tied to the tail of civilization'. Although fighter pilots wrote to *Horizon* to say that so

Leonard Rosoman

long as the magazine continued they had a cause to fight for, Connolly quoted Lord Beaverbrook that there was no place for culture in wartime and added that there was certainly no place for it in the warrior. Writers and painters were right and wise to ignore the war. This provoked a stinging 'Letter from a Soldier' written by Goronwy Rees, who had joined up. The war would not be ignored. It was Connolly's guilty conscience that made him give such bad advice. The people of Britain did not demand that the writer should lay down his pen and take up arms. Yet the war was not the enemy of creative activity for artists, who might see in it what they once saw in the crucifixion of Christ, a tragic and terrible birth. Muttering that T. S. Eliot was better off writing 'East Coker' than serving as Rees's brother officer, Connolly accepted that he and *Horizon* were living in a fools' paradise, lulled by the general false security before the invasion and the bombardment. He wrote to his mother that all the war he had seen was an army lorry colliding with his taxicab near Sloane Square; the accident broke the pelvis of his mistress.

Yet the war and its conditions were finally registering. One spoiled Fitzrovian described how he would sit in his chalk-covered trench and mentally summon the head waiter of the Café Royal or the *patronne* of a little place in Dean Street before rounding off the evening with a visit to the Nest or the Nut-house. Planning leaves in London was the easy way out of war, until he realized that there was no such thing as leave. The war insisted on following him around. The old 1939 way of life simply was not there any more. A 48-hour pass to London was a gap between two worlds. 'That's why – though there are parties and pub-crawls, blinds and blondes – there is no such thing as leave.'

The hiatus in culture in the first months of the Bore War could not last. When the theatre of war had opened in September 1939, the London shows had closed their curtains. Black-out regulations had killed the house lights, while a fear of an imminent blitzkrieg had kept the seats empty. But by October, half a dozen theatres unlocked their doors, particularly the Prince of Wales and the Windmill with its tableaux of nearly naked girls. Its proud slogan would remain 'We Never Closed' until the competition of strip shows and pornographic films in Soho would close it twenty years later. But during air raids, its girls would sleep in the theatre to keep the show going; if bombs fell close, they would rush to the foyer wearing only a couple of roses, a tin helmet and a first-aid bag. Leading casts and plays, John Gielgud in *The Importance of Being Earnest* and Emlyn Williams in *The Corn is Green*, toured the provinces until the theatre managements recovered their nerves and invited them to London, while Welsh villages were graced with the roles of Medea, Lady Macbeth and Candida played by Sybil Thorndike. The closure, however, of the Ivor Novello musical *The Dancing Years* at Drury Lane gave Basil Dean his chance to establish there the headquarters of the Entertainments National Service Association, which was founded by the government to provide entertainment for troops sent to all the stages of the global conflict.

The Old Vic company and many other groups toured for ENSA between spells of acting in London. For the first time, state patronage began to support the theatre and a company which might serve as the nucleus of a national theatre. The embryo of the Arts Council of Great Britain was also formed, the Council for the Encouragement of Music and the Arts, appointed by the Ministry of Education to subsidize enough entertainment to keep up the morale of the civilians unable to move far from their homes because of travel restrictions. CEMA gave grants to the Old Vic and to tiny companies such as the Pilgrim Players, who travelled in two cars bringing religious plays to the people. The actors were paid at the rate of the common soldier and lived worse than he did. 'The Plague sent Shakespeare to inn-yards – banqueting-halls – the village green ... Should we go there? Taking conditions in Britain as we found them. How hard! How exciting!'

For the first time in British history, war conditions developed state patronage for drama in London and the provinces and the overseas theatres of war. A third organization, the Army Bureau of Current Affairs, developed the dramatic documentary to educate the troops, many of whom had never before seen live theatre. J. B. Priestley wrote for this experimental new form of drama for the people. His *Desert Highway* was a resolute combination of facts and the imagination. A popular theatre with a mass audience seemed possible in the early years of the war, although the heartland of the English theatre remained in the commercial theatres near Shaftesbury Avenue and St Martin's Lane, the boundaries of Fitzrovia. There escapist American musicals and comedies would run throughout the bombardment of London: realistic plays dealing with the conflict, such as *Lifeline* about the Merchant Navy or *Salt of the Earth* about Occupied France, would be flops. Only established playwrights, Terence Rattigan in *Flare Path* and Mary Hayley Bell in *Men in Shadow*, could create successes by using the war as a background for conventional emotional drama or thrillers. There would be quite enough spectacle in the mighty battle in the skies above London to make theatre audiences wish to escape reality in the playhouses on the ground.

The call-up to national service did not spare even male ballet-dancers. All the original members of the Sadler's Wells *corps de ballet* joined the forces in spite of a plea from George Bernard Shaw to exempt them. And although the coming of the war nearly destroyed the company, artistic isolation helped the establishment of a future National Ballet. For war audiences flocked to see its illusions as an escape from conditions outside. During the Battle of Britain, the company would tour England with two pianos replacing the orchestra. They would dance to audiences of factory workers and men in uniform. They had lost the Sadler's Wells Theatre to the Finsbury Borough Council. 'We're a *madhouse*,' the theatre manager said. 'Five tours, either in the country or being organised, and a hundred and sixty homeless people living in the theatre and giving a *lot of trouble*.' Finally, the Sadler's Wells ballet would come to roost back in London at the New Theatre, which it would share with the Old Vic company, bombed out of its Waterloo Road premises. There Robert Helpmann's dancing of *Hamlet* in front of the artist Leslie Hurry's nightmarish sets would provoke applause and controversy. As one Helpmann

36

supporter wrote, 'Hamlet always has been ruined by the words.'

Opera fared less well in the war. Despite being declared bankrupt after a previous attempt to run Covent Garden, Sir Thomas Beecham, still backed by Lady Cunard, was again at the helm of the Opera House in 1939; but he could not keep it going as many of its maestros and *divas* came from enemy Germany and Austria and Italy. The building had been degraded to a storage space for furniture in the First World War. Now it became one of the more popular dance-halls in London, crammed with visiting servicemen and ministry secretaries and factory girls. The change from arias to tangos and foxtrots was a sign of the times; as the popular radio professor C. E. M. Joad said, the distinctive cultural expression of English genius in the opening years of the war was light music.

The start of the war certainly created the opportunity for a more popular culture. Light music, indeed, dominated the airwaves, emanating from the BBC, which considered Sandy Macpherson on his electric organ an adequate response to Lord Haw-Haw's venomous innuendoes from Nazi Germany. And the empty spaces on the walls of the great galleries encouraged the showing of people's art. In December 1939, the Royal Academy gave its first open show of contemporary art with more than two thousand exhibits including a portrait in feathers of the young Princess Elizabeth. One leading painter, John Piper, suggested that this might kill art with kindness. When an exhibition by members of the armed forces was assembled to hang on the bare walls of the National Gallery, the ageing art critic Herbert Read fulminated: 'Even a worm could lift his head above this level. What stretches before us is the sordid scum left by a receding civilization. Aesthetic criticism has no function here: it is an affair for the social pathologist. But to that science the art critic is inevitably driven day by day, and I doubt whether the war has left him with any other relevant basis.'

Read had been influential in shifting the emphasis of British art from the stifling formalism and classicism beloved by Roger Fry and the Bloomsbury Group towards a neo-Romantic vision of painting, its distant roots in the Celtic and Gothic past, in Fuseli and William Blake and Samuel Palmer, but its modern stimulation in the apocalypse of the world war. Peter Watson, the patron of *Horizon* and *Poetry London*, financed the young neo-Romantic painters, the Scots lovers Robert Colquhoun and Robert MacBryde, along with Lucian Freud and John Craxton, to whom he wrote, 'Nostalgia for the past is not a valid vehicle for art now, I am sure of that.' As in the First World War, artists were now commissioned by the government, which bought their canvases and drawings. The better of the established surreal and neo-Romantic painters produced major work as a contribution to the struggle. Henry Moore would become obsessed by the sleepers in the underground stations, trying to avoid the bombs, the masses of the people camping deep under the earth. Tambimuttu was to publish Moore's *Shelter Sketchbook* in his Editions Poetry London and to announce Graham Sutherland's sketch book of 1936–42. Sutherland was to become an official war artist, covering aircraft and tin-mines and steel furnaces and open-cast coal operations as well as bomb damage in London – 'perspectives of destruction seeming to recede into infinity'. John Piper also would paint bomb damage in addition to the stylized control rooms of regional quarters of ARP command posts. John Minton would make blitzed dockland the home of ghostly haunted children. And Paul Nash converted the flying dreams of his childhood into pictures of downed German aeroplanes that did not please his superiors in the Air Ministry. A drawing of the wreck of an enemy machine on the ground 'was rather like shooting at a sitting bird. In the slang of the moment, they took a poor view of it.'

The dead sea of dumped German aeroplanes which Paul Nash called *Totes Meer* was the supreme fusion of the Romantic vision and the facts of the fighting – the best war picture so far, Sir Kenneth Clark considered in 1941. Without a doubt, employment as war artists did stimulate the leading neo-Romantics, who were shocked into a perception of the truth of conflict that wonderfully concentrated their minds and defined their paintings. It was no different in the British cinema. Co-director of the blitz film, *London Can Take It*, the former painter Humphrey Jennings would achieve a poetic authenticity in *Fires Were Started*, his depiction of the London Fire Brigade and Auxiliary Fire Service, in which so many writers and artists were enrolled. The documentary techniques spilled over into a distinguished series of war films; one of them was Cavalcanti's chilling work of the imagination, *Went The Day Well?*, in which Graham Greene recounted the occupation of an English village by Nazi paratroopers wearing British Army uniforms. But the apogee of the cinema of the early war years was *In Which We Serve*, produced by the Italian refugee Filippo del Giudice, with Noël Coward playing the role of his friend Lord Louis Mountbatten almost as well as Mountbatten played it, and showing a restraint and power of observation that denied his usual mannerisms. The careful social delineation of the characters of the sailors on the doomed destroyer made the film a lighthouse to the new British cinema with its strong documentary tradition. 'It took a war to compel the British to look at themselves', a contemporary critic wrote, 'and find themselves interesting.'

The documentary film meant pay and salvation to some of the Fitzrovians, particularly those attached to Donald Taylor at Strand Films in Golden Square. The Highlander in Dean Street was one of the Soho pubs frequented by technicians and continuity-girls from the Films Division of the Ministry of Information. There Taylor met Julian Maclaren-Ross, who had already been recommended to him by Dylan Thomas. The two fledgeling scriptwriters soon encountered and appraised each other:

Dylan wore a green porkpie hat pulled down level with his slightly bulging eyes: like the agate marbles we used as Alley Taws when I was a boy in France, but a darker brown. His full lips were set low in a round full face, a fag-end stuck to the lower one. His nose was bulbous and shiny. He told me afterwards that he used to rub it up with his fist before the mirror every morning until it shone satisfactorily: as a housewife might polish her doorknob or I the silver-topped malacca cane that I affected in those days.

Instead of writing a script on the Home Guard, they used to spend their time drinking Irish whiskey in the back bar of the Café Royal, Scotch ale in the Wheatsheaf, gin in the Highlander, and whatsoever passed for drink in the Horseshoe Club. Dylan used to attack Maclaren-Ross for his dandy airs, stating, 'Sordidness, boy, that's the thing.'

A new art form developed, the documentary with staged scenes, which was to become a mainstay of post-war television – that remarkable British invention was shut down abruptly by the British Broadcasting Corporation in the first week of the war with the tart remark that as so many things were passing, too, television was not singled out for neglect. The acted documentary film, however, *Target for Tonight* reconstructed realistic scenes in the fuselage of a grounded Wellington bomber, F for Freddie, to simulate an air raid over Germany. Its propaganda value was great, showing to seventy million people in Britain and the United States. Its success led to a new confusion between the actual and the artificial, the documentary and the feature film, the truth and the forgery, that corresponded to the privations and the hopes of those waiting to go to war. The ageing critic Robert Herring went to one party crowded as usual with the young makers of documentary films. A director was complaining that he could not find a suitable crater to shoot, although there were thousands in the bombed streets. They did not look like craters. 'We shall probably have to make one,' the director said earnestly, 'and I did so want to have no faked stuff.' Herring found the film-makers too earnest and patronized them. It was their first war, and his second. The tedious trivialities of rationing, gas masks, uniforms and economy were second nature to his generation of older people, who had made a mess of peace because they had not met it before.

The Ministry of Information and the BBC were interested only in their version of the truth, all the propaganda fit to broadcast. Louis MacNeice at first fled their service to the United States, justifying himself with the statement, 'There must be plenty of people to propagand, so I have no feeling of guilt in refusing to mortify my mind.' But when he returned home because he thought he was 'missing history' and began twenty-two years of work as a BBC producer and writer, he changed his literary philosophy. 'Freedom means Getting Into Things, not getting Out of Them; also that one must keep making things which are *not oneself*, e.g. works of art.' William Empson also came back from the Far East to work in the BBC, serving with other poets and writers out of uniform, and suffering with them from a moral ambivalence that corroded their sense of integrity.

Although George Orwell stayed in London to serve in the Home Guard against possible invasion, he was also working at the BBC producing talks to India and employing leading writers and editors from T. S. Eliot to Tambimuttu and Cyril Connolly, who thought Orwell slipped into the war as into an old tweed jacket. All the same, he saw a disturbing parallel between what was happening to the arts in the totalitarian powers that Britain was fighting, and in the Ministry of Information and the BBC and the film companies, which brought up promising young writers, set them to work like cab horses and managed to rob literary creation of its 39 individual character. The refugee writer Arthur Koestler sounded much the same warnings when he saw the intelligentsia absorbed as temporary civil servants into the ministries and the BBC. To him, conformity was dangerous, as it might become a betrayal carried out with a clear conscience. Cecil Day Lewis himself worked at the Ministry of Information, where he had fixed a place to evade army service. As a communist sympathizer at the time of the Stalin–Hitler pact, he was considered as dangerous as a fascist. An internal memo stated that MI5 allowed the use of his material, but forbade a personal appearance at the microphone. He was as bitter as his friend Louis MacNeice about the broadcasts of destruction that reached the ears of those sitting safe behind their radio sets at home:

> Mass destruction, mass disease:
>
> We thank thee, Lord, upon our knees
> That we were born in times like these
>
> When with doom tumbling from the sky
> Each of us has an alibi
> For doing nothing – Let him die.
>
> Let him die, his death will be
> A drop of water in the sea,
> A journalist's commodity ...
>
> Die the soldiers, die the Jews,
> And all the breadless homeless queues.
> Give us this day our daily news.

By the second year of the war, one writer produced by another was to dominate the wireless, reading 'Postscripts' to the nine o'clock news. The novelist and playwright J. B. Priestley was managed by Norman Collins and delivered three times a week his commentary on the war, 'designed to have a very broad and classless appeal'. His popularity became second only to Winston Churchill, whose jealousy was said to have made the Minister of Information, Duff Cooper, terminate in 1941 the 'Postscripts' for a British audience. In so far as the war was a people's war with the citizens of London suffering as much as the troops once the blitz began, Priestley seemed to be the voice of the people with his admirable stagecraft and techniques at the microphone, sounding intimate and easy with just a flavour of Yorkshire in his vowels. He also revived an informal Authors' National Committee and suggested that first-class writers should be sent out to cover military campaigns and so produce something imperishable. But the second authors' committee also fell victim to the fissiparous and anarchic tendencies of most writers, particularly the Fitzrovians. Even Priestley himself rather enjoyed sparkling under the bombs when they fell at last. He was no longer suspicious of gaiety. He felt 'free, companionable, even – except where waiting for the explosion – lighthearted. It took bombs to deliver us.'

40

Those of military age did not know how long they could keep their jobs in London. For the call-up progressed, as one ironist wrote, with the speed of an elephant trying to compete in the Derby. The registration of the able-bodied up to the age of forty was not completed until June 1941, a full year after the fall of France and the evacuation of Dunkirk had finally ended the Bore War and convinced the British people that the real war would begin at home. All the waiting and the training would soon prove its purpose. The expected apocalypse was upon Britain. As Spender noted, the getting together of Stalin and Hitler, two monsters out of the Book of Revelation, had been an apocalyptic event. 'One imagined the vast armies and air forces of these beasts overrunning the land and darkening the skies, raining down bombs on the cities of the West.' The 'thirties had been wound up like a company going bankrupt. And the flight of Auden to America in 1939 had been a public act of great significance that underlined what Spender and his colleagues now knew. People could no longer oppose fascism as individuals who might influence history. 'They joined armies in which they were expected to forget that they were individuals.' Spender himself joined the fire service to fight the bombs to come.

The first year of the new war decade was fundamentally changing the assumptions of the intellectuals of the 'thirties. Resistance to authoritarianism had become acquiescence in its necessity as the government, the ministries and the armed forces issued their rules and regulations. The fiction that a bourgeois Marxist sympathizer could escape his class and become 'proletarian' with his fellow believers was developing into a real ability to cross class barriers, if he wore the same uniform and had to do the same duties. Slumming was becoming serving together, pretending to be comrades was having to be mates. The impassable barrier of public and private school lingo that the Auden group spoke was being replaced by common war slang with its ack-ack and prangs, boffins and spam. The paradox was that the individual protest against the class system of the 'thirties had created a false comradeship, whereas national conscription into mass units enforced a necessary community and a common language. The refuge from the snobbery of background was not picking up the red card of the socialist parties but putting on the khaki or blue of the forces.

A further contradiction was that the regimentation of war did not produce another cultural élite, but broke it. *The Times* itself welcomed the eclipse of the highbrow. Commenting on Lord Elton's attack on 'that weak and arrogant contempt for the common man', a leader writer condemned the hasty brilliance and esoteric parlour games of the arts in the two decades between the wars. The public had grown bewildered and then bored. 'The arts, even while sometimes declaring themselves communist, despised the common man, and he retaliated.' That age was past. Civilians and soldiers were now inextricably mixed in a common danger and purpose. The young artists of the future were being trained on the battlefield of Britain. Whatever changes of taste the war might produce, nobody could foresee. But they would not be unintelligible outside a Bloomsbury drawing- 41

room and differ from the stoic virtues the whole nation now practised.
From the cusp of the period, David Gascoyne gave the toast:

> And so let's take a last look round, and say Farewell to all
> Events that gave the last decade, which this New Year
> Brings to its close, a special pathos. Let us fill
> One final fiery glass and quickly drink to 'the Pre-War'
> Before we greet 'the Forties', whose unseen sphinx-face
> Is staring fixedly upon us from behind its veil;
> Drink farewell quickly, ere the Future smash the glass.

" I SEE NO NEWS—I HEAR NO NEWS—I SPEAK NO NEWS "

Standard paper-weight for all the 1066 desks in the Ministry
of Nonformation.

Michael Barsley, *Ritzkrieg*

THREE

Exiles in Khaki

18 miles

1 ½ pints

170 million candles

Life in the Army

11 buttons

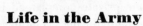

Day's march .. 18 miles
Major General's pay £1,652 p.a.
Weight of tin helmet 38 ounces.
Hours of work (recruit)
                    34 per week.
Paces per minute 70 slow march
Searchlight's power
        170 million candle power
Buttons on coat (infantryman) 11
Eyesight minimum requirements
    for infantrymen
        4/10 in. letters at 20 ft.
Minimum height (recruit)
                    5 ft. 2 in.
Men in a platoon 39
Weight of shell (large) 1,938 lb.
Water bottle capacity 1½ pints
Weight of rifle .. 8 lb. 10 oz.
Cost of uniform (officers) .. £40
Morse buzzer signaller
            10 words a minute
Length bayonet blade .. 22 in.

34 hours' work

Eyesight minimum

5 ft. 2 in.

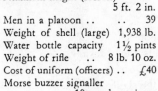

38 ounces

£1,652

1,938 lb.

'There is only one logical solution,' a conscientious objector said to the chairman of the Appellate Tribunal of England and Wales. 'A conscientious objector who does not want to help the war must commit suicide.' The chairman thought so, too, unless the objector left the country – as Auden and Isherwood had done. Actually, fewer than three men in two hundred applied to be registered as objectors, although many of them were self-styled artists. But the tribunals did not allow the appeals of most who refused to serve. Julian Symons, for instance, said that he objected to fighting in a capitalist war; this was held to be so eccentric that he was called up into the army, in which he served for three years until he was invalided out. He could only complain in 'Conscript', printed in *More Poems from the Forces*, that the organization of madness proceeded by orders:

> On the parade ground clerks and electricians
> Forget the antique laws by which their lives
> Ran in the cooling capitalist groove.
> *The commando training prepares for death.*

The problem of military training was that it prepared recruits for boredom, not for extinction. It made no difference whether a person was a conscript or a volunteer. He became, as one private complained in *Horizon*, a number, two identification discs on a string round the neck, a uniform and a military haircut with his dress, his feet, his face and his penis inspected by authority. However much he might feel for his mates in suffering, it was not *our* war, but *their* war – the war of officers and politicians and big businessmen and propagandists. 'We do what we are told, or else jankers and the glasshouse. We are not the people's army, the ragtag fighters, but members of His Majesty's Forces, who go where they are ordered.' Poets like Cecil Day Lewis might find a fine unity in the Home Guard or the Auxiliary Fire Service, but that did not extend to the conscripts in the training camps, who resented – as Patric Dickinson found before catching typhoid and a disability pension – being taught to be morons by morons. The atmosphere of khaki was a corrosive stultifier:

> Dusty traditions, dusty hopes,
> Dusty ideals and thoughts, dusty desires,
> Dusty daily every minute Dust
> Working its way within the skull,
> Khaki catalysing soul. And still
> They grumble we have naught to say.

The routine of military life made writing difficult. Keidrych Rhys, the editor of two admirable anthologies of poems from the forces, defended in 1940 the author in uniform, born into the wrong times, accepting conscription with grace, betrayed by the intellectuals of the depression, and having no respect for a literary culture dominated by two Old Etonians, John Lehmann and Cyril Connolly, who consciously or unconsciously opposed the war. 'If poets *must* be used in Army, Air Force and Naval jobs in which they are wasted, with resultant harmful effect on their state of mind, then you cannot possibly *expect* crops of marvellous poets *right now*.' All the same, Rhys found many good poems to publish by established and unknown writers in battledress. It was possible to scribble and serve. He did not agree with Joan Wyndham's artist who would not join up, thinking he was doing just as much to save civilization by sitting on his bottom thinking the right thoughts, as by rushing round with a gun thinking the wrong ones.

Thirty artists, however, were recruited by the Ministry of Information to record war activities, although poets were merely drafted into the ranks. It was an enlightened decision because most of the conscripts, when given lectures on painting, could not understand why there were war artists, when photographs could be taken instead. In fact, the conditions of service in the forces inspired the commissioned artists. Keith Henderson, painting a dawn patrol at an aerodrome in May 1940, had to restrict his palette to the little light: his colour scheme was black and dim white with vermilion lamps against a grey-blue distance. Then, in a sudden alert in a hangar, he saw an animal rabble in gas masks, goggling and swarming round the snouts of giant insects, the goggle-eyed aeroplanes. To experience active duty was to be given new vision.

It was the same for the conscripts. Military training might be corrosive and stultifying, but it provided material for writing on methods and machines. From the drill book and arms instruction, philosophic reactions derived. And from the weapons themselves, a certain love blew like smoke from the barrel of a gun. A new poet, Henry Reed, wrote a fine war trilogy of poems, on 'Naming of Parts', 'Judging Distances' and 'Unarmed Combat'. He simply translated the manual into the immortal. Alun Lewis, the best of the Welsh war poets, wrote an ode on being moody and dull during manoeuvres, 'All Day It Has Rained ...' But while the writers of the 'thirties hymned and feared the aeroplane, the war servicemen praised against their better instincts the Bofors and Lewis and Bren guns, the artillery and ack-ack battery, the Lee-Enfield and the grenade. A new poetry of machines developed as though weapons had a beauty despite their function of murder. Francis Scarfe lauded the 25-pounder as a little dragon that could kill wherever it willed: it had that in common with love. And as for the grenade, he held it in his palm as a child holds an apple, glad of its weight until it grew warm and ready for tasting.

> May they who take you
> Into their flesh,
> Whose ears are split
> By your mad laughter,
> Not know how long
> I weighed your evil
> And flung for shame.

R. N. Currey, who learned from the world of guns and radar 'that for which we seem to be bound – the world of machines and modern witchcraft', wrote of a boy   45 trying out his new weapon as if it were a mathematical delight.

> Rifle-virgin, delicate
> To this yard of metal, slender
> Strange and lovely as a mate,
>
> Trigger gravely-curved and tender
> As a lover's lips, a rod
> And a thimbleful of thunder
>
> Carrying life-and-death, and shod
> With the speed of instancy,
> Exquisitely just as God
>
> Neat as trigonometry ...

Field-glasses set greater eyes on the user and caught the privacies of nature in a crystal cage. The firing-range did not produce thoughts of enemies or trite slogans of hate in H. B. Mallalieu, but a concentration of the will upon a target.

> The butt is firm, at home against the shoulder.
> The bull obscures village and room from sight.
> There is only this minute: each wholly a soldier.
> I sense the birds above me flying into light.

Finally, all the training for war and the waiting to fight and the bonhomie of serving with fellow soldiers was a camouflage. The weapon was the truth for John Manifold:

> Therefore if I must choose I prefer to sing
> The tommy-gun, the clean, functional thing,
> The single-hander, deadly to rigid line,
> Good at a job it doesn't attempt to conceal.
> Give me time only to teach this hate of mine
> The patience and integrity of the steel.

Few had the ferocity of John Gawsworth in 'Bayonet Instruction': 'Of course, if the blade sticks, fire in a round. You'll get release then easy from the wound.' But all were being trained to kill. It was their objective and their duty. The commissioned and the non-commissioned officers taught the men the skills of murder for a just cause, in hope of peace and early release. The battery subalterns on the Home Front felt distinctly distant from the masses. For them:

> Unheeding now through summer days they give
> Their drilled attention to the killers' art
> Rehearsing in their minds the life they'll live
> When some day soon their second life will start,
> And ripping, every time they thrust, the drab,
> Embittered present with a bayonet jab.

The creation of the new officer class was a subject that *Horizon* could not leave alone. Its anonymous commentator thought that while the war was making other classes liquefy and unite, a vast deadweight officer class would stand out like the old broad-gauge railway long after other tracks had narrowed into uniformity. '*In the "People's Army" of to-day officership is no longer a responsibility: it is a privilege, and those who win it are the privileged classes. That is why, despite the removal of petty barriers, there is for the first time class antagonism between leaders and led within an army which has for the first time a cause common to all.*'

That hostile feeling might be present during the ennui of training, but it would not exist during the necessary unity of combat against a common enemy outside the army hierarchy of pips on the shoulder or tapes on the sleeve. The first major writer thrown up by military experience, Julian Maclaren-Ross, described the bad feeling caused by promotion from the ranks. His sketch 'The Tape' led the twenty-five tales of army life that make up *The Stuff To Give The Troops*. It tells of a soldier, Phil, who refuses to become a corporal because he doesn't like authority. When he gets his tape on his uniform, he tries to stay in with his old soldier mates, but he cannot. 'You couldn't keep discipline if NCOs didn't keep theirselves to theirselves, stands to reason, and Phil said what about democracy and what the hell were we fighting for?'

Phil lost in the end to the principle of authority, just as Maclaren-Ross did when he tried to be a fellow writer, though an ordinary soldier, with Second Lieutenant Alun Lewis. He saluted Lewis, who thought Maclaren-Ross was making fun of him. The officers' mess proved impossible as a meeting-place, and even in the local pub Lewis's Sam Browne made it difficult for him to drink with Maclaren-Ross in his webbing belt. Lewis was uneasy about leaving the ranks, but he had thought he would be able to do something for the men as an officer before he found that he was more helpless than ever. So Maclaren-Ross asked him

how his brother officers treated the idea of his being a poet. At first they'd regarded it as rather rum, made contemptuous little jokes about Shakespeare and asked him to make up smutty limericks, but then a photograph of him was found in an old copy of *Lilliput* and the Mess was impressed. Fame could reach no higher: unless, of course, the photograph had appeared in *Men Only*. Now his writing was regarded as a harmless pastime, so long as it didn't interfere with his efficiency as an officer.

When they parted company, Maclaren-Ross raised his hand to salute Lewis, who shook it instead. Maclaren-Ross found himself accused of consorting with officers by his regimental sergeant major, who observed that soldiers could not be made out of civilians – writers and suchlike. Lewis was reprimanded for consorting with a private by his commanding officer. The army system did not allow brother writers to cross the barriers of rank. When Lewis was killed in action in Burma at the time that Maclaren-Ross was being court-martialled and invalided from the army, Keidrych Rhys asked the uncomprehending War Office about the death of Second Lieutenant Lewis, only to hear, 'At first you said a poet or something. Why didn't you say he was an officer?'

In Fitzrovia, none of the shibboleths of rank existed. Conscientious objectors and civilians and military men could congregate as old comrades of words and pictures. Leave in London was the way out of the segregated mess and the common canteen. There Maclaren-Ross decamped after his discharge to become, in the sailor poet Alan Ross's opinion, Soho's longest-serving combatant. 'Soldiers, sailors and airmen, of all nationalities, drifted in for a few days and then were gone for long periods, but Julian, a tall, dark figure holding court at the far end of the Wheatsheaf bar in teddy-bear coat and sun-glasses, gold-topped cane beside him, was always there.'

Even in the months of delayed action before the blitz, uniform conditions of war were being imposed on the whole nation. Food and clothes rationing were universal and accepted, black-out regulations necessary and unpopular. Outside a few insiders and profiteers, everybody had to put up with it. Civilians had to register at shops to receive their variable weekly average of two shillings' worth of meat, four ounces of bacon and cheese and fat and tea, eight ounces of sugar and two eggs. Clothes coupons had to be hoarded to buy a coat, while petrol was practically unobtainable. The black-out turned familiar streets into dark ravines with shaded traffic lights, buses creeping along like dimly luminous monsters, taxis all black inside and cars with headlamps no brighter than cat's eyes. As Mass-Observation discovered: 'Nothing, no amount of experience, makes you really used to the black-out. And however little it may change your habits, the consciousness of it, waiting for you out there, behind the black material on the window, is a threat to any of the pre-war happy-go-lucky. Each evening expedition is now an event, maybe a dangerous adventure.' Mass-Observation also noted that lovers and prostitutes liked the black-out. It conferred on everybody an equality of clandestine anonymity before the radiance of the incendiaries that were to come from the sky. Kenneth Allott enjoyed the common cloak of the night laid over London for fear of sending signals to German bombers:

> Walking the dark this night might be anywhere,
> Anywhere, that is, where the war is here:
> The searchlights prying on the loves of clouds
> Like constables, the guns waiting to hiccough,
> The tea-drinking basements waiting for the All-Clear.

In the pubs and in the streets, in the defence units and in the factories where men and women were drafted because of special skills or disabilities which kept them from the armed forces, there was little antagonism of class or background. It did seem a people's war on the Home Front, and authority lay in a local warden or policeman or fireman, wearing a tin hat or a helmet or an armband. To those who were serving on dangerous duties, however, the safety of city life seemed almost intolerable, particularly to the sailors on leave from the freezing convoys, their shipmates sunk by U-boats, or to the bomber pilots, flying hopeless missions over Germany, only to return to the laconic announcement that some of our aeroplanes were missing. Particularly hated were the civil servants who lived in 'Safe Areas'. As one naval rating wrote:

> You people in safe areas,
> Overfed, over-pleasured, over-glutted
> With rotten ideas
> Of what is life or death!
> I have seen you feed
> In restaurants, where music
> Creeps into and saps
>   Your selfish minds.
> I have seen you drink
> Your gin and bitters
> In pubs that advertise
> A well-concreted shelter.
> I have heard you speak
> With pride
> Of reserved and nationally important jobs,
> That keep you bended over office desks ...
> Oh! how I wish you were conscripted
> And should you run away to safety,
> Then die.
> For nothing belongs to anybody in war,
> Not even safety.

That was true when the bombs began to fall, for few areas were safe, no occupation without threat of destruction from the sky. Curiously, it was safer to be training in a military camp in the countryside than living in a city expecting the blitz. Poetry and painting were being produced during the tedious period of wasting time in rural barracks, and these were finding a market and an audience in London, where the publishers and the galleries were still concentrated. When, at last, the terrible rain of bombs broke on the metropolis, a phenomenon had begun, something approaching a popular poetry and story and art. Little illustrated magazines filled with sketches and verses from people in the forces began to sell to the conscripts and civilians, loitering on duty, awaiting Armageddon. The literary and artistic cliques of the 'thirties were fled or mute; new editors wanted serving contributors to describe their war experiences to a lingering audience with short periods to fill in between rosters and schedules. The writer Keith Vaughan, whom John Lehmann encouraged to become a painter, described people like himself as exiles in khaki, an army in occupation of their own country. 'Dressed alike, eating alike. Every town and village has its contingent like its cats.' But the exiles did not want to be banished from London, which was ready to broadcast their descriptions of their routine and give them the artistic stimulus which they craved.

Leaves to get to London, trains and stations spawned another literature. The 24-hour or 48-hour pass was the dream of the men lost in the country camps. The night-train took them to their urban loves. As Alan Ross wrote:

> Each makes the wish obliterate the fact,
> Imagines the loved face, and not the unlovely act.
> The train takes you where you have to go.

Stations saw scenes of infinite partings in the early mornings, when the young women left the men with whom they had spent the night hours, perhaps their final ones together. Henry Green captured the essence of leaving in *Caught*:

When these girls were left behind alone as train after train went out loaded with men to fight, the pretty creatures must be hunting for more farewells. As they were driven to create memories to compare, and thus to compensate for the loss each had suffered, he saw them hungrily seeking another man, oh they were sorry for men and they pitied themselves, for yet another man with whom they could spend last hours, to whom they could murmur darling, darling, darling it will be you always; the phrase till death do us part being, for them, the short ride next morning to a railway station; the active death, for them, to be left alone on a platform; the I-have-given-all-before-we-die, their dying breath.

Wishing to become a poet before he died, the young airman Timothy Corsellis arranged to meet Stephen Spender on one leave, and wrote a poem to him. He could not stand the limbo of instruction for a combat that did not come. 'Thou shalt not fly' was the daily directive and war was as remote as Abyssinia:

> Then came the queuing, the recurrent line of pungent men
> Dressed in dirt with mud eating their trouser legs,
> The collar that is cleaner than the shirt
> And the inevitable adjectives.
>
> The papers ran out early today,
> There was no butter for the bread at breakfast,
> Nobody calls us at dawn,
> We never strain or sweat,
> Nor do they notice when we come in late.
>
> When I was civilian I hoped high,
> Dreamt my future cartwheels in the sky,
> Almost forgot to arm myself
> Against the boredom and the inefficiency
> The petty injustice and the everlasting grudges.
> The sacrifice is greater than I ever expected.

He gave the greatest sacrifice, his own life when the fighting did begin, and left Spender with the regret that he had never answered the poem dedicated to him.

Regretting his lovers in Austria, John Lehmann plunged into the military underworld that brought soldiers and men of letters together in the lull before the blitz. He encountered several guardsmen in the strange period before the bombing began, when

the black-out heightened the sense of adventure as one slipped into pub after pub. My sexual hunger was avid as it was with so many others at a time when death seemed to tease us with forebodings of liquidation in terrors still undeclared. One curious manifestation of this was in the public urinals. As never before, and with the advantage of the black-out, a number of these, scattered all over London, became notorious for homosexual activities. Heaving bodies filled them, and it was often quite impossible for anyone who genuinely wanted to relieve himself to get in ... This was not my scene, but the pubs frequented by the soldiery were: those caverns of light and potential sensuous adventure that hid behind the blacked-out windows and the heavy double curtains of the doorway, in a totally darkened though sometimes moon-dramatised cliff landscape. Faceless uniformed figures passed me, fingers brushed my fingers, but I hurried on, ignoring the solicitations of blindfold Eros until I was in a place where I could see and choose for myself ... More and more of one's younger friends suddenly appeared in battledress or bell-bottoms, on leave from their training camps to say goodbye, to spend a few nostalgic days or weeks with their families and friends, with those who had loved or been loved by them before the clock struck. An atmosphere of heightened emotion dominated; kisses were exchanged with those one would never in normal times have reached the point of kissing; declarations of devotion and admiration were made that might never have come to the surface otherwise; vows to keep in touch, to form closer and more meaningful alliances when peace returned, came from upper lips that were usually stiff. Cheerfulness without bombast, or even hatred of the enemy, prevailed on the surface.

So *In the Purely Pagan Sense* described the encounters of young serving men with a leading literary editor in the first year of the war. The Charlotte Street café regular and artists' model with hennaed hair, Quentin Crisp, agreed. Along with some of the younger Fitzrovian painters, he had been exempted from military service as an overt homosexual, said to suffer from sexual perversion although he gloried in it. He lived in the world of bookies and burglars, artists and actresses, poets and prostitutes who haunted Fitzrovia. These were now joined by the war deserters, who lived in the cafés and stayed for weeks on end in a cellar called 'The Low Dive', until the military police swooped on them. Crisp liked the time because the women had gone butch and took to uniforms, and he could at last wear women's trousers and black, lace-up shoes with firm, medium heels. London by night became 'one of those dimly lit parties that their hosts hope are slightly wicked'. But when the bombs started to fall, 'the city became like a paved double bed. Voices whispered suggestively to you as you walked along; hands reached out if you stood still and in dimly lit trains people carried on as they had once behaved only in taxis.' Railway carriages were the playground of exhibitionists. 'The whole of London was one long towpath, one vast movie house.' This was 'the feast of love and death that St Adolf had set before the palates of the English – parched these long dark twenty-five years'. And along Piccadilly, the regular tarts still walked their beats, carrying gas masks, which seemed to offer a grim sort of sex, a threat of terminal disease behind the smiling question, 'Hallo, dearie – want a little love?'

This was the world of London on leave, to which the exiles in khaki had to return to publicize their perceptions and frustrations. There they met the editors and

51

patrons and sympathizers who would listen to and perhaps broadcast their discontents. And those who were not summoned to duty or were excused from it allayed their guilt by trying to print the works of those who were. *Horizon* published Alun Lewis's poem 'All Day It Has Rained' and two more of his works, then called him to the office for a meeting. There he found 'the strange nervous *Horizon* gang.' He felt his khaki was too rough, his boots 'much too heavy to be near them.' Stephen Spender particularly impressed him as a mixture of hawk and dove, but they would never lead the people to the new world. Cyril Connolly, after all, had endeavoured to ignore the war and was called to task and to a grudging participation. The time of security was over. Nothing belonged to anybody in war, not even safety. In his 'Ballad of the Safe Area', Francis Scarfe had his civilian narrator thinking 'of poets lost in barracks or crawling about on muddy stomachs' while he drank their toasts in beer and whiskey. But the bombardment came even to his street and his house. And when he tried to help the victims of the land-mines, he was sent away. There was nothing for him to do, the wardens did not like him trying to be a hero. He had not trained monotonously for it.

In point of fact, putting on the uniform of the exile in khaki was already the denial of all property in the past. Wearing battledress produced a sense of classless anonymity, just as the actual loss of all possessions might lead to a feeling of freedom. In 'Soldiers and Civilians', the refugee Alfred Perles, now working in the Pioneer Corps, testified to the liberation of losing all that he owned when a bomb destroyed his London house, which was suspended in the air like a nightmare Tower of Pisa with his library and clothes and manuscript notes floating on a malarial bog in the basement. He felt curiously elated and newborn into his khaki battledress in Oxford Street. He walked into a pub and almost shouted 'Heil Hitler' in gratitude for being totally freed to become an unknown soldier. He was protected from all curiosity, malevolent and benevolent. 'Only I knew that I had just lost all my terrestrial goods. It did not matter. After all, I had lost nothing essential. As a matter of fact, all I had lost was essentially inessential. Out of a sudden, I realised that all one possibly can lose must needs be inessential.'

FOUR

War Like a Wasp

Writing his testament and prophecy five centuries later than François Villon, John Bayliss warned wayfarers travelling through Coventry and London. It might be better to die quickly than grub among ruins, seeing the remains of children or friends or lovers lifted out by the rescuers.

> And I say to you who have seen
> War like a wasp under a warm apple
> rise and sting the unwary,
> that its breed shall multiply
> and fill the air with wings, and dapple
> disaster on the bright sky,
> and worse things shall be than have been.

Waiting for the blitz may have been false alarms and prolonged tedium, but, when it came, it fulfilled its fears and prophecies. 'The clear September of that year was good for bombers,' Seán Jennett wrote, one of the poets who worked for the Grey Walls Press and later for Faber & Faber. 'We remember it because the sky screamed and we were mere items of wreckage in the ruined day.' On the 7th of September, 1940, the German bombers struck dockland and the East End on the principle that they should shatter the morale of the working classes, who might cause a revolution at home. One of the writers working in the Auxiliary Fire Service and made famous by the war, William Sansom, objected to the contemporary slogan, 'London Can Take It'. There were other courses open – riots, mass flight, desertion from the civil defence forces, strikes and staying away from the offices and factories. Yet London stood firm. The only revolt was the invasion of the underground stations to act as the public shelters; the government had not built enough of them.

A new civilization was born under London, a new art provoked from it. On the fifth day of the blitz, the East Enders stormed the tubes of East and Central London. 'It's a great victory for the working class,' one man told Bernard Kops. Soon up to one hundred and fifty thousand people were sheltering there every night, or living there because they were homeless. The government had to acquiesce in the action of the people. 'They lay anywhere,' Sansom wrote. 'In rows like huddled fish they lay on the platforms. They slept in the passages and on the escalators. Women, children, men, suitcases, blankets, pillows, rugs, coats and even sheets lay packed in a solid mass. The trains came and went, the people tried to sleep and slept.' The trains pushed hot air ahead, so that a reeking warm blast swept through the platforms. Although only four in a hundred Londoners went down the underground and nine in a hundred slept in public shelters, the tube dwellers caught the public eye and imagination. Not only did they inspire Henry Moore's greatest drawings, but a poetry and a mythology.

> Knees, necks, a litter of loose arms,
> Awaiting to-morrow in yesterday's clothes, privacy's
> Last surrender.

Tambimuttu himself praised the man in the street, now in the underground, in one of George Orwell's talks to India. Hailing the new spirit of comradeship among the shelter people, he even claimed that many went down there not to escape the bombs, but because they liked being together and having a conversation.

More squalid than the underground stations, which allowed a certain movement, were the improvised public shelters, set up beneath railway arches or in sunken warehouses. The more notorious of these were at Tilbury and the Isle of Dogs. Up to fourteen thousand people filled the Tilbury shelter, which Ritchie Calder said was unequalled 'by anything west of Suez. Every race and colour in the world were represented there – Whites, Negroes, Chinese, Hindus, Polynesians, Levantines, East Europeans, Jews, Gentiles, Moslems, and probably Sun-Worshippers were all piled there in miscellaneous confusion. Seamen came in for a few hours between tides. Prostitutes paraded. Hawkers sold clammy fried fish, which cloyed the fug with greasy sickliness. The police broke up free fights. And children slept.' On the Isle of Dogs, an American journalist found only twelve toilet units for eight thousand people, carpeted, blanketed, draped everywhere. The stench was appalling, lice thrived. He was shocked and numbed, then he proceeded to the shelter at the Dorchester Hotel. There in the old Turkish baths were neat rows of cots covered with fluffy eiderdowns. On one curtained alcove a sign was painted: RESERVED FOR LORD HALIFAX. The other places, Cecil Beaton noticed, were occupied by 'cabinet ministers and their self-consciously respectable wives; hatchet-jawed, iron-grey brigadiers; calf-like airmen off duty; tarts on duty; actresses (also), *déclassé* society people, cheap musicians and motor-car agents.'

The wealthy and literary Canadian diplomat Charles Ritchie felt safe in the Dorchester: it was a fortress propped up with money bags: no bomb would dare penetrate its privileged enclosure. He lived himself at Brook's Club in St James's, and he found the shelterers in the tube hardly riotous, although there were stories of drunks throwing each other on the live wire. He had never seen so many different ages and types of people asleep underground. Their sprawled attitudes made him think of war photographs of the battlefield dead – 'their stark and simplified faces. What one misses in the sleeping and the dead are the facial posturings prompted by perpetual vanity.'

The contrast between the public shelters for the rich and the poor provoked one outburst. A Communist Member of Parliament led a hundred East Enders into the Savoy Hotel shelter when the sirens sounded; but the All Clear was heard a quarter of an hour later, and all the demonstrators had to leave, tipping the commissionaire, or so it was said. Remarkably, there was no other protest. London could take it in its various refuges for its polyglot population. There was, however, a certain shame in seeing the terrible contrasts on a night out on the way to a 'Blitz Dinner'. As one Able Seaman on leave described it:

> The Hun was droning overhead, lady
> And Taxis wouldn't ply
> As to the Savoy Grill we went – by Underground.

The stench and heat and aching light, lady
And trains that rattled by –
Showed sights we dared not see, for we were pleasure bound.
West End lights were low and soft, my lady –
Silver the music's sigh.
Expensive food lulled flesh, dulled minds to war's dread sound.
Deep I looked in your sad eyes, sweet lady –
Afraid that you would cry
These few to scorn, their selfish set confound.
And silent and ashamed we rose and returned
By way of the Tube, through humanity spurned.

Oddly enough, such reactions were rare. Most Londoners and visitors to London found a new openness and equality. Radicals such as Julian Symons thought he had reached a Utopia, rather like life in Russia in the months after the revolution. He was happy because existence was so impermanent. Money and property were meaningless, as they could be gone tomorrow. The journey to work was an absurdity and an adventure. Living was the next meal and drink. 'Barriers of class and circumstance disappeared.' The critic V. S. Pritchett could ask, 'Is it not merely externally a war but really a social revolution?' The early rumour that the Nazi Air Marshal Goering had promised not to drop bombs west of Aldgate was soon dispelled when high explosives twice hit Buckingham Palace and devastated large areas of the West End, including the Cavendish Hotel. Queen Elizabeth was photographed against the same sort of splintered wreckage faced by many housewives, while Rosa Lewis, wearing her collection of army badges up to her shoulders, moved temporarily with a hamper of champagne to the air-raid shelter at the neighbouring Ritz. Even Ritchie Calder, who had seen a segregation and a class system in the shelters, admitted that the raids and the communal feeding of the homeless were a great social leveller. The bombs flattened all without benefit of rank or place.

'There were no longer two Englands,' John Braine later declared in his biography of J. B. Priestley, 'Blighty and the Front, the safe civilian world and the hellish military world. The blitz at one stroke abolished the distinction between soldier and civilian.' It was particularly so in the fire-fighting services, where even middle-class writers like Peter Quennell found a curious acceptance and a respect for privacy from his fellow firemen, brought up in overcrowded homes with a natural tendency to keep their distance. They were tactful and light and easy, Stephen Spender noted in his *Citizens In War – And After*, to make up for the heavy stupidity of the wet and cold fire-fighting equipment. During the period of the first blitz, which came to be known as the 'Old Blitz', there was a necessary companionship, a refusal to complain, a minimum of grousing. 'The stubborn individual will', William Sansom wrote, 'merged into a grim, effective communal will – from the free lifts advertised in all cars to the old lady with a saucepan for a tin helmet who handed out her tea in the fire-glow of splintered streets.' While having a haircut in the City, George Orwell asked his barber if he carried on shaving people during air raids. Oh yes, the barber said, he carried on just the same. And one day – Orwell commented in his diary – a bomb would drop near enough to make the barber jump, and he would slice half somebody's face off.

A perception of common suffering extended beyond community. Spender found in the fire service a touching refusal to hate German thought and arts. As for the German people, they were separated from their leaders. During one air raid, a fireman said to Spender that he supposed the Germans hated being bombed just as much as the Londoners did. There was a bond between all people who were being attacked from the sky. Even airmen were sorry for the victims whom they killed so blindly. Spender understood that, too, for he was comforted during bombing raids by the thought of how random the dark plain of London under black-out must seem to the aeroplane on high. Each person was so small compared with the immensity of the whole city. Firemen like himself, indeed, attracted the pity of RAF pilots, who felt they were lesser targets than those who fought the fires which the bombs began. 'You're the chaps I feel sorry for,' Spender was told, 'when we're on a raid.' Charles Ritchie even thought that the war had caught the British in the same trap as the Germans. Unnatural weapons dominated all. 'The pilot is the tool of his plane, the gunner of his gun. That is what makes modern war a new predicament ... The Germans know the same joys and sorrows that we do. They are the mad dogs who have bitten us and infected us with their madness.'

The blitz brought another pardon to London. The soldiers in the rural monotony of their camps and the provincials in the envious righteousness of the shires forgave the great Wen, the ravening shrew of a metropolis. London could take it, as the phrase went, and take it London did, nightly, cruelly, murderously. The suffering and courage of its citizens altered regional antipathies. The poet J. C. Hall journeying to the capital from Wales and mountainous indifference, travelled to where his hopes were, 'to the heart of love, to the heart of danger'. The general refusal of the cockneys to evacuate their home streets, even if it meant night after night in the squalor of shelters or the underground, persuaded countrymen that even urban dwellers had roots. Most of the three-quarters of a million evacuees of September 1939 had voluntarily returned to London from the unfamiliar isolation of the provinces. They would rather incendiaries fell on their heads than apples.

> You can't dismiss cities with an idealist cry,
> With a sigh; you may bomb them, smash them.
> But cities don't easily die.
>
> Houses, people and parks, buildings and shops,
> Spire and steeple, and the simple satisfying sun,
> Are real; are remembered like good crops.

For the provincials and the new artists, the fires over London burned open new opportunities, which only the post-war architects were stupendously to put to waste   57 again. Between Christmas and New Year's Eve of 1940, the German bombers tried to make a conflagration of the whole City of London. In Paternoster Row near St Paul's and its great dome, twenty-seven publishing firms had their offices and warehouses, including Longman's and Collins, Hutchinson's and Eyre & Spottiswoode. Five million new books were incinerated on the 29th of December, and fifteen million volumes more in the raids to come. Old literature was put to the torch in a way that Hitler had never even achieved in Nazi Germany. As Sagittarius mourned:

> Red roared the fire through the heart of London's City,
> Hurled from the clouds by a brute and savage foe,
> They who their own land robbed of light and learning
> Kindled the bombs here, a brand for London's burning,
> Lighted the bonfire of Paternoster Row.

So the blitz paradoxically opened the door to new writers by clearing out the stocks of new books by established authors. A. P. Herbert, whose satirical poems in *Punch* and the *Sunday Graphic* were a feature of the war, had already derided the government for leaving out all printers and writers from the Schedule of Reserved Occupations, those crafts in which workers had to stay on the necessary jobs and so were exempt from service in the armed forces. 'They, whose trade it is to tell the truth,' Herbert commented, 'will not be wanted in the next Big Fight.' This had been made even more explicit on the eve of the blitz by the Chancellor of the Exchequer stressing the urgent and imperative need to limit civilian consumption of books. If he had merely said that reading must not occur again, people would understand that books should be treated like boots. But with the destruction by fire of the inventory of most of the leading publishers, there were few books to sell or to tax. An opportunity had been created for fresh authors to the limits of the paper ration. It was also an opportunity to read past writers. It was a disaster that the intellectual production of the country should be brought to a standstill, Margaret Kennedy declared in *The Author*, 'but a country must draw on its resources. It must read old books, just as it wears old clothes. Fortunately books last better than clothes.'

Established editors and writers were also affected by the blitz. Cyril Connolly had to change his literary values; he even found Proust disappointing. The bombs had not only emptied the drawing-rooms, they had blasted the reputations made in them. War shrank everything. There was no time to read the leisurely masterpieces of the past without being irritated by the amount they took for granted. 'We are living history, which means we are living from hand to mouth ... It is as unfair to judge art in these philistine conditions as if we were seasick.' Although very little new was being written, much of the old was being forgotten. William Blake had commanded: Drive our harrow on the bones of the dead. Such a silent revolution was happening. And there was a judgement on the new writers by the old. For T. S. Eliot's *The Waste Land* had become actual, the waste land of the city of London with its burned bricks and broken glass, fallen arches and rubble, charred baulks of timber and shattered tiles. Graham Greene felt at home at last in bombed London, because life there was what it ought to be. Life had at last become just and poetic, for those who believed the bombardment was the right end to the muddled thought and the sentimentality and selfishness of generations.

If a cracked cup is put in boiling water it breaks, and an old dog-toothed civilization is breaking now. The nightly routine of sirens, barrage, the probing raider, the unmistakable engine ('Where are you? Where are you? Where are you?'), the bomb-bursts moving nearer and then moving away, hold one like a love-charm. We are not quite happy when we take a few days off. There is something just a little unsavoury about a safe area – as if a corpse were to keep alive in some of its members, the fingers fumbling or the tongue seeking to taste. So we go hurrying back to our shelter, to the nightly uneasiness and then the 'All Clear' sounding happily like New Year's bells and the first dawn look at the world to see what has gone ...

An old world was gone, a new world created. For artists even more than writers, the landscape was translated. The black-out reduced the colours on the palette, the dim blue light allowed in railway carriages and buses, torch beams dimmed to a sliver, traffic lights masked to three crosses of red and green and yellow, only a cigarette-end displaying a nocturnal orange spot on the street. In the offices, dim green-shaded bulbs sent out a tenuous glow against the curtains tacked over the windows. Henry Carr and Eric Ravilious, James Boswell and John Piper caught the dim atmosphere of the shrouded streets, the shadowed brightness of the control rooms. But it was the bombing itself that converted the painters to visions of the Apocalypse, until then a term appropriated by a group of minor romantic poets, whose fires would burn down soon after the blitz. Walking through the City after the raids, Graham Sutherland would never forget 'the silence, the absolute dead silence, except every now and again a thin tinkling of falling glass – a noise which reminded me of some of the music of Debussy'. In a bombed factory for women's hats, the entrails of machines hung through the floors, 'looking extraordinarily beautiful at the same time'. Stephen Spender believed Sutherland and Henry Moore and John Piper to be the painters of the devastation with their landscapes of twisted girders and broken humanity, but the artists of the Auxiliary Fire Service themselves, particularly Leonard Rosoman and Paul Dessau, were sufficient to the holocaust thereof. John Minton, too, made up a cosmology of the devastation in the East End with shell-shocked children wandering through his delineated ruins like waifs from Delvaux or Balthus in a metropolitan wilderness. To John Lehmann on a taxi ride through the devastated City of London, the sights were more extraordinary than the ruins of Rome in the old prints of Piranesi.

During the raids, the skies were full of an extraordinary geometry. In Spender's words:

> Triangles, parallels, parallelograms,
> Experiments with hypotheses
> On the blackboard sky,

Seeking that X
Where the enemy is met.
Two beams cross
To chalk his cross ...

His experience of actual and continual bombardment stimulated Spender into writing finer war poetry than the refugees Auden and Isherwood had written when they had skirmished in Spain. Then, he had been their lesser associate. Now, he inspired the younger war writers. Three who were to die visited him at the *Horizon* offices, the burned Richard Hillary, Timothy Corsellis and young Michael Jones, who was to be killed in a training accident, but who described to Spender the streets full of glass like heaped-up ice, the collapsed houses of the East End, and St Paul's in silhouette against the far fires of dockland.

Unfortunately, London during the blitz did take on a new beauty. By night, William Sansom found that the great buildings of the City were turned into cold, ancient, lunar palaces carved in bone from the moon. Then the darkness flared into sudden relief

in the yellow flash of gunfire, in the whitish-green hiss of incendiaries, in the copper-red reflection of the fires, in the yellow flare of the burning gas main, in the red explosion of the bomb. In such light the gilt tracery of Big Ben's tower flashed into colour, the sombre drab alleys round Covent Garden blazed with a theatrical daylight, the corrugated skylines of Park Lane and Knightsbridge showed black against the deep red sky, the streets of Pimlico and Soho saw the high scarfing columns of a naked gas flame flaring like some giant idealization of the naphtha flames that through the years had lit their fairs and their stalls.

These were the lights – but there were also dark streets, streets where suddenly a house of blackness collapsed with a roar, shifting down heavily like some bricked elephant lumbering to its knees, thickening the darkness with a poisonous cloud of dust, shrouding the moment after its fall with a fearful empty silence broken only by small sounds, the whispering of broken water pipes, slight shiftings of debris, moans and little cries of the injured; then into the torchlight of the wardens there would stagger those untrapped, lonely figures in the dust-fog bleached grey with powder and streaked and patched with black blood; or – there would be nobody, and not a sound, only a living silence in the knowledge that under a smoking, spawning mass of timber and brick and dust there lay pressed and stifled the bodies of warm people whose minutes were slowly ticking away, whose rescue was absurdly blocked ...

The worst elements of the bombed streets were the rank smells and the rabid cats. A raw and harsh stink pervaded the air, a compound of soot and dust, cinder and the lingering acidity of high explosive. Gas escaping from broken pipes tweaked at the nostrils, and the sweet reek of blood and corpses made the lungs retch. Meanwhile, hordes of mad cats leapt and screeched, trying to find their old snug-holes in the rubble of their owners' houses. Light as birds on the treacherous debris, the cats often led the firemen to buried bodies. And on the streets, glass glittered like frost on grass and broke underfoot in a strange grinding tinkle.

The morning after the raids revealed the houses disembowelled, the intimacies of private lives broadcast to the glare of day.

> They say that women, in a bombing-raid,
> Retire to sleep in brand-new underwear
> Lest they be tumbled out of doors, displayed
> In shabby garments to the public stare.
>
> You've often seen a house, sliced like a cheese,
> Displaying its poor secrets – peeling walls
> And warping cupboards. Of such tragedies
> It is the petty scale that most appals.

So Norman Cameron commented in his poem 'Punishment Enough' and Bertram Warr, serving in the Royal Canadian Air Force, found no comment on the war from the damaged houses in 'Stepney 1941':

> Shall we knock? Shall we get their reactions to the war?
> This one will do. But it's empty; no door even
> To knock at. And this too; the whole row
> And not a soul, all empty and windowless,
> With walls standing around regarding one another
> Naked, as they bear the weight of shocked ceilings.
> Let us not speak, for we look into hearts
> That are drained and stilled, as though
> God had … Hell, like a lot of tarts
> They are, with their legs cocked, showing the works.
> Let's get out of this. Look, there's a cat lurking
> In that debris! See, beside that smashed divan.
> Here, puss, pretty puss, here. Why, look at it run!
> Crazed, and that savage eye, already it has forgotten.

The writer and artist Mervyn Peake served as a sapper in a bomb disposal group. To him, the ruined houses were not skeletons, but opened bodies showing their coloured muscles and burst skin, vacant wombs and organs as rubble. Yet the very extent of the destruction also revealed the old anatomy of London itself. On a December night on Ludgate Hill, James Monahan could serve as the coroner of chaos and see among the desolation the sinews and ligaments of the ancient roads and patterns of the city, 'each criss-cross, curve, each cul-de-sac, each square, a blueprint, magical across the waste'. The heart of history was still beating, the dome of St Paul's still stood serene above the autopsy performed by a blitz that had sliced open the fundamental design of bygone London.

So the general devastation changed the perceptions and the visions of artists and transients in the capital. The bombs also stimulated the senses, awoke the eye. Men and women, after all, were alive and aware, while bricks and plaster were not. The arts revived with a fresh significance. 'This arose spontaneously and simply,' Spender wrote, 'because people felt that music, the ballet, poetry and painting were 61 concerned with a seriousness of living and dying with which they themselves had suddenly been confronted ... A little island of civilization surrounded by burning churches – that was how the arts seemed in England during the war.' The troops and the displaced still swarmed to that last centre of civilization despite its battered geography and nightly disturbances. Alan Ross found London an *émigré* capital, where, at rare intervals of paradise, people were allowed to return.

We lived in two mental dimensions. On leave we indulged, ruthlessly at first, sentimentally later, our most primal, parched appetites. At the same time we carried in our minds, like pock-marks or scars, the pitted land-and-seascapes to which we had always to return, and whose reality insisted on disturbing us like the image of an operating theatre on patients let out on parole before operations. The other, reversed process of these dimensions was, back at sea or in the desert, that we wore them like flowers on the drab uniformity of our serving minds the images of our leaves.

But London itself was a pool, imaginary or real, which held us, infinitely, because like an older, experienced mistress it both satiated and expiated us. We returned to our military obligations on level terms with ourselves.

The mental picture of leaves in London during the blitz were larded with women. All around the clubs and pubs of Fitzrovia and Chelsea were 'The Lost Girls', independent and adventurous young women, described by Peter Quennell as wayward and lonely and courageous, perfectly capable of existing without any thought for past or future. 'I trust you don't get too drunk in Soho and claw the lads in consequence,' John Gawsworth wrote back to one of them. 'My neck still bears marks of your talons and my Commanding Officer looked most oddly at it on Special Inspection – but passed on!' Not all were products of war conditions, such as Joan Wyndham or Barbara Skelton or Theodora Fitzgibbon, who have written the better memoirs of the period. Many kept the habits of the pre-war *garçonnes* and variety girls and models, the women whom Alan Ross called 'The Nightclub Naughties a decade before the Forties'. But as a spate of grateful poems showed, war made them give themselves up to brief encounters. At the Bag o' Nails, the girls did not even make servicemen subsidize their favours, if they had spent their pay. 'The girls were so nice to you,' a transport officer in the Irish Guards said. 'They were all afraid, so they were much nicer to you, but only during the war.' As Francis Scarfe wrote in his 'Lines Written in an Air Raid':

> Look, friend, how the hostile day
> Raffles reality above our love.
> Say to me all you never meant to say
> For I know, now, all you were ever thinking of.
> Look in my eyes, and not the other way
> To the sky, where the clouds are set as gigantic chess
> And the planes between as players' fingers move.
> Kiss me, before all breaks. Let me touch your dress.
> If we must die, then let it be of love,
> And set the whole world trembling as we kiss.

Tributes for 'The Girl in the London Blitz', taken on the cold earth, and to the hotel encounter in 'Two Pairs of Shoes' festoon the war anthologies. The brilliant Keith Foottit wrote the second poem before dying in a bomber over Germany at the age of twenty-two. 'There's no time to lose, dear, / There's no time to lose, / Already they are polishing / Our two pairs of shoes.' Short leaves and snatches at emotion, desperate partings and the imminence of death produced writing that was more stoic and laconic than romantic. Even the ballads were more bitter than sweet, as when the two lovers walked down a Tooting street to the three-roomed flat at the Radio Store:

> The wail of a bus as it changes gear,
> The smell and the cries of the fading light,
> The raucous song of men on the beer
> All, all are gone, and we have tonight.
>
> And the man who is weary of marching days
> Lists to the music the great bed makes,
> 'Forget your dull drab khaki ways,
> Sleep the sweet sleep from which no man wakes ...'
>
> – Till the daylight fades in the lurid sky
> And the night dew bathes the rotting dead.
> 'What does it matter, we all must die,
> In a blood-stained field or a quiet bed.'

Three novels best describe the state of mind of Londoners surviving the blitz. *Caught* by Henry Green is partially autobiographical; he was a member of the fire service at the time and told of the conflagration from the point of view of the firemen. *No Directions* by James Hanley depicts a night in a Chelsea apartment house during the raids, but it is too disjointed and surreal and drowning in streams of consciousness to suggest more than the absurdity and chaos of the bombardment. Nigel Balchin, however, in his undervalued *Darkness Falls from the Air* captures the frenzied dance of death, by which many assuaged the time of sudden mayhem from the air. By making his narrator a civil servant with a taste for bohemia, Balchin implies a criticism of the false insouciance and real strain suffered by those in London, who chose to try to ignore war conditions and random deaths. The limited hero thinks it would be all right to be in the armed forces – either you got killed or you sat around with tarts and laughed your head off. It was better than slaving at a ministry trying to persuade your boss to do his job. He wines and dines expensively with his errant wife, occasionally sauntering out into the blitz, which carries on regardless of them as they carry on regardless of it. But bombs impinge and explode in spite of the weary comments on the shattered night-life of the West End. 'Look – one joint that has been hit by a bomb is very like any other joint that's been hit by a bomb,' and, 'Air raids always seem to make people get tight.' Aimless fights break out, brawlers are wounded more often than bomb 63 victims, the raids are left to go on cheerfully while the narrator goes to sleep. But eventually he has to reach the blazing East End, where his wife is trapped in a fallen building. She is dying in agony, he gives her a shot of morphia. 'I lay there for a bit with my fingers on her pulse, though I hadn't been able to feel it for a long time. Then her eyes opened again and I knew that was that. I shut them because of the dust.' With prose barer than Hemingway's, with a terse recognition, the civil servant knows that he can no longer disclaim the facts of the war. The novel ends with him on the Embankment, extinguishing an incendiary with a sandbag. 'It went out, and then it was darker than ever.'

The blitz forced the civilian and the artist, the civil servant and the secretary, the fireman and the housewife, the soldier on leave and the factory worker, to recognize that they were fighting the same war. Their number might be on every incendiary, on each piece of shrapnel, which people used to collect like sea-shells from the beaches that were now framed with barbed wire. Their experience was common with all experience in a world war. 'Ordered this year,' Roy Fuller wrote:

> A billion tons of broken glass and rubble,
> Blockade of chaos, the other requisites
> For the reduction of Europe to a rabble.

The question for artists was whether the conditions of the war stimulated writing, as in the case of Fuller and Spender and Sansom, who had written only advertising copy before, and in the case of the painting of Moore and Sutherland and Piper, or put an end to them. In one of her stories, a character of Elizabeth Bowen's said of the blitz, 'It will have no literature.' The statement was in total contrast to the overheated declaration of Basil Woon in *Hell Came to London*: 'A thousand literary masterpieces will germinate from the bloody debris of London.' Neither statement was true. Many fine paintings and poems and stories, a few excellent film documentaries and novels resulted from the blitz, which was only a series of blazes in five long years of blasts. 'But time is a firework,' one poet declared, and his poem was 'a fuse or pin in the bomb.' Those who dared, lit the fuse or pulled the pin. And those who edited the works that derived from the blitz and from military service wondered about the result of all that suffering and devastation. Tambimuttu put the question at the end of a rare poem:

> What we must love or fight or hate about
> Is when the bombs and bands are ushered out
> Where O where will we find us after wreck?

FIVE

A True Bohemia

Leonard Rosoman

During the war, Fitzrovia was a true bohemia as it never was before or after it. Until 1939, its writers and artists had attracted people who hung on to them or who could be cadged off. Poverty was a choice rather than an imposition, a sacrifice to the arts, not a necessity. But war brought universal equality from rationing to pay scales: few had more than a few shillings to spare. The bombs did not select, either; only the draft boards did. Those who could stay in Fitzrovia and Soho were the lucky ones, although they could claim that the blitz and fair shares for all put them on a level with the servicemen, who were drawn to their company on leave. However bad the disease of 'Sohoitis', the condition of drinking there and getting nothing done, a Fitzrovian had more chance of scribbling a story or finishing a painting than a visiting guardsman or an airman. In a bitter attack on the pacifist Alex Comfort, 'As One Non-Combatant to Another', George Orwell pointed out that one man's personal safety was another man's loyal service:

> For while you write the warships ring you round
> And flights of bombers drown the nightingales,
> And every bomb that drops is worth a pound
> To you or someone like you, for your sales
> Are swollen with those rivals dead or silent ...

The ranks of literature were, indeed, most depleted, and thus most self-conscious. 'There were not a great number of us,' John Lehmann testified: 'Nearly all who remained knew one another (or very soon got to know one another) personally, and living more or less under siege conditions with very little opportunity of movement far afield, we were continually meeting to discuss together, so that ideas were rapidly absorbed into the general bloodstream and hostile camps and schisms never lasted long or remained very serious.' The group, for instance, which came to encapsulate the poetry of the 'forties, the New Apocalypse led by Henry Treece and J. F. Hendry, was conceived in the late 'thirties at Cambridge and died soon after the publication of its third anthology, *The Crown and the Sickle*, in 1943. It never had the influence or the power it was said to have.

The Scots poet G. S. Fraser, then serving in the army in Perth, wrote the important preface to *The White Horseman*, the first anthology of the New Apocalypse based on D. H. Lawrence's cry for 'the royal me, the sacred ego'. Edited by Hendry and Treece, it featured their own poetry and that of Fraser and Nicholas Moore, the son of the Cambridge philosopher. Fraser never met his editors; he stressed later that the New Apocalypse was a confused movement springing from a confused reaction. It was not the product of a clique. It was a movement towards completeness and freedom for man, against false politics and the State Machine. Based on Freud and the positive element in surrealism, the work of the New Apocalypse should have permanent clinical value for the human race. The movement was also a romantic denial of the Auden generation of poets, who were all members of the English ruling élite unlike the mainly regional and working-class poets in the new anthologry. The Auden group could only touch the uneasy conscience of its own class, not of the workers who were claimed as comrades. Its social conscience was out of touch with the slow and sure rise of the British Labour movement. Its heroic and militant poetry of the Spanish Civil War was irrelevant to the glum, dour patience needed by a young soldier training to defeat Hitler. The war, anyway, had made partisan poems of immediate political relevance a practical impossibility. Now all people had to withdraw into themselves, to become stoics. Only personal poetry was possible when society had disintegrated. 'We have not *asked* to be thrown back on our own imagination.' The army itself was not a society or a world: it had only a jargon, not an idiom. The integrity of the self, the writing of personal messages, that was the New Apocalypse. The war had killed off the social poet.

In fact, most of the poetry in *The White Horseman* was obscure, self-conscious and adolescent. Nicholas Moore's 'The Flag' made a fairytale out of Freud and the blitz.

> Anger walks like Aladdin
> Talking to the town with abandon,
> Rubs his lamp over London,
> And the bombs come rattling down.
>
> O Aladdin-Hitler I hate you
> With your lucky map and your language.
> If I out of my languor
> Can wake, I will wake and shake you ...

Posted to Cairo, G. S. Fraser dissociated himself from the New Apocalypse, saying that it was a crossroads. The poets in the anthology, who included Norman McCaig and Vernon Watkins, went off in their separate directions. Only Treece and Hendry remained as leaders of a movement without followers, marking time and preventing their own development. The brief members of a group that was never really a group had to survive the mockery of their fellow poets for being associated with a late and bad flowering of surrealism, a hangover of the 'thirties that was wrongly used to belittle some of the better poets of the war.

As for the New Romanticism, another term which was used to denigrate the achievement of the 'forties, it was hardly a literary movement, although the term was applied with some truth to three disparate major poets already working in the pre-war decade, George Barker and David Gascoyne and Dylan Thomas, and to the predominant group of Fitzrovian painters. The New Romanticism, however, had no truth when used to describe the contributors to *Now*, edited by George Woodcock, who was an anarchist pacifist himself and published the Trotskyite Julian Symons, the Marxist Roy Fuller, the Welsh nationalist Keidrych Rhys and many pure opportunists like Ruthven Todd. As Symons said, 'For anybody 67 wanting to know what non-communist literary radicals thought and hoped during those years *Now* must be an indispensable document, as *Horizon*, for example, is not.'

Yet Lehmann was correct. When Britain itself was a hostile camp aimed at Germany and bombed by Germany, with London as its epicentre, there was no place for intellectual schisms. It was 'a five-year sentence in gregarious confinement which we were all serving', wrote Lehmann's rival editor on *Horizon*, Cyril Connolly. The war made such demands on the time of writers that Connolly and Lehmann were always complaining that they never received enough material, particularly as Tambimuttu and Woodcock and Rhys and Wrey Gardiner were competing in order to fill the pages of their own little publications. And paradoxically, by 1941, a vast captive audience had been created for magazines, which printed short stories, diaries, poems and sketches – the only writing of consequence, in Orwell's opinion, in wartime. There were fewer established writers able to practise their craft, more opportunities for new writers with the occasional piece to publish, and an insatiable market, waiting in the black-out for the next diversion from the war. With a shortage of books because of bombing and limited paper supplies, nearly all magazines and anthologies sold out every issue. It was a golden age for the Fitzrovian writer who managed to write something, and many did.

Particularly successful were those who had military experience and escaped from it. The raw material of their new writing was forced upon them with later leisure to exploit it. A nucleus of Fitzrovia later in the war, Julian Maclaren-Ross and Keidrych Rhys and Paul Potts, a Canadian who hawked his hand-printed poems round the Soho streets, all served until they were discharged after being processed in an army psychiatric hospital. As one of the Fitzrovians noticed, the bulk of the intelligentsia had been conscripted without much regard for their special talents, and only now were some writers returning 'via the glass house and mental homes to Soho, there to join us the asthmatics, the consumptives and the conscientious objectors who had been left behind'. Potts, the holy fool among the Marxist poets, had already served time before the war. He had literally believed the rhetoric of his peers, as 'Inside' revealed:

> I sat around listening to men
> Talking revolution,
> All about free love and no private property
> Especially no private property
> So I went out and lived the way they talked
> Now when I get done for ninety days
> Did they send in a cigarette
> Did they write me all the news
> On long white sheets of paper?

Potts was one of those who was aware of the revolt against class among the new Fitzrovians. In his praise of George Barker and David Gascoyne and Dylan Thomas, he pointed out that they were all products of suburban secondary schools unlike the public schoolboys of the Auden group. 'No important poet under thirty-five has been to a senior university,' Potts asserted, 'no real poet of our generation is what a film script-writer would call a gentleman.' It was a point of view supported by Henry Reed, who saw the rebels against the Auden group in almost a dialectic process 'against the politically-conscious, over-intellectual writers of the early 'thirties'.

After their time inside military psychiatric hospitals, the discharged Fitzrovians joined those who avoided serving because of physical disability, such as Nina Hamnett's friend who came back to the Wheatsheaf, saying, 'None of the fighting forces will have me so I have returned to the old corps, the "Saloon Barrage".' Even John Lehmann, cruising on the last night of the blitz in the Fitzroy Tavern, bought Nina Hamnett several drinks before he picked up a sardonic young man in uniform, who spent the night chuckling macabrely as the bombs crumped down. He tended to remain on the outskirts of the pub groups, his eyes narrowing over his cigarette-holder, assessing 'the relative pleasures of company against the nuisance value of unwanted or rejected contributors to *New Writing*'. Those who were excused military service because they were already serving the BBC or the Ministry of Information could also congregate in Soho, Louis MacNeice and Cecil Day Lewis and George Orwell, who resented being made to put out propaganda, wasting his brains on war and feeling mean because other men were dying. And finally, littérateurs like Lehmann and Connolly were exempt because they were leading magazine editors, at last considered a reserved occupation for the very few.

The forced gregariousness, the necessary intimacy of writers and artists in those war years discovered its milieu in the pubs, which also had their golden age. As Theodora Fitzgibbon explained in *With Love*:

They were the only places in wartime London where one could entertain and be entertained cheaply, and find the companionship badly needed during the war. For people of our age with no solid, regular accounts behind us, it was difficult to come by even a bottle of sherry. Food was very scarce indeed, and food for the occasional dinner party had to be hunted for and often took many hours and much traipsing about. Many middle-aged people used to drinking at home found their only source of supply was the pubs. Bombs dropping on London could not be so easily heard when one was in them, and the company lessened apprehension. I loved pubs, they were new to me and I liked being able to find friends I wanted to see in a certain place at a certain time. Dylan (Thomas) had previously pointed out to me that the link between host and guest was a tenuous one, but that it never arose if one met in a pub.

Dylan Thomas, indeed, was one of two wartime Fitzrovians who would rise to international fame without rejecting his pub past; the other was Francis Bacon. But as the Irish writer and Fitzrovian Anthony Cronin observed, their success was a result of a defiance of the world and its fashions rather than a cultivation of them. For most Fitzrovians, success passed them by or they lost interest in it. But 'none of these people made a virtue or a life-style out of rejection or bohemianism ... They knew that artists as well as many other people had been poor and that some people must accept poverty as preferable to the waste of time and the corruptions inherent in the struggle to avoid it.' It was the uncreative, Cronin believed, who were most likely to confuse a mere life-style with a creative discovery. Those who clustered round the real artists and poets frequently did.

Fitzrovia was an initiation for young men and women, a world of sought encounters. 'One unlearned a lot and developed social skills,' John Heath-Stubbs said. 'It was a school of life which lasted till the late 'forties. In a night, how many distinguished people you met.' When the fledgeling novelist Peter Vansittart wanted to win some sort of reputation without earning it, he roamed the statutory Soho pubs, where he saw Paul Potts, who had bought a hat so he could raise it to a man currently unpopular. He stepped over the drunken Dylan Thomas. From a safe distance he watched the two unpredictable artists, Robert MacBryde and Robert Colquhoun. He dodged for weeks buying Julian Maclaren-Ross a drink as he held court, using his gold-knobbed cane as a sceptre and a truncheon. David Wright found Tambimuttu and Michael Hamburger, then on leave, in the Swiss pub and was introduced to Dylan Thomas, drunk and helpless and woebegone, nattily dressed like an unsuccessful commercial traveller. At the French pub, where old Gaston Berlemont presided with his grey handlebar moustache beneath the photographs of famous prize-fighters and music-hall stars, Dylan Thomas met everybody who would buy him a drink, just as the crown princess of the Wheatsheaf, Nina Hamnett, jingled her money-box at anyone who could buy her a drink and then said, 'Have you got the mun, deah?' Graham Greene was drinking in the Horseshoe with friends during the 'great blitz' of Central London, and he found all the Soho restaurants closed except for the Czardas in Dean Street: he ended on fire duty all night in Bloomsbury and, unshaven in the morning, was berated by a chemist when he asked for razor-blades: 'Don't you know there's a war on?'

Encounters proliferated in Soho pubs and drinking-places throughout the war. Stories of meetings in them were legion. But the questions were these. The meetings, were they inspirational? Did they produce better music or writing or painting, or were they merely a relief from the disciplines demanded by the arts? In Maclaren-Ross's case, he wrote after midnight and after drinking, and his early material came from his army days; only at the end of his life did he write his *Memoirs of the Forties* about his times in Fitzrovia. What is clear from that book is that pub life was full of fun and games, verbal and physical, like Maclaren-Ross's own match game called Spoof. But also clear is the convenience of the pubs for young and unknown writers, particularly those from the armed forces on leave, in meeting their peers and their editors. Tambimuttu did use the Swiss and the French pubs as his offices, although his backers Nicholson & Watson had provided him with real ones. It was in those pubs that he met Keith Douglas and edited the fine posthumous book of war poems, sketches and prose – Douglas's *Alamein to Zem Zem*. Whatever Tambimuttu's own view of the inertia of Soho, however great his drunken misuse of his own talents, he was available in the pubs to commission, encourage and deliver some of the better poetry of his decade.

Even Old Etonian editors could not forgo the pub entirely. Although Lehmann and Connolly also frequented the last of the salons, the clubs and the dinner-parties, shortage of drink and occasional loneliness and the need to meet their contributors such as their fellow Etonian George Orwell sent them on expeditions to the pubs, where Orwell insisted on drinking beer as a true working man should. 'Voices from young men under arms,' Lehmann wrote, 'poets and lovers of poetry cramped into the discomforts of the creaking, grinding military omnibus; voices overheard in pubs, confidences over glasses of mild and bitter; voices rise and are gone like clouds on a windy autumn day. Day-dreams, forebodings, meditations and visions ... What is the prospect? A mad world after the war – or no end to the war because the world has already gone mad? Somehow or other, one must build a fortress for poetry, for art.' Actually, it was from the roof of the fortress for art of *Horizon* that Orwell saw the great fire raid on the docks, with the Marxist novelist Humphrey Slater saying, 'It's just like Madrid – quite nostalgic.' Connolly did not agree. After looking at the enormous conflagration beyond St Paul's, he said, 'It's the end of capitalism. It's a judgement on us.'

Judgement did not descend on them or on capitalism. The poor were generally safe in their pubs in Fitzrovia as the rich were in their clubs. The nearest Connolly approached destruction was in a restaurant, which an incendiary hit and set fire to his good winter overcoat: he found himself 'eleventh away from the blaze in the chain of bucket-passers'. Only in Chelsea were two of the artists' pubs blasted, the Six Bells and the Crossed Keys. In the West End, judgement did descend on Madame Buhler's café in Charlotte Street and on the Café de Paris, already a deep crater in the ground which had begun its life as a bear-pit before it was remodelled as a restaurant and a ballroom on the design of the liner *Titanic*. Its customers, as Constantine Fitzgibbon pointed out, were another generation of the same sort of people for whom that doomed liner was built. As it was underground, it was falsely advertised as London's safest restaurant. This did not prevent two hundred-pound bombs falling through the twin roofs above the Café de Paris, killing thirty-four of the band and waiters and dancers, while hundreds more revellers were injured. On the balcony restaurant above, the glasses were unbroken with champagne bubbles still rising under a layer of plaster dust. One diner remembered wiping off the dirty foam before drinking the champagne and noticing that the waiter who had been pouring the wine was lying dead at his feet. Ken 'Snakehips' Johnson was killed. A witness saw his head rolling across the dance floor; but his trumpeter survived and went on to another night-club, where he blew his trumpet for his lost band-leader. He thought it was the best thing to do. Other people thought, the *New Yorker* correspondent noted, that the incident would cramp the style of restaurateurs, but when the next big raid came, all the popular places were as full as ever.

Drinking together did not escape social judgements. As the humorist Nicolas Bentley wrote:

> Blessed are the rich
>   Who can afford the clubs
> Where they can go drinking
>   When the poor have left the pubs.

Drinking hours and early closing time at the pubs, instituted as a measure to discipline working men in the First World War, did separate the pleasure and the leisure of the rich and the poor. What most shocked the bohemian Philip O'Connor about the mood of wartime London was that the left began playing 'the right luxury game of debauchery and drunkenness', at least the circle of writers and painters that he knew, and they played it in the meeting-places of the rich. For O'Connor, the feeling of community and comradeship between classes in wartime was only an embarrassing *manner*, 'a charade of being together that owed its continued existence to an immense fund of social sentimentality'. Some of the poems from the forces collected by Keidrych Rhys were in agreement: Bertram Warr writing on the 'Working Class' as the walkers on the pavement with their twice-turned collars and patched crotches, who saw that

> They have gashed the lands with cities
> And gone away afraid when the wounds turned blue.

And Pilot Officer David Bourne was disgusted with the night-clubs, which he could occasionally afford to frequent:

> Sagging on the bar, lean women smirked
> Their scarlet lips like blood on a mushroom
> Their greasy hair glistening, tinselled in the glaring light
> Gripping greedily in their blood-stained talons
> Beakers of thick and filthy liquid,
> Trained cigarettes drooping from their mouth-gashes.
> Pasty playboys ooze among the screeching throng,
> Seeking eagerly the women's vulgar leers –
> Smarmed like tight toads,
> Croaking lewdly in their husky tone.
> A haze of cess-pool air hangs from above
> Poisoned humus of a drugged society.

Although such denunciations were more harangue than verse, they did reveal the skull grinning beneath the skin of *bonhomie*. Louis MacNeice was as ambiguous as usual about the actual benefits brought about by contacts between the classes through the use of 'Alcohol', a poem printed in *Horizon*:

> On golden seas of drink, so the Greek poet said,
> Rich and poor are alike. Looking around in war
> We watch the many who have returned to the dead
> Ordering time-and-again the same-as-before.

Those Haves who cannot bear making a choice,
Those Have-nots who are bored with having nothing to choose,
Call for their drinks in the same tone of voice,
Find a factitious popular front in booze ...

Take away your slogans; give us something to swallow,
Give us beer or brandy or schnapps or gin;
This is the only road for the self-betrayed to follow –
The last way out that leads not out but in.

He was suggesting an inward journey, a self-exploration for those like himself who had falsely believed that they and the masses were one, and now knew that most English working-men supported 'the capitalist war' led by Winston Churchill against the Nazis, even if Soviet Russia had become a belated and willy-nilly ally on its old crusade against fascism. The turnabout of Stalin after Hitler's attack on Russia in 1941 caused some hilarity. As Sagittarius pointed out in 'Strange Bedfellows':

Capitalist circles here,
Forgetting their habitual fear,
Encourage with a Tory cheer
The battling Bolsheviki ...

Faced with the common enemy
Extremes must as allies agree,
For there is no security
Unless it is collective.

Cyril Connolly was even more acute when he pointed out that the alliance with Russia in 1941 solved the problems of those who were still covert communists after the Nazi-Soviet pact. 'They may now have been able to serve their own and their adopted country without a conflict,' he wrote of Guy Burgess and Donald Maclean. 'They were double patriots ... But few in power thought that the alliance with Russia was more than an expedient to defeat Hitler.'

The people crammed together in the pubs and the clubs also thought that there was some security in being collected together. Extremes met among them, too, the right and the left, the soldier and the conscientious objector, the pilot and the civil servant. Uniform itself covered up class differences; the debutante in the ATS or the WAAF looked the same in khaki or blue as the miner's daughter. The civilian population itself took on a drab and equal look because there were not enough coupons to buy new clothes. It was not quite, as the *New Yorker* maintained, sixty-eight coupons between the British and loin-cloths. But it was necessary to dress in old suits and overcoats until these were worn down to the same drab grey-black of the unpainted streets. All the silk for women's underclothes had been commandeered for the blimps, which floated like silver whales in air over the London parks. 73

The one outside the American Embassy in Grosvenor Square was manned by the sole crew of women in barrage-balloon defence, but their only hope of getting the cotton off their legs was if the blimp came down, and they could cut a piece from its shimmering flanks to cobble into stockings. In hope, they called it 'Romeo'.

The temporary communities where the armed forces and civilians met led to celebrations of canteens and messes, dance and music-halls, pubs and clubs. It was the first such tribute by poets to their haunts among the people rather than their drinking bouts with one another. The Mermaid Tavern was no longer lauded because Ben Jonson and William Shakespeare and their like passed their time there, but pubs in general were praised as refuges from the pervasive war.

> And nothing to say and the glasses are raised, we are happy
> Drinking through time, and a world that is gentle and helpless
> Survives in the pub and goes up the smoke of your breath,
> The regulars doze in the corner, the talkers are fluent;
> Look now in the faces of those you love and remember
>   That you are not thinking of death.
>
> But thinking of death as the lights go out and the glasses
> Are lowered, the people go out and the evening
> Goes out ah goes out like a light and leaves you alone,
> As the heart goes out, the door opens out into darkness,
> The foot takes a step, and the moment, the moment of falling
>   Is here, you go down like a stone ...

So Julian Symons wrote for Tambimuttu to print in *Poetry in Wartime*, while John Arlott was writing on the music-hall for *Modern Reading*, edited by the influential Reginald Moore – the theme was old, but came 'from the basic-slag of life, of debtor, or lodger, or faithless wife'. Mervyn Peake saw in 'Palais de Danse' a woman as powdered clay, but one of a bright million lost in the music with their limbs singing, as they watched:

> The sons of swingtime with their feet tap-tapping
> The hollow platform wait the millionth moment
>
> When to let loose on us the tinsel tiger.
> Arise the fag-end boys from the tin-tables,
> And slide into the hollow of the rhythm.
>
> The crimson jazz is bouncing on the boards!

For women without children, life in London was imminent, transient, of the moment. Relationships were as impermanent as the small drinking-clubs were. 'They all had very fancy titles like "The Stars and Stripes", "The Canadian Maple Leaf", Czech names and Polish names, and they all sold atrocious liquor. They were, in fact, clip joints.' There the loose girls and the street-walkers went with the men in uniform from home and abroad, to enjoy the few hours they could have in company, if the bombs allowed and in defiance of the bombs. 'The war was still reasonably new,' a girl from the Coconut Grove said to Constantine Fitzgibbon. 'It was exciting, a terrible thing to say, but it was. After all, when you're twenty-three years old a stimulus is a stimulus.' Social and sexual distinctions were swept away. 'It was God's gift to naughty girls,' Fitzgibbon's later wife Theodora wrote, 'for from the moment the sirens went, they were not expected to get home until morning when the "all clear" sounded. In fact, they were urged to stay where they were. When it came to the pinch, where their parents were concerned, fate was far preferable to death.'

The war was a stimulus for the men, too. Theodora Fitzgibbon paid her husband a tribute, when he asked her two decades later after their divorce why he and Dylan Thomas and so many of the Fitzrovians were dead or alcoholics or old before their time. She replied, 'When I first met you, Constantine, in Chelsea during the war, you and your friends wanted to drink all the drinks, sleep with all the girls, paint all the pictures, act in all the plays, write all the poems, *and* beat the Germans. And you did. Are you really surprised?' She had married him for the reasons that many people married quickly in the war – 'the fear that one or the other of them (this was a civilian's war, as well as the soldiers') might be killed and never see each other again; also for economic reasons. The army allowance for wives was, I don't care what anybody says, an incentive.' Among the artists and bohemians, at least, a mate serving in uniform could provide a regular income.

Other worlds joined the artists' communities in wartime – the worlds of intelligence and diplomacy and academe. Theodora Fitzgibbon became friendly with Donald Maclean, who had sought out French artists during his posting at the embassy in Paris, and now spent his time off-duty with British bohemians. He was introduced by the artist Isabel Delmer, the beautiful wife of the journalist of the intelligence services, Sefton Delmer: she later married the conductor and composer Constant Lambert, who summed her up as drawing corks, nudes and conclusions. Lambert was also something of a bohemian with a taste for drink and friends who were writers and artists, especially Michael Ayrton. Guy Burgess, from the *louche* flat in Bentinck Street which he shared with another intelligence officer, Anthony Blunt, made regular forays into Fitzrovia. Once he even appeared without rhyme or reason with George Orwell and the poets William Empson and Norman Cameron at an evening with the cabinet minister Stafford Cripps, who had suddenly expressed a desire to meet some literary people. The epicene Brian Howard, who also shared the flat in Bentinck Street and was the model for both Ambrose Silk in *Put Out More Flags* and the intolerable Anthony Blanche in *Brideshead Revisited*, had also inveigled his way into the secret service agency MI5, which he betrayed nightly in the Café Royal or the Gargoyle or the Ritz Bar. There, when rebuked for his indiscretions by a senior officer, he defied authority by replying, 'Mrs Smith to you, darling.'

In the pubs and clubs of London, rank hardly mattered in spite of occasional attempts by the military to restrict saloon bars to officers. The stimulus of war levelled all in some areas of the city just as the bombs had levelled all in other areas. There was a common reaction to the opportunities of the time among every class of men and women, who took it as it came, to hell with the morning. It did not always, however, lead to an expected success, as the historian of France and America, Denis Brogan, discovered, when he was working for British intelligence on Vichy. Walking with a wealthy Fitzrovian girl during the 'great blitz', he pressed her to make love before both of them were killed. 'I would love to,' she replied, 'but you are not the sort of man I could afford to be found dead in bed with.' Peter Quennell had a different experience with his 'Lost Girl', who was stimulated by watching a fire raid. 'That night fear and pleasure combined', he wrote, 'to produce a mood of wild exhilaration. The impact of a bomb a few hundred yards away merely sharpened pleasure's edge; and next day we wandered, agreeably bemused, around the shattered streets of Mayfair, crunching underfoot green glaciers of broken glass strewn ankle-deep upon the pavements.'

So the various social worlds of the capital mingled under war conditions. Many of the young women spent their time scurrying between friends and lovers, meeting them indiscriminately at whatever places they could afford. Barbara Skelton, then caught between simultaneous affairs with Peter Quennell and the Polish artist Feliks Topolski, found herself on a continual round between the Bunch of Grapes and the Queen's, the Belle Meunière and the Ivy, the Gargoyle and the Nest. 'What were we but a pair of opportunists,' she told Quennell, 'huddling together in a vain attempt to ward off the blows of life?' When she lunched at the Ritz she felt shabby. 'Oh! To be smart or rich or something.' But she was depressed by seeing all the homeless lying about in the tube, which she had to take on the way home. Eventually she met Donald Maclean in the Café Royal, and he helped her get a job as a cipher clerk in the Foreign Office, which resulted in a posting to Cairo in Egypt, where she became the mistress of King Farouk. After the war, she married Cyril Connolly, who thought her the equal of his *Horizon* assistant Sonia Brownell, later Mrs George Orwell, in sexual attraction.

It was one life story among many of that time in Fitzrovia. Barbara Skelton particularly bridged the gap between authors and artists, as Fitzrovia did in general, with its true bohemian blend of members of all the arts, writing and painting, drama and cinema, music and dance. While actors and film technicians and musicians and members of the opera and ballet companies had to come to the district for their work and contacts, most of the leading young painters chose to spend their time in London's wartime Latin Quarter. Augustus John and Nina Hamnett had done much to shift the artists' drinking-clubs to Fitzrovia from Chelsea, although the river borough still boasted the Gateways and the Studio, the Pheasantry and the cruelly named Crater Club. Nina Hamnett's reputation attracted the younger generation of artists, Robert Colquhoun and Robert MacBryde, John Minton and Lucian Freud, John Banting and Keith Vaughan, Francis Bacon and John Craxton who thought her a kind of hangover from pre-war artistic Paris, now that the war had stopped painters from going there for inspiration. Another attraction was the ultimate bohemian artist, Gerald Wilde, held to be the inspiration for Joyce Cary's quintessential Gulley Jimson in his wartime novel *The Horse's Mouth*. Cary actually bought Wilde's pictures, although the differences between him and Gulley were greater than the similarities. In fact, Wilde imitated Gulley's life-style more than he inspired it; but in one thing he was the true Fitzrovian. When Jung heard of the way Wilde existed, he analysed the painter as a man for whom money was poison. Like the hero of another novel, *The Small Back Room* by Nigel Balchin, Wilde was conscripted to take fuses out of high-explosive grenades. The experience made him half-demented, led to the torment of his greater paintings like *The Charnel House*, and gave him a bleak philosophy, usually expressed as 'Life is pure unadulterated hell.'

A peculiarly flaccid tripod – Ruthven Todd remembered – approached him one night in Soho by the light of a parachute-flare dropped from a German aeroplane. It was Augustus John, Nina Hamnett and Norman Douglas, linked by arms over one another's shoulders, 'drunk as sponges, on the way to the Gargoyle for an unneeded drink'. Hamnett seemed to span all social barriers, lunching with Nancy Cunard to discuss old friends like Ronald Firbank and Virginia Woolf and James Joyce, whom Nancy reckoned one required some drink to understand. She also acted as Joan Wyndham's introduction to the Fitzrovian pub world, although Joan's aristocratic father Richard Wyndham warned her off in case she became an expensive drinker like Hamnett; then he took his daughter off to the Gargoyle, which was owned by her cousin David Tennant; there Philip Toynbee was being sick on the sofa and Alexander's Band was playing the suggestive 'If You Want It You've Got To Buy It'.

> You can have it in a saucer
> You can have it in a cup
> You can have it lying down
> You can have it standing up.

A few months later, Joan Wyndham found herself at a party given by the Roberts, Colquhoun and MacBryde, for John Minton, who was on leave, 'the pretty dark one with the funny teeth'. She fell foul of the Scots laureate, Hugh MacDiarmid, on the subject of Robert Burns, but Colquhoun made her gloriously drunk by taking away her wine cup with the words, 'That piss is nae guid! Hae some whisky!'

John Minton and Lucian Freud may have been rich enough to patronize the Gargoyle, but the other neo-Romantic painters could afford only the Wheatsheaf and the Marquis of Granby, the Swiss and the French pubs, when they travelled into Soho from their flats in 77 Bedford Gardens on Camden Hill. Minton used that address intermittently as a studio, Robert Colquhoun lived there with MacBryde. So did the wise Polish painter and colleague of Paul Klee, Jankel Adler; the graphic artist Ronald Searle; and Kaye Webb, the art editor of *Lilliput* and patroness of them all, commissioning illustrations for her popular magazine. Robert Colquhoun and Robert MacBryde, however, were the cynosure of the 77

Fitzrovian painters, the Joe Orton and Kenneth Halliwell of the war decade. They were lovers, both extreme Scots nationalists, aggressive and touchy, proletarian and generous to a fault. Colquhoun had been conscripted into the Royal Army Medical Corps in 1940, and MacBryde had tried to get him out, asking the War Artists' Advisory Committee to commission paintings from him. When the committee had refused, MacBryde had denounced it as a body which neglected North Britain. By flaunting his homosexuality, never an open subject within the British Army, and by staging some nervous collapses, Colquhoun had secured his discharge and headed with MacBryde for London, a city which they would exploit and denounce for the rest of their lives. The Maecenas of his age, Peter Watson, subsidized them for a while; theft and minor work for civil defence bought the drinks. They rammed their regionalism down the throats of their benefactors, wearing kilts and dancing Highland flings and denouncing other Scotsmen working in London as quislings and collaborators with the bloody English. As a painter, Colquhoun had a touch of imaginary genius, a gift for Celtic design, while MacBryde was – as Paul Potts wrote – the greatest artist of them all in his medium, the love of human beings. 'He could turn a cup of tea into a feast. He loved children, dancing, singing and giving you money. He'd give you a pound note as simply as most people would give away a cigarette and more quickly than some. He hated bad art, the Hanoverian dynasty and Lyons tea shops; loved Turkish baths, patrons and cooking.'

MacBryde's great gift, as Paul Potts saw it, was that he was working class and a gentleman, which made him that much more a gentleman than an ordinary one. Potts himself came from the middle class and had left a private school too young. 'If you are going to be poor, you are lucky to be working class. Poverty is harder on those who fall into it than on those who can't climb out of it. Compare George Gissing to an unemployed miner in the thirties.' Temperamentally, Potts thought he was not cut out to be poor and precarious. Dylan Thomas once told him, 'You know you are a rich man without any money, while I am a poor one with a lot, I hope.' Ironically, it was Potts and not Thomas who came to be known as 'the poet of the people'. He personally hawked his verse in penny broadsheets round the Soho streets and sold it to the poor. He thought it to be a sacrament, while journalists thought it a stunt; some of his poetry was printed next to Ezra Pound's in *The Faber Book of Twentieth-Century Verse*. He had a just sense of his worth, writing that the difference between himself and a great artist was that he was not one. Like many other Fitzrovians, he was merely a person trying to be a poet. And like a true bohemian, he declared, 'When one is confronted with the mechanics of other people's success, one's own failure looks a little less shabby.'

John Lehmann was a mechanic of other people's success, a man cut out to be secure and well-off. There were emotional tragedies in his life including the death of a beloved Greek poet Demetrios Capetanakis; but the nearest he came to personal disaster was the explosion of a time-bomb in Mecklenburgh Square, which ended the Hogarth Press's domination of Bloomsbury a year after hostilities had begun. To Charles Ritchie, the bombing of Virginia Woolf's house and her death by suicide for fear of madness – a fear far worse than the fear of any bombs – meant the collapse of civilization. Certainly, the Bloomsbury ethos appeared to die with her, although John Lehmann was to continue with Penguin *New Writing* and become the most successful magazine editor of his decade. As early as 1942, the editor of the *Fortune Anthology*, the Apocalyptic poet John Bayliss, found it absurd that 'against a background of real war we have a miniature battle of the books, with Mr Lehmann striding over all like the Colossus of Rhodes, and editors of mere magazines blowing darts at each other between his legs. The problem has become who can compete with *New Writing*?' Lehmann did ignore, however, the supreme artist of his age and the illuminator of the agony of mankind under blitz and holocaust, Francis Bacon, who was actually working nearby in Mecklenburgh Square as an asthmatic servant for a solicitor in order to make ends meet – only the solicitor could not see why Bacon finally gave up his job to go back to painting, and declared: 'I can't understand why he's leaving because he doesn't do anything.' Lehmann himself employed Sonia Brownell as his secretary and admired her darting, gaily cynical intelligence and insatiable curiosity about all the gossip of the literary world; but he lost her to Cyril Connolly on *Horizon*, where she provided an intimate link between the two camps, which were thought to be opposed to each other. Actually, Lehmann and Connolly met throughout the war at parties and at clubs, and they had an area of agreement: the independence of literature should be defended, while the experiments and grouses of young servicemen should be printed. Lehmann, however, thought that Connolly was too moody and intermittent to be a professional editor like himself. *Horizon* had a 'chancy brilliance'.

The literary success despised by the Fitzrovians was assured by an invitation to Lehmann's wartime *soirées* on the sixth floor of Carrington House in Piccadilly. The guest list put Gatsby's to shame. Graham Greene was there, before he left for West Africa, full of sardonic tales about bureaucracy that failed to work; these were complemented by Cecil Day Lewis's horror stories about the Ministry of Information, where Laurie Lee also laboured. William Plomer was there, working in intelligence for the Admiralty with Ian Fleming, while George Orwell and Louis MacNeice would come over from the BBC. The Auxiliary Fire Service was heavily represented, Henry Green and Stephen Spender and William Sansom, whose novels Lehmann would get published. Connolly was often there, talking to Lehmann's sister, the novelist Rosamond, who always declared that she was like the Alcazar and never surrendered to the Marxist poets besieging her, but actually was the mistress of Day Lewis. Nancy Mitford would come along after closing Heywood Hill's bookshop in Curzon Street, and the historian Veronica Wedgwood, and Elizabeth Bowen, whose post-war novel *The Heat of the Day* would brilliantly distil the oppressive atmosphere and ambiguities of the war years. 'Take it from one of the best living novelists,' she said, 'that people's personalities are not interesting, except when you are in love with them.' Henry Reed, the poet of the instruction manual, would talk with Raymond Mortimer, the literary editor of the

New Statesman, which employed V. S. Pritchett, up from the country, and Philip Toynbee, who had written brilliantly on *Post D* during the blitz. Rex Warner would attend after the success of his novel, *The Aerodrome*, and the old Rose Macaulay, who had lost her manuscripts in a bombing attack. Among the young servicemen on leave were the writer and painter Keith Vaughan, the sailor and poet Alan Ross, and a sprinkling of aliens in Britain, all contributors to *New Writing*, Czechs and Greeks like Demetrios Capetanakis, Canadians and Americans. It was the place to go. It was the place to be and to be made.

Higher and rarer than Lehmann's parties were the last of the salons. Lehmann himself admired the feared Edith Sitwell's *Street Songs* and her *Green Song*: the war, indeed, seemed to have injected blood into the rich anaemia of her verse. He visited her at the Sesame Club and began a long association of sympathy and admiration, for admiring Edith's every statement was the prerequisite for her company. The actor Alec Guinness found this out to his cost. 'Beethoven is *deadly*,' she announced at lunch. 'Beethoven is a bore.' Stephen Spender meekly agreed, as did Dylan Thomas, but Guinness rebelled. 'I imagine Beethoven will be played and loved,' he said, 'long after everyone at this table has been entirely forgotten.' Guinness was neither forgiven nor invited back to lunch at the Sesame Club for a decade, until Edith Sitwell was received, as Guinness had been, into the Catholic Church.

The Ladies Colefax and Cunard continued to run their wartime salons, but these were more political than literary. Emerald Cunard's estranged daughter Nancy busied herself with collecting an anthology of poems on France and its fall. Like Cyril Connolly and Storm Jameson and many of the painters, she felt that the German occupation of Paris had cut off British culture from its necessary Gallic stimulants. And a social figure from the First World War arrived back in England to hold court in the Ritz, as Emerald Cunard held it in the Dorchester. It was King Edward the Seventh's last regular royal mistress, Mrs Keppel. 'To hear Alice talk about her escape from France,' a friend said, 'one would think she had swum the Channel with her maid between her teeth.' She was the empress of the Ritz during the war, or so Harold Acton thought, himself displaced from Italy to active service in the Royal Air Force. Through her salon flowed the *beau monde* of the arts, Acton and Noël Coward and Cecil Beaton. On her death-bed soon after the war, she was asked whether she loved nature. 'Yes,' she replied, 'the nature of the Ritz.'

Others held court at the Ritz in their fashion. Some were the *poules de luxe* who had fled France with their jewels and furs, provoking from James Agate the remark, 'How are the Fallen mighty!' Another was the aristocratic and drunken Edomie, otherwise known as Sod. Her exceptional kindness endeared her to many. In the war, the painter Michael Wishart remarked, Sod became 'a shrine of pilgrimage to homosexuals on leave from active service. During the bombardment, the downstairs bar at the Ritz was known as "l'Abri" (the shelter). It was here that Sod held court. To many she meant home. She was the buggers' Vera Lynn.' She bridged the bohemia of the 'forties, ending as an attraction in Muriel Belcher's Colony

Room, where she drank her meals until the last gulp.

Another wartime salon in the Dorchester was held by the press baron, Sir Edward Hulton, who had begun the successful *Picture Post*, the popular iconography of the war. The corridors of the Dorchester were thought to be the safest and best-supplied shelters in London. When leaving, late-night visitors often had to step over rows of famous bodies laid end to end. Hulton had married the daughter of a chamberlain of the last tsar, Princess Nika Yourievitch, and she shared the Francophile tastes of Cyril Connolly and the other exiles from European culture who enjoyed her dinner table. Once Connolly rebuked her for buying a new Rolls-Royce during the war, saying that it was not going to make her happy. She replied, 'Yes, I do realize that, Cyril. But when I'm very *un*happy it will comfort me to go and look at my Rolls-Royce.'

The war conditions of the rich were different from those of the poor. The artists were conscious of it, but then even Robert MacBryde loved the patrons like Peter Watson who bought Robert Colquhoun's pictures. Although the state had just begun to subsidize the theatre and painting, private patronage still ruled. Colquhoun was not to receive his first commission on a Scottish subject from the War Artists Advisory Committee until 1944. And most of the artists went to the grander clubs and hotels, when they could afford it, when they were asked. There was a movement across class barriers and habits, which J. B. Priestley noticed in his favourite Soho restaurant, the Ivy. In a piece printed in *Horizon*, he confessed that he was glad to see the leaders of the Labour Party eating regularly there. Although he was against privilege and for the people, he did not want to be governed by men who sat in back kitchens eating bread and margarine. They would console themselves for their ruined digestions by grabbing ferociously at power. The Ivy was very civilized and full of theatrical and film people, artists whom the Labour Party never considered. Priestley declared that he had spent much of the war with writers, musicians, painters, sculptors, theatrical and film producers, philosophers and scholars. 'If Labour had ever given them even one encouraging glance, they never mentioned it.' That is why the sight of Labour leaders in the company of established artists gave Priestley so much pleasure. He hoped the Labour politicians were meeting to plan the new England, which should have plenty of restaurants like the Ivy in it. Perhaps they would call intellectuals and artists to their table to lay the foundations of Blake's Jerusalem – 'oh, happy day!'

This was Priestley's dream, and it was not all fantasy. The post-war Labour government would subsidize education and the arts. State funding of British culture would develop. The contacts of the Labour leaders among the intellectuals and the artists in Fitzrovia were significant. Rationing and shortages encouraged them to visit the same restaurants and pubs. The war levelled up as well as down. Yet for most of the Fitzrovians it was a time of hand to mouth, chop and chop about, take what you could get before the bombs fell or the call-up came or the goods and the girls ran out. Senses were heightened, perceptions changed, new visions possible. The consciousness, which the Marxists had talked of raising in the 'thirties, was raised from class differences to winning a war in common. Meanwhile, there was the skimping and the exuberance of life every day, the expectation and the denial of imminent death every night. The novelist and radio producer Desmond Hawkins captured the atmosphere in his 'Night Raid', one of the more evocative poems of Tambimuttu's *Poetry in Wartime*:

> The sleepers humped down on the benches,
> The daft boy was playing rummy with anyone he could get,
> And the dancing girl said, 'What I say is,
> If there's a bomb made for YOU,
> You're going to get it.'
> Someone muttered, 'The bees are coming again.'
> Someone whispered beside me in the darkness,
> 'They're coming up from the east.'
> Way off the guns muttered distantly.
>
> This was in the small hours, at the ebb.
> And the dancing girl clicked her teeth like castanets
> And said, 'I don't mind life, believe me.
> I like it. If there's any more to come,
> I can take it and be glad of it.'
> She was shivering and laughing and throwing her head back.
> On the pavement men looked up thoughtfully,
> Making plausible conjectures. The night sky
> Throbbed under the cool bandage of the searchlights.

Lilliput

DECEMBER 1942   ONE SHILLING

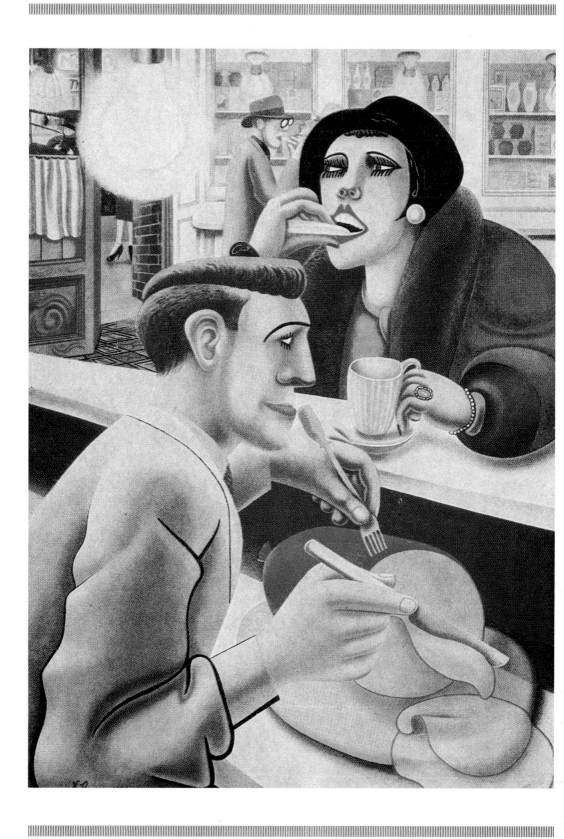

West End – Two Doubles, painted for
Lilliput by James Fitton.

The Pay Off from Edgar Ainsworth's 'In
Darkest Soho'.

OPPOSITE: *Snack Counter* by Edward Burra.

OPPOSITE: *St. Paul's from the River* – John Minton's painting from *Lilliput* in 1947.

Two Sisters, a drawing in coloured chalks by Robert Colquhoun, reproduced in Michael Ayrton's *British Drawings* of 1946.

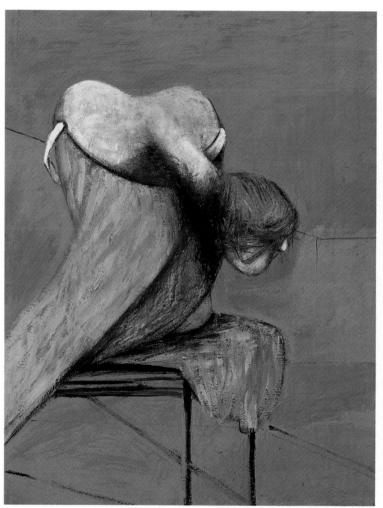

Three Studies for Figures at the Base of a Crucifixion (1944) by Francis Bacon.

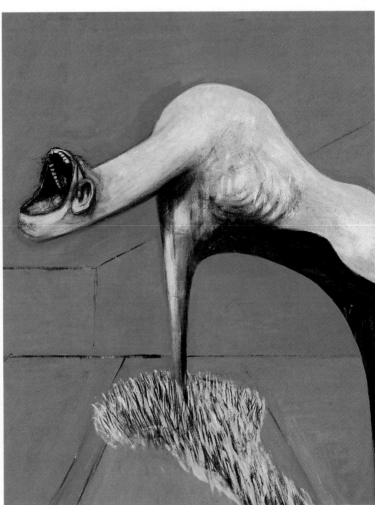

This is an illustration by Michael Ayrton for a poetry anthology,
Poems of Death, 1945.

SIX

Strangers in a Strange City

Leonard Rosoman

'Now we know where we are!' the captain of a Thames tug shouted to A. P. Herbert, who hoisted the naval signal A T I, *There is no need for alarm*, on the news of the fall of France. 'No more bloody Allies!' In 1940, the national mood turned against the refugees from Europe, the aliens who were bringing their special skills and culture to London. They seemed to be infiltrators, come to undermine British institutions. Even the poet W. R. Rodgers warned those who were trying to escape, that staying put might be preferable to long exile:

> The roads of Europe are running away from the war ...
> Turn back, you who want to escape or want to forget
> The ruin of all your regards. You will be more free
> At the thoughtless centre of slaughter than you would be
> Standing chained to the telephone-end while the world crashes.

Only known sympathizers of the Nazis were interned on the outbreak of hostilities. But with fears of a fifth column of enemy agents in the capital and with Winston Churchill talking of 'malignancy in our midst', measures were taken in May and June of 1940 to detain many of the European refugees and residents of London, particularly those who had fled from Central Europe or were of German or Italian origins. The fugitive intellectual Arthur Koestler was gaoled in Pentonville prison for six weeks on arrival in England; his important novel *Darkness At Noon* was being published and reviewed in London while he was still incarcerated; on his release, he said that when he wrote a Baedeker of the prisons of Europe, he would give Pentonville three stars in spite of the state of its plumbing. Anti-Italian riots were reported in Soho, when Mussolini decided to enter the conflict on the side of Hitler. George Orwell went to inspect the damage, but he could find only three shopfronts destroyed: the Italian grocer Gennaro's was plastered with placards declaring, THIS ESTABLISHMENT IS ENTIRELY BRITISH, whilst the Spaghetti House was renamed BRITISH FOOD SHOP. Unfortunately, many of those with Italian names, some with families who had lived in Fitzrovia for generations, were arrested and sometimes deported. The *Arandora Star* sailed for Canada packed with internees behind barbed wire draped over the ship's railings: it was torpedoed with the loss of six hundred lives.

Most of the aliens, however, were quartered in makeshift camps – in the totalizator on Kempton Park racecourse, in the Ascot Winter headquarters of Bertram Mills circus, in a disused cotton mill in Bury, in tents on a Shropshire heath, or chiefly in guarded boarding-houses on the Isle of Man. They were not badly treated. The London intellectuals who campaigned for their release were surprised that the confined, upon their return to the capital after their vetting, were as brown as tourists to the Riviera instead of black-and-blue after beatings in an English concentration camp. The Home Secretary was convinced that the wholesale temporary internment of aliens had prevented the Germans from having a single effective spy in Britain; but their incarceration did not help government propaganda that the war was a crusade for liberty. 'Nothing Alien Is Human' was another shaft from the pen of Sagittarius:

> When we intern the friends of liberty
> We cancel Ministerial eloquence,
> When we deport the alien refugee
> We shake the friendly alien's confidence,
> Until between us and the enemy
> They find in fact so little difference
> That when we sound the hour of their release
> They may be reconciled to Nazi peace.

The arrival of an intelligentsia from Europe represented a threat to the English version of that mentality. Geoffrey Grigson, who was unkind enough to many British writers, confessed to a general unkindness to the new cultural *émigrés*. 'We were jealous,' he wrote in his recollections of the Café Royal, 'and failed to keep any of the best and most creative of them.' Although the *émigrés* would rather have stayed in London, on the European side of the Atlantic, they were never given the funds or the prestige that they deserved. At Herbert Read's studio in Hampstead, Walter Gropius could be found, interrogating and finding society in London almost as grotesque as Lilliput. Moholy-Nagy came with the leaders of the Bauhaus school, but soon he was tempted along with Gropius to the United States, where dollars from Chicago would give him an Institute of Design. Both British insularity and brief internment soured the relationships between many of the Central European refugees and the native intellectual establishment. While displacement was the commonplace of this century – Joseph Brodsky was to declare – social insignificance was what writers in exile could not stand. It was this insignificance that the Londoners in wartime were particularly good at conferring on the refugees.

The foreign intelligentsia and the internees in their tens of thousands were relatively insignificant in a London flooded by hundreds of thousands of foreign allies. The drab streets of the bombed and gutted city were brightened by all the rainbow colours of multitudinous uniforms and insignia. 'French sailors with their red pom-poms and striped shirts, Dutch police in black uniforms and grey-silver braid, the dragoon-like mortarboards of Polish officers, the smart grey of nursing units from Canada, the cerise berets and sky-blue trimmings of the new parachute regiments, all the other gaily coloured field-caps of all the other regiments, the scarlet linings of our own nurses' cloaks, the vivid electric blue of Dominion air forces, sandy bush-hats and lion-coloured turbans, the prevalent Royal Air Force blue, a few greenish-tinted Russian uniforms and the suave black and gold of the Chinese navy.' Soon they were joined by the markings of the Americans, the military police in their helmets whiter than snowdrops, the army officers in their piebald olive jackets and mushroom-pink pants. The streets of Fitzrovia were a kaleidoscope of combat on leave of absence. *They Came to London*, a novel by Paul Tabori who had himself come there, hymned the refugees in their coats of many colours, waiting to return as soldiers to their home cities and lands. 85

Before the Americans entered the war, those European refugees who were fighting for the Allied cause felt superior. In an open letter to Henry Miller printed in *Horizon*, the French intellectual Alfred Perles flaunted his commitment. Although his only heroic deeds were shovelling dirt all day for a detachment of the Pioneer Corps detailed by the War Office to clear up air-raid damage, he was thankful for his fate. He would rather be an unknown British soldier than a best-selling writer in the United States. Europe might stink, but it was capable of suffering, while America could not suffer. 'Culture, if it is to die, will die in Europe, and there is no hope that it might come to life in the U.S.A.'

This judgement was spectacularly wrong. In the cinema and in popular music, American culture already dominated. England had no cinema stars with the appeal of Ginger Rogers or Joan Crawford, Humphrey Bogart or Fred Astaire, and swingtime was ruled by Benny Goodman and Glenn Miller. In literature, more and more American authors were being praised and printed and reprinted: William Faulkner and Ernest Hemingway and William Carlos Williams at Editions Poetry London, and Scott Fitzgerald and Nathanael West at the Grey Walls Press. The influx of American airmen and soldiers to London also led to American poets finding a place in little magazines and in critical acclaim. Randall Jarrell and Richard Eberhart, Richard Wilbur and Louis Simpson and Lincoln Kirstein were particularly noted for their war poems, and no British war poet achieved the laconic and effective lines of Jarrell's short elegy on 'The Death of the Ball Turret Gunner':

> From my mother's sleep I fell into the State,
> And I hunched in its belly till my wet fur froze.
> Six miles from earth, loosed from its dream of life,
> I woke to black flak and the nightmare fighters.
> When I died they washed me out of the turret with a hose.

Before and after the American entry into the war, there was an intriguing examination of the 'special relationship' between the two English-speaking cultures. Important at its time, praised by King George the Sixth and printed in dozens of editions in Britain and the United States, was Alice Duer Miller's narrative poem, *The White Cliffs*. Along with the later Greer Garson film, *Mrs Miniver*, it served as some of the more cogent propaganda across the Atlantic during the war years. Mrs Miller had married an aristocratic husband during the first week of the First World War, when 'all the men wore uniform, as English people can, unconscious of it'. Their honeymoon had been brief, for 'lovers in war-time / Better understand / The fullness of living, / With death close at hand'. Her husband was killed in France, a child was born, her mother-in-law, the Lady Jean, helped bring up the child, but never wholly accepted her dead son's wife or her cultivated background. In a notable exchange, the Lady Jean patronized Alice, saying that although she was an American, she did not speak like one. This was meant to be a compliment, but Alice answered with anger:

> 'Not at all, I speak –
> At least I've always thought this true –
> As educated people do
> In any country – even mine.'
> 'Really?' I saw her head incline,
> I saw her ready to assert
> Americans are easily hurt.

Yet despite it all, Alice Duer Miller ended by stating that the seed of the tree of liberty which grew in the United States was an English seed.

> I am American bred,
> I have seen much to hate here – much to forgive,
> But in a world where England is finished and dead,
> I do not wish to live.

A similar arrogance and endurance, patronage and love, displayed this time by a teenage girl aristocrat, provoked the best story written by a visiting American soldier of his experience in wartime England, *For Esmé – With Love and Squalor* by J. D. Salinger. According to him, her gift of her dead father's broken wrist-watch saved his sanity in the darkest days of his war.

During the great American invasion of London, it was suggested that the words of the popular song 'A Nightingale Sang in Berkeley Square' should be changed to 'An Englishman Spoke in Grosvenor Square'. The centre of American life in the capital was the Rainbow Club, the huge Red Cross Centre that overlooked the shuttered statue of Eros in Piccadilly Circus. It had been constructed from two landmarks commandeered by the government, the Monico and the adjoining Lyons Corner House. It was converted into a home from home, with a juke-box and a shoe-shine parlour and a Back Room, where Lady Charles Cavendish, once known as Fred Astaire's sister Adele, wrote letters for the GIs to the folks back home. Outside in Piccadilly and the streets of Soho, prostitutes were parked more frequently than taxis, lined up more regularly than blacked-out street lamps. American pay was ten times that of the British or European soldier, American rations were larger and more lavish and seemed to include nylon stockings, so the GIs could buy a better time for women on the loose with their men away from home. The notorious GI who stood in Piccadilly and asked every passing woman the same monotonous question, 'Wanna f—k?', was surprisingly successful. The sexual conquests of the Americans led to resentment on the part of the native soldiers, who were trained to kill and had no enemy to fight except Allied soldiers and their own people. Sticking bayonets into dummies, garrotting by piano wire, breaking necks by reflex action, unarmed combat, these were new skills without use. And when jealousy provoked violence, when misogyny found the enemy in the other sex, when male hatred and puritanism and lust were unleashed on women, military training in techniques of killing had terrible consequences. One poem by the perpetual Fitzrovian Philip O'Connor, 'The Murder of the Prostitutes', 87 suggested the extent of the alienation of the serving men, waiting to attack the real enemy and finding only stray tarts to stab.

> A meeting of the bought and sold –
> drearily enough and often told.
> But tonight the hellish disappointment at military inactivity on a 2nd front
> was breeding murder in the backward mind of two soldiers
> so that when they asked two Piccadilly girls
> for themselves at a pound
> it was only a profound social apathy
> that prevented one scenting death ...

Such violence against women was random and, although it was frequent, it was not reported. It was bad for morale. The current myth was that the Poles and the Free French were particularly attractive to English women – and the Italian prisoners-of-war, working on the land. The only tribute paid by insular London literary society to any of the allies – except for Cyril Connolly's occasional laurel wreaths in *Horizon* to the lost and decadent pleasures of the culture across the Channel – was Nancy Cunard's anthology *Poems for France*. Inspired partially by Spender and Lehmann's regretful anthology of 1939, *Poems for Spain*, she scurried round London collecting pieces from poets and those who had never written a poem before. She claimed to be inspired by some verses in *Tribune*, written by Jack Beeching, a member of the British Communist Party who was working in the Fleet Air Arm as a radio mechanic. His 'Spring Offensive' began with images of lambs and daffodils and tractors and 'the hopscotch of bull and cow', and ended with shells and bayonets and dead men. It had a simple quality, which was more than could be said for the lucky dip and bran-tub of the rest of the poems for France. Only William Plomer and Sylvia Townsend-Warner and John Manifold seemed able to produce verses that comprehended the enormity of the disaster and the endurance of the Resistance. Vita Sackville-West wrote an aristocrat's lament for 'The Wines of France' that should have squeezed vintage tears from any connoisseur. Her lines ended with a true appreciation of the tragedy taking place in Gaul.

> But stay. We had forgot. The hideous
> Science of men has triumphed over beauty.
> Vanished, the strange, the coloured grace. The Boche
> Is making petrol from the wines of France.

While drinking with Augustus John and Norman Cameron in the Pier Hotel in Battersea, Nancy Cunard frequently wondered why no great poem had ever been written in praise of wine in wartime. Certainly, she had not published one. Her approach to editing an anthology was another proof of the barriers of class and nationality that still divided London, however hard a radical and a rebel like herself tried to deny them. To include on her list of contributors the Lords Vansittart and Dunsany with the headmaster of Eton was not aimed at lowering class-consciousness. Her mother, Emerald, Lady Cunard, might be estranged from her; but at least her salon at the Dorchester introduced many of the visiting Americans to British intellectuals who were thought to be amusing, particularly John Lehmann and Peter Quennell and James Pope-Hennessy. Often there was the mysterious American intelligence officer known as 'The Sergeant' throughout society. In fact, he was Stewart Preston, the forerunner of another graduate and teacher from Yale, Norman Holmes Pearson, who was in love with London and its literary and musical life. Claridge's and Prunier's, Quaglino's and Boulestin's were his favourite restaurants: E. M. Forster asked Pearson his opinion of his unpublished homosexual novel *Maurice*, Graham Greene exchanged intelligence information at the Ritz, Benjamin Britten and Ralph Vaughan Williams discussed their compositions, Norman Douglas and Elizabeth Bowen gave him tea, and the Sitwells entertained him often along with the reclusive and wealthy writer Bryher and the American poetess H. D., whom he admired although she lived with her patroness Bryher. He was ubiquitous and proved that a posting to London for an American could be a trip to Parnassus.

'The Sergeant' may have found the English cultural scene at a certain level as comfortable as an old slipper. But many Americans in London, particularly when visiting Fitzrovia, thought themselves among aliens from another stratosphere. Nina Hamnett was fortunate enough to encounter a hopeful American writer from the US Eighth Air Force, Julius Horwitz. He was looking for bohemia as if it were a sleazy Utopia, and his imagination had already wrapped the dowdy painter in the Worth cape which she often wore to hide her shabbiness. His leaves in Fitzrovia were front seats in the theatre of art and living. He understood the reasons why the Fitzrovians took to the bottle like lambs to the ewe.

They're always drunk or rapidly approaching. They see the comedy, realize their own helplessness and hate their selfish compromise with morals and society. Insanity or drunkenness. Their talk is seldom the intellectual sauerkraut of polite gatherings. Always dirty stories or funny stories; songs and love affairs. Flighty. Their own minds are too damn heavy with unsolved problems to bring them into their fun.

The American airman frequently went to the Café Royal, which he found full of Yankee queens with their RAF lovers, people from the film world, successful writers and successful mistresses. The Café did not serve the prostitutes waiting outside the Rainbow Club in Piccadilly. By government regulation, no meal could cost more than five shillings, but with wine and cover charges, the bill usually came to a pound. In the West End, there was always a way round the laws of wartime.

Nina Hamnett's drunkenness and self-degradation were witnessed by the American. The back room of her squalid flat, which he shared at arm's length, seemed to be a flop-house for most of the errant Fitzrovians, while she herself would wake up in her bed with another woman, or the sailors she particularly fancied 'because they go away'. She became the central character of Horwitz's novel about his leaves in London, as Nora in *Can I Get There by Candlelight?* In   89 the book, she took her leave of him on the corner of the Tottenham Court Road, that boundary between Fitzrovia and Bloomsbury, the old false bohemia of the wealthy. 'I got this far,' Nora said, 'this far and no farther. It's remarkable why anybody bothers to stay alive. But here we are. Good-bye.'

For other regulars at the Wheatsheaf and the Marquis of Granby and the Bricklayer's Arms, the Americans were an added attraction. Quentin Crisp knew that Hamnett and the Fitzrovians were living literature and art, so he set himself out to be a cameo, although perhaps his greatest pose was nude in Goldsmiths' College, when he remained motionless after a bomb dropped and blew in all the windows of the life class. It was not stoicism, but an inability to move his locked limbs after long stillness. He loved Fitzrovia because there alone was an effortless acceptance of other people's identities, however strange they appeared. Visitors were never thrown out unless they fought too much or drank too little. With significant gestures and memorable phrases, he tried to give good value for what he was receiving. And gratefully receive he did.

This brand new army of (no) occupation flowed through the streets of London like cream on strawberries, like melted butter over green peas. Labelled 'with love from Uncle Sam' and packaged in uniforms so tight that in them their owners could fight for nothing but their honour, these 'bundles for Britain' leaned against the lamp-posts of Shaftesbury Avenue or lolled on the steps of thin-lipped statues of dead English statesmen. As they sat in the cafés or stood in the pubs, their bodies bulged through every straining khaki fibre towards our feverish hands. Their voices were like warm milk, their skins as flawless as expensive indiarubber, and their eyes as beautiful as glass. Above all it was the liberality of their natures that was so marvellous. Never in the history of sex was so much offered to so many by so few.

London began to assume the aspect of a gigantic caravanserai, Peter Quennell noted. Through the metropolis a host of travellers moved, sometimes under an alias, bound for known or unknown destinations. By 1944, there would be nearly one and a half million Allied troops quartered in Britain, of which a million were Americans. Most of them came to London on leave or on their way to embarkation elsewhere. The artists among them, hopeful or professional, were drawn to the notoriety of the Soho pubs, where their welcome was mixed and paradoxical. Some of the violence, which the British soldiers felt for their women who indulged the rich Allied invaders, was also felt by the poor writers and artists drinking the war away to assuage the guilt of not putting on the uniforms, whose wearers sought their company. Dylan Thomas was always picking fights with soldiers, which he never won. The beatings he took were his war wounds and satisfied his masochism. Julian Maclaren-Ross also provoked bar brawls by his rudeness and affectations, but the gold or silver knob on his cane was effective against the wild blows of drunken soldiers: he and Keidrych Rhys nearly attacked the New Zealand writer Dan Davin, then a staff officer, on their first encounter in the Wheatsheaf: hostilities were put off with the remark, 'Why didn't you tell us you were a writer? We thought you were an officer. Have a drink.' William Sansom explained in his journal why the continual violence of the war was so rarely described. For him, the experience of fire-fighting was too fierce to set down. In dealing with the core of the violent act itself, language failed.

Wearing their chips as conscientious objectors like epaulettes on their shoulders, the Roberts Colquhoun and MacBryde were usually bloody to foreign soldiers and bloodied by them, yet curiously the intrusion of Poles and Free Frenchmen and Americans confirmed their emotions as Celts. The Scots and the Irish and the Welsh often felt aliens in London. The presence of so many offshore foreigners increased their separation and sense of regional identity. As Idris Davies wrote in his poem on the 'London Welsh':

> We have carried our accents into Westminster
> As soldiers carry rifles into the wars,
> We have carried our idioms into Piccadilly,
> Food for the critics on Saturday night ...
> We have also shivered by the Thames in the night
> And known that the frost has no racial distinctions.

Alun Lewis was a Welshman, but he did not think that birthplace or heritage made a person feel alienated. Being a soldier was enough to create an alien, a stranger among strangers.

The soldier doesn't bother. He is a migrant, an Arab, taking his belongings with him, needing surprisingly little of the world's goods. He leaves his violin and his Cézanne and his garden behind. His wife, too, and his children, as time passes. Hitler's soldiers have been taught two simple things: Obey Commands; Forget Home. In the long run, these two rules are easier to learn than to resist. That is the danger. That is why I say: to women, feel less; to men, feel more. I may be exaggerating this danger. Certainly the soldier's heart leaps for leave. But when I go home on leave I feel vaguely 'out of it.' The new carpet doesn't thrill me as it should; the troubles and little quarrels with neighbours are no longer my troubles; they are the preoccupations of strangers. I feel sympathetic, I listen and suggest. But I don't interfere, I don't trespass on them. And perhaps they think I don't talk much, don't open up, don't confide. Until one of them divines the reason, and knows me as a stranger, and takes me in as a stranger, into her lonely arms. We talk quietly of strangenesses, night marches, bivouacs, odd and far-off incidents, Europe. Till our loneliness is complete, and we are united in loneliness, just the two of us, as it used to be when first we sought each other, losing and finding each other, never quite giving in, never quite defeated.

The soldier says: 'Life is a series of meetings with strangers. We are all strange, to ourselves as well.'

A fear of embarkation into the unknown, a sense of utter dislocation made the soldier passing through London towards the front overseas feel a stranger in a strange city, even if the city had been familiar, even if it were in his own country. The best-known of the air force poets, John Pudney, whom Michael Redgrave made famous by reciting his 'For Johnny' in the film *The Way to the Stars*, resented his embarkation leave in London. Time played tricks, evenings hung ponderously, then a whole day flew off like a squib and was gone. He hated other poets who were working in the ministries and who stressed how hard they were working 'in the stern discomforts of governmental corridors'. They gave him introductions to civilized friends in Groppi's Hussars, to other poets and civil servants like themselves who were not fighting in the desert, but spending their war in Cairo's most famous tea-rooms or in the *louche* bars there, setting up a minor Fitzrovia in the Egyptian capital. They despised Pudney in his blue uniform, as if his posting abroad were a foolish act of his own free will. Military service made him appear a buffoon as well as a man apart.

Exiles from Europe and Allied soldiers on leave in London found themselves imprisoned in the total alienation of the war. Not only were foreigners segregated in the capital, but also the military persons passing through. Soldiers and sailors and airmen had already been divorced from London by their training in brutality, their camps in the country, the breakdown of their relationships with families and wives and neighbours. If they flocked to Fitzrovia to make tenuous contacts with an uneasy and flamboyant society that was vagrant and wayward by its very nature, the dislocated were meeting the dispossessed, those who had lost their identity within uniform were dealing with those who were protecting their intolerance of uniformity. Everyone was changed by the war, John Lehmann thought – 'like the man who found he was an insect one morning in Kafka's horrible and prophetic story – into something completely alien to one's old self'. Peter Watson also told his artist friends such as John Craxton that Kafka was the most satisfactory person to read during the war. Combatants and civilians became aliens to each other and to themselves. There were misunderstandings between them, there were conflicts and aggressions in the pubs and the clubs. Yet the overriding necessity of fighting the war and winning it did induce a desperate sense of temporary community, a lunge at a fellow-feeling among deprived artists. In the last analysis, everybody was in the same boat, even if it were sinking like so many of the convoys across the Atlantic. Under war conditions, which estranged individuals from themselves as well as from others, all were evacuees from peace, exiles from the city or country which they once had known and loved. The best of the Scots poets, Edwin Muir, described the inevitable rejections faced by those whom the war had forced into becoming 'The Refugees'.

> For such things homelessness is ours
> And shall be others'. Tenement roofs and towers
> Will fall upon the kind and the unkind
> Without election,
> For deaf and blind
> Is rejection bred by rejection
> Breeding rejection,
> And where no counsel is what will be will be.
> We must shape here a new philosophy.

SEVEN

Where Are the War Writers?

Leonard Rosoman

About this time of year, Cyril Connolly wrote early in 1941, articles used to appear called 'Where are our war poets?' The answer was 'under your nose'. The same phrase was used by Keidrich Rhys in his introduction to *Poems from the Forces*, when he attacked the pre-war, editorial-chair attitude of the editor of *Horizon* and the unflourishing, unchanging state of letters in liberal England. Writing a month after the retreat from Dunkirk, Rhys found that the appearance of a poem by a soldier in print was still a bit of a wonder. Julian Symons had conjured up a pamphlet, *Some Poems in War-time*, in the spring of 1940; but otherwise only Rhys's appeal to people serving in uniform had produced a worthwhile collection of poems. He was not expecting to print the counterparts of the First World War poets, Rupert Brooke and Robert Graves, Wilfred Owen and Isaac Rosenberg, Julian Grenfell and Siegfried Sassoon. But he was printing some established and some new poets, all of whom the war had engulfed and affected. The names were impressive and needed no justification: Christopher Hassall and Gavin Ewart, Alun Lewis and G. S. Fraser, Roy Fuller and Alan Rook, and the discoveries, Timothy Corsellis and John Manifold, Charles Hamblett and Mervyn Peake and Bertram Warr. By 1943, when Rhys had edited *More Poems from the Forces*, the list of names was even more impressive, including Brian Allwood and David Bourne, Robert Chaloner and Herbert Corby, R. N. Currey and Keith Douglas, Stephen Haggard and Norman Hampson, Sidney Keyes and H. B. Mallalieu, Norman McCaig and F. T. Prince, John Pudney and Henry Reed, Francis Scarfe and Gervase Stewart, Julian Symons and Henry Treece, Vernon Watkins and Richard B. Wright. It was a roll-call of poets of some achievement and great promise; but many were to be killed in the war and others were to fall silent. Few were to continue with their poetry throughout the vicissitudes of the peace.

Rhys did not publish the poets in uniform who merely used the properties of their present existence, 'the menacing siren, the holocaust, shrapnel, Junkers, searchlights, metal Messerschmitt, deadly Dornier, magnesium-bomb and primrose flare, the daylight raid and stutter of guns, the destructive steel and similar clichés ...' He understood how poetry might be bad because of conditions under active service. Another poet, Patric Dickinson, now invalided out of the forces and creating his own anthology of war, agreed with Rhys. The whole ghastly paraphernalia of death was not directly assimilable into poetry. 'You may make symbols of it but once you are among its terms poetry seems to desert you or at best becomes a sort of conscript prose in poetic uniform.' Yet he and Rhys did not believe that poetry might be better in the hands of those who withdrew from the war and served only behind their desks. *Poetry from the Forces* was the work of poets going to the war, stated the colonel who wrote the preface to Rhys's anthology. War had horrors enough, but it had its compensations. Horizons contracted. Death was no longer a certainty, but a probability, for many servicemen would survive raids and battles. Yet the poets in uniform had literally taken their lives into their hands and had accepted the war with their bodies. By their acts, they opposed the mental resignation to death and resentment of life of pre-war writers.

By reviewing for *Horizon* and Penguin *New Writing*, Stephen Spender had become the most influential critic of his time. He agreed that the conditions of war necessarily affected contemporary poetry, even if its subjects were not always about war. He made this clear when reviewing *Another Time*, Auden's first book of poems to be published in England following his flight to America. Spender questioned Auden's poetic future. He was floating off into generalizations when he should be coming to grips with reality. His poems were vague and diffuse. Abstract books of advice from America were meaningless to an England 'being blasted by the concrete and the particular'. The whole of the Auden group of poets of the 'thirties except for Spender was also blasted by the ageing novelist, Sir Hugh Walpole, who claimed that they belonged to an earlier age of pessimism and cynicism and despair. 'After Dunkirk, new poets were born.' John Lehmann protested about this attack and met Walpole; but he himself bitterly regretted the absence of Auden and Isherwood, and he believed that they would lose from not experiencing what those who stayed in England would experience. Only Louis MacNeice, who had returned from America ten months after the outbreak of hostilities, really came to the defence of the evacuee poets. Although some people born in Britain might better themselves as writers and persons by being in England, only a minority would. A Malraux or a Hemingway might thrive on scenes of violence or suffering, but none of the British expatriates were like them. War did not necessarily improve writing or people.

What the expatriate writers had certainly done was to desert their followers and abdicate their position as leaders. 'He told us that the duty of all was to fight Fascism,' one of Auden's pupils said to Spender, 'and then he went away.' The feeling of betrayal was stressed by Christopher Lee in 'Trahison des Clercs':

> One sailed for New York: a second followed;
> one at that moment broke his heart for a woman,
> showing the pieces to strangers in cafés,
> making of this world's calamity
> a mirror of his own sensitiveness;
> the fourth held his tongue. These the men
> – flown, flying, broken or checked pen –
> the poets we took for leaders, who should speak
> for those who could not, make
> bridges and barricades for all of us ...

The bridges and barricades were now being made by the new poets after Dunkirk, although the older ones were not giving way gracefully to them. Stephen Spender took issue with *Poems from the Forces*, declaring that the war had made only a superficial impression on the poets as it had on the war artists, who had just put on their first exhibition. The boredom of military training was present, but not the blood of Dunkirk and Libya, not the meaning of the war or any effective statement against it. 'The poets regard the war from the *outside*: it is not *their* war they seem to say. They disclaim all responsibility for it; they don't like it, they don't understand it, and they don't wish to do so.' Spender thought that the blame lay in the war itself, not in the poets in uniform, who had only time to put down statements, not to explain their ideas and experiences. 'A nation at war is a nation of trivialities.'

On behalf of the new poets, Alex Comfort took up the cudgels against Spender. The poets in uniform were not incompetent, they were just unutterably weary. They were members of the military community in which they lived. They could not have an integrated purpose in the war. A return to romanticism and the idea of the tragic myth might solve their problem. Spender did not agree. The war had split writers into three generations: those who were blind to events between the wars and were now the old literary establishment, T. S. Eliot and the like: those like himself and George Orwell who had been acutely aware of the approaching war and felt relief when it came as a fulfilment of their prophecies: and now the generation of the war's victims, too young to be responsible for it, but bitter against the previous generations who had put them into it. They must become the war poets, for the previous generation had lost its voice in the course of the 'thirties, or so Cecil Day Lewis claimed at the opening of his translation of Virgil's *Georgics*, dedicated to Stephen Spender:

> Where are the war poets? the fools inquire ...
> We were at war, while they still played with fire
> And rigged the market for the ruin of man:
> Spain was a death to us, Munich a mourning.
> No wonder then if, like the pelican,
> We have turned inward for our iron ration ...

Spender himself was engaged sufficiently in the fire services not to believe that turning inward was the only solution for writing poetry in wartime. He also made another telling prophecy. He foresaw literature falling into the hands of a generation which had little sympathy with the new or with the war conditions forced upon it. For the next ten years, a young writer would mean a writer produced by the war, who had written nothing before it, whose work bore the birthmark of October 1939. Spender did not take his argument beyond that point. Yet young writers were likely, indeed, to react against the decade of privation that was being imposed upon them. They would not see the war as the First World War poets saw it, a nightmare of horror and slaughter that must never be repeated again. It was being repeated again but in a far-flung, diffuse way in many theatres of conflict stretching from the Libyan desert to the Far East. The environment of combat was not concentrated on the muddy Western Front, but spread over sand and mountain, jungle and dust. And machinery rather than men would win the victory. In his examination of why the poets of the First World War seemed better than those of the Second, Robert Graves stated: 'The internal combustion engine does not consort with poetry.' Mechanization did not lead to good verse. Mass mobilization was different from volunteering to fight, many modern soldiers were conscripts. Most of the army was not engaged in combat, but bored stiff with inactivity, seeing the beauty of the English countryside through a tent-flap during a dreary exile from home. As for the soldier poet, 'he cannot even feel that his rendezvous with death is more certain than that of his Aunt Fanny, the firewatcher'.

Graves himself had survived death in the trenches for years in Flanders and had brought back poems from his exposure. He had the right to judge. But he was wrong, or so Herbert Read pointed out: both Spender and Graves implied that poets were creations of events – the First World War had produced one kind of poet because of its nature, the Second World War had not yet because it was not the same kind of war. In fact, there were new and good war poets. It was merely that the public had not been given the opportunity to notice them. Of course, this war was different, but it had already thrown up young poets, who were better than those of the First World War at the same stage of development. Keidrych Rhys agreed. Spender and the old magazine editors were biased against the younger generation of poets and were playing at literary games that were irrelevant to the times. When the new verse was properly published, the public would see its merits.

In the short term, Read and Rhys were correct about the young war writers. The slim volumes of John Pudney on the air force and Alun Lewis on army life sold in many editions; Alan Rook's 'Dunkirk Pier' and Henry Reed's 'Naming of Parts' became famous in field tent and household; and the autobiography of a burned pilot, Richard Hillary, *The Last Enemy*, made him a national myth and hero. Yet in the long term, the older generation of Spender and Graves were to be proved right. Even the better young poets of the war, particularly Roy Fuller, were to reject the whole decade because its deprivations were imposed upon them, and because it was linked with the romantic or individual escape from its imperatives. Fuller's first book, *Poems*, was actually published during the war in December 1939, yet he claimed to be of the 'thirties, stating in his memoirs, 'Only in the nick of time was I saved from being forever labelled a Forties poet.' He was, in truth, one of the finer of the war poets. On his cold convoys to Russia as a sailor, another young war poet, Alan Ross, memorized Fuller's wartime verses by heart. They provided a shared experience, a common bond, cherished by Ross personally, though he understated the achievement of the poets of the Second World War. Weariness and endurance seemed to be their fate. They accepted responsibility and action without belief or hope. They fought on a basis of necessity because war was inevitable and unavoidable. They defended 'the bad against the worse'.

Cecil Day Lewis's famous phrase came from his poem 'Where are the War Poets?' It was his personal *mea culpa*, because he was working at the Ministry of Information, producing more propaganda than poetry, and certainly not serving in any front line. In fact, he had been drafted for twenty-four hours into the Signal Corps depot in Yorkshire, but his mistress Rosamond Lehmann talked to the influential Harold Nicolson, who had already helped to secure scarce paper supplies for *Horizon*, and her lover Day Lewis found himself back at his ministry desk again:

> They who in folly or mere greed
> Enslaved religion, markets, laws,
> Borrow our language now and bid
> Us to speak up in freedom's cause.
>
> It is the logic of our times,
> No subject for immortal verse –
> That we who lived by honest dreams
> Defend the bad against the worse.

This was the excuse of the civil servant, not the poet as combatant, who was actually defending his country against the enemy. It was also the voice of the Auden generation, which found the just cause of the Spanish Civil War transmuted into the drudgery of surviving a long war at home. Unfortunately, Day Lewis's dry claim that capitalism had stolen the vocabulary of freedom and thus stifled the war poets did not apply to those who put on uniform, even if they were Marxists. When he wrote 'A Wry Smile' in his packed Nissen hut, Roy Fuller wanted to bring

> The poets from their safe and paper beds,
> Show them my comrades and the silver pall
> Over the airfield, ask them what they'd sing.

None of the civilians had been shamed or tortured as he had by the government and by sergeants. Fuller did not envy the safe poets or pity himself; but they were missing his experience. 'They reflect time, I am the very ticking.' The problem for the poet in uniform was how to translate the habitual monotony of his experience into poetry. Julian Symons considered that, while he was drilling:

> How into this to introduce that picture
> We call a poem? To give the chaotic
> Elements of our lives a single meaning,
> The rational correctness of a square?
> There is nothing we do not know here, and nothing
> That is worth knowing ...

On the march, the soldier poet had to 'forget his shoulder's triggered load' and 'train that gunsight if he can or fiddle, if he can, a poem'. For Sidney Keyes, the 'War Poet' could hardly approach his craft because of his circumstances:

> I am the man who looked for peace and found
> My own eyes barbed ...
> When I reach for the wind
> Cast me not down:
> Though my face is a burnt book
> And a wasted town.

But the last word on being a war poet came from Donald Bain, who served in the Royal Artillery and the Gordon Highlanders before being invalided from the army before the end of the war. He agreed in essence with Edwin Muir's criticism of the very concept of war poetry propounded by Spender and Graves. Muir felt that the war was so huge and implied so much that no single individual could formulate a response to it. The stationary trench fighting in Flanders had become a symbol of the First World War as a whole; but the global conflict of the Second and the bombing of cities were terrible illustrations of something far vaster, which might be felt, but for which there was no image. The war was too invisible and gigantic to comprehend. There could be no war poets, or, as Donald Bain described them, only minor ones:

> We in our haste can only see the small components of the scene
> We cannot tell what incidents will focus on the final screen ...
>
> We only watch, and indicate and make our scribbled pencil notes.
> We do not wish to moralize, only to ease our dusty throats.

So much for the war poets' answer to the question: 'Where are the War Poets?' They were under people's noses, they were writing tens of thousands of poems, they were publishing them more and more frequently as the public taste for anthologies of poetry and little magazines grew after 1941 into a national appreciation of the relevant short piece and the appropriate slim volume. The readers did not accept the limitations that the war poets tried to impose on their role. Some heroic and immortal verse was being published, the real stuff of the odd twenty popular anthologies of the war that appeared during and after the conflict was over. Hamish Henderson's 'Elegies for the Dead in Cyrenaica' and Alan Ross's narrative poem of a naval action from the point of view of a sailor, 'J.W. 51B: A Convoy' are some of the greater epic poems in the English language: the shorter poems of Keith Douglas from Egypt, Alun Lewis from India and Roy Fuller from Africa contradicted the assertion that the diffusion of the world war did not concentrate the ink wonderfully. Sun and sand, indeed, seemed to illuminate poems more precisely than mustard gas and mud.

The uncompromising Keith Douglas asserted that only those who had experienced battle could write war poetry. It was too narrow a definition. Many of those serving in uniform never fought in combat, particularly those in the fire services; yet the act of attacking a blazing warehouse could be more dangerous and searing an exposure than fighting from *Alamein to Zem Zem*, Douglas's posthumous work of prose, illustrations and poetry, published by Tambimuttu. In his important anthology, carefully called *Poetry in Wartime*, Tambimuttu took up the catholic position that times of war affected civilians and soldiers alike, and thus the poetry was of its pervasive period. Julian Symons had a similar attitude in *An Anthology of War Poetry*, also published in 1942, when he stated that there was no specialized department of war poetry, which was 'quite simply the poetry, comic or tragic, cynical or heroic, joyful, embittered or disillusioned, of people affected by the reality of war'. He was distinguishing himself from the widest and weakest 99 definition of war poetry, taken by the leaders of the New Apocalypse, particularly J. F. Hendry, whose own books of poems written in wartime, *The Bombed Happiness* and *The Orchestral Mountain*, produced nothing of note except the concept implicit in the title of the first book that there might be a liberation and joy in destruction. When cities fell and dry rot attacked the tyranny of the times, 'the silence of the mad and bombed is its own balm'.

Treece himself eventually followed the rest of the members of the New Apocalypse in leaving the movement to Hendry alone when T. S. Eliot began to edit his poems at Faber & Faber. The poetic establishment seemed to have partially accepted the New Romanticism and Eliot co-operated in publishing some of its poets with Herbert Read, in charge of poetry at Routledge. Even Stephen Spender approved of *Lyra*, an anthology of new lyrics edited by Alex Comfort and Robert Greacen, and published by Wrey Gardiner at the Grey Walls Press: he found a more interesting and discriminating choice of poets in *Lyra* than in *Poems from the Forces*, although the effects of the war were hardly mentioned: the poets all seemed victims of the times with a sense of deprivation in love. Spender also praised Herbert Read's clarion call in his introduction to *Lyra*; the war was, indeed, apocalyptic and a world revolution, in which all conventions were being tried under fire. 'Painting and poetry, drama and the film – all are involved in this insurrection-ary test.' A new political, economic and practical world was being forced upon Britain. The old literary conventions could not be dragged into this new age.

Such were the claims and counterclaims of the editors and practitioners of war poetry, from those who wore uniform and managed to write, to those who shrank from uniform and sought to build a fresh language from the blitzed conventions of the old. Their opportunity was certainly there. As another poet and editor, Peter Baker, wrote in Wrey Gardiner's *Poetry Review* in May 1943, the new poetry was democratic, as all true poetry should be. By true poetry, he meant emotive or romantic poetry. To him, the romantic poet was essentially a democrat, whose reason did not rule his emotions. The poet was now speaking of and for the people, who were able to read his work at last in the flood of fresh publications. The new poetry was hardly, however, being published in the dominant literary magazines, *Horizon* and Penguin *New Writing*. The critical standards of their editors did not allow it. John Lehmann, for one, regretted it, feeling that he was in a telephone exchange, in which confused messages were always arriving of immense human appeal, but unpublishable, 'burning shrapnel fragments of experience and reflection-in-action, from places where the meaning of the war was most keenly felt'. Yet though these pieces were more real and significant than newspaper reports, they were incomplete and lost in a tangle of clichés. To write of war on the march was not to write well. Schools for poets were needed – Spender complained in 1943 – not schools of poets. The total effect was an 'all-pervading blur in the arts'.

The guilt of not experiencing the global war prompted a remarkable manifesto in *Horizon*, 'Why Not War Writers?' Signed among others by Connolly and Koestler, Orwell and Spender and Alun Lewis, who was actually serving on duty,

Horizon

A REVIEW OF LITERATURE & ART

Montgomery Belgion
G. M. Brady
F. Buchanan
Adam Drinan
Lucian Freud
Clement Greenberg
Terence Heywood
Laurie Lee
L. S. Little
Nicholas Moore
V. S. Pritchett
Frederic Prokosch
William Rogers
J. A. Spender
Stephen Spender

MONTHLY: ONE SHILLING NET
APRIL   VOL. I, NO. 4   1940

Edited by Cyril Connolly

the manifesto demanded that writers should be treated like artists and photo-graphers and journalists. British authors should be sent to the Americas, the Dominions and Russia so that they could report back by stories and plays and poems. Foreign writers should be brought to Britain. The proposal aroused some irony from a combatant correspondent, who stated that there was plenty of leisure in the armed forces, particularly in the ranks, and that genius overcame privation and inconvenience. The way to write was to serve, as H. E. Bates was doing, the first short-story writer to be given a commission in the Royal Air Force to describe the life of the air crews under the name of 'Flying Officer X'. He wrote enough stories to fill two volumes, both of which sold some quarter of a million copies. He received his pay, but no royalties or fees, nor did he expect any. He had 'the privilege of experience and the exhilaration of living with men of action', which could not be assessed in material terms. The best-selling thriller writer and librarian of the House of Commons, Hilary St George Saunders, was also employed to turn out exemplary booklets of documentation, such as *The Battle of Britain* and *Bomber Command*. The novelist and flier David Garnett worked on official documents and wrote *The War in the Air*. And Spender himself was commissioned to do a book on civil defence, while Saunders's subordinate at the Ministry of Information, Cecil Day Lewis, who was also a thriller writer under the name of Nicholas Blake, helped to write and edit forty more of the illustrated booklets ranging from *R.A.F. Middle East* to *The Campaign in Burma* and *Ark Royal*. He did, however, also manage to write two dozen poems; his 'Word Over All' was a success; the book of the same name sold 11,000 copies in several editions. He admitted that experiencing the war directly during the blitz had perhaps led to better poetry than when he pretended to be a militant about the Spanish Civil War without doing much more than drinking with his local communist cell in the Red Lion in his village. He used to give a speech to schools about a night raid on London, when he watched a little girl talking to her doll while the bombs fell close around them. It gave him the inspiration for one of his better poems, 'In the Shelter'. 'I was watching the little girl. She bent closer over the doll as the bombs shrieked down; she was murmuring to it, comforting it. She seemed extraordinarily alone there, in the midst of the crowded shelter. Alone, but not lonely ...'

War writers were not generally employed by the state. The paper ration for books was cut from sixty to less than forty per cent of pre-war levels: in the three years after 1940, the number of book titles published fell by one half. The quality of paper declined, being repulped from old volumes or processed from straw. The pages were yellowish, and Orwell was right in complaining that writing-paper looked like toilet paper, which in turn felt like sheet tin. The way out of the dilemma was to find a provincial printer with a stock of pre-war paper and to found a new publishing house or little magazine. There were a hundred new magazine and anthology titles registered in the six years of the war and enumerated in *The Little Reviews Anthology*: its editor Denys Val Baker considered that the leading old ones were the *Adelphi*, the *Poetry Review*, *Scrutiny* and *Life and Letters Today*, while the new ones were *Horizon*, Penguin *New Writing*, *Kingdom Come*, *Bell*, *Our Time*, *Poetry London*, *Wind and the Rain*, *Transformation*, *New Road*, *Here and Now*, *Wartime Harvest*, *Counterpoint*, *Oasis*, *Opus*, *Arson*, *Million*, *Voices*, *Poetry Quarterly* and *Seven*. There was a tremendous increase in poetry magazines and short-story anthologies, such as *Argosy*, *English Story*, *Modern Reading*, *Selected Writing* and *Writing Today*. *Poetry London* asserted that there was more poetry being written, made public and read in Britain than in any other country. Much of it consisted of regional poetry, a reaction from the war to old cultural values, and of writing by distinguished *émigrés* like Koestler, who were living in England. There were also numerous books of short stories being published by individual writers on the war, particularly William Sansom, Julian Maclaren-Ross, James Hanley, H. E. Bates and Alun Lewis, along with the Welsh writers, Dylan Thomas and Glyn Jones and Rhys Davies. 'Since the war began,' the refugee philosopher Canetti noted in 1943, 'thoughts and sentences have gotten terse, conforming to the tone of commands … We brush many sentences away like leaves on a road.' The bulletin, the sketch, the newsreel, the spare poem, these were fit for the spurts of attention possible in wartime.

There were popular books on the war, which were read in their hundreds of thousands. Tom Harrisson of Mass-Observation culled war books for two years for *Horizon*. He became totally bogged down and engrossed in bad reading. He got through so many accounts of flying from *Bomber's Moon* to *Winged Love* to *Wellington Wendy* that he felt he had never owed so little to so many. He read books on the army, the navy, politics, conflict in the country and overseas, but most of it seemed the chaotic effluvia of a world confused. There were certain periods of war literature: first, war in the country and evacuation novels: second, diaries and notebooks from established writers designed for friends in America to show what a hard time, relatively, they were having; then, Dunkirk books and RAF books and blitz books; and finally, espionage and political and peace books. One note ran through all these works. While before the war, they had a slant to the left, now they were right-wing. 'In wartime it is socially difficult to criticize; easy to be uninformed and uniformed.' The scapegoats of popular wartime literature were the reds, the intellectuals and the Jews; the heroes were the cockneys, usually taxi-drivers or char-ladies, fighter pilots and war cripples. Most of the books were written about officers, few about the ranks. One novel alone seemed a work of art, Rex Warner's allegory *The Aerodrome*. There were excellent documentaries, particularly Paul Richey's *Fighter Pilot* and an anonymous air controller's *Readiness At Dawn*. These were equalled by 'Gunbuster' in his *Return via Dunkirk*, a detailed account of an artillery unit escaping from the Germans. Hailed by his publishers as the literary discovery of the war after his first novel ran into twenty-one editions, 'Gunbuster' disappointed with his successive books, *Battle Dress*, *Zero Hour* and *Ground Barrage*. He proved the dictum that every soldier has one novel in his knapsack, if he can write it.

The supreme novelist of the First World War may well have been Ford Madox Ford; of the Second, it was Henry Green. Unique in the breadth of his social connections, an Etonian who worked for years in his father's foundry in Birmingham, his early novel of factory life, *Living*, was the only true statement of working-class values (other than George Orwell's self-conscious *Down and Out in Paris and London*) to appear from the pens of the Auden generation, whose experience of the lives of workers was vocal, but minimal. Green had no tin ear for dialogue. His gift lay in catching the rhythms and repetitions, the hesitations and the pauses, the indirectness and the falling away of the speech patterns of all classes. His rich people are never as absurd as those of Ronald Firbank or Evelyn Waugh; his poor people never as comic or peculiar as those of Dickens. In the four novels which he wrote between 1938 and 1945, he captured the vernacular and the feelings of the time. The first sentences of *Party Going* create the uncertainty and unease of the prelude to a war. There is dense fog outside the departure tunnel of a London station. A pigeon flies into a balustrade and falls like a bloody bomb at the feet of a sick traveller, who washes the bird's body and wraps it in a brown paper parcel before trying to set off for a holiday with a party abroad. The fog stops all trains from running, the streets seem like conduits. Seen from seven thousand feet high, as from the cockpit of a bomber, the blocked main roads of traffic would seem like worms crawling from the station. The dead bird dropping from the fog like Aldous Huxley's dog from the flying machine that explodes beside two lovers on a roof, and the aerial view of London seen as an open sewer full of worms of vehicles, presage an expected blitzkrieg of poison gas and incendiaries. As in Jean Renoir's pre-war film *The Rules of the Game*, the privileged few in the party take refuge to play their sexual games in a sequestered building, a terminus hotel. Their paradigm of slaughter is not shooting rabbits, but commenting from the hotel windows as in a view from a gibbet that the mob of stranded passengers outside sounds like numbers of aeroplanes flying by and would make good targets for a bomb. The rich few feel like Renoir's transatlantic airman, in danger of running fatally into earth. On the station, their abandoned luggage looks like gravestones, the porters like undertakers' men, and the crowd like ruins in the wet, places where life has been, the debris of the city. And all the while, the wealthy people going to the South of France gossip and drink and play, bathe and dry and powder their beauty in solipsistic snobbery. 'Do you think it's the revolution, Madam?' a lady's maid asks and continues, 'and I have your bath-salts unpacked and your bath is ready for you now.'

If *Party Going* described the social *toilette* of the privileged before the deluge, Henry Green's next novel *Caught* paid tribute to the Auxiliary Fire Service, in which he served during the actual blitz in London. There is little sense of class distinction among the auxiliaries. 'It brings everyone together, there's that much to a war,' one of them says while they are waiting interminably for the big air raids to come, and when these do come in the blazing docklands at the climax of *Caught*, the feeling of camaraderie is only reinforced. As the hero tells his wife, 'In some fantastic way I'm sure you only get in war, we were suddenly alone and forced to rely on one another entirely. And that after twelve months' bickering. Each crew was thrown upon itself, on its own resources. The only thing to do was to keep together.'

If the auxiliaries do not keep together, and they know they must even during their training, they will not live apart. There is no room for solitary action, no reprieve from one mistake. 'You're dead,' the old fireman says. 'You're a smell, you're fried.' Their solace in 1940 is that the London girls are willing to give themselves to the new heroes, first to the pilots and then to the fire-fighters, who are seen as suicide squads. War, many of the women think, is sex.

This was a time when girls, taken out to night clubs by men in uniform, if he was a pilot she died in his arms that would soon, so she thought, be dead. In the hard idiom of the drum these women seemed already given up to the male in uniform so soon to go away, these girls, as they felt, soon to be killed themselves, so little time left, moth deathly gay, in a daze of giving.

That same afternoon the train to Portsmouth had wives dragged along the platform hanging limp to door handles and snatched off by porters in the way a man, standing aside, will pick bulrushes out of a harvest waggon load of oats.

Limp, dancing as never before entirely to his movements, long-haired sheaved heads too heavy for their bodies collapsed on pilots' blue shoulders, these clubs were like hotels, from double bedrooms of which the guests came, gorged with love, sleep lovewalking.

Loving was Henry Green's next novel, set in an Irish castle. If in *Party Going* the war is imminent, in *Loving* it is an irrelevance. The mistress of the castle feels that doing up the house is her war-work, and her servants feel abandoned to IRA or German hooligans when she deserts them to visit London during the air raids. The butler dies, the nanny is dying, and eventually even the servants realize that there is a danger in being neutral. Two of them leave to marry and live happily ever after in England. In *Back*, however, published in 1946, the fighting is nearly over. The problem is readjustment for a repatriated and one-legged prisoner-of-war, whose beloved Rose has died while he has lived behind barbed wire. The armed forces have come back to what they did not expect – to joblessness, to petty bureaucracy, even to disdain from superiors who are guilty at not fighting. They are always being told that the civilians have had their share of the war this time. Those who have not fought now order them about as officials in the interminable ministries with initials proliferating like weeds. Finally, Henry Green's prisoner-of-war does return to a life of peace, but only through the love of another woman, who takes no more or less than she has expected.

Henry Green was the prophet and judge of the war, but Joyce Cary became its bardic novelist in a major quintet written in Oxford, a city safe from bombing. One of the novels, *Charley Is My Darling*, dealt with a group of delinquent evacuees from a slum, who are lost in a Devon village during the first year of the war. It has a coarse and lyrical strength, very different from Cary's flight into his early memories, *A House of Children*, in which he tells of the sudden transformations of childhood, the metamorphoses of boys and girls from one character to another, almost overnight. 105

Then there is a sudden leap to his trilogy of masterpieces. When he was asked how he made the jump to *Herself Surprised*, *To Be a Pilgrim* and *The Horse's Mouth*, he wrote, 'To me it is a jump not from one boat to another but from one rope to another on the same boat, say jib to main sheet.' The main sheet was the author's disappearance within his three main characters, the cook Sara, the Protestant lawyer Wilcher and the Blakeian painter, Gulley Jimson. He writes from the interior of his protagonists, confining his language to the paucity of their moralizing, the sensuousness of their touching and feeling, and the richness of the painter's vision of glory on earth. In one sense, Cary's trilogy is a celebration of English history and his own lifetime from 1888 until the start of the Second World War. In another sense, he shows a command over vocabulary that has never been equalled outside the work of James Joyce. The publication of *The Horse's Mouth* at the end of the war proved that the publication of *Finnegans Wake* on the eve of the war did not conclude the literary genre called 'modernism', but heralded its passage to modern times.

Other than Orwell, whose extraordinary novels of ideas, *Animal Farm* and *1984*, had their impact after victory in Europe, Rex Warner was the only remarkable English novelist to make original use of the struggle between fascism, communism and democracy during the war. Although his first two sardonic fantasies, *The Wild Goose Chase* and *The Professor*, had smacked of the liberal disillusion of the late 'thirties, his *chef d'oeuvre* of 1941, *The Aerodrome*, is a symbolic allegory of power and its corruption through mechanical force, with airmen playing the parts which the pigs were to play in *Animal Farm*. Family ties and ordinary existence are negated, but life still remains 'most intricate, fiercer than tigers'. The sequel to *The Aerodrome* was more muted, an inquiry into the real causes of the death of the unknown soldier who is all soldiers, *Why Was I Killed?* Actually a scholar of ancient Greece, Warner lacked the passion and invention of a Green or a Cary, and certainly their mastery over the everyday words that people used. The other considerable novelists who made their reputation in the war years, Nigel Balchin and F. L. Green, reproduced with extraordinary accuracy the staccato style and clipped rhythms of contemporary speech. *The Small Back Room* is an admirable study of the bickering in a scientific research department, and of the endurance and courage needed to defuse a lethal German booby-trap. *Odd Man Out* was to be made by Carol Reed into an exemplar of the post-war British cinema, but as a novel it is remarkable for its study of an Irish revolutionary hunted through Belfast and pursued by a drunken painter, as obsessed with capturing the last light of dying as any Gulley Jimson. The later work of Balchin and F. L. Green never achieved the trenchant immediacy of their wartime novels. They seemed to prove the suspicion of John Lehmann and the insistence of Keith Douglas that direct war experience might be necessary for a description of the period. Two lesser novelists, James Hanley and Gerald Kersh, whose *They Died With their Boots Clean* promised a stark view of the war at last written from the ranks, lost their balance in the mixed brutality and sentimentality of their later perceptions. Their bleak vision did not survive the transition into peace.

Many of the better novels about the war were written from the luxury of hindsight, particularly Evelyn Waugh's trilogy *Men At Arms*, and the relevant volumes in the sequences of novels from the pens of C. P. Snow and Anthony Powell. Waugh had immediately joined the army, leaving *Work Suspended* – its two chapters were published in 1943 with the declaration that if he ever found again 'the leisure and will to finish it, the work would be in vain'. Its world had ceased to exist. Yet Waugh did publish in 1945 his first serious novel, which changed his reputation, *Brideshead Revisited*, above all an elegy for a world that had ceased to exist. His minor comic novel of 1942, *Put Out More Flags*, had been an exaggerated attack on many of the anomalies and farcical incidents caused by requisitioning and rationing, delinquent evacuees and crooked government employees. But *Brideshead Revisited*, which began and ended with the visit of an army officer to the commandeered and finally dilapidated stately home of the Marchmain family, has an ending as resonant as the close of *The Great Gatsby*, not of boats beating against the current and borne back ceaselessly into the past, but of a small red flame lit by the vanities of the 'thirties that led to victory in war at the price of the destruction of the ruined mansion, never to be restored to its former hedonistic state of grace. Waugh himself considered the novel as a souvenir of the Second World War, not of the decades before it, which appeared to be the substance of the book.

Two women writers were changed by the experience of the war. In her collections of short stories of 1941 and 1945, *Look at All Those Roses* and *The Demon Lover*, Elizabeth Bowen displayed the same elegiac spirit as Evelyn Waugh, a regret for Edwardian aristocratic values that could not last the blitz and the times. The subtle and degrading effect of war – its poet Henry Reed noted – held together the tales in *The Demon Lover*. No story in the book did not convey 'that feeling of the deterioration of the spirit which, when the tumult, and the shooting, and the self-deception subside, is seen to be war's residue'. The adultery which had been squalid in peacetime was still more squalid in war, which called for brute courage, but might leave behind nothing but brutes or ghosts. 'Left to oneself,' said the heroine of 'Pink May', 'one doesn't ruin one's life.' In a post-war novel, *The Heat of the Day*, Elizabeth Bowen revived the intense atmosphere of the air raids and the black-out. From a melodramatic plot, she constructed an evocation of precarious existence that still grips and records feelings of the period, of 'The Bombed Happiness'. Rosamond Lehmann, however, the other major woman writer most affected by the period, was personally involved. Separated from her second husband Wogan Philipps, later the only communist peer, Lord Milford, she was involved with Cecil Day Lewis, who dedicated to her his major book of war poems, *Word Over All*.

> We speak of what we know, but what we have spoken
> Truly we know not –
> Whether our good may tarnish, our grief to far
> Centuries glow not ...

Her novel, *The Ballad and the Source*, was set before the First World War, but its theme, an examination of the truth, the difference between a fiction and the fact, was relevant to her time, particularly as Day Lewis was concerned with the effect on his own serious writing of the continuous propaganda which he was editing at the Ministry of Information.

Involved in intelligence duties during the war, Graham Greene had *The Power and the Glory* published in 1940; but he wrote only an 'entertainment', *The Ministry of Fear*, with a thrilling plot set against a precise and raffish decor of blitzed London. In the manner of Evelyn Waugh, Greene's posting to and experience in West Africa would confirm his talent; the writing of *The Heart of the Matter* would prove him to be an illuminating and serious novelist with a rare insight into the psychology and guilt of love. His study of duty overseas and its emotional consequences would condemn Somerset Maugham to the triviality of a minor imperial scribe: out of his time, he was not worth more. Service abroad would initiate in Greene a series of books set in hostile foreign situations from Vietnam to Cuba to Paraguay, that would make him the premier novelist of his age.

Two prose works were the thesis and the antithesis of the war years. *The Last Enemy* by Richard Hillary made him the Rupert Brooke and Saint-Exupéry of his time. His Oxford blitheness; his heroism as a fighter pilot; his degradation as a burned victim; his resurrection by the skin surgeon Archibald McIndoe; his recognition and denial of his disfigurement while rescuing the bombed and the dying with the famous line, 'I see they got you too'; his love affairs with Merle Oberon and Mary Booker; his final apotheosis when he insisted on flying again; this life was catharsis through suffering, redemption through love and courage. Arthur Koestler confirmed the hagiography of Hillary in an article for *Horizon*, 'Birth of a Myth'. He recognized that Hillary's life and death were symbolic – and concluded that the myth devoured the man. 'It is the myth of the Lost Generation – sceptic crusaders, knights of effete veneer, sick with the nostalgia of something to fight for, which as yet is not. It is the myth of the crusade without a cross, and of desperate crusaders in search of a cross.' Koestler's praise of Hillary was published by Cyril Connolly, whose own work, *The Unquiet Grave*, was the antithesis of Hillary's autobiography. On one thing only, he agreed with Hillary: the last enemy was oneself. Although Palinurus, the old steersman of Aeneas who fell asleep and drowned before reaching haven in Italy, is the official spokesman and moralist of the book, Connolly is issuing an elegant apologia for a wasted life more self-lacerating than *Enemies of Promise*. He begins by stating that the true function of a writer is to produce a masterpiece. Any other task, even serving in a war or editing *Horizon*, is of no consequence. Any other contribution to the war effort is no more effective than peeling potatoes. By unstated implication, Connolly himself is most at fault: his pre-war novel, *The Rock Pool*, was his only published novel, although drafts of six unfinished novels were to mask his future. All he could do was to regret Mediterranean civilization and his own sloth and self-pity. He could also condemn all other war writers for becoming the servants of the government's bribe of comradeship, the 'gregarious herd-sense and herd-smell which keeps people from thinking and so reconciles them to the destruction of their private lives'.

The greatest difficulty for all writers in wartime was to protect an inner truth and isolation from an outward show and obligatory gestures. For the many who were working in intelligence, the Ministry of Information and the BBC, the dilemma was intolerable. They had to subscribe to falsehoods in the name of winning the war, but what if the means sullied the victory? As Clifford Dyment wrote:

> From many a mangled truth a war is won
> And who am I to oppose
> War and the lie and the pose
> Asserting a lie is good if a war be won?

> From many a mangled truth a war is won
> And many a truth has died
> That has lived undenied
> For always there must be loss that a war be won.

> From many a mangled truth a war is won
> And when no thought is pure
> Who of us can be sure
> Of lie and truth and war when the war is won?

All were avid to hear the broadcast news, which was certainly the most truthful news being broadcast across the world at that time. All devoured the daily newspapers, and the British press was still technically free. Yet all information was subject to censorship, official or inhouse. Writers and poets were made censors. After fifteen months of being a censor, W. R. Rodgers complained that he had been bombed four times, was short of gas and water and light, and found the rules difficult to keep.

> Yet the Blue Pencil is a mere toy to wield,
> There are worse knots than the tangles of Red Tape.
> It is not difficult to censor foreign news,
> What is hard to-day is to censor one's own thoughts, –
> To sit by and see the blind man
> On the sightless horse, riding into the bottomless abyss.

In an ironic editorial in *Horizon*, Connolly proposed that every artist, turned administrator for the duration, should be prevented from writing because of the lack of creative material as well as the pressure of his work. The dilemma of the serving author would be solved by a moratorium on art. 'All writers who feel that they are in the war and responsible for winning it should be excused literary activity, and even forbidden it. This alone would remove their guilt.'

Such a prohibition might have prevented the writing of the most famous poem of the struggle, 'Lessons of the War', for Henry Reed served in the army for only a few months before being released to work at the Foreign Office. Some serving soldiers, 109 such as the poet and editor of *Kingdom Come*, John Waller, agreed that taking part in warfare was too tedious and embarrassing to allow for writing. The true artist should eschew military training and do work more important than the mere waging of war for whatever cause. The poet G. S. Fraser claimed that an organic human being in uniform had to sham dead. People in the forces were effectively prisoners in war. And even those who managed to use the experience of war as a subject of poetry found it difficult to find an appropriate tone or style to define something which Alan Ross termed 'a mixture of fear, farce and tedium, and worst of all, the absence of any real feelings at all'.

It might come hard, but poetry of value was being ground out by all three of Spender's generations, the literary elders, the prophets of the conflict, and its victims. John Lehmann asserted its worth. The last three of T. S. Eliot's *Four Quartets*, 'East Coker' and 'The Dry Salvages' and 'Little Gidding', were as exciting to him as news of great military victories. They were proof that the spirit of man might still celebrate place and life and eternity. Eliot himself noted that these were patriotic poems before crossing out his confession. And he told John Lehmann that 'Burnt Norton' might have remained alone if it had not been for the war. He was involved in writing for the stage and might have gone from *The Family Reunion* to another play, but 'the war destroyed that impulse for a time, the conditions of one's life changed, and one was thrown in on oneself'. So he wrote 'East Coker' and began to see the two poems as part of a quartet. Then Edith Sitwell wrote *Street Songs* and *Green Song* in an astonishing late flowering of her genius. The realities of war had made her lose the extravagance and solipsism of her earlier work. Her poems were now 'tragic, and often bitter with a kind of savagery of bitterness'. 'Lullaby' and 'Still Falls the Rain' were 'two of the most original poems *about the war* that were written during the war'.

> Heed my ragged lullaby,
> Fear not living, fear not chance;
> All is equal – blindness, sight,
> There is no depth, there is no height:
> Do, do.

Both Sitwell and Eliot were producing poetry equal to 'the spiritual demands of an apocalyptic age'. As for members of his own generation, Spender's prophets of war, Lehmann thought that they were writing better than ever during the struggle. Day Lewis and MacNeice and Spender himself were producing some of their most beautiful and intellectually vigorous work. There was not a break from their work before the war, but a maturity. Certainly, some political illusions had been shed; but politics had never dominated their poetry to the exclusion of everything else. Spender has said that his generation did not think about modernism. 'We were journalistic. Modernism was irrelevant to us. We were very interested in what was going on, even gossip. The Modernists didn't know anything about that.' Thus the experience of the war, the daily news of it, profoundly changed their poetry for the better. In Lehmann's opinion, Day Lewis's poems in *Word Over All* were 'more remarkable technically and more profoundly felt than what went before or what came after', while Spender's work in *Ruins and Visions* and the wartime poems collected in *Poems of Dedication* had moments of extraordinary illumination, as MacNeice's poetry had greater depth and power after his return from America.

Lehmann then quoted the words of his late friend Demetrios Capetanakis, that while war was not frightening physically, it was metaphysically, and poetry of a high order had to come out of it. Alun Lewis and Keith Douglas were the victims of the war, two of many young poets of the highest quality who were killed. They answered the cry of 'Where are the war poets?', but their answers were not the answers of the poets of the First World War. They were different. They had technical vitality and deep seriousness. Many of the surviving war poets were fastidious artists: Roy Fuller, Lawrence Durrell, Terence Tiller, Henry Reed, Norman Nicholson, Laurie Lee. What was admirable was 'their effort towards a new integration – their attempt to map some system of thought and feeling wide enough and deep enough for our culture to exist in'. Hills that had blocked the view had subsided in an earthquake, great mountains were glimpsed behind. There was an apocalyptic sense everywhere in the poetry of the time, although even Dylan Thomas was not a member of the minor poetic school called 'Apocalyptics'. There was a 'sense of the old certainties dissolving under the pressure of some deep upheaval of the spirit'. And the young poets, many of whom died in the war or fell into silence after it, tried to restate a faith 'in imaginative creation, but above all in the value of the individual and the reality of moral choice against man-made machines of organisation and the crudity of material "Progress": against a world based on values of power only ...'

Lehmann was the midwife, not of the expected revolution of the 'thirties, but of the revolutionary poetry of the 'forties. His defence of it, and Spender's contemporary criticism of it, proved its validity and emphasized its birth from the crucible of its creation. There is an illusion that the First World War killed off the best young minds and the best young writers, while the Second spared them. It is untrue. In a recent and judicious anthology of the poetry of the last world war, *The Terrible Rain*, the work of eighty-seven poets in uniform is included: twenty of them died on active service, mainly in the Royal Air Force or with the Fleet Air Arm. Some fifty poets in all published some of their work before being killed in action: a roll-call of their names concludes this book. Death in the sky replaced death in the trenches. Poets who were pilots were killed where infantry officers had been slaughtered in the previous conflict. Only five major poets in khaki died in the Second World War: Keith Douglas and Alun Lewis, Sidney Keyes and Drummond Allison and John Jarmain. The rest were mostly fliers. As David Wright wrote about his contemporaries with their magnanimity of spirit in Oxford in 1939: 'Nearly all were waiting to join the air force, and nearly all, it seemed, were to be killed in the Battle of Britain or shortly after.' Even the survivors, such as Richard Hillary, did not last long. As he wrote of himself before he died, 'It is odd that I who always gave least should be the one who remained.'

It was not enough to be killed to make a great war writer, but it helped. A poet's death wonderfully concentrated the minds of those who had hardly risked their lives and had avoided serving in the war. At the time, the attention given to writers in uniform was considerable and considered; the posthumous attention to victims in the forces was lyrical and elegiac. Yet the rejection of the war and of its privations by many of those who suffered it allowed a later generation of writers and critics to undervalue the radical and 'modernist' work of the quick and the dead of that time. They could still ask where were the war writers, when these lay unread under their noses. Those who were in the grave could not defend or improve their works. Those who were silenced by the horror and scale of their war experience often chose to be dumb rather than retaliate in anger and bitterness against those who were caustic about the catharsis caused by the conflict. The war had to be forgotten, the peace lived through, families raised, fame passed to those who did not really serve. As John Pudney wrote in his epitaph for all the dead young pilots, 'For Johnny':

> Do not despair
> For Johnny-head-in-air;
> He sleeps as sound
> As Johnny underground.
>
> Fetch out no shroud
> For Johnny-in-the-cloud;
> And keep your tears
> For him in after years.
>
> Better by far
> For Johnny-the-bright-star,
> To keep your head,
> And see his children fed.

EIGHT

Feeding the War Machine

Leonard Rosoman

You cannot cage a field
You cannot wire it, as you wire a summer's roses
To sell in towns; you cannot cage it
Or kill it utterly ... the field never dies,
Though you build on it, burn it black, or domicile
A thousand prisoners upon its empty features.

So Henry Reed, who had named the parts of the rifle, confirmed that the countryside would outlive all the impositions which machines and men at war put upon it. The country always had. It served the governments in London and accepted their directives. Its armies had not marched on the capital for three hundred years, since it had supported the King in the Civil War. In this new war, the countryside put up its little defences, accepted the evacuees from the metropolis and the military training areas and the internment camps and the Allied soldiers waiting to invade Europe, and it produced more to eat than Britain had ever produced, two-thirds of all essential foodstuffs. A land army was created, both an army in training that disfigured the landscape, and an army that worked the land itself. Those who refused to serve in khaki or blue uniforms were frequently drafted to till the fields; their conscientious objections did not extend as far as refusing to brutalize the earth with spade and mattock. Hundreds of thousands of young women were also drafted to work as agricultural labourers in an official Land Army, which wore a costume of green jerseys and fawn breeches. Some of them were the literati of London and brought the attitudes of Fitzrovia to the farm. In one notorious story, 'The Land Girl', Diana Gardner told of her revenge on a jealous farmer's wife before taking the bus back to town. But on the whole, writers like Phyllis Castle, who had lasted only one week in the WAAF, deciphered the land and its language and stuck to it. 'At first I used to lean on my fork and watch the Bristol bombers right across the sky and long for a really big bomb to break the monotony ... Now at the end of three weeks I'm perfectly contented.'

The evacuees from the cities and the military forces massing in their country camps and the Land Army itself brought urban opinions to rural minds, who spoke their minds in return. A common resistance to the threat of invasion broke down the antipathy between hedgerow and street, while the blitz on the capital and on many of the ports and provincial cities made country people believe that, for once, the urban dwellers were getting the worst of it. As Anne Ridler wrote in 'For this Time':

Now country people look towards town,
And awestruck see the crimson stain
Spread on the cloud, and *London's burning*
Say in grief as once laughing ...

Bombing made for a community of suffering, as did rationing. And there again, the cities were worse off. There was always food to be found without coupons in the villages, while it was scarce in the market-places. Living near the land meant eating better. Even serving in the rural Civil Defence and Home Guard units – the choice of many temporary expatriates from London such as John Lehmann and Cecil Day Lewis – was preferable to serving on the streets. Patrols were like nature rambles, night duty was an opportunity to exchange arable and intellectual cultures. As Day Lewis wrote of his 'Watching Post' with a farmer as his fellow guard, both of them had found their natural law in preparing to resist the invader. And in 'The Stand-To', Day Lewis found himself, as he never had during his Marxist youth, one of thirty comrades:

> Last night a Stand-To was ordered. Thirty men of us here
> Came out to guard the starlit village – my men who wear
> Unwitting the season's beauty, the received truth of the spade –
> Roadmen, farm labourers, masons, turned to another trade ...
>
> I write this verse to record the men who have watched with me –
> Spot who is good at darts, Squibby at repartee,
> Mark and Cyril, the dead shots, Ralph with a ploughman's gait,
> Gibson, Harris and Long, old hands for the barricade,
>
> Whiller the lorry-driver, Francis and Rattlesnake,
> Fred and Charles and Stan – these nights I have lain awake
> And thought of my thirty men and the autumn wind that blows
> The apples down too early and shatters the autumn rose.

The provincial towns were invaded with soldiers and airmen looking for distraction and finding only small hotels and pubs and a local cinema. Willy-nilly, a company of sorts grew between them in their passing and the local societies. Never had so many street-wise conscripted civilians been thrown into such country conditions and communities. In one of the more affecting stories of the war, 'They Came', Alun Lewis told of a Welsh soldier, whose wife was killed by a bomb when he was on leave in his home town: he returned to be consoled by the villagers in the pub, by his mate who was an alien East Ender, and by the night-time in the countryside. The errant bands of soldiers from their huts met the permanent countryfolk in their nightly rituals in their pubs, and no longer felt divided. Their common task was to feed the war machine. Even a Welsh separatist like Keidrych Rhys, serving as a gunner with nine other men in a bell-tent near Dover, found himself resolved 'of race contradictions and all regimentation'. Peace was now the ambush; but mounting guard at night on a farm where they helped the farmer to harvest his corn by day, made Rhys feel one with his fellow English gunners and the farmer's family in the common legacy of the land.

The war, however, did foul the face of England, but it also increased paradoxically the appreciation of England's beauties in contrast to the necessary and ugly appurtenances of the military machine. The onset of war – the wireless philosopher C. E. M. Joad complained – destroyed nature rather than the enemy.

All over the country, lanes are being turned into roads, trees and hedges are being cut down, turf is being gashed by lorries, margins and verges destroyed by tanks, fields converted into seas of mud, covered with concrete or asphalt, stacked with dumps or littered with rubbish. Great tracts are studded with concrete posts or bound with barbed wire. Meanwhile barracks, camps, Ack-Ack battalions, searchlight units, aerodromes, air fields, munition works, and all their attachments and appendages in the way of hutments, shacks, rubble, barbed wire, latrines, tents and rubbish dumps, are bidding fair to turn England into a devastated area. It has long been known that with the possible exception of poultry, soldiers create more ugliness, destroy more beauty, and do these things more rapidly, than any other form of living organism. 'It is no use,' said a friend of mine in the Army, referring to the mess that has been made of Box Hill, 'expecting us to do any different. Wherever we go we shall destroy trees, cut up the grass, make mud, leave tins, stick up wire, and generally make a mess.'

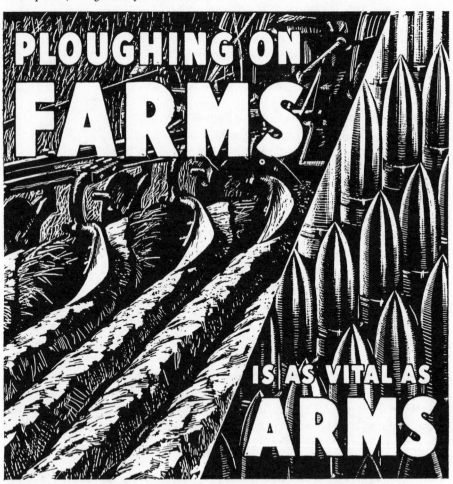

Although the patterns of dog-fights and searchlight beams and flare paths might excite painters and writers, although the dread precision of the actual machines of war had a terrible beauty, although poets might even see in barrage balloons a silver serendipity in the sky, the land was desecrated by the squalid accoutrements of military necessity. A feeling of regionalism, which was being eroded by a national sense of fighting a war in common directed by the government in London, was latent and would emerge more profoundly after the war because of the devastation to the landscape caused by the war machine. This was the paradox of mobilizing the country and the city in mutual service to achieve a triumph over foreign enemies. Never had farmer and trader, villager and slum tenant felt so united, but only in a common cause. When that cause was successful and the skies were clear of German raiders, the old divisions would spring up again because of the wreckage and the anomalies that the winning of the war left behind. The price of unity for victory would be a divided peace.

In reaction from the conditions imposed by war, English poetry hymned a nostalgic and sensuous landscape. The poems of Dylan Thomas and Vernon Watkins and R. S. Thomas spoke of the natural wonders of Wales, while those of Scotland were lauded by Norman McCaig and W. S. Graham and Edwin Muir, who declared that reading Tolstoy on death told him more about the meaning and end of life than any experience of the current carnage. Norman Nicholson, praising the landscape of Cumberland, found that the bombing of the cities meant the celebration of the country by those who were not fighting. 'The face of London might be changed or even destroyed in a night, but Black Combe, three miles from my bedroom window, would be little different whatever happened in the war. There was a political side to this, too. During the War, many of us resented the centralization of power, the standardization, the ironing-out of regional differences and individualities. It may have been necessary at the time, but we saw it as the worsening of a process which had been going on for ten or twenty years.' The war poetry of the enduring countryside was a kind of protest against 'the sheer disregard of London-based government.'

There were other poets who saw in the beauty of the countryside the very fight to the death. It was inescapable. For Clive Sansom, all Nature's agents imaged war: butterflies on sinister flights, bees droning at bomber's pitch, tractors making parallel trenches. Laurie Lee heard cuckoos pumping forth salvoes across an armoured valley, and blackbirds were nervous beneath the hawk's reconnaissance. J. C. Hall saw the manoeuvres of the spring conquering the land like the battalions of Europe. Clifford Dyment viewed gulls as seaplanes, a Fulmar with her throttle full, a Skua snatching him into the air. A walk on the moors was a combat report for Ruthven Todd, throwing puffball spores as explosive for his bombs and watching real fighter planes engage the curlews above the peat-moss. But most remarkable of the poems that saw nature as a kind of war was Herbert Corby's 'Missing'. Its subject was a Hampden bomber that did not return. Countrymen had told the poet that when the wheat was cut, hares went about on the stubble, homeless and afraid. 117

And so did the flight commander at dawn on the aerodrome after the air raid:

> He walks distraught, circling the landing ground,
> waiting the last one in that won't come back,
> and like those hares, he wanders round and round,
> lost and desolate on the close-cropped track.

For the country people sent their sons and daughters into the armed forces just as the city people did. There were proportionately as many casualties from the village as from the slum. Before he died fighting in Bulgaria, Frank Thompson, the son of the poet of the First World War Edward Thompson, acknowledged the death toll in the villages and the old men in the pubs talking about the lost lads who had died in a war of others' making. 'War, like a grocer, weighs and sends us back / Ashes for men, and all our year goes black.' And the bombs did not spare every country place. In point of feeling, when a market town was raided, it seemed worse than London, which had burned down before in its great fire. Charles Hamblett, who served in the Royal Air Force and went off with Tambimuttu's beautiful and diabetic wife Jacqueline, pointed out that he suffered more over bombs that fell on Newmarket than on Soho. The farmers he spoke of in the Wheatsheaf suffered more to see their High Street destroyed than did the Fitzrovians.

> To see your small, damaged town
> Where each stone
> Holds a history of its own,
> Evokes a wild pity
> Deeper than being
> With strange folk; seeing
> The devastastion
> Of their city ...

Yet the war machine fed London, which was the maw of the national effort. It ingested the products of the farms and the factories, the earth and the mines below the earth. Its destruction during the blitz would have meant a decentralization and a democratization, which might well have lost the war. Through London, the soldiers briefly passed along with many of the country people and the land army and the factory workers, either on leave or business. In London were the major ministries and theatres and galleries, most of the publishers and the film technicians, a preponderance of the artists and the writers and the magazine editors. From London, those who could communicate about life on the Home Front were sent out to describe and depict the war effort on the land and on the shop floor. The capital was truly the centre of the spread and scattered community, which the struggle had made of the whole nation.

The writers and artists of the nineteen-thirties may have called the workers their comrades, but they did not work in the factories. The behaviour and assumptions of the bourgeois intellectual were a machine shop or a mineshaft away from those of the proletarian. It was no good clapping him on the back, George Orwell wrote, and saying he was as good a man as Orwell was. A total alteration was necessary in Orwell's character, if he were to leave his class and join with the manual labourer. Among the leading writers, only Henry Green had worked for years in his family's foundry near Birmingham. He welcomed the coming of the war because it would force readers and writers to go out into the unknown territories of the factories at home and to accept other people's strange lives and perhaps to change the style of their own. V. S. Pritchett, indeed, did have to visit his 'fellow prisoners' in an England he hardly knew, the England of factory workers. He became a documentary reporter for the *New Statesman*, spending weeks in shipyards, engineering works, marshalling yards and railway control centres. But he was not engaged. He felt that he was a mere voyeur. And as for James Pope-Hennessy, who was drafted to Ayrshire on the collapse of Cazalet's cushy battery, he told Clarissa Churchill that he had no affinity with the local working class – 'Uninteresting essentially to me, but somehow evoking all my most kindly instincts; and an anxiety to be liked I do not always feel with intellectuals or others. They appeal to me much as did the negroes in the West Indies, though they are far less original, strange and affectionate.'

Those bourgeois intellectuals engaged in factory work were usually women. For Britain was the first democracy to conscript women for national service in the armed forces, industry and agriculture. The five and a half million women at the machines turned out one third of national output. Often they worked at the most dangerous occupations, particularly in the vast munitions works, filling shells with explosives, 'handling cold death with calloused hands'. In the words of a popular rhyme of the time:

> She's the girl that makes the thing
> That drills the hole, that holds the spring
> That drives the rod, that turns the knob
> That works the thingummybob.
> It's a ticklish sort of job
> Making a thing for the thingummybob
> Especially when you don't know what it's for.
> And it's the girl that makes the thing
> That holds the oil that oils the ring
> That makes the thingummybob that's going to win the war ...

Inez Holden wrote for *Horizon* of her experiences on the shop floor, where she was eventually accepted. While in the First World War the battle was between those at the front and those at home, in the Second it was between those who stayed at home and worked, and those who got away into safe or sunny places. There was also a small guerrilla war to be waged against the bourgeois intellectuals, who fought class battles from their armchair and not the factory bench. True belief in dialectical materialism meant actually clocking-in at the machines. The only possible comradeship was with fellow workers.

The editors in London felt no guilt in not working in the factories on war production. Their job was occasionally to report on conditions there and to print stories from authors fighting on the industrial front. John Lehmann particularly felt obliged to deny class barriers and publish short stories written by proletarians in Penguin *New Writing*, but he found few to publish outside the mining stories of B. L. Coombes and Percy Coates, or Gordon Jeffery's account of being docked threepence 'In the Welding Bay'. Lehmann thought that unemployment had encouraged proletarian writing during the depression, but now its sources would be dried up by full employment for war production. Poverty, indeed, was no longer a question of class but of choice. As Coombes was told, Lehmann knew a large number of writers and artists of 'middle-class origin' who were much poorer than the average worker. 'They have chosen to remain so, because they felt that for creative work leisure, at whatever cost, was necessary.' For them, Fitzrovia was their factory.

Extreme as always, the Scots poet Hugh MacDiarmid left his sanctuary in the Shetlands at the age of forty-nine to take on heavy manual labour in a Clydeside factory. During the Nazi-Soviet pact, he and other Marxist intellectuals had disapproved of increased production for an 'imperialist' war; but when Russia joined the Allies after the German attack of 1941, MacDiarmid had to accept industrial conscription and make munitions for the victory of the workers. His ideology was clear in a long poem on 'The Fall of France', parts of which were printed by Nancy Cunard in her French anthology:

> Thus the poet who is a true poet
> Finds in the very life of the proletariat
> The flame which transforms him, and which, in his turn,
> By dint of his poet's gift, he renders back
> To the class which incarnates all poetry,
> The living and animating poetry of struggle ...

MacDiarmid was not alone in writing the poetry of struggle from a factory. In imitation of the lake poets of the Romantic revolution, a group of Marxist intellectuals persuaded Tambimuttu to publish *New Lyrical Ballads* in Editions Poetry London. The remarkable collection included factory ballads by two of the editors, Maurice Carpenter and Honor Arundel, as well as service poems by the third editor, Jack Lindsay, whose 'Squadding' became an anthology piece. The *New Lyrical Ballads* are generally moving, intense and passionate. In all the poetry of the war, they convey the only true feeling of a workers' struggle, whether dressed in overalls or a boiler suit or a uniform. To Maurice Carpenter, red sky at night meant bombers' delight, but:

> Morning brings ravaged homes and my mates' eyes
> Stab with a dangerous light the fog of lies,
> Red sky at morning.
> Warning.

While on the late shift in the machine shop:

> The night roars in these walls
> And screams in steel,
> For we are midwives of a queer nativity,
> And in the quiet night outside
> Hear our winged children drone across the moon ...

Other poems on foundries and lathes, mines and morning shifts, completed the factory section of *New Lyrical Ballads*. One ballad of the war was inexplicably omitted: Norman Nicholson's bitter comment on the pits at 'Cleator Moor', which had been closed during the depression, but were opened again for the duration of the fighting.

> ... But now the pits are wick with men,
> Digging like dogs dig for a bone:
> For food and life *we* dig the earth –
> In Cleator Moor they dig for death.
>
> Every waggon of cold coal
> Is fire to drive a turbine wheel;
> Every knuckle of soft ore
> A bullet in a soldier's ear.
>
> The miner at the rockface stands,
> With his segged and bleeding hands
> Heaps on his head the fiery coal,
> And feels the iron in his soul.

More poignant than the poems of the mines and of the factories of war were the paintings. Up to Clydeside where Hugh MacDiarmid was working, Stanley Spencer went. The impoverished and God-driven old painter was commissioned by the state to depict the shipbuilding at Lithgow's yards in Port Glasgow. He saw there, in the work of the welders and the riveters, an involvement and a sacred sense of community. 'Everything I see', he wrote after a visit to a riggers' loft, 'is manifestly religious and sexual.' His foreshortened view of the burners in his central panel of *Shipbuilding on the Clyde* is a masterpiece of men at work, worthy to rank in imaginative perspective with Uccello's knights at war. He made of manual labour a claustrophobic conflict, a combat of metal and tool, flame and men within a narrow space, that brought a world war into a little room. *Picture Post* ran a feature on him sketching in his pyjamas among the welders and making his biblical statements, 'Seek and the technicalities shall be added unto you ... I am a worm wriggling about the legs of men.'

Commissions from the War Artists' Advisory Committee brought the painter's brush towards the crankshaft and the casing. What Leger had done to show the essence of the machine age, William Roberts achieved in his pictures of munitions factories, as did Leslie Cole in his shaping of keel plates, Frank Dobson in his multiple drills and arc-welding marine boilers, R. Vivian Pitchforth in his damaged propellers at maintenance stations, Keith Henderson in his air gunners in their turrets, Henry Lamb in his command posts, C. R. W. Nevison in his anti-aircraft defences, Raymond McGrath in his wings and hangars, Barnett Freedman in his gun turrets, Leonard Rosoman in his radar predictors, Stephen Bone in his conning towers, Richard Eurich in the great convoy to North Africa – and the three who died in the war also achieved much definition, Albert Richards in his searchlight batteries, Eric Ravilious in the different aspects of his *Submarine Series* and Thomas Hennell in his operation rooms and handling of depth charges. The terrible beauty of the machines of war, the arcs and the angles, the struts and the fins, the cones and the noses, the colour and the camouflage of the engines of death provoked an extraordinary appreciation in the artist's eye of the geometry of his craft, the lines and the distances, the spaces and the configurations that lay between earth and sea, air and fire, life and death, heaven and hell. 'To watch a man sitting, trapped almost, in the flower-like interior of a radar predictor was beautiful,' Leonard Rosoman wrote while on the aircraft carrier *Formidable*. 'The aeroplane folds its wings and crouches on the flight deck. These things must be felt with the senses, not just used in terms of interesting shapes.'

Machines and munitions made by men and women to kill other human beings precisely and bloodily were the material of the war artists, who were the first British illuminators of the lucid means of annihilation. They saw what Laurie Lee saw, creation in the engines of destruction.

> Look into wombs and factories and behold
> nativities unblessed by hopeful stars,
> the sleek machine of flesh,
> the chubby bomb,
> lying together in one dreadful cradle.

And so the war machine was fed, with children of military age, with explosives, with armaments, with rations, with uniforms, with boots, with the paraphernalia of murder. And in London were those who directed the nation in what to make, where to send it, whom to kill – and how to record the whole operation for future generations, if there should be any.

NINE

Air, Sea, Earth and Home

In the next great war, Liam O'Flaherty thought before its declaration, pilots would seize power. There would be flying barons, an aristocracy of the air instead of the earth. They would quarrel among themselves, until all cities lay in ruins and civilization had disappeared. After 1939, most people believed with O'Flaherty that Goering's bombers would destroy all British cities, although the raiders failed to do so. The fighter pilots who defended the urban sprawls did become aerial knights, each a Galahad in his Spitfire or Hurricane, the first of the few. But they seemed a marked aristocracy, bound to die. They thought they were doomed and usually achieved their fate. In proportion to the rest of the armed forces, airmen were suicide squads. Small though their numbers were, the fliers predominated on the list of creative artists who died in the war, nearly half of the number. Death fell from the sky, and brightness from the air.

The pilots seemed to be winged cavaliers of culture, the guards above the ivory dome, with surveillance over all. Stephen Spender wrote a poem linking thinkers and airmen on the edge of the skies of the future. Before they plunged into an iron war, he wanted them to remember their wild good drunkenness where they had abandoned care.

> And then forget. Become what
> Things require. The expletive word.
> The all-night long screeching metal bird.
> And all of time shut down in one shot
> Of night by a gun uttered.

Bullets now mattered more than syllables. The cockpit defended the rostrum. The poetry and prose of flying descended on the editors in London. If there was no Saint-Exupéry, there was Richard Hillary of the burned sacrifice and the drama of human recognition with the victims of the blitz. The air force fought from home bases. Its machines were a form of expression. 'The planes themselves are very lovely,' John Sommerfeld wrote to John Lehmann, 'and incredibly civilized, but nothing else in this life is.' He descibed for Penguin *New Writing* how life worked on aerodromes, sounding like zoos of hungry animals, confused with roarings and growlings. In the dark hangars, pools of bluish light bathed the sleek forms of aircraft, which mechanics dissected, opening their sides to reveal their complex silvery bones. There was a peculiar smell, both sweet and oily, as if cattle were mingled with machinery, while aviation fuel gave off a jungle scent. The pilot, finally socketed into his cockpit, seemed only the final piece that completed the puzzle.

John Pudney became the leading poet of the Royal Air Force with his *Dispersal Point* of 1942 and later with *Beyond This Disregard* and *South of Forty*. He also edited with Henry Treece an anthology of *Air Force Poetry*. The language was most successful when it achieved the terse and laconic communications of the pilots themselves. The verse failed when it took wings into a romantic style; it served best as the true vocabulary of man and machine, the grammar of combat. In one Pudney

Previous page: Leonard Rosoman

poem, the fighter pilot talks: 'I let him have a sharp four-second squirt, / Closing to fifty yards. He went on fire / ... He burnt out in the air: that's how the poor sod died.' Pudney saw a store of bombs as patient, waiting as grocer's goods on shelves for somebody to stroke them or chalk a joke on them to be dropped on Berlin. 'And fun shall be our cloak.'

For two pilot poets who were to die, safety was all and a banal return.

> Snap back the canopy,
> Pull out the oxygen tube,
> Flick the harness pin
> And slap out into the air
> Clear of the machine.

So David Bourne wrote of a 'Parachute Descent' for the boys who wanted to stay in the sky, because their ideas and ideals were too high for earth. But for 'Airmen' who had a safe landing, Brian Allwood recommended silence.

> Has nothing to say, and this is done.
> At night the long youth of the flaring gun;
> Against the great raiders, the great sun.
>
> Returning now the dawn lets him be safe:
> No one has really asked him for his life,
> Eating eggs and bacon with a fork and knife.

The words of the service were understated, and so were the best of its descriptions. Olivia Fitzroy, finding her fighter pilot in a pub, heard that all his jargon was of aircraft or of beer. 'Good show!' he said. 'They're wizard types! ... After this morning's prang ... I thought I'd had it in that teased-out kite.' She asked him what he would do after the war:

> Then saw his puzzled face, and caught my breath.
> There was no afterwards for him, but death.

A contrary wind blew when defence changed to attack. British fighters left home ground to fly over France, while thousand-bomber raids destroyed the old civilization of Germany as well as the factories filled with Nazi slave labour. There was a change of air in wartime poetry. The pilot was no longer sentry and sacrifice. He was abstraction and avenger. He did not guard homes, he savaged abroad. William Blake's Invisible Worm, who flew in the night and the howling storm, now turned. It destroyed the dark secret heart of the Third Reich. And in that terrible retribution, the vision of the fliers and their recorders altered to a common pity, a mutual mercy. Those about to die in the air also broadcast death upon the earth. Revenge was not sweet, but apt. And those who suffered on the ground reconsidered their definitions of their aerial saviours. As the Royal Artillery officer, R. N. Currey, wrote, he now lived in a 'Disintegration of Springtime'. The joyride was over, it was a damned unnatural sort of war. The pilot in the clouds might be sure of 125 his values, but he could not even see the people beneath he was about to destroy. Equally, those on the ground could perceive the pilot as no more than a machine shown on an instrument. He might be somebody's son, 'fragile as Icarus – and our desire / To see that damned machine come down on fire.'

There was an element of vengeance in the fighters' world as well as the bombers'. David Bourne was too honest not to confess to this.

> Twelve jets and spume of flame
> Stumble and leap into the blackness,
> To be held there for an instant.
> Then away and up, stuttering Firefly of revenge ...
>
> And we're off to see the wizard
> The wonderful Wizard of Oz –
> Lost? No. Motherdrome will see you home ...
> To the taxi-in triumphant.

Motherdrome failed to see him home in the end, nor did it see the return of all the bombing crews. They were themselves murderers, who were also murdered in the air. This was particularly clear to the American bombers, when they joined the war, for America had not even been bombed. Randall Jarrell saw himself and the murdering Eighth Air Force as part of the general 'Losses':

> In bombers named for girls, we burned
> The cities we had learned about in school –
> Till our lives wore out; our bodies lay among
> The people we had killed and never seen.
> When we lasted long enough they gave us medals;
> When we died they said, 'Our casualties were low.'
> They said, 'Here are the maps'; we burned the cities.

Yet it was a just war that burned the cities, perhaps the last just war that would ever be fought. The guardians of the air above Britain had become the executioners, but their aim was right. The problem was O'Flaherty's main point: the retribution from the air on the cities of Europe did destroy civilization, particularly in the final holocaust by fire at Dresden. 'I cannot look at any more maps,' Canetti wrote in 1943. 'The names of cities reek of burnt flesh.' Michael MacNaughton-Smith, one of many war poets from St John's College at Oxford, died on a raid over Germany; but the bombing was never an act of pride for him. He was always setting course for Troy to leave it burning, and finally did not himself return. And Patric Dickinson, watching the British bombers fly out in the evening, heard their engines beat the executioner's slow drum. They were killers and would be killed.

> And as I watch and count
> The fair impassive wings
> I see the victims mount
> Self-willed their scaffoldings.

The later theme of the common victim and the common dead also surfaced in the war at sea. At first, it was the convoys which suffered from submarine attack. Ships loaded with refugees were sunk as well as troop transports. G. S. Fraser mourned the children lost on the SS *City of Benares*, the blood of the innocent smearing the sky, while Roy Campbell evoked the soaring headlands of the Cape to be the monument of a troopship that went down:

> Where, packed as tight as space can fit them
> The soldiers retch, and snore, and stink.
> It was no bunch of flowers that hit them
> And woke them up, that night, to drink.

The supreme recorder of the convoys was Alan Ross, who served on the worst run of all, the Arctic voyage to Russia. His long poem on the encounter of his destroyer, the *Onslow*, with the German heavy cruiser *Hipper* is a classic of bardic reportage, never forsaking the talk of the lower deck even when calling up the images of Olympus.

> 'A' and 'B' Guns unable to fire,
> Radar destroyed, aerials ripped,
> And, forward, the sea stripping
> The Mess decks, spilling over tables,
> Fire and water clinching like boxers
> As the ship listed, sprawling them.
> Tamblin, his earphones awry, like a laurel wreath
> Slipped on a drunken god, gargled to death
> In water with a noise of snoring ...

Ross was buoyed throughout the war by reading the works of three other war poets, Roy Fuller and Alun Lewis and Keith Douglas, the last two of whom were killed. His leaves in London were spent in Fitzrovia, where his reputation was made by Tambimuttu and John Lehmann. His prose account of 'Arctic Convoy', however, showed that he could have become a writer on the sea and ships at the level of Conrad:

Not felt, not comprehended, merely seen; only the eye active, detached like a bird's eye, recording. The destroyers attack, drawing the enemy fire. Four swords of flame flick into the greyness, like a fencer's blows. World is a small narrowing circle, squeezed smaller and smaller, time has been interrupted, the clock smashed. Red-flecked, world is reduced to the gunsight's orb, its still centre, a focal grey in a tilted world of sea and sky. It is too late to put the pieces together.

Naval experience turned Ross into a poet as it did Charles Causley, who had been a playwright before becoming a coder below deck. 'It was Hitler who pushed a subject under my nose,' he declared, 'and the fact that poetry could be put together in one's head – when working at other jobs, lying half-asleep in a hammock, sitting in a bar – and written down complete, on a bit of paper the way a play or novel or short-story couldn't, gave me a form.' His ballads of the sea war contained in   127

Farewell Aggie Weston and *Survivor's Leave* were full of realism and naval slang; but he shared in Alan Ross's detachment from hatred of the enemy. In his poems, there was no appreciation of the warship as an instrument of revenge, a feeling in many of those who served in destroyers as well as fighters and bombers. Fresh from Oxford University, naval Sub-Lieutenant Norman Hampson praised the grey machinery of murder of his 'Corvette', which held 'beauty and the promise of the future'. But on 'Convoy', he brought up the theme of a common fate for all sailors, divided as they were by creed and country. Although those who were torpedoed felt hatred for the U-boat men, they also felt pity. Sweating in their fumy cell, the German submariners also dreamed of home and would die – 'to call them guilty is jangling broken words to no sane end.' All were murderers, all shared in the killing, yet the British sailors kept 'the truest course by the best light we know'.

In the sea stories published in the magazines in London, a curious truth emerged, the occasional happiness of men away from home. War seemed good for men and machines, but hell for women and children. Lehmann published in Penguin *New Writing* two stories which emphasized the fear and loathing of men on warships in the night, followed by a delirium and a delight in the day. In 'The Gregale', a ship's commander hates a phrase on the BBC, that somebody is thoroughly enjoying the war, but at dawn, as his ship approaches safety at Malta, he feels excited, within an 'absolute essence of *living*, with fear realised and dismissed, the future accepted for whatever it might bring of evil or good'. In 'The Hours of Darkness', the frightened sailor on watch off the submarine-haunted coasts of Scotland is suddenly filled with happiness, considering his mates and engineers and firemen, set against the immensity of the seas. Then he remembers London, which he has hated and loved; and where he has drunk beer on Saturday nights under the silver barrage balloons and the trolley-bus wires at the bottom of the Gray's Inn Road. The sea is like rolling green hills and the ships should have masses of young green leaves on them.

There were tales of safe landings and of the liberation of the spirit. And as in *The Tempest*, to drown at sea could be to escape into something rich and strange. In 'How It Is with the Happy Dead', the sunken ship on the bottom of the North Sea is as big as the whole world and as quiet as a cathedral. The underwaters accept her, the jellied growths and the shoals of fish, as does the last to breathe, the layer gunner trapped in the wreck. 'He wasn't afraid, why worry? Trawling all your life and then the war – always so near to death – seeing your mates lost overboard or smashed – always so near to death. Afraid? Why worry about a thing you've known of for so long?'

Many worried about becoming justified murderers. Their duty, if not their right, was to kill the enemy. To be killed was an evasion or dereliction. As Denis Saunders wrote in 'Almendro':

> Today I killed a man. God forgive me!
> Tomorrow I shall sow another political corpse,
> Or be dead myself. And strangely

I am satisfied to be applauded killer.
Holy Mary plead my dutied sin's legality ...

For J. G. Meddemmen, the way from the dilemma of murder was a stultification
of conscience, a blunting of sensibility:

It is not easy to waken
A full comprehension
Of what it now means
To be legally killer;
Man is dulled, not shaken ...

Those murdered best who thought least about it.

The duty of killing others, however, was the price exacted by serving in the war
on or over the seas. Entering that service gave a curious liberty, freedom from
worries at home. In a sense, the armed forces abroad were regimental bohemians.
While the Fitzrovians were not domestic creatures by choice, the troops away from
home were not domestic by necessity. Liberated from family responsibility by
service for their country and limited pay, the man in uniform in foreign parts was a
free agent caught within a male collective. His alienation was not from his home
land, but from his home within that land. His nostalgia was extreme for the places
he knew: he even tried to re-create them overseas, a little England in his mess in the
sand and the mud, the sweat and the monsoon. But he was alienated from his family
by his segregated society and the exile of geography. War meant a memory of lost
places, but divorce from the house. For the army, there had already been the long
separation from domesticity in the training camps in Britain, when the differences
between mates of the same sex in their barracks and their women with their
children and neighbours in their streets, had begun. Once there was embarkation
on troopships, the separation became a renunciation. A return to the old certainties
could not be. In his 'Home Thoughts from Abroad', John Bayliss wrote:

War is a dirty business, bayonet and blood
Stamped in the mud among fallen leaves.
The soldier moves aloof in his mood,
Set apart from life, and his wife forgives,
Having no grief to quench her greed:
Kisses, and for her the uniform lives ...

No man spoiled me save my own countrymen.
No man stole from me save my companions.
And I have done as much for them,
For property, once lost, is anyone's.
A moving watch in a dead man's hand
Is better taken, is better turned,
Wound and acquainted with a new touch.

Possessions were meaningless for men serving overseas as were homes and wives.
In that sense, all were bohemians or Fitzrovians. Some sort of identity did matter, **129**

even if it were only inscribed on the obligatory tags around one's neck. The worst tales were those of men who were blown to bits without being recorded. In one story of the wiping-out of a battalion, its intellectual Signals Officer from Balliol College at Oxford goes out to die with his identity discs at last slung around his neck. He remembers that his friend Stinky Lewis has been detonated into fragments without wearing his tags. He must make his own death of a little significance. Indeed, the worst job for those who did not die was clearing up the effects of those who did. One of them, a bomber pilot in the Middle East who was to die over Italy in his turn, remembered his waking eyes seeking out the empty beds:

> And – 'Damn', you said, 'another kit to pack.'
> I never liked that part: you never knew
> What privacies your sorting might lay bare.
> I always tried to leave my kit arranged
> In decent tidiness. You never know ...

The troops sent overseas after three years of training at home had already changed their outlook. As Bruce Bain testified, the inner man was altered in the prelude to exile. The feeling of 1940 had been lost. Then, an urgent need for self-sacrifice and a common danger had united all men in an experience of community. 'To that time of promises and brotherhood the young serviceman looks back with nostalgia and ever-increasing cynicism.' The life of the squad over the years was debasing and trivial, filled with inertia and grating self-consciousness of fellow soldiers. But now the purpose of the war approached in the prospect of combat and strange societies. Bain found himself trained, prepared, matured and launched into a world of pain, hatred and privation which he had only read about. He was prepared for the worst. As his poem *De Gustibus* stated, 'Man is the lord or louse of life.' He was already recording the expected patterns of English cities – the buses, the pubs, the cafés, the Odeons, the very monotony and insufficiency. He would need to recall these familiar landmarks abroad, although he had cut himself free from home ties. He expected nothing, his slate was clean. A few books and literary letters back would be his only link with 'the old centres of thought and feeling, to a dwindling world behind uncomprehending seas'.

The main theatre of the war in the Mediterranean reproduced the situation at home. In Cairo, a miniature Fitzrovia sprang up, which produced its own little magazines, although it corresponded regularly with its peers in London. John Lehmann and Tambimuttu approved of *Personal Landscape*, a literary venture brought out by teachers at Cairo University, particularly Terence Tiller and Bernard Spencer, who were joined by Lawrence Durrell after the fall of Greece. 'English exiles,' Dan Davin's Braun called them. 'England's reply to Goebbels. The British Council's legion.' The novelist Olivia Manning was married to one of the 'legion' and a close friend of Spencer, who also was close to the best serving poet in Egypt, Keith Douglas. She noted an English review of *Personal Landscape*, which said how quickly the poets of the Middle East had lost touch. In fact, they had not, even though a manuscript took three months to reach England round the Cape. But they did come out with a rash of other little magazines, *Salamander* and *Citadel* and *Forum*; a literary war between Cairo and Alexandria – as Durrell told Tambimuttu, 'not since Troy was there such a bash-up'; two army-based magazines, *Orientations* and *Parade*; and finally, *Oasis*, an anthology of poetry from the forces. The last was inspired by Lord Wavell, himself the editor of the best-selling collection of verses, *Other Men's Flowers*. When Montgomery succeeded him as commander in the Middle East, he proved no rival as a poetaster. His selection, *Poems from the Desert*, was as trite as it was touching, ending with an anonymous poem blown into a slit trench during a heavy bombardment at El Agheila:

> I love a game. I love a fight.
> I hate the dark; I love the light.
> I love my child; I love my wife.
> I am no coward. I love Life ...

Hardly poetry, but many fine poems were written in the Middle East, and a new generation of poets was established that seemed of importance back in London. G. S. Fraser served there as a sergeant-major, wearing tennis shoes and a dirty scarf and trousers fastened with string; and he considered that the Middle East 'produced far more – and at times even finer – poetry than all the years of attrition on the Western Front' in the First World War. The real gap in Cairo was between battledress and civilian clothes. The poetry came from a more literate and aware generation, although it derived from four sources; the teachers and propagandists in Cairo and Alexandria, who knew their classics and were in contact with the exiled Greeks, particularly George Seferis; the intelligence officers, remembered by Evelyn Waugh and described by Lawrence Durrell in *The Alexandria Quartet* and called by Cecil Beaton on a photographic trip to the desert 'the Gabardine Swine'; those soldiers rotting on the long lines of communications to the front-line forces after the victory at El Alamein; and those combatants who returned briefly on leaves to Cairo to get on with their writing and links to London. All were united only by exile. The practice of their art was their 'defensive reply to stagnation; publication on the spot was their reply to distances'. G. S. Fraser tried to define a neo-Classic Cairo school of poets as more sad and mature than a neo-Romantic London school, but Tambimuttu would not accept that there were two movements in the two cities. Such thinking was mere propaganda, for all contemporary poetry should represent its times.

Fraser found his friends garish against the background of Cairo. They flourished their eccentricity, but were also dead and alive like posed waxworks. They suffered from inner exhaustion. Durrell agreed with him. 'Egypt would be interesting if it were really the beginning of Africa,' he wrote back to Tambimuttu in London, 'but it is an anteroom, a limbo. In this soft corrupting plenty nothing   131 very much is possible. The Nile flows like dirty coffee under the solid English bridges ...' All the exiles in Cairo had in common was the hyperconsciousness of death. 'One lived not only beside the ancient dead that took up so much room in a world they'd left thousands of years before,' Olivia Manning wrote:

but the recent dead that had a quarter of the city to themselves. That was a show-place by moonlight ... More than that, more pertinent to us, of course, the deaths in the desert, the war, the major premise of our lives there. The men on leave talked to us willingly about it. Dark, dried with sun, thin, avid for a normal life, they congratulated civilians on secure jobs. They looked among us for the life for which they were homesick. We were looking for it ourselves. They looked for it in hotels, bars and restaurants ... Danger had an advantage over them. The news that one of them had been killed often came as no more than confirmation of a suspicion felt on his departure.

The Fitzrovia of Cairo for its *habitués* and men on leave was the terrace and bar of Shepheard's Hotel with its frosted lights aloft and pearl-inlaid furniture, Groppi's tea-rooms and debates at the Victory Club, the Gezirah Club without its rumoured orgies as curfew stopped drinking at ten o'clock nightly, the back-street bars where anything went till dawn, and in particular a small Greek grocer's shop off Soliman Pacha, which became the Café Royal and the Wheatsheaf of the expatriate poets 'because of the creaking, rickety chairs, the smell of oil, the crates on which we balanced our glasses; the bottled beer was always just off the ice, and one could help oneself to olives and crisps out of great bowls. An Arab would come round to the shop during the evening with a brazier like a chestnut brazier, but piled high with little roasted birds, birds that fed on figs and had a sweet, delicate flesh. We would eat these greedily with our fingers, crunching them, bones and all.'

At the grocer's shop, visitors from Fitzrovia were greeted with enthusiasm as messengers of a lost culture. Durrell wrote of the arrival of John Gawsworth, *alias* Air Force Sergeant Terence Iain Fytton Armstrong. 'The death by alcohol invaded him.' G. S. Fraser found 'a certain rakish and piratical air about this sergeant; an air, also, of grave and secret ceremony'. He was a shrewd bohemian who had kept afloat so long on London's deep waters that the Nile would not drown him either. Gawsworth himself wrote of 'The Salamanders' of Egypt, particularly praising John Waller, then serving as a captain at the Ministry of Information in Cairo with his subordinate G. S. Fraser, who 'dims / Behind his Scottish rims: / It is frightfully effectual / To look intellectual.' Fraser in his turn wrote a long 'Monologue for a Cairo Evening' dedicated to Waller, who went in for the serious pursuit of pleasure and was happier with acquaintances than friends. There, rocking at the bar, was round-faced Durrell in a tartan scarf, looking like a jovial commercial traveller, but talking like an angel descending the ladder of alcohol. There also was John Waller, who seemed like 'a florid weather devil', and Kay Garland from the Ministry of Information, who was to die when a bomb fell on the Guards Chapel in London. Also there was the doomed Keith Douglas, in Cairo after a spell of service in the desert, with his shrewd and rustic eyes, and his

poems spitting out shrapnel. It was a drunken evening in memory of culture and
Europe:

> And Europe stinks
> Of the perverted human will, is tortured
> Just as our guts are tortured by our drinks.
>
> And Europe spews up Europe, as we spew
> Cairo on Cairo; Europe crawls to bed
> As Cairenes totter from the crying jag
> With half of history throbbing in the head.

In 'Cairo Jag', Keith Douglas put the antithesis of the big city. His fellow poets at
the university or in the Ministry of Information were safe, as long as Rommel and
his tanks did not break through at El Alamein. His poem appeared in his
posthumous book of sketches, prose and poetry, *Alamein to Zem Zem*, edited by
Tambimuttu for Editions Poetry London; its appearance would create an army
equivalent to Richard Hillary. Douglas was a militarist as a child, always pugna-
cious: he wanted to fight, not booze in Cairo bars, although he had a stubborn belief
in his literary genius. 'Cairo Jag' begins with the question, 'Shall I get drunk or cut
myself a piece of cake ...' but it changes to the perception of another world a day's
travel away.

> The vegetation is of iron.
> Dead tanks and gunbarrels split like celery
> the metal brambles without flowers or berries:
> and there are all sorts of manure, you can imagine
> the dead themselves, their boots, clothes and possessions
> clinging to the ground. A man with no head
> has a packet of chocolate and a souvenir of Tripoli.

It was a new world and another world and nothing to do with Cairo. Cecil Beaton,
with the curious precision of his camera's eye, pointed out that though Cairo
demanded too little of a man, the desert demanded too much. No one could remain
long in either place, for both were unnatural. 'A false reality prevails.' But when
Beaton thankfully flew from Cairo at Rommel's approach, confessing that he was
delighted to be the first of the rats going home, he might have appreciated the true
reality of the desert war. Certainly Terence Tiller did, when he went to lecture to
the battle-weary troops. They sat like shrubs among the cans and thistles, wanting
girls and beer, and all they had was a lecturer on English culture from Cairo. His
clean cleverness was tiny and useless.

> They have walked horror's coast,
> loosened the flesh in flame, slept with naked war:
> while I come taut and scatheless with a virgin air,
> diffident as a looking-glass,
> with the fat lexicon of peace.

The theme of the community of the dead, echoing Wilfred Owen's finest line from the First World War, 'I am the enemy you killed, my friend ...', was found in the more moving of the desert poems, Douglas's 'Vergissmeinicht' and 'Landscape With Figures', and Hamish Henderson's 'Elegies for the Dead in Cyrenaica'. Henderson had been discovered by John Lehmann who published his work in *New Writing and Daylight* and Penguin *New Writing*. A Highlander by election and descent, a socialist by profession, he saw an unlikely link between Marxism and Scots nationalism and the Celtic revival. The themes of his Elegies for the Dead were suggested to him by the remark of a captured German officer: 'Africa changes everything. In reality we are allies, and the desert is our common enemy.' The conflict seemed between the innocent dead – who were all comrades – and the living who could justify their survival only by recognizing the processes of history:

> There are many dead in the brutish desert,
> > who lie uneasy
> among the scrub in this landscape of half-wit
> stunted ill-will ...
> > > Sleep here the sleep of the dust.
> There were our own, there were the others.
> Their deaths were like their lives, human and animal.
> There were no gods and precious few heroes ...

The most important thing for the poet was that the requiem of the dead should be in words of reconciliation and healing.

> No blah about their sacrifice; rather tears or reviling
> of the time that took them, than an insult so outrageous.

In appreciation of the war poetry from the desert, Henderson particularly praised the literacy of the Eighth Army, built up from citizen soldiers. Many became poets as a result of going to war. He mentioned in his despatch Lieutenant W. H. Burt of the Highland Recce Regiment for his 'Stane Jock in the mantrap field / Walking saftly'; and the Gaelic poets George Campbell Hay and Sorley Maclean and the Lallans writer Robert Garioch:

> There is no rancour in my heart
> against the hardy soldiers of the Enemy
> but the kinship that there is among
> men in prison on a tidal rock
>
> waiting for the sea flowing
> and making cold the warm stone;
> and the coldness of life
> in the hot sun of the Desert.

Henderson especially appreciated the poetry of Keith Douglas, even though Douglas was intensely, almost militantly, English. He recognized with Tambimuttu that Douglas crystallized the experience of the war generation as Auden had of the 'thirties intellectuals. Both preferred the rhythms of common speech or slang, but Douglas was less glib, ironic and clever. As he wrote to a friend, he hated, in poetry as well as in the army, Bullshit. 'To be sentimental or emotional now is dangerous to oneself and to others. To trust anyone or to admit any hope of a better world is criminally foolish, as foolish as it is to stop working for it. It sounds silly to say work without hope, but it can be done; it's only a form of insurance; it doesn't mean work hopelessly.' Douglas worked and left behind him enough poems of insight and ruth to justify a reputation that should be greater than those of Wilfred Owen or Isaac Rosenberg in a language that still speaks directly to modern ears. He knew he would die, and laboured to record what he could while he lived. 'I can't afford to wait,' he wrote to a friend, 'because of military engagements which may be the end of me.'

When an undergraduate at Oxford, he had been editor of *Cherwell* and of a miscellany of university verse and prose named *Augury*. In that issue, his tutor Edmund Blunden had written a poem to Wilfred Owen, foretelling Douglas's own work and death:

> Where does your spirit walk, kind soldier, now,
> In this deep winter, bright with ready guns?
> And have you found new poems in this war?

Douglas had also been published by a group of poets at Queen's College, Oxford, led by Sidney Keyes and Michael Meyer, supported by John Heath-Stubbs and Drummond Allison. All of these were included in the important *Eight Oxford Poets* of 1941; but Philip Larkin was excluded, alienating him and other writers who later went to St John's College, Kingsley Amis and Alan Ross and John Wain. In his introduction to *Eight Oxford Poets*, Keyes had called them all *Romantic* writers with little sympathy with the Auden group of poets. In point of fact, Douglas was no romantic, and Keyes himself, who achieved a temporary reputation and a death equal to Rupert Brooke's during the war, was refined by his military experience into refuting romanticism and finding himself isolated as a writer. He thought the Germans were a chosen people: their task was to explore death. He was killed, sending his men back to safety and holding off the advancing Germans with a tommy-gun; he explored his own death. War had, in Keith Douglas's phrase, simplified him when and before he was dead. He had stood up to his own doubt and terror.

> ...Fear finally of tripwire and garrotte
> Reaching possessive from an easy air:
> These bring the careful man into despair.
>
> Then let me never crouch against the wall
> But meet my fears and fight them till I fall.

Of the eight Oxford poets, Drummond Allison was also to die in Italy. His poems were not romantic: he was an extrovert 'rackety *enfant terrible* with tow-coloured 135 hair'. He was more clear-sighted than the poets of the Auden group, confessing in his tribute 'For Karl Marx' that he still had some allegiance to the guilty classes for whom Marx had ordained annihilation. He shrugged death aside.

> Come let us pity not the dead but Death,
> For He can only come when we are leaving,
> He cannot stay for tea or share our sherry ...

In fact, so many of the Oxford poets died that Michael Meyer, who survived to become the arbiter of Strindberg and Ibsen in the English theatre, gave up his conscientious objections to the war and served in the Operations Section of Bomber Command Headquarters – a revenge of sorts for the killing of most of his friends. 'The leaders were dead,' Meyer testified. 'If Keyes and Douglas had lived, they would have been bigger figures than Philip Larkin. He would have been the isolated one.' It had been so at Oxford, for when Larkin had bumped into Keyes in Turl Street, he had found that Keyes was able to talk to history as some people talked to porters, but that they two had nothing to say.

The third of the young war poets celebrated after his death was Alun Lewis. For once, he did not come from a public school and Oxford, but a Welsh grammar school and University College, Aberystwyth. A schoolteacher before the war, he served as an officer in the South Wales Borderers before dying on the Burmese front by a shot from his own revolver that was judged to be accidental death. He published short stories and poetry in *Horizon*, and his work opened the anthology *Poems from India by Members of the Forces*, which was the answer of the Far East to *Oasis* and a later collection called *Poems from Italy*. Lewis was Dylan Thomas's peer from Wales; his war experience controlled his prose and verse. He honed his lyricism with a bayonet. In praising him and Wilfred Owen in a talk on Welsh poets, Dylan Thomas said that both of them knew that, in war, the poetry was in the pity. Yet curiously enough Lewis failed to write about the Bengal Famine, which killed one and a half million Indians in 1943. The immensity of the suffering and the statistics of the dead numbed expression. How bury all those corpses in some verses? How contain the disasters of history in a few words as Auden had failed to do? Lewis was concerned with the deaths of individuals and his own end. Death would find him as it found the young soldier in his story, 'The Earth Is A Syllable':

He'd often thought he'd die; it was a familiar idea; why shouldn't it be, if there's a war on and you're young and you try to be in it, somewhere? It had taken him a long time to succeed. He'd got into the army easy enough, but the war seemed to elude him all the time ... And now that he had caught up with it, here in Burma, well, it hadn't been much of a show. But he'd never liked the idea of Burma. He'd always known he'd die if he caught up with it in Burma ...

This prophecy by Lewis of his own death was published back in London. His actual death brought out black headlines in English newspapers. War poets were now important; they had become newsworthy. Far away as they might be, they were making their reputations in London, where all the lines that led to fame were still printed. Poets such as the admirable Roy Fuller, proletarianized by service on the lower decks and able at last to live with a class to which he did not belong, remained in touch with the Old Etonian John Lehmann from his exile in East Africa. Lehmann pitied the young poets serving abroad, who were at the beginning of their careers and in danger of having no career at all. Their connection to their editors was all-important, the struggle 'to hold on to the literary world of England by the frail capricious threads of airgraph and air letter'. Exclusion from intellectual companionship and the world of argument and discussion, that is what writers in uniform felt most keenly. No Fitzrovia-in-exile could make up for the absence of London, not in Cairo nor later in the Three Arts Club off the Via Roma in Naples, which was 'a classless and rankless honey-pot, a continuous swirl of painters and writers and musicians and lovers of these things'. No flow of Nile or Ganges could compensate for intimate talk by the little Thames.

Poets have one paradox in common with monks. Their practice and way of life depend on being solitary and gregarious. They must be alone to write poems, even if serving as swaddies in a desert army. But they must also meet other poets and editors to celebrate their work and arrange for it to be published. They must write elegies for the death of their peers and eulogies on encounters with their comrades and employers. Dylan Thomas may not have practised his lonely craft for ambition or bread, but he could not have survived or seen his work printed without a subsidized war decade spent around Fitzrovia. Contacts and commissions in London kept the artist going, as well as commemorations. Nearly all the poets wrote or gave work to their peers or editors. J. C. Hall dedicated a poem to Keith Douglas, Vernon Watkins to Alun Lewis, John Heath-Stubbs to Sidney Keyes:

> My friend is out of earshot. Our ways divided
> Before we ever knew we had missed each other ...

Stephen Spender wrote 'Poets and Airmen' in memory of Michael Jones, Timothy Corsellis a poem to Stephen Spender and a requiem to a dead fellow pilot, Nigel Weir – and the editor Patricia Ledward wrote *in memoriam* of Corsellis, before Spender had time to do so.

> Come! let us dance in nightclubs you frequented ...
> Play on, O Harlem band, O swing your blues!
> Rend every stone with your terrible, lamenting cry:
> Those who would sing of life, and hope, and joy,
> Are driven out to hunt, to kill, to die.

Julian Symons dedicated his book of poems of 1943, *The Second Man*, to Roy Fuller; it was written in a time of murder, and sent from bitter England to darkest Africa. Roy Fuller wrote tributes to Alan Ross, who wrote in praise of John Lehmann. George Barker honoured Stephen Spender trudging up the world's steps with his soul upon his shoulder, and T. S. Eliot expecting a bomb or an angel through the roof, and Michael Roberts, the influential editor of *The Faber Book of Modern Verse*. G. S. Fraser wrote long poems to Anne Ridler, who was to   137 succeed Roberts as the editor of the new enlarged edition of *The Faber Book*; it would include Fraser's poems. And so forth. Poets sung of dead and living poets and of poetry editors who might also be poets. Elegy and eulogy were the means of the craft, the commonwealth of verse.

'Provincialism didn't have a chance in the nineteen-forties,' Michael Meyer said. 'You had to be in London. Regionalism and redbrick were a phenomenon of the 'fifties. Until then, it was all London and Oxbridge.' The long sinews and frail ligaments of the global war stretched back to the metropolis. There the editors printed whatever could be returned to them, while they missed and mourned their absent friends. John Lehmann pointed out that forty Etonians he had known died in the war, five from his own house, seven hundred and fifty in all. The privileged filled up their fair share of the cemeteries, while the most privileged of all – those who were spared from the fighting – ran the hub of the lines of communication in London. Even Tambimuttu, named Tuttifrutti for his eclectic taste by Julian Symons, was of service to all who could find him, and that was easy enough in Fitzrovia. As David Wright noted, it did not matter whether *Poetry London* was good or bad. Tambimuttu was 'a kind of peripatetic rendezvous, a one-man Institute of Contemporary Arts through whom, at a time of scattering and regimentation, poets and painters met one another. He kept the lines of communication open. You could call him the Lady Ottoline of the Second World War, not least for his eccentricity and enthusiasm; not to mention the eccentricity of his enthusiasms. Soho, sleazy and rumbustious, was the Garsington where he dispensed Dutch hospitality … One could meet literally anybody there, the King of Poland, a Cambridge Senior Wrangler, or the fighting forces of half Europe.' However widespread the war on air or sea or earth, all roads for artists led to Fitzrovia.

TEN

National Arts

Leonard Rosoman

War may stimulate the arts. It did in ancient Athens in the city's struggle with Sparta. It did in Renaissance Italy when the city states fought one another and the French invaders. It did in London, when the bombs fell upon the metropolis and the armies passed through it on their way to Europe. John Lehmann was excited by the revival of the romantic and visionary tradition in British painting that stemmed from William Blake and Samuel Palmer, and that was now practised by Graham Sutherland in painting and Leslie Hurry in stage design. There was an intensity of imagination in the choreography of Frederick Ashton, Ninette de Valois and Robert Helpmann, with ballet music being created by Constant Lambert and other British composers. In the film world, a fresh realism that did not descend into propaganda; in drama, a revival of interest in Shakespeare, particularly when played by the exciting triad of British actors, John Gielgud and Laurence Olivier and Ralph Richardson. A paradox of circumstance was also feeding the arts in England. The nation and its capital were beleaguered and cut off from European influence, yet stimulated by the European *émigrés* passing through. The defence of the realm was also an anthem to British qualities, in which the refugees from the continent might join. Moreover, the people was moved by the celebration of its country's values in the arts. Stephen Spender noted how popular the new works became:

People felt that music, the ballet, poetry and painting were concerned with a seriousness of living and dying with which they themselves had suddenly been confronted. The audiences at the midday concerts of the National Gallery, or at the recitals of music and ballet in provincial towns and at factories, sat with a rapt attention as though they were listening for some message from the artist, who, though perhaps he had lived in other times, was close to the same realities as themselves – and to the pressing need to affirm faith and joy within them. There was something deeply touching about this interest in the arts; it was one of the few things which can still make me regret the war.

The confluence of the arts was in Fitzrovia. There the artists could meet and commission one another, the painters be engaged for magazine or book illustration or stage and film design, the musicians be asked to compose or play original ballet or cinema scores, the actors find roles on stage or documentary or screen or ENSA tour. The pubs of Dean Street and Rathbone Place were free of the shibboleths of rank and class and sex. Talent and the occasional ability to buy a round of drinks mattered. And there was a feeling of sanctuary for artists, particularly for the young painters. The law tolerated Soho as the red-light district of London. There the prostitutes and homosexuals clustered in relative security. Soliciting and sodomy were criminal offences; but on Soho the police usually turned a blind eye. There was a powerful subculture of wealthy homosexual patrons of the arts, particularly in the theatre and the ballet, in publishing and music; it was focused on Fitzrovia and welcomed the arrival of young artists from the provinces or in uniform. When Robert Colquhoun and Robert MacBryde left Scotland for London, they expected to find commissions from sympathetic patrons and the support of fellow artists such as John Minton. *In the Purely Pagan Sense*, John Lehmann's novel about wartime London, displays the pleasure of being a rich supporter of the arts like himself or Peter Watson, able to enjoy the company of dislocated young men, freed from women and home and looking for solace and wages under bombs and blackout. Lehmann reproduced fifteen of Keith Vaughan's pictures in Penguin *New Writing* and put him on the editorial board; the magazine became a tiny gallery for neo-Romantic art, especially favouring John Minton, who was to share an apartment with Vaughan after the war. Minton had secured his discharge from the all-male Pioneer Corps by confessing to his colonel that he was a homosexual, 'a preference which, in the circumstances, put him under strain'. Vaughan did not agree about the Pioneer Corps and took roots over five years in the camaraderie of other men, feeling despair the day before his demobilization. He was to devote himself mainly to painting erotic studies of male nudes. He was always nostalgic about the nineteen-forties, 'when artists and workers congregated at two or three special Soho pubs, like the French House or the Wheatsheaf, but for some reason this habit broke up'.

The polymath and propagandist among the neo-Romantic artists was Michael Ayrton, whose facets shone like a Koh-i-noor. Invalided from the Royal Air Force with a throat abscess, he became the youngest member of the Brains Trust, a popular intellectual programme on the wireless; the art critic of *The Spectator*, succeeding John Piper; and a stage and opera designer, a book illustrator and a major painter of his generation. By his works, he proved the cross-fertilization of the arts possible during the war decade. For his close friend Constant Lambert, Ayrton improvised sets for the Sadler's Wells Ballet on its wartime tours, for Roussel's *Le Festin de l'Araignée* at the New Theatre in London, and finally for Purcell's *The Fairy Queen* after the war in a revived Covent Garden. He and Lambert invented graffiti as an art form forty years before the event in New York City's subways, once decorating a whole railway compartment with cats and fishes, even covering the roof with their designs while lying on their backs in the luggage racks. Both of them ended by setting up house together in London and going on daily rounds of the local bars in search of strange experiences as well as alcohol. 'This morning's pub crawl,' Lambert wrote to Ayrton from Glasgow where he was on tour without his friend, 'produced two black A T S (and my God what beauties), a lesbian midget in crutches by Dadd, and (believe me or believe me not) outside The Bear and Rummer of all places, a woman in a tartan skirt with *two* bandaged legs both of which were bleeding.' When not drinking with Lambert, Ayrton illustrated many books and plays, including *Macbeth*, *The Duchess of Malfi*, Poe's *Tales of Mystery and Imagination*, Oscar Wilde's *The Picture of Dorian Gray*, and most eerily an anthology of 1945, *Poems of Death*. It fitted his macabre talents. 'After all,' the editor wrote, 'the subject has been forced on our attention for the last five years, and few people have been able to say with Mrs Peachum that they never meddle in matters of death.'

Ayrton particularly championed the work of John Minton and Robert Colquhoun and Leslie Hurry, but he could damn the work of other young contemporary   141 painters such as John Craxton and Lucian Freud and Robert MacBryde. Of the elder painters, he admired Stanley Spencer and Wyndham Lewis, Graham Sutherland and Paul Nash and Edward Burra, who designed Robert Helpmann's ballet, *Miracle in the Gorbals*. He hated what Cyril Connolly loved – the French school of painting. In one celebrated article, he dismissed Picasso as a master of pastiche, who was not concerned with nature or with a single tradition. 'He differs from the artists of the past, as Woolworth's differs from the craftsman's shop.' Ayrton saw the enforced isolation of the war years as the opportunity of British national art. It had been seized upon by his young contemporaries, who were returning to their native traditions. Britain must and would become the torch-bearer of the flame of European art, but within its own heritage. 'I believe that England is just about to emerge from a century of pictorial mediocrity into a period of great painting, and that this fact should be shouted from the rooftops.'

The bright hopes of the revival were Ayrton himself, John Minton and John Craxton, Keith Vaughan and Leslie Hurry, and the Roberts Colquhoun and MacBryde. They were the publicized young names of the decade, successful and patronized, their friends stretching from one end of Fitzrovia to the other. It was not to last and did not, for that generation of painters. 'Apart from any blockages and the tendency to self-destruction they shared with the other war-babies ...' Anthony Cronin observed, '"the English Romantics" belonged to the war and immediate post-war.' Too soon they were too late. The one genius among them, Francis Bacon, did not look to the Celtic past or to his London contemporaries for his inspiration. 'How can you find the techniques of putting over the eternal realities so that they shine violently as reality?' he asked recently. 'You renew your realities. The basics are the same always. The ways of conveying them get tired, very tired. That is why I hate all the late Romantics.' In answer to the calamities of his time – holocaust and fire raid and nuclear fission – he turned to the imprisonment of power in Velázquez and to the scream against atrocity of Goya. His confined and flayed shapes caged in curtains and boxes had holes for mouths. They howled dumbly to be freed from pain and canvas, as the tens of millions of the dead groaned in silence from their untoward mass graves. Bacon's art proved the flaw in the nationalism of the neo-Romantics. The long experience of Europe in its interminable internecine strife informed the truest painter of his age.

Theodora Fitzgibbon used to drink with Bacon and the other young painters in the Colony, the Horseshoe or the Mandrake. She was delighted to have her looks compared to his; they had both been brought up in the same part of Ireland. She knew him for being a brilliant painter, working under great difficulties, but praised his lack of malice and his 'gay equanimity; his troubles were not brought out for drinks'. At the time, his poverty led him to painting with one-inch thick brushes bought from ironmongers. The war was hell on artists' materials. They had to paint as they could in the colours they could find. 'London was dirty, chaotic and dangerous,' John Craxton said. 'People were just about managing to keep things ticking over. It was unbearable. I started to read the works of several contemporary

European writers and I often thought how "Kafkaesque" London was during that period.'

Yet as in Kafka's constructions, there were strange connections between people and places in wartime London. For painters, Fitzrovia was a castle of the arts, where pub rooms led to parties and commissions from a hidden bureaucracy and transient plutocracy. There were not only jobs to be found from the War Artists' Advisory Commission, but also from editors and theatre managers and film companies as well as from private patrons. John Minton aided his friend Michael Ayrton in creating the costumes and sets for John Gielgud's *Macbeth* of 1942 and became the most prolific illustrator of his time, designing for *Lilliput*, *Picture Post*, Penguin *New Writing*, *The Listener*, *Radio Times*, *Vogue* and *Opera*. His style became the literary hallmark of its period, finally achieving the covers of John Lehmann's magazine in a series of drawings of the seasons that ended with scattered folios falling from dark clouds and bombed buildings. In the series of poetry anthologies which Ayrton also illustrated, John Craxton executed superb lithographs for *The Poet's Eye* and Robert Colquhoun for *Poets of Sleep and Dream*. Its promoter, the influential Kenneth Clark, was to suggest to Massine that Colquhoun and MacBryde design his new ballet, *Donald of the Burthens* – and Colquhoun later worked on the Stratford production of *King Lear* that starred Michael Redgrave. John Lehmann arranged for Keith Vaughan to illustrate Rimbaud's *Une Saison en Enfer* with an English text by Norman Cameron, and also sent Minton after the war with Alan Ross to illustrate *Time Was Away*.

Moreover, throughout the war, the private encouragement and patronage of another Old Etonian, Peter Watson, was the gluepot of the Fitzrovian painters. 'He was a man everyone was in love with,' Stephen Spender remembered. 'He paid for everything.' Although he was a depressive and meeting people was agony for him, he had the rare elegance of a Beau Brummel, 'which is to say by elimination'. Or so the young painter Michael Wishart thought, pitying Watson for spending so much time in the pursuit of love, 'a thankless task for so fastidious a homosexual despite his haunted beauty'. The first and last of his objects of passion were homicidal and larcenous, dissipating the collections of modern paintings entrusted by Watson to their care. Through his art editorship of *Horizon*, he introduced its readers to the best of modern British painting, educating a generation during the 'forties. He was braver than Cyril Connolly, saying to Cecil Beaton, who loved him hopelessly, 'I never go to a shelter. I would rather die in my sleep.' He tried to join the Royal Air Force like his baronet brother, but was turned down for being underweight – not a problem that afflicted Connolly, who was even to appeal in the columns of *Horizon* for food parcels to be sent to him and his contributors. When the American critic Edmund Wilson later asked if Connolly took provisions from the parcels addressed to other authors, Watson thought and replied, 'No, only the *foie gras*.'

Watson's little flat in Palace Gate was a refuge and a café of European taste. He bought works and subsidized painting trips for John Minton and Francis Bacon as well as the older artists Graham Sutherland and John Piper, while secretly giving   143 money to the poets David Gascoyne and Dylan Thomas, who made it all disappear 'quick as a sardine.' He set up John Craxton in a studio with Lucian Freud, who had spent five months as a seaman on the dangerous Atlantic convoy run, and he bought the works of both of the young painters. He was admirable in his reserve, his tact, his generosity, his lack of ostentation and his taste in modern art. He used the bounty of his fortune from margarine to ease the lives of his talented friends. He seemed to Stephen Spender almost American, 'extraordinarily chic, like a character from Henry James'. He was the last of the true private patrons of the arts before the coming of state aid for them.

A very different patron was to epitomize the state aid to come. Although he was educated at that Eton *manqué*, Winchester College, Kenneth Clark was born to wealth and rule. He was appointed as the Director of the National Gallery at the age of twenty-nine and knighted five years later, and was the key public patron of painting in his time. When the war came and the gallery was stripped of all its masterpieces, he felt civilization was doomed. Even if Britain won, there would be no place for privileged intellectuals like himself in a post-war world. He became the first chairman of the War Artists' Advisory Committee and served on the arts panel of the Committee for the Encouragement of Music and the Arts; he was responsible for subsidizing Moore and Piper and Sutherland, who was told that painting was the highest form of national service for him. Clark also became head of the Films Division in the Ministry of Information because of a misapprehension that he knew something about 'pictures'. He helped to produce twenty-eight short films before becoming head of Home Publicity. He would have been happier at the National Gallery, Harold Nicolson wrote, 'vaguely doing high-brow war service. Yet he works like a nigger here merely because he loathes Hitler so much.' He was the ultimate bureaucrat, ready to turn his aesthetics and knowledge of the corridors of power to any state purpose. He became the supreme British catalyst and fixer for the élite; later as Chairman of the Arts Council, he was to promote his favourite painters into international reputation. He was wrong about his post-war role, which proved the continuity of his influence and taste. His career was a testimony that those born with a silver spoon in their mouths could transmute it to a golden age.

Along with Lucian Freud, John Minton was the other Fitzrovian artist who had some money from his family, although his commercial artwork earned him considerably more than his connection with Minton china. He was notorious for his drunkenness, promiscuity, frivolity, melancholy and prodigality. He bestowed pound notes like blessings on other poor artists. His oval face swarthy and elongated, his protruding teeth grinning in a loose mouth, his disjointed figure dangling from his shoulders like a marionette, he looked like a Spanish Armada sailor in the blue reefer jersey or pea-jacket he usually wore. Robert Colquhoun shared his lean and hungry and olive look as if both were tanned from being pickled in alcohol; but Robert MacBryde was smaller in the manner of Francis Bacon. The two Roberts wore pullovers, red and blue, and kilts to proclaim their origins. They kept their Scots accents as thick and fat as a haggis, and they attacked

Scotsmen like Ruthven Todd and Welshmen like Dylan Thomas for being phonies and talking with English cut-glass accents. If they could not find anyone in Soho to insult or fight, they fought each other, 'careering in a clinch the whole course of a long bar, with all the club members skipping out of their path, until they reached the doorman at his desk, who then toppled them, still gripped together, into the street'. They were the bother boys of British painting, the counterpoint to Keith Vaughan, who was reserved and withdrawn in spite of occasional drunken sprees cruising in Fitzrovia, picking up male bed-fellows who seemed to cause him more pain than pleasure. It was the same for Lucian Freud, whose passionate pursuit of women as models and lovers so often ended with his picking out their private parts hair by hair in his clinical paintings. 'You know,' Stephen Spender told Ruthven Todd, 'that so far as Lucian's concerned, I'm afraid his grandfather lived in vain.'

The world of ballet particularly patronized the romantic painters. Frederick Ashton asked Graham Sutherland to design *The Wanderer* with a Schubert score and John Piper to create the sets for *The Quest* with music from William Walton. Constant Lambert's ballet *Pomona* had been given a décor by John Banting, an artist with a shaved head and a madman's laugh, who once flourished his fist at Tambimuttu in the Swiss pub for not publishing his illustrated *Little Book of Fishes*, one of many projects promised without performance. He was mollified by a pint of bitter and the Tamil editor's excuse, 'You see, I haven't a European conception of Time.' Leslie Hurry's nightmarish sets for Robert Helpmann's ballet of *Hamlet* were complemented by his exquisite fairytale backdrops for *Swan Lake*. Indeed, Hurry was commissioned to execute the film poster of the classic British thriller of 1945, *Dead of Night*, one of the few occasions that leading painters were called upon by the cinema, although Powell and Pressburger were heavily influenced in their décors by the macabre and romantic style of the decade. Humphrey Jennings, however, had contributed a picture and collages to the Surrealist Exhibition of 1936, and his war documentaries for the Crown Film Unit showed a painter's eye, particularly *The Silent Village* and *Diary for Timothy*. He spent his spare time collecting with Ruthven Todd materials for his historical symposium on the industrial revolution, *Pandaemonium*, which was published posthumously after his death while filming on a Greek island.

The Highlander in Dean Street was the watering-hole for makers of documentary films during the war. There Ruthven Todd introduced the producer Donald Taylor to Dylan Thomas to get him a job as a screenwriter, although Dylan's friends suggested that his girth should make him do his war work as a tank. Humphrey Jennings and Paul Rotha were regulars at the bar of the Highlander; they were also the social conscience of the cinema of the period. Above all, Rotha wanted to know what the war was about, what were the aims that justified all the slaughter. His *World of Plenty* of 1943 contrasted the abundance of food in rich nations with starvation in poor ones. He showed that rationing in Britain was now distributing food fairly between rich and poor people. The suggestion was world rationing and fair distribution for all after the peace came. Another Rotha 145 documentary, *Children of the City*, examined juvenile delinquency in Scotland and its possible treatment by psychiatry or probation or approved school. An example was being set for the future school of television reportage on social evils that was to inform a later age.

Five kinds of film were being made during the war years: instructional films on every subject from putting on gas masks to avoiding venereal diseases, all of them sponsored by the government or the armed services; short and long propaganda films like *Desert Victory*, again supported by the government; propaganda feature films like *The Way to the Stars* made by commercial production companies, but encouraged by the government, which allowed only films 'of national importance'; indirect propaganda films such as *The First of the Few* which needed the co-operation of the armed forces; and escapist films ranging from *Fanny By Gaslight* to *Brief Encounter*, which the government finally permitted because they filled the British quota and were good for civilian morale. In detailing these categories, the producer Michael Balcon stressed that there were no government plans for film-making at the beginning of the war and never any for commercial feature films. But he did attribute the renascence of the British cinema to the stimulus of adversity on the creative mind. It was England's gain and America's loss. British films had direct human impact, even if they lacked the technical gloss of the Hollywood product. And at last there was widespread state patronage of the most expensive medium of all, the cinema. 'You can write poetry and make sketches in a fox-hole, but film production is a clumsy, laborious, collaborative, mechanical business. The film producer's atelier is given the courtesy title of studio, but to the layman's eye it resembles much more what it very nearly is – a factory.' Only the creative process of the manufacture of films saved the studio from the moral degradation of the conveyor belt. 'And then, and even then, not always.'

As a collaborative process, the film industry did provide jobs for many who worked in the arts. Leading actors were required for starring roles, even if they had to be seconded from their war duties. Major composers were asked to put aside their symphonies to back soundtracks. Writers were paid to scribble dialogue and action sequences. Laurence Olivier, who had become a naval parachute officer, was whisked out of service by the wily producer Filippo del Giudice to play a fraternal Russian engineer falling in love with the British way of life: the film was called *Demi-Paradise* and did not reach even halfway to felicity. Ralph Richardson was a naval commander, survived flying the dangerous Walruses and an Albatross, and went drinking with Olivier. '"The trouble with you, Ralph," Olivier said, "is that you can't hold your liquor." And then fell flat on his face.' Richardson was kept on half-salary throughout the war by Alexander Korda and was given leave to perform in five patriotic feature films, including Thorold Dickinson's *The Next of Kin* and Powell and Pressburger's *The Volunteer*. The third of the great triumvirate, John Gielgud, only served his statutory duty in ENSA, touring garrison theatres playing with Beatrice Lillie in Noël Coward's *Fumed Oak*. He was part of that 'theatre of bachelors' which the drama critic Beverly Baxter accused of running and ruining the West End Theatre because so many of the more virile performers were away serving in uniform. Making a film meant only a few weeks on leave, while playing on stage might lead to a long run.

As for composers, the demands of war propaganda trivialized their work. William Walton wrote the score of *The Next of Kin* and *The First of the Few* and Olivier's film of 1944, Shakespeare's *Henry V*. He calculated that he could have composed eleven symphonies in the time that it took him to write incidental music for radio plays or the screen in wartime. It was not a matter of greed, but of duty, the muddled choice put in front of artists by the very conditions of the hostilities. Olivier, for instance, did not object to the horrors of war, but to the irremediable mess it caused in everybody's lives. 'The whole earth is under a sort of pall of sickness, distress, and anxiety and self-disgust in some way or another. So many millions of people trying to feel something they don't feel or trying not to feel something they do.'

For the Fitzrovian writers, particularly Dylan Thomas, screenwriting and radio work were meant to be the drugs which prevented them from achieving their better work. In Thomas's case, this was doubtful. He had always had a passion for the cinema, sharing it with many of his generation. In the words of Cecil Day Lewis's 'Newsreel':

> Enter the dream-house, brothers and sisters, leaving
> Your debts asleep, your history at the door:
> This is the house for heroes, and this loving
> Darkness a fur you can afford.

Dylan and his friends were always in the dream-house; but the actual discipline for Thomas of writing simple scripts for radio and screen documentaries refined his language and clarified his sentences. His letters to his friend and fellow Welsh poet, Vernon Watkins, show him still writing a few and good poems including 'A Refusal To Mourn the Death, by Fire, of a Child in London' and 'Fern Hill'. Dylan never did blame his work in other fields as a way out of his responsibilities. He did not think that living by writing more than poetry was a waste of himself. As he testified to *Horizon* in answer to questions on 'The Cost of Letters':

Shadily living by one's literary wits is as good a way of making too little money as any other, so long as, all the time you are writing B.B.C. and film-scripts, reviews, etc., you aren't thinking, sincerely, that this work is depriving the world of a great poem or a great story. Great, or at any rate very good, poems and stories do get written in spite of the fact that the writers of them spend much of their waking time doing entirely different things. And even a poet like Yeats, who was made by patronage financially safe so that he need not write and think nothing but poetry, *had*, voluntarily, to give himself a secondary job: that of philosopher, mystic, crank, quack.

Dylan's work on ten documentary films may well have influenced the lines of his later and greater verse. All art of whatever sort interpenetrates and informs all other art from the same source. No artist can put his different styles into little boxes: they   147 spill over. That was why so much richness came out of the meetings of such diverse minds and crafts in Fitzrovia. Dylan's waste of words may well have been in his pub performances, where he spoke like a genius between his fifth and thirteenth drink, but it was not in his commissioned work. All he wrote enriched all else he wrote. What he spoke spilled over and was lost. In that failing, he was like his friend George Barker. As John Minton said of him, 'If you haven't heard George performing at the Windsor Castle on Saturday night, I doubt if you know what poetry is. Odes and elegies by the dozen. They sweep them up after closing time.'

Some documentaries with scripts by Dylan Thomas were completed by Strand Films including *Green Mountain, Black Mountain*, in which he celebrated Wales at war, not the ancient war against England, but the terrible near war that had united Wales and England against a common enemy. It concluded bitter memories of dole queues and slag heaps with the refrain: 'Remember the procession of the old-young men. *It shall never happen again!*' He also tried to write feature screenplays with Julian Maclaren-Ross, which would give the reader 'an absolute visual impression of the film in words and could be published as a new form of literature'. Dylan's cinema version of the Burke and Hare murder story, *The Doctor and the Devils*, was published and then made thirty years after the poet's death, but it did not achieve his ambitions. It read like a screenplay and made a mediocre movie. Film work was successful only within its own medium, even if its disciplines might instruct other crafts. It was best for the Fitzrovians to exploit the world of cinema as Ruthven Todd did, meeting Zoltan Korda in the Arts Theatre Club in Newport Street and becoming a film researcher on the strength of a ticket to the British Museum Reading Room and a membership of the London Library. It was Todd's most profitable enterprise and confirmed him in his low opinion of the intelligence of those involved in the making of commercial films.

In fact, the commercial feature in England was revived by the war and achieved a national style based on the realism of the documentary. What was true in British art was also true in the cinema. Forced isolation bred a concentration on tradition. And, particularly, the drain of British technicians and actors to Hollywood was halted. Although some went over there in 1939, 'Gone With The Wind Up', many more returned home like Olivier and David Niven, to serve as they could. Even though some were conscripted, enough remained to create a pool of talent. The realistic cameo performances so brilliantly depicted in *In Which We Serve* led to a dozen fine films being shot in the war. These included *Western Approaches* and *San Demetrio, London* on the navy, Harry Watt's *Nine Men* and Carol Reed's *The Way Ahead* on the army, and Anthony Asquith's *We Dive At Dawn* for the submariners and *The Way To The Stars* for the Allied air forces. The urban scene was not forgotten in Launder and Gilliat's *Millions Like Us*, set in an aircraft factory, and Gilliat's *Waterloo Road*, which examined the underworld of army deserters and profiteers in London. But in David Lean's film of a Coward script, *Brief Encounter*, with its themes of meetings and partings at steamy railway stations and buffets, of the rationing of love by the dreariness of war, the feeling of English life carrying on and slowly wearing down was encapsulated in a small love story of infinite distress and resonance.

War conditions and isolation created a national style in painting and on the screen. In the drama, it led to a revival of interest in Shakespeare, the supreme national playwright. *Henry IV, Part One*, and the apt *All's Well That Ends Well* played at the Vaudeville during the blitz, while Donald Wolfit presented Shakespeare readings at lunchtime in the Strand Theatre. The Old Vic toured the provinces with *Macbeth*, *Twelfth Night*, *The Merchant of Venice* and *King John*, as did Wolfit with his inadequate company, which served as a dungheap behind his incomparable King Lear and other tragic roles. John Gielgud, who had played Hamlet on the eve of war with 'radiant, nerve-tossed beauty', and King Lear for the Old Vic before its theatre on Waterloo Road was bombed, toured as Macbeth in 1942 and brought the production to the Piccadilly Theatre with its sets by Ayrton and Minton. Two years later, he took the Haymarket for a classical season, in which he played Prospero in *The Tempest* as a macabre tyrant, while his Hamlet gained in dignity what it lost in fire. He was rather upstaged by an Old Vic production of *Hamlet* at the New Theatre, which used the flamboyant Hurry ballet sets and Robert Helpmann himself to play the Danish prince with words, not legs. He had to speak, not dance. He gave the part a tension and an unease which had to do with the grace of his movements set against his soliloquies. For once, the silent Hamlet ruled the stage.

Before Olivier took over the Old Vic with Ralph Richardson to create the great Shakespearean productions of the war that gave hope of a future national theatre, he made a film of *Henry V*, putting off his uniform to do so. Again the politic producer del Giudice manufactured the opportunity. The Second Front was opening at last in 1944. France would be invaded once more from England. The time was ripe for *Henry V*, particularly as Olivier wanted to break through into control of the film medium. He insisted that he would not seek a release from the Fleet Air Arm unless he produced and starred in the film. He asked William Wyler to direct it, as Wyler was then a major in the American Army Air Force, preparing to make documentary war films from Claridge's. Wyler refused, as did Carol Reed, and so Olivier took on the additional job himself. 'Shakespeare, in a way, "wrote for films",' he declared. 'His splitting up of the action into a multitude of small scenes is almost an anticipation of film technique, and more than one of his plays seems to chafe against the cramping restrictions of the stage.' Then Olivier quoted the line, 'Can this cockpit hold / The vasty fields of France?' Obviously, it could not, any more than the massing Allied armies could be held in England indefinitely before D-Day and the invasion of Europe. Olivier found it most difficult to spring his leading actors from their military duties and impossible to film the battle of Agincourt among coastal defences and military camps on the downs and beneath aircraft incessantly droning above. Therefore he decided to invade Ireland instead. The battle of Agincourt was fought again on the green fields of Eire, neutral in the war, happy to stage a fictitious bloodbath. So the cameras rolled to film the mock 149 invasion across the Channel as the real one unrolled over the sea to Normandy. The fighting sequences in the film were the finest seen on the screen since Eisenstein had made *Alexander Nevsky*, another apposite parable about Russian resistance to German attack in time past. For once, the cinema met history, as if the newsreel spanned more than five centuries. Shakespeare, indeed, wrote for films.

George Bernard Shaw did not write so well. Persuaded by the equally wily Gabriel Pascal to part with the options on his plays for a five-pound note, he allowed *Caesar and Cleopatra* to be filmed during the war. Shaw believed that both he and Shakespeare, if they had been at the outset of their careers, 'would write for the screen and never dream of turning back to the limitations of the stage'. He insisted that his whole text be filmed and added two new scenes, including a topical reference to British troops occupying Alexandria in the guise of Romans. Backed by J. Arthur Rank, who once asserted he was in films because of the Holy Spirit, the epic was shot in Denham Studios serving as Ancient Egypt. It starred Vivien Leigh, who was prevented by her contract with Selznick after *Gone with the Wind* from playing the minor role of the French princess in her husband's *Henry V*. Flying-bomb attacks interrupted the shooting, one of them nearly killing the producer and half the film unit. The noise of the true war overlaid the studio battles and interfered with the logistics. The English summer weather of 1944 was terrible, and the production finally finished in the real Egypt with a section of the Royal Air Force running two aeroplane engines to whip up a sandstorm round an artificial Sphinx. Only Pascal would have imported a prefabricated Sphinx into the Middle Eastern desert; but artifice overcame sense and managed to produce one of the more resounding flops of its time. Rarely was so much wasted on so little. Shaw, apparently, did not match Shakespeare as a screenwriter.

So the screen took over the properties of the stage, and two hybrids were shot at the end of the war, relevant to the struggle, which had its Egyptian theatre and now its French one. Yet although *Henry V* proved a triumph on the screen, Olivier wanted to tread the boards again in London, preferring the cockpit of the Old Vic to vastier fields. He and Ralph Richardson and the crippled John Burrell, a drama producer at the BBC, took over the management of the theatre company and mounted a classical season including Shaw and Ibsen and Shakespeare. Olivier was rather rueful at the alacrity with which the Lords of the Admiralty let him and Richardson go. Rehearsals in the empty National Gallery were interrupted by the explosions of flying-bombs, although not as interrupted as the whole of drama in London. All theatres were closed for weeks except for the Windmill, and only eight reopened fairly soon. The most unfortunate play was *Zero Hour*; its subject was D-Day, it lasted four nights and took nine pounds at the box office, although the real show was playing well in France and took hundreds of thousands of German dead and wounded. At the Old Vic, the first season was announced with Ralph Richardson in the part of Peer Gynt and Olivier attempting the crookback King Richard III. He succeeded triumphantly, prolonging his convulsive, arching death so long that Richardson, playing Richmond, could not find a still body to put his foot upon. 'The bloody dog' never seemed to die. Olivier's performance was the marriage of neat display with cold reason. 'Here indeed we have the true double Gloucester,' one critic wrote, 'thinker and doer, mind and mask.'

In one role, Olivier rivalled Gielgud as England's leading Shakespearean actor. Gielgud was playing Hamlet at the time, but, as another critic wrote, he 'lacked the male insistence of a Hamlet, who in Elizabethan eyes would have been a seducer'. But with characteristic generosity, Gielgud presented Olivier with Edmund Kean's sword, which the previous great actor had worn when he had played the ill-starred king. In the wake of *Henry V*, the Old Vic company followed the victorious armies to present their plays over the Channel, including the anti-war comedy, *Arms and the Man*. One performance of Shaw's play was given at Belsen for the five hundred soldiers guarding the forty thousand survivors; it was the denial of comedy, the antithesis of truth: Mervyn Peake was sketching the dying and the dead for an English magazine. Olivier was not only creating a national theatre based on excellent performances of the work of *the* national playwright, but also he was bringing European acceptance of the value of the English theatre. The Old Vic company was asked to play for two weeks in the liberated theatre of the Comédie Française, the first time that a foreign troupe had ever been asked to play in the national theatre of France, particularly on the sacred day of the French Revolution, the Fourteenth of July. It was an extraordinary achievement, the contribution of war, that brought the national drama of England to an international standing. The old saying had been that trade followed the flag, but now drama followed the British army.

By sharing the New Theatre with the Old Vic company, the Sadler's Wells Ballet and Opera were also in a position to form the nuclei of two more national companies. As the administrator of all three organizations, Tyrone Guthrie recognized that the war was not disastrous. If it destroyed many things, it also cleared away the rubbish and allowed for new experiments. 'Under the stress of war there is an intense liberation of feeling and thought which only such a violent stimulus seems able to achieve.' For the first time, the government funded all three companies through the Council for the Encouragement of Music and the Arts, the forerunner of the Arts Council of Great Britain. Backed by state patronage, drama and ballet and opera toured the provinces and returned to a base in a London theatre. To his surprise, Tyrone Guthrie found that *Les Sylphides* 'proved exactly the stuff to give the troops. Indeed, what everybody wanted almost as much as food and drink during those years was to see youthful and beautiful creatures beautifully moving through ordered evolutions to a predestined and satisfactory close. It was the antidote to the drabness and dullness and monotony of a life which seemed to be moving in disorder to a predestined and highly unsatisfactory close.'

Many years were to pass and many pitfalls to be avoided before a national theatre, a national ballet and a national opera were to become actual. But the principle of state support for the arts was established during the war and given to the three companies which shared the New Theatre. Although the Sadler's Wells   151

Leonard Rosoman

Opera had an unhappy and inglorious war, it did develop the finest opera to be written for many years by an English composer, *Peter Grimes* by Benjamin Britten, which was presented in June 1945. Britten had been exempted from military duties because of his musical abilities, and he proved that he was of more service as a pianist and conductor and composer than he was as a soldier. His peer, Michael Tippett, was less fortunate; he had to serve three months in gaol because he would not join the Land Army as a conscientious objector. His oratorio, however, *A Child of Our Time*, was one of the more moving works of the war with its theme of the Jewish assassin of a German official and its use of Black spirituals as choruses.

While a national school of painting and a national theatre and ballet and opera were being created by the stimulus of war and the exclusion of foreign influences, British architecture was changed into a national disgrace. City, town and country put on a necessary and ugly face. The pillbox and the bunker, the trench and the emplacement, the mess and the canteen, the hangar and the radar station, the barbed-wire perimeter and the guard-tower, these were brutal, functional, unlovely and unloved. Fear of being bombed converted the British into a nation of troglodytes and cellar-dwellers. Tunnels and caverns honeycombed the chalk cliffs and the hills; munitions stores and military operation rooms lived within stone and beneath soil. The corrugated curved steel sides of two and a quarter million Anderson shelters replaced the garden shed with their dull humps, while, within the house, the Morrison shelter made a metal mesh refuge and a dining-table. And everywhere was the work of Nissen of the hut. The low arcs and oblongs of his designs lay in herds across the landscape wherever there was a camp or an aerodrome. Le Corbusier was irrelevant in wartime, his skyscrapers and office blocks an incitement to air attack. The architecture of combat demanded the sunken and the hidden, the low profile, the return to earth. All was disguised by decaying camouflage: no Capability Brown changed the view to beauty for future generations.

Perhaps the most extraordinary contribution of artists to the war effort was camouflage. In his *Bohemia Junction*, Tschiffely told of the followers of the impressionist and surrealist schools deserting Chelsea during the war to use their techniques in disguising heavy guns and tanks and hangars. The landscape painter Edward Seago was consulted by Field Marshal Alexander about deception of the enemy through combinations of colour, and his advice changed the hues painted on tanks and lorries. Although disability prevented him from serving in the army, Seago was taken out to Italy by Alexander in 1944 as a freelance artist during the campaign in the Apennines and produced a series of war pictures that was an admirable record of the army abroad. He did not mind being accused of 'pictorial reportage' – Rowlandson, Hogarth, Morland and Canaletto had also portrayed the men and happenings of their time. War stimulated the artist into fresh creative visions.

Seago was one of the first British painters to reach Italy and escape the constrictions of a besieged Britain. In the post-war years, many other painters 153 would also escape to the light of the Mediterranean and lose their sense of a national tradition of art. But as long as the war lasted, most artists were forced to stay at home and find their inspiration there like Henry Moore, excluded from Italy and seeing his visions for his supreme *Shelter Sketches* in the underground stations of London.

I had never seen so many rows of reclining figures and even the holes out of which the trains were coming seemed to me to be like the holes in my sculpture. And there were intimate little touches. Children fast asleep, with trains roaring past only a couple of yards away. People who were obviously strangers to one another forming tight little intimate groups. They were cut off from what was happening up above, but they were aware of it. There was tension in the air. They were a bit like the chorus in a Greek drama telling us about the violence we don't actually witness.

The war brought classical influences home to earth. It stimulated a new vision and a national consciousness. As long as it did not last too long and become wearisome to all.

ELEVEN

The Other End

War was so orderly, Elias Canetti noted in 1943, that people began feeling at home in it. 'Many simple people ask you: "Do you think the war will be over soon?" And if you innocently answer: "Yes, very soon," you suddenly notice – and at first, you refuse to believe it – fear and dismay spreading over their faces. They are slightly embarrassed at this and at least know that they ought to be glad for humane reasons. But the war has brought them bread and a good income, for some the first time in their lives, for others the first time in years, and so one single feeling torments them: If only it goes on for a while, if only it doesn't end that soon! Whole nations, down to the lowest strata, have become war-profiteers.' What filled Canetti with the most despair was the daily experience of the war as a bread-winner and as security. It was the answer to a decade of depression and unemployment.

Or so it seemed, when the bombing stopped, and victories began to be reported in Africa and Russia and even against the Japanese in the Far East. But the war still went on with its regular monotony, particularly for the women at home. Again Elizabeth Bowen's *The Heat of the Day* caught the mood of 1943, with the spring teeming with pursuits and astronomic surrenders in North Africa, the Red armies opening their green offensives, Mussolini out and back in, landings and beach-heads, news pictures of Berlin learning in rubble how bad it had been in London, the Big Three leaders smiling at Tehran, and talk of the Second Front soon in Europe. 'War's being global meant it ran off the edges of maps; it was uncontainable … There were too many theatres of war.'

The London theatre of war was putting on other acts. There were a few tip-and-run raids by individual German aeroplanes, but these were more of a nuisance than a deterrence. Wearing his tin hat, John Lehmann would watch the night sky from the roof of his Piccadilly home, the searchlights wavering like the legs of a giant insect until they crossed to trap a streaking silver insect with explosions winking in the raider's path. The sunburned victors of Africa, including Keith Douglas and Roy Fuller, were coming back to London to contradict the hordes of Americans, waiting for the Second Front. They surged past the bombed Café de Paris with its notice: DANGER – UNSAFE PREMISES, on to Piccadilly Circus, where a London bobby now felt safe enough to wear a peacetime blue helmet and watch the military policemen of all the nations parade in twos round the circus 'rather like the animals that walked into the ark – two girl soldiers with red caps and M.P. on their armlets, two American M.P.s, two French gendarmes, and a couple of Dutch *schupos*. "Go ahead," he seemed to say, "you're only playing at being policemen!"' The 400 in Leicester Square was the last place of pleasure left with any character not infested with stout middle-aged gentlemen and their blondes. It always had the same background for Charles Ritchie, 'nostalgic music, half-lighting, eternal youthfulness; guards officers and girls and myself – not so eternally youthful – always well in the foreground.'

Military authority did not wield a big stick in the pubs of the West End. John Lehmann found in the Fitzroy Tavern with its rows of naval badges and military caps and barbaric weapons a kind of invincible London tough high spirits, a general

156

Previous page: Leonard Rosoman

warmth. He would sally out there and to the Wheatsheaf, to the Swiss and the French pubs, 'and others in remoter districts; or if it was after hours, the cafés and late-night snack-bars into which the stragglers emptied themselves. There a floating population of bohemians, actors, firemen, soldiers, sailors and airmen on leave or of the London garrison, and of many nationalities, poets and artists sometimes in uniform and sometimes in civvies, drifted together in chance and ever-changing groups: never have the London pubs been more stimulating, never has one been able to hear more extraordinary revelations, never witness more unlikely encounters.'

As before the war, there was a regularity and security in this new Bohemia. There was money to stand drinks to those artists on leave or avoiding military service. 'I'm Dylan Thomas, and I'm f—ing skint,' the poet with lips like Michelin tyres said to Joan Wyndham in the Wheatsheaf. 'Be a nice Waafie and buy me another Special Ale.' Later, she avoided his beery kisses – it was like being embraced by an intoxicated octopus. There was now little threat of darkness falling on the bars from the air. For those in uniform starved of intelligent company or intellectual excitement, in search of the pick-up of fellow souls as well as bodies, the allure of Fitzrovia grew into a potent musk of beer, gin, chatter and encounter. Alan Ross remembered:

A perpetual waiting for darkness at Rainbow Corner, lonely groups of G.I.'s, chewing or staring or making passes at adolescent girls, painted and screaming like parrots; Bloomsbury girls and writers, drunks and sergeants and itinerant queens in Soho pubs; artists and military ex-Stockbrokers and middle-class girls doing their bit at the Antelope; non-alcoholic excesses at the Astoria Ballroom and Palais de Dance, sailors and Waafs spilling out into unlit streets to catch last trains from sand-bagged, gaping stations. They played 'Deep Purple' and 'Jealousy' and 'Lili Marlene' at Naafi's and Other Ranks' Clubs. They linked arms in the streets and sang 'Yours Till the Stars Lose Their Glory' and 'Frenesi' and 'She'll be Wearing Silk Pyjamas When She Comes'. It was a time of Vera Lynn and the Stage Door Canteen … There had been earlier, more haunting songs like 'A Nightingale Sang in Berkeley Square' and 'Room 504' and 'That Lovely Week-End'. But the specialists in nostalgia were drying up; everyone was getting tired of the war; of uniforms and drabness. Manners deteriorated; imagination sagged; it took an extra two drinks to come up to par.

Everybody was expecting the war to be over soon, and it never was – the Second Front had to begin, and it never did. In the spring, the *New Yorker* correspondent noted, a young or old Englishman's fancy lightly turned to thoughts of invasion, this time towards France, not from it; but D-Day was conspicuous only by its postponement. There was a certain gloating from the BBC carolling about the tonnage of bombs dropped on Berlin rather as if rugby scores were being announced; but this counting did not alleviate the general fatigue. James Pope-Hennessy, now posted to a cellar in the War Office, found London shabby and stale with crowds milling round Piccadilly, 'pleasure-seeking men on leave, who find no pleasure because it no longer exists in this tarnished city'. There was a frightening

157

increase of an evil atmosphere, which seemed to haunt the tube stations day and night. London seemed to be in a doldrum, secure and adequately fed and paid, waiting for something momentous or disastrous to happen, and certainly expecting the end of the war.

The pre-war literary feuds reared up their hydra heads once more. What the blitz had lopped off, the All Clear renewed. Lacking a common enemy overhead, the artists found the enemy in each other roundabout. Class divisions were again apparent. The left-wing and grammar school and regional writers resented the dominance of those Old Etonians on *Horizon* and Penguin *New Writing*. Julian Symons found the battle of 'players against gentlemen, puritans against hedonists, Goths against silver-age Romans' a permanent one in twentieth-century Britain. The war had camouflaged it, not ended it. Julian Maclaren-Ross agreed. An internecine war between various schools of poetry and individual poets was breaking out. Dylan Thomas might say that poetry was not a competitor, but with competitive poets around such as the Scots W. Sydney Graham, the light of battle glowed in his glaucous eyes. The latest theatre of war was in the bar-rooms of Fitzrovia. In spite of the truce which the blitz had induced, a war had always been fought among the people whom A. S. J. Tessimond described as 'The Lesser Artists':

> We are the disembowellers who have used
> Our own guts and our friends' for strings for fiddles.
> We are the eyes and ears at our own keyholes;
> The spies on our own whispered conversations;
> The ghostly watchers of our copulations,
> The third in the narrow bed.
> We are that ill-assorted, arrogant, petty,
> Incompetent-at-living, glib-at-comment,
> Destructive, self-destructive, self-divided,
> Restless, rootless, faithless, faith-demanding,
> Unsatisfied, unsatisfiable crew
> Whom the ironical gods in a casual moment
> Chose for their gift of tongues and touched with fire.

Nobody could have flung down the gauntlet louder and declared the class divisions in the poetic world more than Osbert Sitwell, when he decided early in 1943 that the time had come to do something to keep the arts alive. 'Morale is low at the moment,' he told the wealthy writer Bryher. To revive it, he and his sister Edith would organize a Royal Poetry Reading in the Aeolian Hall in front of the Queen and her two daughters, the Princesses Elizabeth and Margaret, and the salon Ladies, Emerald Cunard and Sibyl Colefax. The invited poets were restricted to the established and the titled. 'The Reading! – the *Reading*!!' Edith lamented to John Lehmann. 'The letters to poets about their collars, the threats to faint ... Life is very difficult.' She herself appeared as if stepping forward from a great tapestry, dressed in black robes and a green hat shaped like a laurel wreath, looking as gaunt and Plantagenet as she claimed to be, and declaiming 'Anne Boleyn's Song' – 'After the terrible rain, the Annunciation ...' which signalled the lull in the bombing and the coming of the Queen to the reading. T. S. Eliot gave a bravura performance of 'What the Thunder Said' from *The Waste Land*, ending his incantation in his 'High Anglican asbestos voice' with the foreboding 'London Bridge is falling down'. One poetess was too drunk to perform, Walter de la Mare was too dwarfish to peer above the lectern, Lady Dorothy Wellesley hit Harold Nicolson with her umbrella and had to be held by Beatrice Lillie, while another poet droned so interminably and inaudibly that he was silenced by a near-riot of applause, which delighted the royal princesses. The competition among the poets was less to recite than to sit next to royalty. In the end, Osbert Sitwell sat with the Queen, de la Mare with Princess Elizabeth, and Eliot with Princess Margaret. 'They sat very still in the front row,' Edith Sitwell said of the royal women, 'and stared at one.' But H. D., the American poetess and Bryher's lover, had the last word. 'It made it so gay, like good Queen Bess times for a lot of assorted poets to read aloud – formal and informal at the same time as only England can manage things in War or Peace.'

H. D. was wrong as only an American could be wrong about English society. The Royal Poetry Reading only emphasized the abyss between the privileged and the others, the old élite and the floating poets of Fitzrovia and the provinces. Even John Lehmann could hardly defend it, finding it hilarious and full of bad performances that reduced the audience to a state of squirming misery. The truth was that such pretentious occasions given by the members of the *ancien régime* of English culture did not disguise the fact that they were hardly helping to restore anyone's morale but their own, and they were doing nothing to win the war or aid those who were actually winning it. A certain guilt, indeed, began to seep into those who had dodged combat as if a Messerschmitt were sitting on their tail. The anonymous 'Neuro' put down his 'Notes on War Guilt' for the uneasy Cyril Connolly in *Horizon*. Guilt had diminished remarkably during the blitz, but if the lull in the air raids continued, it would soon surpass pre-war guilt records. Those who had avoided serving in the forces were now hating their jobs in Food Control, the Ministry of Information, or a cushy reserved occupation. The bombing of London had made most people feel classless in a common front against the enemy. Clear skies revived the neurosis of cowardice, when victories were being won abroad in Africa, and the hospitals at home were full of the valiant wounded. Brilliant propaganda was needed to persuade bureaucrats and civilians that they, too, were helping to win the war. The right kind of fantasy had to be found to stimulate the intellectual's belief that pushing pens or inking paper was also a patriotic endeavour. As the highest common factor of contemporary sophistication, *Horizon* had its role. It must drive home the message – 'the duty of a man with brains is substantially unaffected by the war.' The duty of a professional artist was still his creative art, whether dangerous or not. Intellectuals were always somewhat ridiculous, and were now no more ridiculous than before the war.

Connolly agreed, confessing to his sloth and blaming the tedium of the middle of the war for his own failings. *Horizon* may have gained in seriousness, but it had lost in mental elasticity. 'The emotional strain of war has broken our curiosity, has fatigued us to the point at which we are cynical, impervious, distressed or hostile in the presence of new ideas.' In his mid-war musings, published under the alias of 'Palinurus' in *The Unquiet Grave*, Connolly saw himself at Christmas with no opinions, no ideas, 'no ideals, no inspiration; a fat, slothful, querulous, greedy, impotent carcass; a stump, a decaying belly washed up on the shore ... Always tired, always bored, always hurt, always hating.' He himself was one of the last of the cultured. Only a very few people like himself maintained civilization in a very few places. Some bombs and prisons would blot them out. The civilized got more out of life than the uncivilized, and so were not forgiven. Resentment was triumphant. The frustrated Have-Nots were massacring the Haves. A world neurosis was overcoming any personal neurosis, until humanity would choke on its own bile. 'One by one, the Golden Apples of the West are shaken from the tree.'

Seeing oneself as a falling Golden Apple shaken down by a world neurosis is a lazy way of assuaging personal war guilt. To confess is not to excuse. *Qui s'excuse s'accuse.* Other privileged littérateurs were more honest about their inglorious war. Peter Quennell admitted that he had worked in offices, gone to night-clubs and dinner parties, written one solid book, and been dismissed from the Auxiliary Fire Service for lighting up a cigarette during a blaze. Now and then he had felt mortally afraid, but he had kept his eyes open. Like the Abbé Sieyès in the French Revolution, he could say he had lived. He did not share in the *angst* which Connolly wore on his sleeve, bemoaning to a soldier friend the abject lot of the civilian and the state of London. The young man from the desert had been appalled by the city's shabbiness and expense, its dirt and vulgarity: 'and its carious houses, the contraceptives in the squares, the puddles of urine in the telephone boxes, the sulphurous wines and goat-stew in the restaurants, the bored, pale, ferrety people milling round the streets, fighting and rutting and crawling over the badly dressed prostitutes like bees round their queen'. Receiving friendly and unpatronizing letters from friends fighting overseas churned the guilt inside Connolly round and round until it curdled into a kind of rancorous despair. 'Oh,' he cried out, 'why can't I fight for myself?' Actually, he was forgiven by the most aggressive American author of all, Ernest Hemingway, who was sent to London as a war correspondent to cover the landings in France. He encountered the sybaritic and uncompetitive Connolly and took to him and to his book, *The Unquiet Grave*. He understood Connolly's resistance to the world conflict, his wish to remain a guardian of culture amid a dirtiness of massacre. He later wrote to Connolly, 'I always get involved in wars but I admired the way that you did not. It would be wrong for me not to fight but it was many times righter for you to do exactly as you did.'

A consciousness of the class system also revived with war weariness and the hiatus in the aerial bombardment. Even during the blitz, both the right wing and the left wing had never dropped their guard over the divisions between the rich and the poor nor over the future of the wealthy. In the amusing *Ritzkrieg*, the Colonels Blimp and Bogey were satirized because they saw nothing to choose between communism and fascism, except that fascism was better if there had to be a choice. Their plan of campaign was to turn the war into a stalemate followed by an attack on Russia. The People's War should become the Best People's War, which would end in an aristocratic peace. The satire was not far from the truth in extreme right-wing circles. Even sensitive writers and artists such as David Jones were not deceived into thinking that the blitz had obliterated class divisions in a common experience under fire. Death came with a singular disparity to rich and poor. 'As in peace so in war, the Ritz and the Doss House, so far from being united in death, face death with utterly other emotions. And that is one of the basic problems of our age. The cat is creeping (rather than leaping) out of the bag. They are knocking at the door and tapping at the floor.'

When later she had become Queen Mother, Queen Elizabeth told Stephen Spender that the war years were the happiest of her life and the King's. The bombings of Buckingham Palace, the tours of the rubble of the East End, made them feel one with the sufferings of the people. Spender himself now thinks that the royal example did much to diminish the class war during the opening of the larger war. But in the East End, the awareness of a privileged life in the West soon returned. Down in the docks, the area west of the Tower of London was called the Other End or Up the Other. *They* in their omnipotence, were Other, to 'the inhabitants of dock-back-street-canal-and-sewer-land ... The way we live in England still, divided up and mutually "other", is not only wrong, it's nonsense. We are living a lie which could be exploded in our life-times, if the whole lot of us faced the lie as we have faced the War.'

In spite of regulations and rationing, the rich and the upper classes did better than the rest of the people by the middle of the war, and men went on doing better than women. The differences showed in food, clothes, housing and jobs. The wealthy could afford expensive things to eat off the ration, grouse, snipe, gull's eggs. There was a 'grey market' and a 'black market' in rationed goods; grocers slipped tinned salmon to favoured customers. Those who lived in country houses no longer threw stones at local poachers and farmers, who could always keep them supplied at a price. And above all, the restaurants of London grouped around Piccadilly and Fitzrovia were the shortest way out of the world of the queue. Although the top price of a meal was fixed at five shillings, expensive wine and service charges made courses sold at less than cost a profitable business for those who could supply to those who could pay. Sagittarius had a good time parodying Christopher Marlowe in 'The Passionate Profiteer to his Love':

> Come feed with me and be my love,
> And pleasures of the table prove,
> Where *Prunier* and *The Ivy* yield
> Choice dainties of the stream and field.

At *Claridge* thou shalt duckling eat,
Sip vintages both dry and sweet,
And thou shalt squeeze between thy lips
Asparagus with buttered tips ...

Come share at the *Savoy* with me
The menu of austerity;
If in these pastures thou wouldst rove
Then feed with me and be my love.

The clothes of the well-to-do lasted longer. The cloth was better, the quality greater. The leather patch on the old Harris tweed jacket became the mark of affluence. And even with coupons and Utility clothes, the poor had to buy quick and shoddy replacements for their dress, while the rich could save for months to buy one good item. In housing, the wealthy might suffer from billeting or requisition; but, on the whole, the evacuees had returned to their homes when the German bombers left English skies and the large houses that were requisitioned were impossible to run without servants, who had nearly all been directed to the factories. The number of maids and skivvies declined by half during the 'forties, and those who left that form of 'service' never returned. The demarcations of the shop floor, the higher pay of males in the same jobs, these were preferable to the class antagonism of domestic work. The divisions of downstairs and upstairs were traded for the disputes and camaraderie of the conveyor belt.

Most women did achieve security in the war from their new jobs or their husbands' military pay; but they became the weariest from its daily drudgery. Many of them worked in factories, brought up children, and acted as air-raid spotters at night. They hardly slept, they slaved. And there was always the emotional deprivation of the men away, the men at risk, the men who would not return. Two women poets writing at the time captured the ambivalence and endurance of this new condition of women. *In These Five Years* told of Daphne Nixon's endeavour to serve in uniform, stay who she was, and change to meet the circumstances:

To be a woman now
it is expected that you live
like men,
and work like men
yet struggle always to remain
fundamentally feminine.
But in our new born hearts
has grown the urge to act
in equal parts of fight and fear,
we want no time to weep,
only the wasted hours bring despair ...

And then the women shared the fear and the guilt of the men in reserved occupations, who knew other men were fighting and dying for them. It was worse

THE PENGUIN
NEW WRITING

No. 31

EDITED BY

JOHN LEHMANN

ABOVE AND RIGHT: John Gawsworth, who claimed to be the King of Redondo, drinking in Soho and studying to be a poet and editor.

OPPOSITE ABOVE: The regulars drinking with the Navy in the Fitzroy Tavern, a photograph by Dan Farson.

OPPOSITE BELOW: Carole Lynne, Richard Murdoch, Pat Kirkwood, Christine Norden and Bonar Colleano, the 'forties stars of stage and screen and radio, drinking in The Coach and Horses, Soho.

PREVIOUS PAGE: This cover of John Lehmann's The Penguin *New Writing* was designed by John Minton.

Cecil Day Lewis (top left), Laurie Lee
(top right), Stephen Spender (left) and
Alun Lewis (above), portrayed in wartime
by Bill Brandt, who also took the portrait
of Dylan Thomas in the Salisbury Tavern
(opposite).

ABOVE: W. H. Auden, Cecil Day Lewis
and Stephen Spender at the Venice
conference of PEN International in 1949.

RIGHT: Cyril Connolly with Lady Caroline
Blackwood outside Wheeler's fish
restaurant in Soho.

OPPOSITE: Louis MacNeice, portrayed by
Bill Brandt.

FOLLOWING PAGE: An illustration by Biro
for *Airman's Song Book*, a collection of
songs by C.H. Ward-Jackson, who also
wrote *It's a Piece of Cake* and *No Bombs at
All*.

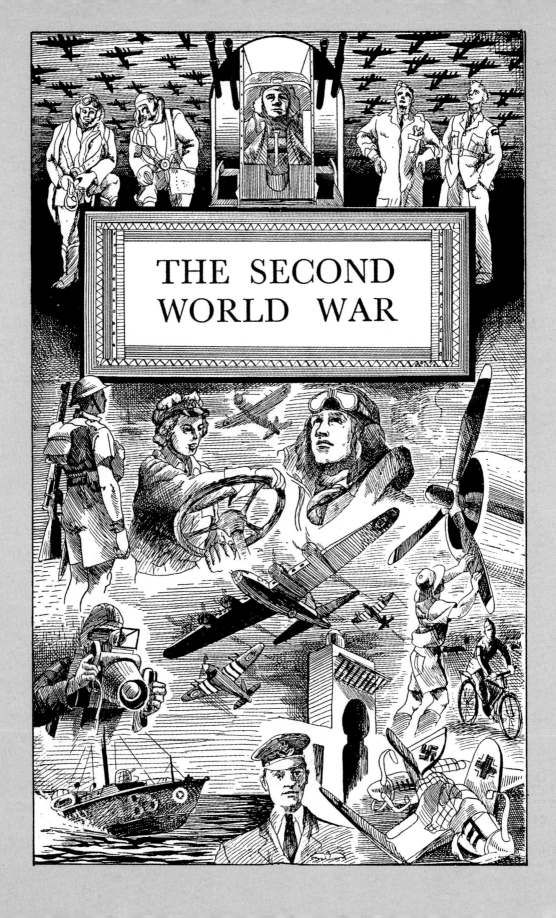

THE SECOND WORLD WAR

Lilliput

ONE SHILLING

MARCH 1944

Lilliput mixed art and war in witty contrasts. The top pair of illustrations is entitled 'Tank Trap', while the bottom right photograph shows Henry Moore in his studio working on one of his shelter drawings (opposite left).

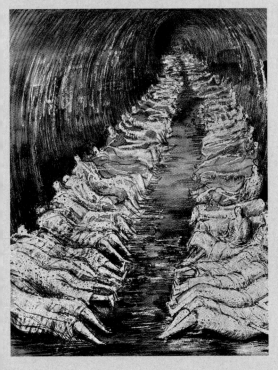

Photographs from *Lilliput* of an ARP warden, Theodora Fitzgibbon posing as an artist's model, Windmill girls in their dressing room, and an anti-aircraft battery.

OPPOSITE: Michael Ayrton's illustrations for *Poems of Death* and E. A. Poe's *Tales of Mystery and Imagination* (bottom right).

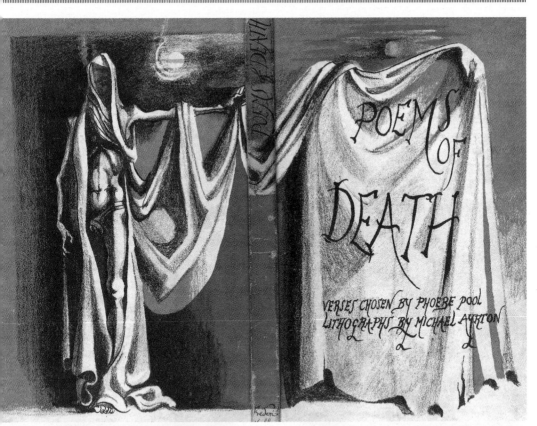

POEMS OF DEATH

VERSES CHOSEN BY PHOEBE POOL
LITHOGRAPHS BY MICHAEL AYRTON

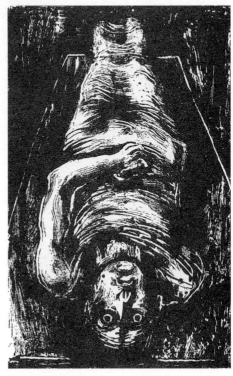

OPPOSITE: *Battle of Britain* – Paul Nash
makes contours and aerial tracks of the
fight for supremacy in the sky.

ABOVE: *A Black Aeroplane on a Red Deck* – Leonard Rosoman's gouache of his
experience on an aircraft carrier.

OPPOSITE: *Crashed Gliders at the Landing
Zone of Ranville* by Albert Richards.

OPPOSITE: *Barrage Balloon* – a drawing by Edward Seago from his book, *High Endeavour*, the story of a circus artist who is trained to be a pilot.

ABOVE: *Shipbuilding on the Clyde – Burners*. The centre panel of Stanley Spencer's vision of shipyard workers during the war.

OPPOSITE: *Two Nuns and a Peasant Family* – from Edward Seago's *With the Allied Armies in Italy*, the artist's account of the Italian campaign of autumn, 1944.

FOLLOWING PAGE: *Negro Club*, a painting from 'In Darkest Soho' by Edgar Ainsworth; it appeared in *Lilliput*.

for the women if it was a loved man, one who would not come back. Addicts of the six o'clock news, the women waited to hear of another battle, whether defeat or victory did not matter, there were the inevitable dead. So Joyce Rowe spoke of 'Dieppe':

> Yet, when all's said and done, who'd have it otherwise?
> Not they.
> Women wait long enough for paradise
> and if it's now – or in a million years –
> it makes no odds. Their blood flows, and my tears
> if I could shed them.
>
> There's the pips.
>
> And News again of men and planes and ships.
> But I already know and feel my lips
> grow cold, and my heart a hot, hard ball
> wedged in my throat. I know they could not all
> Come back.

Although written after the war as part of that revisionism, which along with Evelyn Waugh's trilogy *Men at Arms* depicted the conflict as a comedy as well as a betrayal of values, *The Heat of the Day* is supremely accurate about the moral ambivalence felt by women during the doldrums before the Second Front. Elizabeth Bowen dared to deal with an attractive but treasonable hero, whom the heroine Stella loves despite his treachery to his country. Even during the blitz, Stella defines the conflict as 'a crooks' war'. She will not sleep with the security agent who accuses her lover of working for the other side. But then her lover confesses that he is guilty. He does not believe in his country. Its vaunted freedom and democracy are a racket. 'Freedom to be what? – the muddled, mediocre, damned.' He himself was born wounded. 'Dunkirk was waiting there in us – what a race! A class without a middle, a race without a country. Unwhole.' He chooses the fascists because they have started something, they have cut the cackle. Finally, he deliberately falls off a roof to his death, and the book ends with the attack of the German rockets on the city, 'droning *things*, mindlessly making for you, thick and fast, day and night, [that] tore the calico of London.'

No better descriptions have been written of encounters during the early air raids, when life was of the moment and the past did not matter because the future was so precarious. Yet the real weight of *The Heat of the Day* was the illustration of war weariness in the middle of the conflict, of people losing their sense of a joint struggle in the everyday matter of living at all. Stella felt 'it was not the country but occupied Europe that was occupying London – suspicious listening, surreptitious movement and leaden hearts. The weather-quarter tonight was the conquered lands. The physical nearness of the Enemy – how few were the miles between the capital and the coast, between coast and coast – became palpable. Tonight, the 163 safety-curtain between the here and the there had lifted; the breath of danger and sorrow travelled over freely from shore to shore.' And with it came the dragon's teeth of doubt of country, commitment and justice. It did prove finally to be a crooks' war with the verdict, 'No right *or* wrong to it after all, perhaps?'

Even during the conflict, a similar scepticism was being expressed about the aims of the war and the future peace. The young men fighting might be betrayed again as they were after the previous world war. 'If the war lasts as long as the Great War,' J. B. Priestley warned, 'and we have done no planning for reconstruction, then disaster will follow the peace, as it did last time, simply because nobody will be lively and up-and-doing except the crooks. The rest of us will be suffering from a profound mental and spiritual exhaustion.' There must be no more muddling and wallowing from one vast tragic farce to the next. C. E. M. Joad gave the same advice in his political fable, *The Adventures of the Young Soldier in Search of the Better World*, with illustrations by Mervyn Peake. The Young Soldier began by hearing Sir Stafford Cripps on the wireless, talking about What We Are Fighting For. The answer was 'to make a better and happier world'. The Young Soldier then asked many people how the better world was to be made and received a chorus of defeatism, revenge and regimentation from Captain Nick and Mr Escapegoat and Mr Speakeasy, the Reverend Hateman and the Red-Tape Worm. This modern Pilgrim's Progress ended with the comfortable Philosopher giving the Young Soldier some down-to-earth advice and refusing to help him make a post-war Utopia. Like Joad himself, the Philosopher was only a signpost. He did not march along the road down which he pointed. As Joad himself was in trouble for persistently travelling without paying for a railway ticket, he was hardly the man to indicate the way to the better world. Nor was the signpost valid, for the dominant philosophy of the period was already in that state of affliction named Logical Positivism, which spent its time questioning the meaning of meaning, not the meaning of the future.

Actually, Joad's fellow member of the wireless Brains Trust, Sir William Beveridge, was providing a blueprint for the better world. The Beveridge Report, which would become the foundation of the post-war welfare state, sold more than half a million copies. Its proposals for family allowances, for a National Health Service and National Assistance, for grants and pensions, were popular even in conservative circles. Tommy Handley himself on his wireless show *It's That Man Again* said he had spent three days and nights reading *Gone With The Want* by that stout fellow Beveridge. The plan seemed to provide social security from cradle to grave. Such a promise of a better world after the war enthused soldiers and civilians alike, and even the Resistance in occupied Europe. Winston Churchill's National Government was compelled to adopt most of Beveridge's recommendations in principle. That was the best way to suggest that the peace might be won as well as the war.

Among the literary élite and the Fitzrovians, the vision of the welfare state merely confirmed their worst fears. The war was already making the state omnipotent.

Captain Nick, *above*, Mr. Speakeasy, *left*, and the Red-Tape Worm, *right*: Mervyn Peake's illustrations to C. E. M. Joad's *The Adventures of the Young Soldier in Search of the Better World*.

This would inevitably lead to an extreme socialist regime and the crushing of the individual. In the forces, the Army Bureau of Current Affairs was giving three hours of education a week to the troops on subjects like 'What Are We Fighting For?' A Theatre Group travelled with drama-documentaries such as *Where Do We Go From Here?* The message was always the same: keep left. Backing for the drama and ballet and music from CEMA was not political, but it did presage state funding after the war, national ballet and opera and theatre companies, which might be under the control of a new Ministry of Culture. The pervasive spread of the Ministry of Information with its thousands of pamphlets and films, the ubiquitous voice of the BBC which was swallowing into its entrails so many writers and poets as producers of its programmes, these were the prophecies of state control after the coming of the peace. Any private Muse would be gagged and bound and directed to the diffusion of official culture. 'We are turning all our writers into commentators,' Cyril Connolly complained, 'until one day there will be nothing left for them to comment on.' If the tyranny of the state were not broken after the war, nobody would have an hour to call his own.

Connolly himself believed that Britain would turn to some form of communism. It was the only effective religion for the working class. Its coming was as inevitable as Christianity. He was as pessimistic about the future of 'The Intelligentsia' in England as Koestler was on its past in Europe. Koestler thought that Stalin and Hitler had hardly needed to destroy the intelligentsia of Europe of the 'thirties. The fellow-travellers of the Pink Decade were only the fifth wheel on the cart of state, left in the cold, deprived of responsibility, the decadents of the revolution. The Nazis knew what they were doing when they exterminated them with the dictum, 'When I hear the word culture I fire my pistol.'

Not all of the intellectual leaders of the Pink Decade were pessimistic about a future socialist state. Stephen Spender expected it; the regular pay which he received when in the Fire Service and briefly in the army made life easy. 'All pay was pocket-money,' he recently said. 'I wouldn't mind living in a socialist state, as long as I was an officer.' The problem was that socialist and national socialist states under Stalin and Hitler had the reputation of liquidating their intellectuals and choosing their officers from party hacks. Spender also did not believe that the planners would succeed after the war. Their plans were not linked with the combat. Realists ran the war and wanted the destruction of cities. Plans for the peace had nothing to do with war. In fact, when Spender applied to a military selection board to visit German universities after the victory and teach them the value of freedom and democracy, he was told by one officer, 'We can assure you, Mr Spender, that after this war there will be *no* culture in Germany.'

Culture in Britain under state control was supported by the Marxist group which published the illustrated magazine *Our Time* during the last four years of the struggle. John Lehmann's sister, the actress Beatrix, was on the editorial board, along with the Fitzrovian painter John Banting and the composer Alan Bush. But the chief editors were Randall Swingler and Montagu Slater and Edgell Rickword, who had edited *The Left Review* in the 'thirties. They supported the state and left-wing organizations, which were growing up as the nuclei of committees of the arts. They believed along with Connolly and Spender that there was an upsurge of culture in wartime and that it was now widely diffused mainly through the help of the government. The question was, who was to bring the arts to the masses when the bullets and the bombs stopped?

One institution alone was the shape of things to come. The British Broadcasting Corporation grew and multiplied during the war. Although it was a monopoly and funded by the state, its first Director-General John Reith had won for it a kind of independence, refusing to broadcast government propaganda against the workers during the General Strike of 1926. Although he had retired before the outbreak of hostilities, and even with the restrictions of war censorship, a tradition of free speech and irreverence for authority remained within the studio complex off Portland Place. The necessities of the time expanded the programmes and their makers. A steady recruitment of writers and poets as radio producers began the slow shift of London's bohemian pubs from the south-east of Fitzrovia to its north-west corner off Upper Regent Street, where flourished the George and the Stag's Head and the Horse and Groom, otherwise known as the Whore's Lament, so-called after the tears shed by the ladies of the bar when the American forces eventually left for France. The wireless staff grew from four to eleven thousand, while fifty hours of broadcasting every day increased to one hundred and fifty hours in forty-seven foreign languages rather than the pre-war eight. Six times as many transmitters were used with three times the power in kilowatts. Broadcasting was a national priority and received all the resources it needed.

The news readers and announcers, particularly Alvar Liddell and Bruce Belfrage and Stuart Hibberd, were dressed formally and invisibly in evening dress: if one of the three bombs that hit Broadcasting House had proved fatal, they wanted to die with their dinner jackets clean. Their names and voices became as familiar as Winston Churchill's own. A reputation for impartiality, whatever the demands of military strategy or national morale, gave the corporation a global primacy in credibility. The Battle of British Broadcasting was victorious on the far-flung radios of the world, which were tuned in to hear something near to the facts of the struggle. The war of the airwaves against fascism was won by telling the limited truth.

The fight to maintain morale was also won by comedy. Not only were the enemies abroad made into fools, but also the bureaucrats at home. Even with a war on, everybody disliked authority, except those who wore the peaked caps. The enduring legacy of the broadcasting monopoly was a paradox – a mocking of the power structure, which had created the state wireless system and had to dictate in order to win the war. Tommy Handley became the master of the assault on officialdom. He dealt with post-war planning as His Washout the Mayor. He intended to dehouse all the people in his borough, if the Germans hadn't already. His motto was: 'Loosen the Green Belt, tuck in the blueprints and paint the town 167 red.' The endearing and zany humour of Handley and Jack Train, Arthur Askey and 'Stinker' Murdoch provided the escape into mirth that released the British people from their endless complaints against the necessary regimentation and rationing of the war. The whistle of 'Lillibullero' may have once mocked an English king off his throne, but the laugh every eleven seconds on an ITMA show kept the present His Majesty's Government in power. It was Hitler's war – said the later producer of the Goons and Tony Hancock – 'which changed us more than we wanted to change, and exhausted us more than we knew. It took people of uncommon energy to turn mere survival into a celebration of life. Our "common cause" is gone, but let's hope a trace of common bolshiness lingers.'

Mervyn Peake

TWELVE

The Summer of
Pilotless Planes

Mervyn Peake

Living on the small island of Britain before D-Day, the *New Yorker* correspondent noticed, was like living 'on a vast combination of an aircraft carrier, a floating dock jammed with men, and a warehouse stacked to the ceiling with material labelled "Europe".' People had waited for the invasion of France for so long that, when it came, it was like the rising of a late curtain. There was more of a sense of relief that the postponement was over than a joyous feeling of imminent victory. The immediate effect in London was to clear the hotels and clubs and pubs and restaurants of the transient millions of men. Their long confine in beleaguered Britain was, at last, a gaol-break across the Channel. As Arnold Rattenbury wrote in his 'Calendar Song' about the long years of preparation at home, eating apples in Bedfordshire no longer mocked him with the red and green wounds of Englishmen overseas, nor did tumbling leaves shame him with the thought of parachutists dying afar:

> But O, when they woke me up in June
> and told all thumbs to touch the news
> I heard my boats grind into France
> and the prisoning seasons let me loose.

Leading the invasion fleet were the slow and vulnerable rocket-ships, some of them wooden, liable to become an inferno on one spark, yet capable of extraordinary destruction. The captain of one of these, William Golding, was to become the greatest writer about the sea after Conrad and was never to recover from his sense of imminent death and of the power of human evil and utter devastation. Safe in England, longing for a return to Europe behind the invasion forces, John Lehmann published one of his rare war pieces about D-Day in Penguin *New Writing*. It was written by Denis Glover, a naval officer who took in Commandos for the first assault. He was reassured by Golding's rocket-ships, which he called battle-wagons. 'War elephants of the fleet, unhurried and packing a wallop ...' They hurled packets of one-ton 'bricks' into defined areas. The flaming explosives destroyed everything within one square half-mile. 'All the mad dogs of hell barking over a bone on the beach, the invisible beach; and the shattering roll of the bombs.' To Golding, the annihilation by his 'bricks' of a Proustian shore from *Remembrance of Things Past* lit a fire in his mind that never burned out.

Back in the security of London, the citizens were afraid of Hitler's retaliation, his secret weapon. They had only a week to wait before the first of the German aerial rockets, the V1s or doodlebugs or buzz-bombs, were fired from the Pas de Calais. Soon they were dropping at the rate of some hundred a day across Kent and Essex and the East End on through the City to the West End and the South London suburbs. Once again, there were theories that poor districts were being bombarded more than rich ones and that the new levelling of housing would make accommodation an appalling problem for the workers, but not for the wealthy. Only the second fear was true. The summer of 1944 was a cotton and cardboard one for Elizabeth Bowen with workmen putting up calico windows inside the shells of a million blasted houses. But the largest massacre by the pilotless planes was of the privileged up in the Guards Chapel in Wellington Barracks just off Buckingham Palace: it was packed for a morning service, and the whole congregation was killed. John Lehmann saw the bomb fall from his sitting-room window on Piccadilly. He could see only a small column of black smoke. 'It was extraordinary how little it affected the general view.'

The flying-bombs certainly affected the psychology of the Londoners, particularly those who could express their fears. The robot planes were the last pinpricks to Cyril Connolly. 'To all guilty people (and by now all civilians are guilty), they are the final appointment in the dentist's chair, and, casualties apart, they have made London more dirty, more unsociable, more plague-stricken than ever. The civilians who remain grow more and more hunted and disagreeable, each sweating and palpitating like a toad under his particular stone. Social life is non-existent, and those few and petty amenities which are the salt of civilian life – friendship, manners, conversations, mutual esteem – now seem extinct for ever.' Yet conditions seemed that intolerable in London only to those who were as frightened as Connolly. Although there was another evacuation of one and a half million women and children from the capital, it was of short duration. And the very repetition of the sound of the secret weapons – the disagreeable splutter like an out-of-tune motor cycle – became a normal background noise, unless the engine stopped, when many people fell to the ground to avoid the blast and flying glass. Women in queues seemed no more uneasy than if they had just heard a wasp in the room. In fact, as the humorist George Stonier noticed, the secret weapon became public gossip, and the prevalent high-pitched buzz came from people talking about it.

Nonchalance was somewhat on the surface, rather like wearing a poppy on Remembrance Sunday. Still working in the fire service, William Sansom found that the flying-bombs were particularly hated because they were automatic, random and wanton. 'The new things were supernatural. The idea of a grey-clad pilot with Nazi-blond hair seemed almost affectionate in comparison.' Until the new weapons fell, people thought every raid had a direction, a chosen target. Now fate had become arbitrary. Although a flying-bomb seemed to approach in a straight line, when the motor stopped overhead, it could drop anywhere within a mile or two. It would not spare a child, a woman, a cat or a dog. 'It was absolutely reasonless, the first purely fatal agent that had come to man for centuries, tempting him to cross his fingers again, bringing a rebirth of superstition.' Theodora Fitzgibbon agreed. 'It was a curious time and life became a valuable stroke of fortune, for we had no idea when death would fiendishly fall from the skies. Sometimes it seemed the war would go on all our lives, increasing in devilish intensity. Equally unnerving was the sinister thunderous noise of the death-laden flying fortresses passing overhead on their way to cities such as Dresden for intensive morale-breaking raids.' Revenge from the air had become a two-way flight.

So the time of the Golem, of Count Frankenstein's monster, of Wellsian 171 mechanical dictators and of the robots in *R.U.R.*, appeared in the sky. The rockets that looked like children's space toys trailing their tiny streak of fire overhead were the revenge of the sorcerer's apprentice in Berlin. Ruthven Todd called them 'the toy hornets of the mad mechanic's brain'. They emphasized that this was more a war of scientists than of human beings. Victory would go to the best technology. Science – Canetti complained – had turned itself into the religion of killing and was hurrying to wipe out mankind before it could be defrocked. The club of radical scientists who advised the government during the war, the Tots and Quots, did not disagree at their frequent dinners in Fitzrovia that science and war were connected. In fact, the total destruction of Nazi Germany was necessary to create the post-war socialist-planned society foreseen by Professors Jack Haldane and Desmond Bernal, whose sympathy for Russia fuelled their hatred of the Third Reich. Although considered a security risk, Bernal worked closely on the equipment needed for the D-Day landings, while frequenting the notorious flat in Bentinck Street where Guy Burgess and Anthony Blunt lived and passed on information to Moscow. But in 1944, killing Germans successfully took precedence over political beliefs. Few heeded Spender's warning about Bernal and his fellow believers in scientific planning: 'In Russia it is the politicians who plan the science.'

As the Allied armies advanced through France, the short-range V1 rockets gave way to the long-range V2s, more powerful and more feared. There was no overt crack in civilian morale as Hitler hoped, but there was a wariness. 'Every night a flying-bomb came over,' Inez Holden wrote, 'the same ritual was observed. At the sound of an express train in the air we became silent, like actors took up our places as near the wall as possible and out of range of window and looking-glass. We stood, each in our own chosen place, completely still till the thud punctured the silence, then continued with our conversation.' The perennial Fitzrovian Philip O'Connor was reduced finally to fear and mania by the flying-bombs. He crouched in a shelter between two studios. 'Every morning seemed posthumous in our lives, every night an encounter with all approximations to death.' A flying-bomb hit the roof of Faber & Faber in Russell Square; fortunately T. S. Eliot was not on fire-watching duty at the time. The publication soon afterwards of the complete edition of *Four Quartets* showed the value of his experience under bombardment in creating the most illuminating long series of poems of the war.

> Ash on an old man's sleeve
> Is all the ash the burnt roses leave.
> Dust in the air suspended
> Marks the place where a story ended.
> Dust inbreathed was a house –
> The wall, the wainscot and the mouse,
> The death of hope and despair,
>   This is the death of air.

To young poets arriving in Fitzrovia, the war had come to them for the second and last time. It was 'the summer of pilotless planes' to David Wright, 'of searchlit nights and soft, when once upon a scare' he ran out with one of the Lost Girls, Julian Orde, under the flying-bombs. She was the granddaughter of the Duke of Wellington, a poet herself and a Fitzrovian, a friend of the two Roberts, MacBryde and Colquhoun, of Sydney Graham and Dylan Thomas. She was bombed and dreamed of being bombed.

> I saw the table break in three,
> I saw the walls cascading down,
> I saw the hard hair of my lover
> Drift out upon the flowing green ...

Escaping from school, Michael Wishart found that when the doodlebugs swarmed in the sky, pubs served children like himself to shelter them from flying shrapnel. Bombs reduced St Anne's Church opposite the French pub in Soho to a crater, which soon became a reservoir and a cesspool, upon which floated a miniature armada of phosphorescent French letters. 'Aware that each moment might be their last, everyone dropped his inhibitions and prejudices into the gutter, where they belonged, and indulged in a non-stop *danse macabre.*' As in the blitz, the time of the buzz bombs made the pubs actually seem safer. Better to die in a fug of company than under the stairs alone. The old Augustus John was back at the Gargoyle, when he was not painting at his studios in Tite Street in Chelsea. He sat by the vast windows as if no explosion would ever come, no rocket would detonate nearby and shower him with broken glass. As one of his models said, the bombs buzzing overhead 'might have been blue-bottles for all he cared'. Even Roy Fuller, back from service in Africa, found that at the end of a war, the little noises of a house were far more alarming 'than the ridiculous detonations outside the gently coughing curtains'. To the artist and the poet and the veteran, the flying-bombs were rather a nuisance, hardly a threat.

One aerial rocket gave Edith Sitwell her finest hour in front of an audience of the timorous literati. She and her two brothers were reading from their poetry at the Allied Forces' Churchill Club to the Ladies Cunard and Colefax and John Lehmann and the rest of the smart social and military world with artistic pretensions. As Edith declaimed her poem about the blitz, 'Still Falls the Rain', a warning whistle sounded in the club. The noise of the approaching flying-bomb became a roaring overhead, but Edith read on, raising her voice above the racket of the destructive machine in the sky. She pronounced:

> Still falls the Rain –
> Then – O Ile leape up to my God: who pulles me doune –
> See, see where Christ's blood streames in the firmament:
> It flows from the Brow we nailed upon the tree
> Deep to the dying, to the thirsting heart
> That holds the fires of the world ...

Her performance seemed magnificent to John Lehmann, like a British admiral giving cool orders in the middle of a sea-battle. She was asserting that poetry was more important than Hitler's mechanical revenge. The flying-bomb roared off, the poem ended: 'Still do I love, still shed my innocent light, my Blood, for thee.' The shocked audience burst into a storm of applause louder than the explosion of the rocket far away.

As with T. S. Eliot, the experience of the war both clarified and enlarged Edith Sitwell's poetry. The publication of her *Street Songs* of 1942 and *Green Song* two years later gave her literary acclaim even from her previous opponents. 'Although her voice is entirely her own,' Stephen Spender wrote, 'it has become the voice of a world-wide suffering.' Even if she still used symbolic verse, she had translated the private and the precious into the language of universal pain. Her embroidered robes, episcopal jewellery and exaggerated diction no longer prevented her from speaking with the voice of common sensibility. Only a few radicals such as Julian Symons dared to criticize the poetry of this bardic phoenix rising from the ashes of the bombing in London. To them, her work was still removed from real life. But she had their measure, complaining to John Lehmann: 'The dregs of the literary population have risen as one worm to insult me.'

The flying-bombs did not destroy London or the morale of its citizens, but they closed London's theatres almost as effectively as the blitz had. Only eight of the capital's thirty theatres remained open and the actors played to handfuls of people nightly. *Blithe Spirit* at the Duchess, *Arsenic and Old Lace* at the Strand and *The Last of Mrs Cheyney* at the Savoy ran through the attacks of the pilotless planes, while the nude tableaux at the Windmill Theatre never closed. As before, London's loss was the provinces' gain. First-rate companies toured the safe country capitals far from the reach of the rockets. And at the National Gallery, the Old Vic company rehearsed under Laurence Olivier and Ralph Richardson for the finest repertory season ever to be mounted on the wartime stage, *Richard III*, *Peer Gynt* and *Arms and the Man*. Some of the actors took refuge under tables when a bomb buzzed overhead, but Olivier and Richardson never tried to hide. 'It was shaming,' admitted the Old Vic producer Tyrone Guthrie, 'how relieved we all felt when a bang, and the ensuing shattering of timbers and glass, would proclaim that someone else had "had" it.'

The ending of the rocket attacks signalled the flowering of English acting in the triple bill of the Old Vic company at the New Theatre. Its excellence was almost matched by John Gielgud mounting a rival repertory with his company at the Haymarket, where he played *Hamlet*, *Love for Love* and *The Circle*. After the closing of most of the playhouses by the second blitz of the rockets, their reopening seemed to herald a renaissance of the drama in England with its triumvirate of male leads performing at the peak of their powers. Although Gielgud's company worked in the commercial theatre while the Old Vic was subsidized by the state, the seeds of a future National Theatre appeared in the autumn of 1944 with the popular and critical success of both repertories. A standard was set for future classic productions in reaction from the drabness and conventionality of most wartime theatre. The very privations of the conflict seemed to have provoked a new and daring approach to mounting classic plays. Only dramatists of genius were missing or on active service. The worthy efforts of Barrie and Priestley were still the best the British could do, with Priestley's *They Came to a City* more of a vision of future social justice than a play of thunder and emotion.

The rocket attacks on London persuaded Priestley that the second blitz had recreated the classlessness and conviviality of the first. A practical utopia could be created after the war, and he was the man to do it. He highly irritated the poet William Empson and Woodrow Wyatt by insisting at a drunken party that his radio broadcasts were the reason that the war was being won. The government did not understand the British people, but he did. His two companions ended by driving him round and round the statue of Eros in Piccadilly Circus, trying to get him back to his flat in the Albany. They could not and dumped his unconscious body in a gutter in Jermyn Street, where Wyatt prodded him with his foot and said, 'He's only a silly old dramatist.' To their surprise, he reached home later and went on writing, talking and complaining for years.

Like Cyril Connolly, Priestley did not think that literature had risen to the occasion during the war. His reason was that writers such as himself had to do so much propaganda that they could not do their best work. Connolly's reason was that boredom and destruction had led to a general decline in all the arts with a belated recognition of their importance by the state. Ignoring the triumph of the subsidized Old Vic company, Connolly accused the state of sitting 'by the bedside of literature like a policeman watching for a would-be suicide to recover consciousness'. It would do anything for the patient except allow him the leisure, privacy and freedom from which art was produced. In England, writers had been exhausted by a total war at home. They must follow the armies back to France and Europe to recover their inspiration. Better for writers to be occupied and liberated and suffer the experience of a real war than to be worn out by long hours, air raids and propaganda work.

Actually, D-Day and the flying-bombs had brought the consequences and violence of the combat back to Britain. The wounded came back directly from battle, covered with blood, not tidied and convalescent after months in hospital. There had been the gruesome sight of the burned pilots who had been shot down in the Battle of Britain like Richard Hillary and had been reconstructed by plastic surgery at the hands of Archibald McIndoe. But they had been grouped at the Queen Victoria Hospital in East Grinstead, where they would sing to the tune of 'The Church's One Foundation':

> We are McIndoe's Army,
> We are his Guinea Pigs,
> With dermatomes and pedicles,
> Glass eyes, false teeth and wigs.
> But when we get our discharge
> We'll shout with all our might –
> 'Per Ardua ad Astra,
> We'd rather drink than fight.'

Yet these maimed victims were few and segregated, while hundreds of thousands of wounded Allied soldiers and German prisoners were now being shipped back from Europe to home eyes and hospitals, which were inundated. Not since the worst years of the trench stalemate in Flanders in the First World War had so many disfigured and mutilated people appeared in England. It was a gory sight and a nightmare to the war children.

Going back to Blighty, the casualties brought back their violence as well as their wounds. On his hospital ship, surrounded by the cots of the blind and the amputees, Hugo Manning had time to reflect on the nature of war. It was not useless, it did solve certain things. Its lesson was heard where reason was dead, for violence was immediate in its appeal. War provided an outlet for suppressed aggressive and erotic impulses. It could be very attractive, 'a costly and treacherous teacher, a mirror of the monster that man at bottom is'. If Hitler was the perfect specimen of the monster, everybody had helped to make him through laziness, selfishness and fear. 'We were Frankenstein making the monster. We must destroy our "masterpiece" now.'

The casualties on the hospital ship had also been made into monsters. They loved to talk of their wounds, their illnesses, and also of the disloyalty of women. They feared betrayal by the women at home and entered into a state of fantasy and jealousy rather like the mosaic of hysteria and madness in Strindberg's *The Father*. One sergeant with both legs recently amputated and a fractured arm in plaster insisted on going back to England to see his wife and the child of three whom he had never seen, and he did not know if it was his child. Violence infused those who were returning home in the last year of the war, maimed physically and psychologically by their experience and their training to kill. Robot rockets were not the only instruments of Hitler's revenge on England, but also the scarred soldiers who were being returned to the shores of Britain, primed for a domestic explosion.

That explosion happened to Dylan Thomas, who had taken Caitlin and his children to New Quay in Wales, 'a long way from London, as the fly bombs'. An argument developed in the local pub with a Commando captain, back from a brutal year of killing with the partisans behind the lines in Greece. When the bar closed, the captain advanced on Thomas's plywood bungalow and fired eighteen rounds from his sten gun through the walls and the ceilings, because he wanted to put 'the wind up those buggers'. Thomas took the gun from him, but the captain produced a grenade and threatened to blow them all up, so Thomas gave him the gun back. Then the police came and the captain was charged with attempted murder. 'Caitlin, I, and three others being the attempted murderees,' Thomas wrote to Vernon Watkins, '(though that isn't quite right, as we certainly didn't attempt to be murderees) ... It's all very nasty, and I'm as frightened as though I had used the sten gun myself ... Caitlin and I go to bed under the bed.'

At the Assizes, the judges said there was no evidence of attempted murder and the jury found the captain not guilty. It was the same up and down the country.
Particularly among the wounded and the disturbed who had come home, trained to

kill on a reflex action, there were hundreds of assaults and murders in pubs, homes and streets. A pat on the back from an unseen stranger could lead to a whiplash reaction and a broken neck. David Niven, returning from Commando duty, found one of his men accused of such a murder in a bar-room incident. He wrote to the court about the training in instant killing and the exemplary war service of the accused. The man was acquitted. Magistrates and judges all over Britain were recommended to exercise mercy on the sudden uncontrolled violence that spurted from the warriors coming home, behaving as violently as Ulysses had to Penelope's suitors in Ithaca. In India, for the first time, psychiatric camps were set up to reverse the reflexes of the taught killers, to deprogramme their training in murder, to fit them for the peace to come.

Meanwhile, Fitzrovia still beckoned the disturbed and the wounded. Many returned in the last years of the war discharged from wards or military psychiatric hospitals. Julian Symons damaged his arm and was invalided out early in 1944: he spent one riotous evening with George Woodcock and the *Now* group singing 'The Internationale' in a subterranean way on the tube train home. But it was in hospital that he felt the uselessness of his war service, the mutilation of his ideals of the 'thirties that were now amputated. Touching his arm in his corner of the war in the ward, he saw:

> The gap stretched out between our lives and hopes,
> An intellectual generation
> Withered:
>
>   It is for us,
> The future: and yet like a disease
> Evades our diagnosis. If I could give power to
> My burning thoughts! This ink turn acid and the pen
> Become a gun: pointed against the murderers,
> The corrupt class, the scum
> Of a top-heavy civilisation:
> If I could extinguish the voice that says
> *Man can endure corruption and be happy.*

The doyen of Fitzrovia, Julian Maclaren-Ross, had passed through military psychiatric hospital on his way back to his seat at the bar of the Wheatsheaf, where he was to be found every evening from the time of his demobilization to VE Day and the surrender of Germany. His nasal and relentless repertoire of film stories was joined by Nina Hamnett's nightly reminiscences of pre-war Paris, when Modigliani had said she had the best breasts in Europe, and she would haul up her striped jersey to prove it, although the rest of her was disastrous by now. 'Soho-itis,' Alan Ross remembered, 'the Marquis of Granby and the Wheatsheaf, the Fitzroy and the Black Horse, the Burglar's Rest and the Highlander, magic cobbled area after months at sea, where the beer spilled and fists occasionally flew, but where the bearded Paul in his kilt and sporran, dirk and gold earrings, banged   177 on the piano and girls with long hair materialized out of the shadows. There was nowhere else where I ever wanted to be, certain that it was here that life had real meaning, that art and literature and sex and all came magically together among friends, even if no work ever seemed to get done.'

Even those who had fled the flying-bombs to the provinces returned to their old haunts. Dylan Thomas, indeed, came up to be best man at the wedding of Vernon Watkins, but never reached the church on time, lost in his usual alcoholic inefficiency, writing back apologetically on the train to Wales 'in the windy corridor, between many soldiers, all twelve foot high & commando-trained to the last lunge of the bayonet ... Reeking & rocking back from a whirled London where nothing went right, all duties were left, and my name spun rank in the whole smoky nose ...' Drinking, the threat of random violence, sudden death from the air, the company of fellow poets and artists, the tarts and the Lost Girls and Tambimuttu's acolytes, whom he would give to his friends like Alan Ross, barking, 'Take your clothes off immediately, my friend has been at sea and hasn't seen a woman for three months, come on, hurry, hurry' – these were the lures of Fitzrovia in the last year of the war. It was the place for the wounded to be healed nightly, the violent to assuage their anger, the disturbed to feel creative without needing to produce anything very much. In his letter to the deaf David Wright on his sixtieth birthday, the blind John Heath-Stubbs recollected their youth at the end of the conflict in those convalescent homes of the unquiet spirit that were the Wheatsheaf and the Fitzroy Tavern, the Swiss and the French pubs:

> But our friendship really began in Soho,
> Our second university – so many lessons
> To learn and to unlearn – days of the flying bomb,
> The hour of the spiv and the wide boy.
> Passing through those streets was rather like
> The jaunt that Dante took through the Inferno;
> Yet we discerned there an image of the City.
> A certain innocence coinhered with the squalor.
> I doubt if it does so still, even for the young.

THIRTEEN

Terrible Victory

Keith Douglas

'One cannot breathe,' Canetti wrote, 'everything is full of victory.' And a terrible victory it was. Victory in Europe in May 1945 was followed by the revelation of the atrocities in the death camps of Belsen and Buchenwald and Auschwitz and Dachau. The photographs and newsreels of the dead and the dying survivors of the Nazi extermination policy appeared to demonstrate the abiding evil in man, who now applied reason to massacre. In Britain, a Labour victory in the July election offered an opportunity for a social revolution, a blueprint for change, if the scientific planners could be trusted. But what of science and plans for the future of man, if the only way to victory over Japan in August was the obliteration of Hiroshima and Nagasaki by two atomic bombs? The atom, the tiniest thing had won, Canetti noted: a paradox of power. No longer valid was any thought about death. 'With an enormous leap,' man 'has achieved a power of contagion such as never before. Now he is really omnipotent, now he is truly God.'

With the terrible victory, two visitations appeared from the United States, prophesying woe. The first was the eminent critic Edmund Wilson, commissioned to write articles for the *New Yorker*; the second was the unrepentant refugee, Wystan Auden. The American Wilson found London just after the war had the same atmosphere as Moscow before it. He commented particularly on the darkness of the city as though the black-out were still operating, on the fronts of the bombed-out houses in the Tottenham Court Road which were like masks, and on the tepid and stagnant air of Piccadilly where the aimless tidal movement of the soldiers and tarts had clotted. 'The aims of the war accomplished, the tension of the war relaxed, these human amoebas were left to drift about on the back eddy of England. What had the war worked up to? Nothing, vacuity – these unintegrated human organisms with no training in directing themselves.' Elias Canetti agreed. Piccadilly and the tiny side-streets leading to it were full of the chaos of war, the many deserters from a very lofty cause, on leave in an everlasting quest for pleasure.

They only have more truth at night as shadows, outside the pubs; they are like dead men who do not realize they are dead ... They reach for one another, and so I know there are female shadows among them. A few shouts interfere, they feign more life than is their due. Did I once listen only to voices? My uncanny strength lay in chaos; I was as sure of it as of the whole world. Today, chaos itself has exploded. Nothing was structured so senselessly that it could not collapse into something even more senseless; and wherever I sniff, everything is heavy with the stench of extinguished fire.

In front of John Lehmann, Wystan Auden reappeared wearing an American accent with his new American officer's uniform, which was more offensive than Edmund Wilson looking like a drab business executive. Auden had been seconded by the Strategic Bombing Survey to report on the effects of bombing on the civilian population of Germany. Having fled the air raids on London, he returned cockily to assess the Allied raids on the enemy. He declared to Lehmann that the British Empire had been liquidated and was bankrupt: Soviet Russia and the United States of America were the two superpowers. 'There was no word from Uncle Sam

Auden about what we had endured, the various skills, the faith, the unremitting industrial and military effort ... not even a personal word of sympathy to a former friend about the discomforts of flying bombs and flying glass.' Conscious that his skedaddle across the Atlantic had lost him the primacy among younger English poets, Auden said with pleasure that the American Navy had just ordered eleven hundred copies of his *Collected Poems*.

In spite of American dominance of the aimless lassitude after a long war, and of the evidence of the horrors of the concentration camps and nuclear fission, there were three celebrations of three victories that summer, the first over peace in Europe, the second over the Labour Party winning the election, and the last over triumph in the Far East. On VE Day, mobs crowded Piccadilly and the Mall and Whitehall, waiting to see the King and the Queen and Winston Churchill. Bonfires were lit in the parks, making a red glow rather like the blitz, and the Fitzrovians danced through the flames or jumped into the fountains of Trafalgar Square. Every lamp-post had a climber on its top, while the boarded statue of Eros supported a hundred successive mountaineers including the poet Michael Hamburger, drunk after a party given by Tambimuttu in the Gargoyle. Torrents of red wine flowed in the French pub, where the ends of the moustache of the proprietor, Gaston Berlemont, were nearly vertical with excitement. And in little Fitzrovia in Cairo, old literary enemies made temporary friends. One of them clasped the hands of G. S. Fraser and said, 'Tomorrow the knives and the poison. But tonight the truce, the temporary forgiveness, the full glass.'

To Quentin Crisp, nothing was worse than peace breaking out. On the terrible evening of VE Day, he weaved his way through the West End in a prolonged conga chain as if he were doing the lancers with the whole world. 'Death-made-easy vanished overnight and soon love-made-easy, personified by the American soldiers, also disappeared ... Even mere friendship grew scarce. Londoners started to regret their indiscriminate expansiveness.' People forgot when moments of shared danger were past. Crisp was banned from the public houses of Fitzrovia, even from the Wheatsheaf, because the police threatened to raid it as 'a funny kind of place' if Crisp were still served there. 'I, who had once been a landmark more cheerful looking and more bomb-proof than St Paul's Cathedral, had ceased to be a talisman. I had become a loathsome reminder of the unfairness of fate. I was still living while the young, the brave and the beautiful were dead.'

It also seemed that the war was not yet over, and, if it were, that its strange security would be lost with demobilization. To Henry Treece, the London mobs on VE Day and the weak beer were flattening. He agreed with an airman at a Piccadilly bar, who said: 'Wish I'd stayed in Camp. We've got all we want there.' Their new world of regular pay and male camaraderie was about to end, while the war in the Far East might still continue for years. 'If one knew this was the *real* end of the war, one might abandon oneself completely ... But VE Day is only an incident in an already too long war.' By now, as Theodora Fitzgibbon said, the climate of Britain was one of exhausted brutality.

The overwhelming victory of the Labour Party in the July election caused consternation as well as celebration. To the aristocracy, soon to be denounced in Parliament as 'lower than vermin' by arrogant politicians who claimed they were the masters now, the result heralded another French Revolution. As Virginia Graham wrote in 'The Tumbrils':

> So we are for it! There is no hope.
>   Death in a carriage-and-pair stands at the door.
> We should be afraid if we hadn't been so
>   Frightened before.
>
> Nobody likes the sound of tumbrils.
>   Yet we hope to greet ours with aplomb,
> For it cannot possibly make as much noise
>   As a V bomb.

At an election lunch in the Savoy, the waiters were all tipsy and served the various courses out of order with vanilla ice-cream after the fish. 'Oh, delicious, a sorbet!' said Lady Colefax, before plunging a spoon into their mistake. After tasting it, she commented that the working classes now thought it was their time to inherit the earth. Cyril Connolly, however, briefly changed salons and sides and made one of his few gestures towards democracy, hailing the new Labour government as reasonable people, 'people like ourselves who are "we", not "they", and who are unlikely to become over-excited by power or to use the word "intellectual" as an insult, like some of the millionaire hoodlums whom we have just put out'. He completely forgot his pre-election praise of Conservative Members of Parliament for the help given to *Horizon* – 'they swallow our pink pills with stoic grace' – and his denunciation of their opponents – 'Labour's record of assistance to the artist is lamentable. It seems to regard Art as a complicated secret weapon of the rich.' When the votes were cast, Connolly followed the election returns.

In Fitzrovia, the Labour triumph soon brought out the knives and the poison after the truce of victory in Europe. John Heath-Stubbs was in the Wheatsheaf with Julian Maclaren-Ross and Dan Davin, who were drinking to toast the results. He himself had voted for Churchill, because he was frightened of a communist revolution in England after the war. He said that he was not getting drunk to celebrate because he had voted for the Tories. 'He's a young poet,' Maclaren-Ross explained to Davin, 'and he voted Conservative – and that's what the future has in store for us.' Many of the radical artists may have believed that a social revolution was imminent, but they were not in the House of Commons, where the young editor of *English Story* had just been elected. Woodrow Wyatt was puzzled by the sloth of the new government in implementing the welfare state and the Beveridge Report on the grounds that everything had to be done as in the army, in an orderly fashion. 'What is the use of having an orderly revolution,' Wyatt asked, 'if it turns out not to be a revolution at all?'

There was no answer to the question because the orderly revolution would turn out not to be a revolution. That was made certain by the consequences of the third terrible victory that began the atomic age. Britain's bankruptcy and Russian intransigence over the terms of the peace led to the Labour government's inability to finance social change and to the first signals of a Cold War before peace had hardly begun. It seemed that the fall-out from the nuclear explosions had blighted all hopes of post-war Utopia. Progress had its bad side, Canetti noted. 'From time to time, it explodes.' By inventing nuclear fission and allowing politicians to use it as the ultimate weapon, scientists had lost their moral position as the creators of material advancement. C. P. Snow, himself a government official as well as a novelist and a scientist, knew that scientists lost when they became soldiers. Although scientific work on weapons of maximum destruction was not intellectually different from other scientific work, there was a moral price to be paid by the scientist obeying the orders of the state. 'Soldiers have to obey. That is the foundation of their morality. It is not the foundation of the scientific morality. Scientists have to question and if necessary to rebel.'

To many artists after Hiroshima and Nagasaki, scientific socialism and scientific planning seemed to imply the same Frankenstein brain, which had created the V2 rockets as well as the atomic bombs. Indeed, the first weapon would soon be adapted by the Americans to carry the second and be called the missile. Few went as far as Roy Campbell in his devastating epigram about 'The Beveridge Plan':

> Through land and sea supreme
> Without a rift or schism
> Roll on the Wowser's dream –
> Fascidemokshevism.

But fear of science and scientific socialism was to become widespread among many of the artists and the people of Britain in the post-war years, a haunting legacy of the justified fear of the atomic bomb, which seemed to have split apart the very basis of all life in this world. Everyone could now share in the fear of the soldier in the desert, who complained:

> They tell us that the worst we have to fear
> Is fear itself. I know no greater lie.
> I fear not fear. I fear no fear of fear.
> I fear one fearful thing – I fear to die.

Immediately, the dropping of the atomic weapons produced little reaction in England except relief for the final end of the war. Nothing was yet known about the lasting effects of radiation. The celebrations of VJ Day were more ordered and restrained. There were no wild parties or drunken orgies, as when Berlin had fallen. And for the British, the sufferings of their returning prisoners-of-war from the Japanese internment camps made for a bitterness as great as that felt for the victims of the German concentration camps, although the images from Belsen were already broadcast. 'I can't manage to feel much sorrow for the innocent 183 people of Hiroshima and Nagasaki,' Joan Wyndham noted, '– I think the concentration camps took all my tears and I have no more left.' To one of her friends, the total destruction of cities was nothing new. '*Carthago* – or Hiroshima – *delenda est.* What's the difference?' It certainly did not make an artist despair of all life, although it might make him more aware. As John Heath-Stubbs wrote later to George Barker:

> We met on VJ night. Supposedly
> Celebrating victory. The cloud over Hiroshima
> Cast turbid reflections in the beer.
> We have lived in that shadow ever since.

David Gascoyne, indeed, told Stephen Spender that the falling of the atomic bomb had broken down the barriers which enclosed people's minds. Now they lived 'within a situation so overwhelming that they shared a single consciousness'. Spender did not disagree, but he pointed out that the tragedy of the 'thirties was the blindness of the many, while the tragedy of the 'forties was the ineffectiveness of the few.

The feeling of mental and physical exhaustion at the end of the war among British artists was allied to a sense of powerlessness. The monstrous regimentation of the war was only to become worse in the state socialism of the peace. And from that lassitude and impotence, a myth and a justification would grow that would become a truism of art and literary history. The events of the war were too appalling to describe or depict. They were beyond the capacity of the artist, who would never comprehend the agony of the holocaust nor the obliteration by the atom bomb. In his own reaction from his memory of tossing his 'bricks' of fire and annihilating all living things on a Proustian beach and watching the destruction of his fellow rocket-ships off Walcheren, William Golding later wrote a full assertion about the impossibility of bearing witness: 'The experiences of Hamburg and Belsen, Hiroshima and Dachau cannot be imagined. We have gone to war and beggared description all over again. These experiences are like the black holes in space. Nothing can get out to let us know what it was like inside. It was like what it was like and on the other hand it was like nothing else whatsoever. We stand before a gap in history. We have discovered a limit to literature.'

This limit to literature was exceeded by Golding in many of his own novels; their sense of moral evil and human frailty reek of his war record. And although he personally avoided Belsen and Hiroshima, he could not avoid the pictures and descriptions of them. In point of fact, the direct experience of Belsen along with the photographs and newsreels taken by the Americans of the concentration camps changed British painting. The age of nuclear fission decomposed English literature. Mervyn Peake was then writing his two eerie and Gothic illustrated masterpieces, *Titus Groan* and *Gormenghast*, the best of their kind since the works of Thomas Love Peacock. He was sent in 1945 to Belsen to prepare a series of drawings for the *Leader* magazine. He had already foreseen what he would witness in his *chef d'oeuvre*, his drawings for Coleridge's 'The Rime of the Ancient Mariner', which Tambimuttu reproduced in *Poetry London*. Peake's Night-mare Life-in-Death was Belsen incarnate. When he returned from the camp, his wife found he looked inward, 'as if he had lost, during that month in Germany, his confidence in life itself'. His first collected drawings, which Wrey Gardiner published at the Grey Walls Press four years later, depict the effect of the vileness of these sights of the emaciated doomed and the apparatus of mass murder. Peake was sensitive enough to recoil from using the suffering of other people for his art. In a poem, he talked of drawing a young girl as she was dying.

> If seeing her an hour before her last
> Weak cough into all blackness I could yet
> Be held by chalk-white walls, and by the great
> Ash-coloured bed,
> And the pillows hardly creased
> By the tapping of her little cough-jerked head –
> If such can be a painter's ecstasy
> (Her limbs like pipes, her head a china skull)
> Then where is mercy?

Graham Sutherland had the same compunction about drawing the victims of the blitz and had often taken photographs of the destruction rather than sketch the sufferers among the ruins. He directly experienced the horrors of war, when his last assignment as a war artist was to depict the wrecked flying-bomb launching sites north-west of Paris. He found a panoramic devastation, houses reduced to black spokes, and in the caves the fragments of bodies, which he drew, but which were not exhibited by his state employers. He never saw the concentration camps, although he said that in some ways he would have liked to have seen them. 'I remember receiving a black-covered American Central Office of Information book dealing with the camps. It was a kind of funeral book. In it were the most terrible photographs of Belsen, Auschwitz and Buchenwald … The whole idea of the depiction of Christ crucified became more real to me after having seen this book and it seemed to be possible to do this subject again.'

Sutherland thought that the disasters of the time did affect painters, who were a kind of blotting paper, bound to soak up the implications of modern chaos. At the Lefevre Gallery show of April 1945, five of his paintings were hung with Francis Bacon's seminal triptych, his howling Furies that formed *Three Studies of Figures at the Base of a Crucifixion*. Influenced by Bacon's work and the Grünewald altarpiece of the Isenheim Christ that had inspired the Expressionists, and by his own studies of twisted trees and thorns in Wales, Sutherland set about his magnificent *Crucifixion* for St Matthew's Church in Northampton. His agonized Christ was pierced with thorns of light and caged with bars and arcs of wire. To Sutherland, the thorns were the cruelty, while the tortured body of the Saviour was derived from Grünewald and the Belsen dead who looked 'like figures deposed from

185

EDITED   BY   TAMBIMUTTU

Poetry LONDON X

MERVYN PEAKE

Drawings for

The Ancient Mariner

Her lips were red, her looks were free
Her locks were yellow as gold
Her skin was as white as leprosy,
The Night-mare Life-in-Death was she,
Who thicks man's blood with cold.

186

crosses ... the continuing beastliness and cruelty of mankind, amounting at times to madness, seem eternal and classic'.

Sutherland had long been an admirer of Bacon's work, even of his early *Crucifixion* of 1933; the reproduction of it in Herbert Read's important *Art Now* was dirty from much thumbing in Sutherland's copy of the book. Bacon had hardly painted again before the last year of the war, although he was living in Millais's old studio in 7 Cornwall Place, South Kensington, with his ancient nanny as his housekeeper and hat-check girl for the illegal gambling parties which he threw to bring in some money by hazard. He began painting again in the old billiards room, because a bomb blew off the studio roof. Sutherland brought in Kenneth Clark from the National Gallery to see Bacon's work, but Clark would not buy a picture, merely commenting on the apparent chaos of Bacon's way of life, 'What extraordinary times we live in.' Films and photographs were always a major influence on Bacon's style, from the wrestling male nudes in Eadweard Muybridge's *The Human Figure in Motion*, through the black hole of the mouth of the screaming bloodied nurse in Eisenstein's *Battleship Potemkin* and the donkey carcasses of Buñuel's *Un Chien Andalou*, to photographs of Hitler and the Belsen newsreels, which he saw at the Rialto Cinema by the bombed Café de Paris. Unlike the ordered and accurate Sutherland, the anarchic Bacon would never admit to his direct influences, claiming sometimes to work while drunk and at other times saying that chance made him paint as he did. In a discussion with this author, he admitted to the direct influence of the Belsen newsreels, but only through 'an intense, active unconsciousness. I see the violence of existence. We must recall it.' Technique was all to him. He did not draw, but painted direct on to the coarse side of the canvas. As it happens, he did do a series of concentration camp pictures, which were owned by Keith Lichtenstein, once the proprietor of the Gigolo café in Chelsea. They directly showed the horror of the holocaust, but they do not appear in the present catalogue of Bacon's paintings, so many of which he has destroyed himself, including the picture owned by Peter Watson, on the pretext of completing it. The gaping mouths of his figures in torment, the white streaks that enclose them like torture cages, the distorted bodies swollen by death or greed, these did derive as did the drawings of Goya from images of human bestiality in blurred photographs from the war. As a trenchant critic wrote, Bacon discovered 'in the art of painting the felicities of the death warrant [and] covered the lamp-shades of his immediate predecessors with human skins'.

Bacon denied that his violence in painting had anything to do with the violence of fighting. He had been accustomed to living through forms of violence which had offended him – the military violence of his Irish boyhood and brutal early affairs with the grooms in his father's stables, the emotional violence of his life in Weimar Berlin and Paris in the 'thirties and wartime London. Yet he looked beyond the violence of war 'to remake the violence of reality itself ... the brutality of fact'. Although contemporary pictures of pain and wounds influenced his images, he wanted to create a universal statement about the suffering of man. His human 187 corpses, his figures of Christ hung like mutton in a butcher's shop, show a belief in the absolute mortality of man without hope of redemption. 'Of course, we are meat, we are potential carcasses.'

Although the crucifixions of Bacon and Sutherland were signals of the true horror of their time, they were attacked in important articles by Geoffrey Grigson. He had already seen in Sutherland's blasted and fiery landscape illustrations for David Gascoyne's poems, published by Tambimuttu, a brooding over personal death and universal decay, not a Blakeian sense of the Pilgrim stretching out his arms against the skeleton path of despair. While Henry Moore's *Madonna and Child* in the church at Northampton affirmed tenderness and humanity, the statue faced 'the twists and cruelty of Sutherland's little-headed, crucified Christ, a Christ who suggests no resurrection'. Sutherland represented a Catholic pessimism, a personal obsession with the violence of mankind and the organic decay of nature. He had a lust for death. 'No resurrection: and an evil time. No doubt it is an evil time.'

That remaking of the reality of violence, that depiction of the brutality of the terrible end to the war, led to contemporary praise of Sutherland and the later beatification of Bacon by most of the art world. Neither of them, however, joined Leslie Hurry in direct political art based on the atomic explosions at Hiroshima and Nagasaki. Hurry used William Blake's coloured clouds and swirling lines of energy as a background to writhing, imploring bodies. His art for the atomic age was to culminate in his backdrop for Bridget Boland's play, *Atomic Bomb*, one of the last productions which ENSA sent out to inform the armies before their demobilization. Afterwards, Hurry's pacifism joined with John Minton's, and they were to find themselves with Picasso at the anti-nuclear peace conferences called by the left wing after the beginning of the Cold War against Russia.

Edith Sitwell, who had been transformed in her own mind by the war from a voice of the cultural élite to the prophetess of the people, saw the atomic age as the occasion for her most important utterances. She would speak out against the imminent dissolution of mankind. Her distinguished and enduring trio of poems, 'Dirge for the New Sunrise', 'The Shadow of Cain' and 'The Canticle of the Rose', turned total destruction into the fire of resurrection. She saw herself as hanging between Christ and the gap where the world was lost.

> And watch the phantom Sun in Famine Street
> – The ghost of the heart of Man ... red Cain
> And the more murderous brain
> Of Man, still redder Nero that conceived the death
> Of his mother Earth, and tore
> Her womb, to know the place where he was conceived ...

Yet the atomic bombs were poor forerunners of Judgement Day. Christ had not died in vain. 'He walks again on the Seas of Blood, He comes in the terrible Rain.' The mushroom cloud was nothing to the ultimate Fire of Christ, which would burn away the cold in the heart of Man. The Saviour was the terminal and redeeming light, even of nuclear fission.

To Alan Ross, the poems contained in Edith Sitwell's *The Canticle of the Rose* stood with Eliot's *Four Quartets* as the most ambitious and important poetry of the 'forties. The war had integrated her humanity, tenderness and pity with great public events. She had become involved for the first time in the affairs of her age. Her poems were commentaries 'on contemporary themes of universal significance; on war, particularly atomic war; on death, birth, love and old age; on the passing of human beauty and decay'. She could comprehend nuclear fission in terms of its significance to mankind. She answered Robert Conquest's call for someone else to do what he could not do, write *the* poem of war.

> ... For I must believe
> That somewhere the poet is working who can handle
> The flung world and his own heart. To him I say
> The little I can. I offer him the debris
> Of five years undirected storm in self and Europe,
> And my love. Let him take it for what it's worth
> In this poem scarcely made and already forgotten.

Isolated in her strange way of life with her brothers, who despaired elegantly of post-war Britain and the atomic future, Edith Sitwell with her religious vision did not join in the gloom of the Fitzrovian editors and writers. Although Wrey Gardiner in *Poetry Quarterly* saw hope of literary fraternization between the peoples of the world because only the Americans had the atom bomb and could impose universal peace, he wrung his hands at the recrudescence of rival literary gangs fighting again in London, 'the same sordid picture of ignorance, corruption, and collusion'. George Orwell found that the brief dominance of the crowd grouped round *New Road*, *Now* and *Poetry London* gave him 'the impression of fleas hopping among the ruins of a civilization'. As he was about to publish his own devastating assault on socialist scientific planning, *Animal Farm*, his pessimism about the present and the future was salutary. The past was also being dismissed, with Cyril Connolly saying that many war poets did not try; they were like boys playing about on a billiard table who wondered what the cues and pockets were for. And Robert Herring dismissed contemporary poetry altogether: war was only an agent of waste, a loss of energy: it stimulated nothing, only the whole of life did. It had destroyed all creativity, which was fleeing London to the regions. To him, poetry was returning to Wales and Scotland in order to revive. Constantine Fitzgibbon agreed, describing the atmosphere among the demobilized and the Fitzrovians in 1945 'as one of exhaustion shot through with violence and hatred. We read about the concentration camps, and we wondered which pub would have beer tonight. We were horrified by Hiroshima, which seemed to make it all meaningless, and we wanted out.'

Those who were already out were those who were occupying Germany, although some sybarites like James Pope-Hennessy avoided going to Frankfurt by meeting a dream brigadier who told him, 'After all, there's a war off now.' Those who wanted to get out were those who joined in the Gadarene rush of the piggish men of 189 letters to their beloved France after its liberation. John Lehmann, despite help from the Publishers' Association and the British Council, found himself out-distanced on the run to Paris by Cyril Connolly and Raymond Mortimer and 'other literary lights of the London wartime firmament'. Connolly, who always con-demned in *Horizon* the artistic achievement of the English compared with the French, spent three of the happiest weeks of his life staying with the Duff Coopers at the British Embassy in Paris on the far side of the Channel, no longer a barrier after five years. Trying to justify his happiness in that ravaged land, he made his most unfortunate comparison, writing that it might be equally unfeeling for a visitor to Belsen or to Dachau to experience elation. Certainly, he did print in the same number of *Horizon* Alan Moorehead's personal description of a visit to Belsen, where he felt revulsion and perceived that the most terrible thing on earth was not positive destruction or the perverse desire to hurt. It was the indifference of the Nazi killers. 'Only the mental danger remains. The danger of indifference.'

That indifference was never to be allowed to grow because of the witness borne by the survivors of the holocaust, many of whom were trying to make their way to Palestine, from where the British administration was attempting to turn them away. As one Jew wrote in the *New English Review*, he had lost all his family in crowded cattle trucks, before reaching by curious ways his promised land of Israel in the making:

> Where all is for the Young who would retrieve
> By work and sacrifice some of God's grace.
> But I grew old in pain, and I believe
> We are but helpless children of our past
> And that our lives and children's lives are cast
> For ever in the anguish of our race.

Testimony of the holocaust continued to be given until it was to become a perpetual dirge on the evils done by mankind to man, a warning that they must never be done again. Particularly in the United States, where the largest surviving Jewish community lived, and especially among the American poets who had now left England for Germany and saw the camps, the nightmare of their experience made them the witnesses for the prosecution. The poems of Howard Nemerov and Randell Jarrell no more shirked the atrocities of their age than those of Edith Sitwell. As Jarrell wrote of 'A Camp in the Prussian Forest', where he laughed at the futility of his gesture of remembrance:

>   ...One year
> They sent a million here:
>
> Here men were drunk like water, burnt like wood.
> The fat of good
> And evil, the breast's star of hope
> Were rendered into soap.

I paint the star I sawed from yellow pine –
And plant the sign
In soil that does not yet refuse
Its usual Jews

Their first asylum ... I laugh aloud
Again and again;
The star laughs from its rotting shroud
Of flesh. O star of men!

If some poetry and paintings could comprehend the horrors of the war, the images of Belsen and Buchenwald and of the radiation victims of Hiroshima and Nagasaki corroded the realism of the war pictures of the renascent British cinema. Any documentary of the blitz, any newsreel of battlefield and victory, any celebration of courage and endurance as in *The Way to the Stars*, could not but seem a gloss on the inhumanity and bestiality of human behaviour, where both Axis and Allied powers had chosen to use the ultimate weapons of extermination, evolved by reason without compassion and invention without control. No national cinema dared to confront the scenes of concentration camp and fall-out victims until a decade had passed in impossible forgetfulness. Then, in France, Alain Resnais with *Nuit et Brouillard* and *Hiroshima, Mon Amour* began to prove that the cinema could also be a sufficient testament to the terminal horror and the ultimate suffering. The final solution of the Nazis could never be final as long as witnesses found the creative strength in the arts to provoke mankind from its indifference.

In Oxford Street, which split Fitzrovia in half, Belsen was made into waxworks. For sixpence, the crowds could see an exhibition which showed in still detail 'All the Horrors of the Concentration Camp'. It was the British tradition to reduce the gruesome and the intolerable into wax effigies in order to attract a paying audience, to shock, to thrill, to titillate, and incidentally to inform. Outside the newsreels and photographs of 1945, the waxworks were the only immediate attempt to keep the concentration camps in the public consciousness. Otherwise, the reaction from the war began in the first weeks of the peace, a wish for oblivion, a denial of the past as soon as possible, a search for whatever pleasure and laughter could still be found in a society in which even bread was soon to be rationed for the first time. The people looked for their cake in entertainment. The British cinema would soon be known not for its war epics, but for its escapist comedies. The playwrights would turn from realism to the verse drama; even T. S. Eliot was to take again to the stage in *The Cocktail Party*. And in spite of the effective bankruptcy of Britain when Lend-Lease ended (for nearly half of the nation's essential imports now came from North America), the opera and the ballet were expected with help from the state to revive their engaging fantasies of song and movement. John Maynard Keynes, who was restructuring American financial aid in peacetime for the Labour government, was also Chairman of the Council for the Encouragement of Music and the Arts; he persuaded the 191

Treasury to continue to fund it under the name of the Arts Council of Great Britain. 'I do not believe it is yet realized what an important thing has happened,' he said in a broadcast in 1945. 'State patronage of the Arts has crept in.'

It was the curious last legacy of Bloomsbury. For Keynes was always the economic guru of Bloomsbury, which bequeathed the principle of government patronage to the arts although its own ethic had been so individual, free and hedonistic. Yet state aid was the best hope for the arts after the terrible victories by the fearsome engines of destruction in Europe and in Asia – also in England, where the victory of the Labour Party could not save the nation from the realities of the atomic age and the Cold War to come. 'A Warning to Politicians', Patric Dickinson's poem on the end of the war, met blind eyes and deaf ears in Westminster:

> The bells proclaim the immediate joy,
> The horror and the killing cease;
> They drag within the walls of Troy
> The wooden horse of Peace.

FOURTEEN

Breaking from the Cage

For civilian and serviceman alike, the war had been confinement and displacement, which did not terminate with the slow demobilization. Some were confined from the beginning until their end. In his fierce ballad, 'Sixty Cubic Feet', Randall Swingler told of the prison life of a working man.

> He was the fourth his mother bore
>   The room was ten by twelve
> His share was sixty cubic feet
>   In which to build himself.
>
> He sat and learned his letters
>   With forty in a room
> And sixty cubic feet of draught
>   The Council lent to him.
>
> At fourteen he must earn a wage
>   He went to pit from school
> In sixty feet of dust and gas
>   He lay and hacked the coal ....

Called up into the army, the young miner slept with seven others in a rainy tent:

> He lay and coughed his heart out
>   In sixty feet of damp
> At last when he could hardly stand
>   They marched him out of camp.
>
> They brought him from the hospital
>   They brought him home alone
> In sixty cubic feet of deal
>   That he could call his own.

In army huts and bivouacs and barracks, in troop trains and ships, in armour and fuselages and under the sea, in trenches and turrets and gun emplacements, men were penned, forced into close company, bored and sometimes afraid. 'There are too many men,' Bruce Bain wrote from his troopship. 'There is no privacy. You cannot be alone for a minute.' Lavatories lacked doors, elbows bumped when using a knife and fork at crowded mess tables, there was no space at the ship's rail even to stare out at the monotones of the sea. The soldiers were already accustomed to the same 'lonely world of greys and greens, Nissen huts and hangars'. Crouching and ducking between a web of hammocks in an iron tomb below decks, each had to find a place in the hanging rows of cords in the thick sweaty heat. Sailors' Homes were even more cramped, as Roy Fuller found, in their solitary confinements.

> A honeycomb of cabins, boxes, cells,
> To which each man retires alone.
> A snatch of singing, like a groan,
> Broken off quickly. Sour, damp smells.

Previous page: Tom Purvis

The machines of war were the ultimate constriction. The whine of the gears, Thomas Skelton noted inside his Armoured Fighting Vehicle, penetrated his ears inside his headphones. Metal plate shut off the desert silence. The noise rolled inside not out.

> Heat shuts up with engine fumes
> And noises sewed up in steel.
> Man in a visor behind his subterfuge
> Facing other iron casings ....
> 'Ahead is target', 'Guns Fire'.
> Inside hot shell cases scald my back,
> Acrid smoke plucks nose and throat.
> What safe hell hole is this, commander?

There was claustrophobia even in a gunpit open to the sky. When the barrage opened at El Alamein, the ground shook over Jack Partridge 'like hundreds of pneumatic-drills breaking up Piccadilly Circus while you lay, with Eros above you, in the middle'. The usual alternative for those who felt enclosed was – did they prefer the shelling or the bombing? Louis Challoner forgot that the airman above had his own imprisonment in his cockpit, because a flying machine appeared as a bird of prey in the sky.

> I'd rather look death in the face
> Borne by a bomber's speed and grace –
> Swinging down its rainbow arc
> Like a falcon to its mark –
> Than grovel like a nerveless slave
> With nothing but his skin to save,
> Crouching beneath the ugly Hell
> Made by the calculated shell.

Some like Robert Joly of the Grenadier Guards were buried alive in the war, the fate of many civilians in the blitz. He felt that he was another Lazarus risen again. 'You have been, Lazarus, of all men the one who the end of things has seen – is death's coming so terrible then?' On his way to his own death in the last months of the war in Europe, Joly found himself in the further confinement of a hospital, which seemed to cramp his very contemplation, 'cabin in meaningless bounds what every day torments me with its restless determination to be expressed'. Yet the worst confinement of all imposed by the conditions of the conflict was psychological, a concentration of feeling upon the tight circle of fellow soldiers, who would keep a mate alive. Victor West hated the indifference which made him treat all his past friends with cold, impersonal disinterest. War had made inevitable a false, local loyalty only to the necessary group tied to him. He grew armoured against loss. The survival of his own miserable hide inhibited any feeling except for the joy of survival.

195

We eye what's pitifully left of 'A' Coy.
Shrug. Crowd round the steaming brew.
Only the Section counts.

The many incarcerations of the war, psychological and physical, were tolerable because there was a purpose, the defeat of the enemy. But that victory involved the possibility of death. The paradox was that the most deleterious cage, a prisoner-of-war camp, meant a curious kind of safety from bullet or explosive. John Jarmain, one of the better poets to die in the war, watched Italian prisoners reach their dull security:

They file away, these who have done their last,
To that grey safety where the days are sealed,
Where no word enters, and the urgent past
Is relieved day by day against the clock
Whose hours are meaningless ...
They are herded now and have no more to give.
Even fear is past. And death, so long so near,
Has suddenly receded to its station
In the misty end of life. For these will live,
They are quit of killing and sudden mutilation;
They no longer cower at the sound of a shell in the air,
They are safe ...

It was a safety rather like the Nissen hut or the barrack room. Captain Robin Campbell lost a leg in a commando raid on Rommel's headquarters and was captured. He found the worst ordeal the total loss of solitude, sharing a room about twenty feet square with fifteen other prisoners and sleeping in a double-decker bunk. In order to survive, he adapted the same carapace as Victor West, who himself spent years as a prisoner-of-war – 'a kind of reptilian insensitiveness – like crocodiles in their tank at the zoo, which walk over each other without either appearing to notice the other'. There was, however, the curious complacency of the prison camp. The anxieties and responsibilities of ordinary life were left on the other side of the barbed wire perimeter. There was no money, so a prisoner lost the habit of possessiveness. Clothes and food were free, although rationed. The only problem was a dreadful staleness, and sometimes a form of starvation. As Robert Garioch noted in his Lallans poem, 'The Presoner's Dream', the captive's friends were sleep and time, but their enemy was hunger.

Thaim that hauf-stairve their presoners
are no exactly murderers;
    whan the taen sodger dees
they scrieve wi sooth in registers
    some orthodox disease.
They arenae monie sophisters
    wad prieve sic truths are lees.

The many forms of confinement of the serviceman caused him psychological problems, when demobilization released him from his enclosures – unless he was returning to the same lack of privacy and cheek-by-jowl living spaces. Yet the civilians at home had also suffered crowding and boxing-in. Their herding into the mass shelters or the underground stations or the cellars of houses or private Anderson shelters during bombing raids engendered a fear and a neurosis similar to those trapped in sunken submarines or flaming aircraft or tanks. Small subterranean areas produced panic and claustrophobia during bombardments. Many people were entombed alive like the unfortunates in the stories of Edgar Allen Poe. This fear of being buried while breathing led to the mass evacuations of London, when all joined in the general displacement and tearing up of roots that was the common fate of children, women and men during the war.

The word 'evacuate' was normally applied to troop or bowel movements, but during the war it was used for children sent out of cities. Mel Calman the cartoonist, never recovered from his evacuation and spoke for all his contemporaries:

I have this image of a small boy with a label tied round his neck.
The boy has no features and is crying.
He is carrying a cardboard box, which contains his gasmask.

I remember that labels with our names on were pinned to our clothes before we left London. I think I felt that I had no identity and was a parcel being posted to the country. The labels frightened me as much as the idea of leaving my parents. A child of seven, if lost, can tell people his name. A label assumes that he does not know his name, or worse, has no name and is given one at random from a list of names.

Perhaps the gasmask felt like a second face, a mask that would replace my own face as soon as I left London. I remember that the gasmask looked inhuman with its celluloid eyeshield and metal snout. I remember that it smelt of rubber and that I could not breathe properly inside it. The shield misted over with condensation and it felt warm and suffocating inside this second face ...

Even nowadays whenever I travel anywhere and have to say goodbye to my own children, I identify with that small boy. I remember the label and the gasmask and feel anxiety gripping my bowels. I write my name on the luggage labels and hope I do not return to find my home bombed to ruins and my identity lost somewhere underneath the rubble.

Soldiers also wore their identity discs round their necks, and if these were lost or blown off their bodies, they lost their names among the unknown dead. They wore gas masks, too, and flying-helmets and tin hats and visors and goggles and frogmen masks. Their bowels went sloppy before attacks and under bombardments. They were shunted about more than their evacuee children, whom they hardly knew for the five years of the fighting, and they returned home perhaps to a house in ruins, but certainly to strangers named as their family. Both in displacement and confinement, the men at war shared much with the women and the children. And the effects of the moving and the caging were to take years of working out after the war in shifting and restlessness, broken marriages and broken hopes of peace at home.

Fitzrovia continued to attract the displaced because it had always been kaleidoscopic and rootless and unconfined. The deserters were drawn there as well as those of the demobilized who craved to be free. Vernon Scannell served with the Gordon Highlanders in the desert and Normandy, until he was wounded. Demobilization took too long for him, and he deserted with the ambition of becoming a poet and writer. The Fitzroy Tavern and the Wheatsheaf lured him with the promise of meeting some of the famous artists of the time; with their thirty-foot bars along the side of a narrow crowded space, they were curiously similar to the squash in an army mess hut; but Scannell was too poor and lonely to buy the notorious regulars a drink or force his ignorance on them. 'Mine was a young man's loneliness,' he wrote, 'expectant, temporary, holding within it a vague promise of dissipation, of a marvellous encounter which would open the way into new and exciting territories.' That encounter never came, but the frequent raids of police in Black Marias looking for deserters in the pubs and cafés of Fitzrovia drove Scannell off to Leeds, where he was eventually arrested and put back in the army. Two years after the war ended, there were still twenty thousand deserters on the run, who could not tolerate the disciplines of military service or the engagements of civilian life. The war left them permanently displaced. As John Manifold wrote of 'The Deserter':

> Born with all arms he sought a separate peace.
> Responsibilities loomed up like tanks,
> And since his manhood marked him of our ranks
> He threw it off and scrambled for release ...
>
> Strong in his impotence he can safely view
> The battlefield of men, and shake his head
> And say, 'I know. But then what can I do?'

Most members of the armed services did wait for the process of formal demobilization. They had to pass through government clothing stores called dispersal centres. There they were given a large cardboard box with a striped or tweed 'demob suit', a shirt with two collars and a pair of cuff-links, a tie and a hat, two pairs of socks and one pair of shoes. Christopher Hassall caught the feeling of wry relief on demobilization in his poem about the choice of a hat in the days when a man felt naked if his scalp was uncovered in the street.

> Arriving at a counter heaped with hats,
> 'Here comes another head,' thought I. 'So shrinks
> Their number as more heads approach, and we
> Don our old differences, hat by hat ...'

The new civilians were given eight weeks of resettlement leave and directed to resettlement offices, which would advise them how to get a job. The government had passed an act requiring every employer to give back to a demobilized serviceman the post he had held before the war. But companies had been bombed or gone out of business, while those who had risen in the armed forces from private to commander could not return to a post as a clerk, taking orders from those who had sat out the war safely behind their desks. In his novel *Back*, Henry Green described the difficulty of a repatriated prisoner-of-war in accepting the authority of those promoted during his enforced absence, while they accused the returned soldiers of coming back 'nervous cases' as they had from the First World War. No one was normal at the end of a struggle that had gone on for so long.

As well as those released from the armed services, another eight and a half million men and women had to be set free from their work in the war factories, which had to convert themselves to production for peace and exports, requiring five million workers to man them again. This vast displacement and re-engagement made the streets and pubs of London look like mass waiting-rooms for travellers without destinations. The metropolis was a limbo in the doldrums, where the transients met each other for the brief sanctuary of sharing in old times. For one of the displaced, 'the immediate postwar Bohemia crystallized the fragmentation of the decade. There were no coherent groups, no public image. They had met in Soho, Alex., Egypt, India – and they confused meeting with achievement. It was the false security of the herd.'

One young demobilized officer, D. Van Den Bogaerde, had written a poem, 'Steel Cathedrals':

> It seems to me, I spend my life in stations.
> Going, coming, standing, waiting.
> Paddington, Darlington, Shrewsbury, York.
> I know them all most bitterly.
> Dawn stations, with a steel light, and waxen figures.
> Dust, stone, and clanking sounds, hiss of weary steam.
> Night stations, shaded light, fading pools of colour.
> Shadows and the shuffling of a million feet.
> Khaki, blue, and bulky kitbags, rifles gleaming dull.
> Metal sound of army boots, and smoker's coughs.   .
> Titter of harlots in their silver foxes.
> Cases, casks, and coffins, clanging of the trolleys.
> Tea urns tarnished, and the greasy white of cups.
> Dry buns, Woodbines, Picture Post and Penguins;
> and the blaze of magazines ...

Now in his demob suit, he took the train to London, wanting to become an actor. 'How do you,' he asked himself, 'at twenty-six, green as a frog, join the team with all the years since nineteen missing?' The civilians on the train patronized him in their guilt at failing to fight overseas; they stressed what a bloody awful war they had suffered on the Home Front, where they had been under siege. With sights of Belsen still fresh in his memory, Van Den Bogaerde tried to contact other actor friends such as Peter Ustinov, but none of them could help him secure a job. It was very hard. Those who had avoided military service were hanging on to their roles like grim death, while thousands of people who had discovered a talent at army concert parties were now trying to get on stage. Finally Van Den Bogaerde was recommended to try the Actors' Reunion Theatre, where an ex-Buffs officer, Allan Davis, was casting for a religious children's playlet, only to be shown to theatrical agents and casting directors. Davis took one look at Van Den Bogaerde and gave him the part of Jesus. Davis knew the plight of the actors returning to the theatre after five years' military service and trying to displace those 'with golden ulcers who did not fight'. The young Jesus was noticed and took the advice which his director gave him in the Salisbury, the actors' pub in Fitzrovia. 'You have great quality,' Davis said, 'but you must be careful and not let anything go to your head.' Under the stage name of Dirk Bogarde, he rose to the head of his profession.

Few of those released from military or factory war work had the success of Bogarde in achieving what he wanted. To most of them, demobilization was demoralization. They left the cocoon of a world run by orders with set standards and without domestic responsibility. For many, as Alan Ross noted, the end of the

Osbert Lancaster

war marked the beginning of their decline. Although they were to deny it, their war experience had been an emotional height. 'In their bones they knew that they would never feel quite so much, or ask and get so much from life, ever again.' The society to which they returned before the new welfare state was instituted was 'a thin image on a colourless slide'. Many were so wearied by the long struggle that they did not wish to compete for the jobs already filled by the non-combatants. 'Anything for a quiet life after all the hurly-burly,' one demobilized officer noted in his *Portrait of a Decade*, 'and if there happened to be a glass close to their elbows – well, so much the better ... personal and family relationships forged during, and even before, the war came under unfamiliar stresses once the conflict was over.'

So the armed forces returned from the various cages and imprisonments of their services to the smaller cages and engagements of their domestic life. Housing was in desperate straits after the devastation of the bombing and the lack of main- tenance of the war years. Military architecture, indeed, became civilian space. Bryher recognized that England and most of the world needed rehousing, but the prefabricated house, which was the government's solution, was only a glorified Nissen hut. The soldiers seemed to be returning to their habitual living area, although 'families want warmth and comfort after their work rather than genteel Nissen'. And many a tent and campfire was preferable to the derelict and blasted rooms and flats, which were all that were available to the unattached and the displaced.

Different prospects of the peace were based on the facts of fighting the war. The socialist victory in the election of 1945 encouraged those who had found true comradeship in the closeness of the ranks. Henry Treece wrote to G. S. Fraser in 1945 about how his faith in his fellow men had increased since he had joined up. Five years of experience had shown up an incontrovertible truth that politicians could not discount. 'All round me I see a rough kindness and co-operation, every one of us united to win a war, to get a square deal for each other and ourselves. And in every case, this kindness and co-operation is not, cannot be, imposed from above.' It was that democratic co-operative spirit which would make a square deal in the peace. Roy Fuller put the same point more theoretically. He had joined the proletariat by serving on the lower deck in the Navy. It confirmed in him the belief that there had to be a social revolution, 'not least for the middle-class intellectual. It extricated me from the great problem of the 'thirties – how to live and write for a class to which one didn't belong.' Even though Fuller's belief in the necessity of a social revolution faded when he was given a commission, the large socialist majority in the House of Commons led by middle-class intellectuals did promise that a sort of revolution might still be achieved, which would end the class and caste system of pre-war Britain, so broken down by wearing a common uniform.

The problem was that the long service of the war had also broken down the strength of those who should have helped to make the social revolution. Not only among the Fitzrovians did meeting and talking and drinking take the place of achievement. When the demobilized came back, they did not feel it was their task 201 to build a New Jerusalem in England's green and pleasant land. In a remarkable confession in his *Poems of an Ordinary Seaman*, David Kendall wrote:

> After these years of war we cannot think
> easily of the inevitable days
> the grey drab houses scowling in the smoke:
> we lack the courage to begin again
>
> to make our new land, vision out our dreams
> our fingers bleeding, building up the walls;
> unhampered by the old world's decadent form
> the shining towers rise into the sky ...
>
> no, the risk is too great; the sacrifice
> too much a burden on these weary years
> flung against weapons and the dead dull toil –
> return, and level out our lives ...
>   Our minds are full
> of war: let us erase the slate.
>
> We have a right to live, enjoy our age,
> sink back, for once, upon the cushions, make
> our own particular castles, leave the rest
> work for the future – we have had enough.

FIFTEEN

And We Shall Build
Jerusalem

Lynton Lamb

Will it be so again –
The jungle code and the hypocrite gesture?
A poppy wreath for the slain
And a cut-throat world for the living? that stale imposture
Played on us once again?

Cecil Day Lewis pointed out that the glorious dead would not stop the old usurpers reaping what they could not sow.

The living alone can nail to their promise the ones who said
It shall not be so again.

The vote of the forces, particularly the army, had given the Labour Party its mammoth victory. Overwhelmingly, those in uniform had filled in a ballot for a socialist Britain after the war. It was Labour pressure in the Coalition government under Winston Churchill which had forced the Reconstruction Committees of the Cabinet to approve three White Papers based on the Beveridge Report and to call for a national health service, social insurance and family allowances, and a policy for full employment. The Conservative R. A. Butler had put into law an exemplary Education Act, while Labour's Hugh Dalton had seen to a Location of Industry Act. What was to be called the 'Welfare State' was the price that the trade unions and socialist politicians had demanded in return for allowing the direction of manpower during the war. Now the social debt had to be paid to the quick for the sake of the dead.

Economic facts contradicted the hopes of building a New Jerusalem at once. John Maynard Keynes had warned the government that it was badly in debt and overstretched because of the 'gay and successful fashion' of slopping out money to anyone who asked. Britain was overplaying its hand as a great power. A financial Dunkirk loomed unless the armies were quickly demobilized, the policing of the empire was reduced, exports rose and the United States continued to loan billions of dollars to pay for reconstruction. Keynes did secure an American loan to replace Lend-Lease, although it was denounced by a Conservative Member of Parliament as selling the British Empire for a packet of cigarettes. Churchill's speech in Fulton, Missouri, speaking of the Iron Curtain that had descended because of the Russian occupation of Eastern Europe reminded the United States of the value of the British alliance. Although Keynes himself was soon to die and Britain was to be plunged into a series of crises in 1947, the wise and generous provision of further aid under the Marshall Plan meant that the United States would again come to the rescue of Britain in finance as well as in combat.

The demobilization of Britain's armies was accelerated to the pace of a galloping tortoise. By the summer of 1946, three million military personnel were released, still leaving two and a half million serving men. There were mutinies, particularly in Malaya, where a Parachute battalion refused to obey orders, but eventually the army was slowly cut to size, although the Labour government did not give up conscription and replaced it with the unpopular compulsory National Service in order to police an empire that became unnecessary, when India was granted its bloody independence and Pakistan split away. The Labour Party believed too much in bureaucracy and planning to apply radical surgery to end the imperialism which it abhorred. It still felt responsible for its subjects in Africa, Asia and the Caribbean, who would rather have had an inefficient independence immediately than a planned transition later.

Control of the economy had become a shibboleth during the war, and some conditions even became worse. For the first time, bread was rationed for two full years; it was probably the single greatest psychological mistake of the government in proving that it was competent in office. Its performance on the housing front was little better. More than a million new homes were needed to replace those which had been bombed, while another three million houses were dilapidated and over eighty years old. Forty thousand people were put into disused army camps, while others went into the one hundred and fifty thousand 'prefabs' built to last for ten years and still in use thirty years later. A spontaneous public protest began, 'squatting' in unoccupied houses as once East Enders had squatted briefly in the shelters of the Savoy. It was in answer to Aneurin Bevan's protest about the inadequate wartime scheme for an immediate attack on peacetime housing, 'Not much of a blitzkrieg, is it?' Yet when Bevan became Minister of Housing and Planning himself, he could not fulfil the needs or the hopes of the people.

The real blitzkrieg had created something of a *tabula rasa* for the New Jerusalem. Vast districts of London, Bayswater and Kensington in particular, had been created for destruction, in Cyril Connolly's opinion. 'Behind the stucco porches and the lace curtains the half-life of decaying Victorian families guttered like marsh-gas. One has no pity for the fate of such houses, and no pity for the spectacular cinemas and fun-palaces of Leicester Square, whose architecture was a standing appeal to heaven to rain down vengeance on them.' In the City of London and in the docklands of the East End, the greatest opportunity for reconstruction had been created since the Great Fire of London in the reign of King Charles the Second. The City was to be rebuilt by its speculators without reason, without care, without spirit, without soul, and with parsimony. The docklands and those who lived within the ruins were to be ignored by Labour and Conservative governments for two generations, even though Limehouse was Prime Minister Clement Attlee's own constituency. Housing policy after the Second World War eventually made true what was suspected during the blitz, that in giving shelter to the threatened and the homeless, there was one policy for the rich and another for the poor. Geography formed an underclass and an overclass in London, one in the East End, the other in the West. Stephen Spender was correct to suspect those who were grateful to German slum clearance, because the dreamers of planned cities did not make them rise above the bomb-damaged ruins.

Yet the impoverished Labour government did create the 'Welfare State' and set the pattern of British social policy for the next forty years. Curiously enough, the 205 term 'Welfare State' at first had a pejorative use; it was taken to mean a society in which people depended on the government for nearly everything from cradle to dole to grave. It implied an intrusive and dictatorial state and the end of private initiative and freedom. It was not so. The measures taken by the Labour government to carry out the plans of the Beveridge Report were admirable in creating a more just and equitable society in Britain with fairer shares for all. But the methods by which the Welfare State was created with repressive controls and prying officials called 'snoopers' damned good intentions by pettifogging means. Most people were not prepared to put up with the authority of wartime in the presumed relaxation of the peace.

'It was a period of Reconstruction – social, architectural, emotional,' Alan Ross wrote. 'A time when ex-officers looked for jobs and nobody wanted them. When houses needed rebuilding and licences to build were unobtainable. A time of shortages and the Black Market and soldiers who had learnt the technique of underground morality in Germany exploiting it in London. There were no homes for heroes, but a living wage, social security and a National Health Service. Public ambition took the place of private enterprise.' For Anthony Powell, 'it was a grisly period in a bomb-defaced weary squalid town, still suffering shortages of every sort ... fortitudes now relaxed – harder to put up with than the war'. For G. S. Fraser, returning from his lugubrious and stimulating Egypt, 'people of all classes dressed and ate much alike, class barriers seemed blurred, life had a certain improvised, camping-out quality. But it lacked colour. There were no settled tendencies or leading reputations. People did not discuss politics or religion but personal relationships and the books they hoped to write.'

Writers and artists were split throughout the post-war years about the new Utopia which was promised and never came. The severe winter of 1947 was followed by a year of crises and became the nadir of those who still believed in a socialist future. Three months of Arctic weather led to electric power failures: the black-out returned to London's streets, and the elevators no longer ran down to the tubes. Cold breakfasts had to be eaten by the light of candles, typists and children suffered from chilblains in unheated offices and schools. Two million people were made unemployed because factories closed, and even the renascent television system was shut down by the BBC to save power – the same action had been taken on the declaration of the war. Floods followed the thaw of the ice and the snow in the spring, so that the Wash spread over most of the reclaimed Fens. The conspiracy of the bad weather could make the unfortunate Labour government say, 'Avec nous le déluge.' Peter Watson, returning from a winter trip to America with Connolly, who had had more success over there than any visitor since Oscar Wilde, wrote to his young lover, 'What a hell each return to this dying country means.'

For the writers who feared government control more than state benefits, post-war privations fulfilled their worst expectations. To the old guard who had been asked their views on Reconstruction, such as John Cowper Powys and Gilbert Frankau, tyranny was suppressing free thought and free art. 'People are putting up with regimentation at the present time,' Frankau said in 1944, 'because they appreciate the necessity for it, but as soon as the war is over compulsion and restriction will have to go. Hang it all, we're fighting this war for freedom, and we're not going to be dictated to by a bunch of civil servants – or social dreamers – when the dictators of Germany and Italy have been eliminated.' At the opposite end of opinion stood J. B. Priestley, who hoped that the peace would achieve the society he had preached during the war. He did not want 'the survival of the slickest', but fair shares for all the people. Interestingly enough, he had opposed the idea of classes during the war, saying that the people were not the masses and had superseded the class system. Those who thought themselves members of a class did not belong to the people. 'Go to the nearest A.R.P. post and you find there people, not members of classes. The bombs kill people, not classes. Nevertheless, they may blow classes clean away.'

Priestley foresaw that Britain would be living in crises for years after the war was over. Democratic industrial Britain had fought and won the war, and its reconstruction would take a decade. He hoped that the collapse of the class system would act like the blowing-up of a dam, releasing untold energies and opportunities. He ignored the fact that during the last long sapping years of the war, class consciousness had begun again to put up the barricades of behaviour. Also the Marxists had emerged as comrades of influence during Britain's belated alliance with Russia; at the time of the siege of Stalingrad, indeed, polls had shown that the Russians were more popular friends than the Americans. Until the millions of murders arranged by Stalin and the ideology of the Cold War became broadcast, there was a brief resurgence in communist influence immediately after the peace, however resolutely the Labour Party banned card-carrying members from joining it. Alan Ross might think that the Marxists had shut up shop and that there were no minority causes left for the writer, only a retreat to imaginative romanticism and private conflicts. But other writers believed that the rebellion of the army vote and the comradeship of the ranks might lead to an extreme socialist society, a little Russia in Belgravia.

Great changes did not come as blueprints, Jack Lindsay thought. Communal life, also resistance, sprang from many ways.

> It first appears
> in mess-room, sleeping-hut, in common fears
> and hopes. It is completed some time after.
>
> The sense of a different union at last coheres
> in anger that can kill. Terror shakes it,
> fails and finally forms it. Life is good
> in that murderous circle of brotherhood.

That good life and communal feeling could be translated with a social revolution into a just peace, until, in Paul Potts's dream, 'the world is Blackpool in August in the afternoon'. The problem was that, for the Marxists, class was truth, class was scientific thought, class consciousness was necessary, the masses were the people. Even if the Labour government provided a more just and socialist society in Britain, it was conceding imperialism abroad at the speed of a sloth, while the Foreign Secretary Ernest Bevin opposed Stalin and supported Truman, the sole possessor of the atomic bomb. In the words of Sid Chaplin, one of the few working-class writers to be published regularly in the war magazines, 'What's the good of building a green and pleasant England if it's going to be blasted apart in ten years time by somebody with an atom bomb? At present our foreign policy is simply sucking up to the big bad boy with the atom bomb. Make Bevin resign. *He is no bloody good.* He is incapable of understanding the Russians who are fighting to save socialism, and that is what he should be doing. And he cannot see that he is selling socialism body and soul by lining up with the Yanks.' In a more pessimistic vein about the future of imperialism, Donald Bishop wrote some lines for a Well-appointed Lounge, which he called a 'Colour Bar'. He noticed that the promised post-war plenty was not for poor men and all men. In the lounge full of the well-dressed and well-fed, he could see that plenty was strictly

For only the white men – and not all the white men,
But only the right men, the happy and few men,
May have and may hold. Yet what if the future,
That uncertain creature, should alter their colour,
Should grieve them, should leave them black and blue men,
Or, cashless and fleshless, to depend for their whiteness,
On the pie and the vulture, the sun and the sand?

The Marxists, however, fared badly after the Cold War began. Their newspapers and magazines such as *Our Time* achieved small circulations: they could not recapture the social cachet among the intelligentsia which they had achieved in the 'thirties. The belligerence of the Russians in Eastern Europe and the imposition of communist governments there, while competing with the Americans in securing their own atomic bombs through spying and subterfuge, seemed to make a Third World War almost inevitable. The atomic bomb, Cyril Connolly thought, would make for London as inevitably as eels for the Sargasso Sea. And this time it might be the unthinkable war, against communism instead of fascism. Would it be so again – and against the society of pre-war hope, so much lauded by the Auden group of poets? Alan Ross had once believed in their message, but now he wrote 'A Lament for the "Thirties" Poets', for Wrey Gardiner's *Poetry Quarterly*. The 'forgers of language' and political thought had been trusted then, but they had lost their disillusions along with their admirers:

Let us not, ten years later, now
Have to admit we were wrong,
Our disillusioners mere fakers
Of unruffled and pedantic songs, who oblivious
And outgrowing history, grow silent to us –
Their world and their words subsiding like flat champagne.

Many of the intellectuals looked towards Western Europe for the salvation of future culture and the peace. Lehmann and Connolly crossed the Channel as soon as they could and printed as much French literature as they dared in *Horizon* and Penguin *New Writing*, which came to an agreement with *La France Libre* to exchange articles and stories and poems. *Horizon* devoted several issues to new work by French writers and favourable assessments of French literature by English critics. The Marxist magazine *Our Time* published a special French issue, while most of the other little magazines from *Now* to *Cornhill* to *New English Review* printed a flood of European translations. It was as if, in the first months of the liberation of the continent, Europe would liberate English culture from its besieged isolation of the previous five years.

John Lehmann, however, thought that even French culture could be *de trop*. He took Philip Toynbee to task in *Horizon* for claiming that French literary output had been incomparably and undeniably superior to British during the war. He quoted work by Bowra on *The Heritage of Symbolism*, Tillyard on the *Elizabethan World Picture* and Bronowski on *A Man Without a Mask*, as well as Connolly's own book, *The Unquiet Grave*, among fifty other distinguished works of non-fiction. As for novels, among many good ones there were Virginia Woolf's *Between the Acts*, Elizabeth Bowen's *Look at All Those Roses*, Rosamond Lehmann's *The Ballad and the Source*, Rex Warner's *The Aerodrome*, Henry Green's *Caught*, Nigel Balchin's *The Small Back Room*, William Sansom's *Fireman Flower*, Gerald Kersh's *They Died with Their Boots Clean* and Philip Toynbee's own *School in Private*. As for poetry, the war had given Britain some of the best work of T. S. Eliot, Edith Sitwell, Edwin Muir, Cecil Day Lewis, Stephen Spender, Louis MacNeice and David Gascoyne, as well as many volumes of achievement and high promise from young poets, some of whom had been killed. In 'The Battle of the Books', Britain might well be the winner, especially as it 'for one fateful year survived alone in this hemisphere and fought on alone against barbarism'.

The European expatriates, however, who gathered round Wrey Gardiner at the Grey Walls Press, were particularly conscious of their duty to the continent across the Channel. Fred Marnau, a particular associate of Gardiner, edited *New Road* for him. It was dedicated to fresh directions in European art and letters, and its number of 1945 was spectacular in its editorial assertions. Europe was 'a pesthouse and humiliated bodies and lost souls'. It was fundamentally a romantic continent. Where it could not fight, it waited. 'All the terror camps in the world will not alter that.' In an extraordinary frontispiece, a map that pinpointed the seats of European cultures in all the capitals as far as Moscow, Marnau printed his list of dead and living contributors which ranged from Pushkin and Lermontov and Dostoevsky, from Stefan George and Apollinaire and Picasso, even from the Americans Henry Miller and Kenneth Patchen, to the spirit of the original Soho poet William Blake, and comprising Alex Comfort and Nicholas Moore, John Bayliss and Ruthven Todd, Wrey Gardiner and David Wright, the Grey Walls faction *in toto*. It was a great pan-European vision with little content of merit, a 209 sublime effort based on small Fitzrovian talents. As Wrey Gardiner characterized Marnau in his depressive answer to Connolly's *The Unquiet Grave*, which was named *The Flowering Moment*, Marnau had achieved 'the necessary loneliness of the solitary hunter in the dark wood of civilization ... the lonely tragic voice of defeated Europe. We see the world change before us from the strains of war to the emptiness of something else, something inferior, more ridiculous, the dying song of an ending and a beginning.'

In *Horizon*, the sage Maurice Bowra took an equally pessimistic view of the effect of war on European poetry. He found that nothing had equalled the poems that resulted from the disturbance of the First World War, such as Mayakovsky's *130,000,000* or Eliot's *The Waste Land*. This dynamic, electrical art was already becoming more traditional and serious before the Second World War, the effect of which was merely to reduce the poetry of the leading Europeans such as Eluard in France, Alberti in Italy and Pasternak in Russia. All were shaped by the need to express to their various countries and causes their thoughts in an accessible shape. War did not refine, it simplified – as Keith Douglas had asked it to do for him.

In one of his more extraordinary turnabouts, Cyril Connolly became optimistic about the Anglo-American future of culture. A new Renaissance was possible because America would help England respect the artist and the regions in the way that it valued the culture of its federal states. A Renaissance had already begun in Wales and Scotland and Ireland. Regionalism was the remedy for provincialism and for the excessive influence of London, which confined all art to the capital and gave it a purely urban outlook. The American influence would liberate England from such prejudices.

Connolly was talking against *Horizon* and himself, for both were metropolitan and European to an extent, and hardly regional. He recognized what should be part of the post-war reconstruction, but would not be because of the continuing grip of the metropolis. Regionalism was briefly a force in literature at the end of the war due to an uncertainty about the direction of publishing in England, but its time would not come until future decades, and then through the enlightened patronage of state and local organizations. In the confusion of the first years of the peace, the artists simply did not know what to do, where to live, or who would employ them. G. S. Fraser remembered 'young writers sharing sparsely furnished flats, giving parties, with mulled Algerian wine and weak bitter beer, talking eagerly through the night, trying to call into existence, as if by magic, a "London literary world". They would eventually meet older writers but these were as much at sea in the new post-war world as their juniors.'

The problem was still the paper shortage for the manufacture of books and magazines. In a pamphlet named after Jonathan Swift's *Battle of the Books*, leading authors and members of the trade pointed out the crisis in the industry. Before the war, there had been too many books with too few readers. The destruction of the stocks of the publishers in the blitz and the avid consumption of everything in print by the population during the war had led to a dearth of books. The new Labour government seemed as philistine as its predecessors about lifting paper rationing, with a spokesman named Belcher declaring in the House of Commons that 'books should not have priority over all other forms of the paper industry because we need to wrap up our food in paper containers'. Although a few Labour Members of Parliament such as Woodrow Wyatt denounced 'the barbarian attitude' of certain government departments to the book trade, wood pulp for pages and cloth for binding and boards was low in the priority of an administration which perversely encouraged publishers to produce volume after volume of English literature for export. England's books, as Osbert Sitwell pointed out, had done more to make it loved in the world than all its politicians or military victories. Books were food. 'You cannot live by bread alone: equally a man cannot live without books. If he does, he is a brute, not a man.' Slow strangulation by short supplies of material, Henry Green wrote, was killing off the English author. 'And in fifty years' time, if all creative work is not stopped meanwhile by the increasing shortage of paper, it will be realised that men and women are writing as well now as they have ever done in this country.'

The paper shortage particularly damned new publishers and new writers, fresh from the services after their demobilization. Rupert Hart-Davis blew a trumpet for the disadvantaged ex-combatant. After the First World War, there had been a renaissance in British publishing led by new firms such as Faber & Faber, Jonathan Cape and Victor Gollancz. Now these firms were hogging the paper supplies to make themselves even more powerful, while newer publishers set up during the war, such as Wrey Gardiner's Grey Walls Press, were being artificially preserved because they had acquired a paper ration. This was ridiculous, but the position of the neophyte publisher was pitiable, rationed to six tons of paper a year, which could produce less than twenty-five thousand novels. The minimum supply of paper to keep going at all was fifteen tons a year. Those who had fought were being penalized for not serving out their time in Soho during the war. 'No trade can remain healthy without the introduction of new blood and new ideas. For six years almost the only newcomers in the publishing trade were opportunists, most of them without experience, all without paper rations, who cashed in on the national book-famine and flooded the shops with cheap and nasty rubbish printed on black-market paper. Many of these mushroom firms will surely fade away, now that black-market paper is harder to come by, and the reading public more discriminating.'

As for the young demobilized author, his position was nearly hopeless. If he wrote his war novel, he would find no publisher to accept it, because of the paper shortage. There was no way for him to earn a living by his pen except in writing catalogues or technical articles, or radio versions of the classics for the BBC, or pieces for American magazines, whose bounty was part of their general aid to the arts. By restricting paper supplies, the Labour government was gagging the voice of those who had voted for it. 'Can they in the present state of the world have paper,' Henry Green demanded, 'or can they not? Can we continue to be more and more silent in the one universal language, that of art? Is it democratic to have only limited editions? And is not the present paper situation, as it worsens from month to month, a kind of censorship which may grow as rigid as some of the worst, but more open, forms elsewhere?'

Paradoxically, censorship by paper rationing preserved for the time being the new Fitzrovian publishers as well as the old established firms. Tambimuttu and Wrey Gardiner, and R. A. Caton of the Fortune Press, were granted a few more years of their precarious activities. Caton went on scurrying from printer to printer, always trying to find a cheaper one with a stack of forgotten paper stashed away. Incredibly, he was still printing the poets of the future, either individually or in anthologies, so little was the demand for their services elsewhere – Kingsley Amis and John Wain, Charles Causley and Gavin Ewart, Francis King and Thom Gunn, Philip Larkin and Ted Hughes, Sylvia Plath and Elizabeth Jennings, and even Wallace Stevens and Dylan Thomas, Julian Symons and Roy Fuller. Caton's taste was as extraordinary as his parsimony. His authors were expected to buy or tout hundreds of copies of their books, and they never received a penny from them in royalties. Amis retaliated by including Caton as a villain in five of his novels, eventually finishing him off in *The Anti-Death League* by having him shot to pieces.

Yet in the doldrums after the war, Caton was one of the few to publish new war poets. He lived in a basement off Buckingham Palace Road, stuffed with unbound copies of his poetic or erotic books. He wore a hat jammed over his mulish face even indoors, with an old RAF raincoat and two pairs of stained cotton trousers put on against the cold. He seemed a sinister man to Nicholas Moore, one of his unwilling poets. 'He had a rather irritable, fussy manner, mainly about money; he would have liked some from you: he didn't want to pay you any. But on reflection years afterwards I don't think he was a crook. He knew nobody liked him and it pained him, I think, enormously. I think he yearned to have a friendly social and literary relationship with one of the poets he published, but presumably – because of his manner and his rather unprepossessing appearance, and the way he treated them, he never achieved one.' Philip Larkin told Julian Symons that he should write Caton's biography and have the last word, but Symons demurred, merely recording that Caton asked him in the street if he knew a certain lubricious author because Caton 'could have done with a bit of homo for the autumn'. And on a last meeting, Caton produced something from his case which he was sure would interest Symons – '*The Pleasure of the Torture Chamber*. Well, that was Caton.'

The Grey Walls Press with its assured paper supplies was taking other measures to survive, which were eventually to end in its ruin. Admirably and internationally, it was printing the works of leading American authors, such as Scott Fitzgerald and Nathanael West. But Wrey Gardiner remained wedded to the authors brought to him by his editor Alex Comfort, many of whom were apostates from the Apocalypse – indeed, its prophet J. F. Hendry was left as its last and lonely post-war survivor, saying of Henry Treece's defection to New Romanticism and the list of Faber & Faber, 'Who could romanticise death-camps?' During the war, as Derek Stanford had noted, Wrey Gardiner, working from his Crown Passage headquarters and doss-house, had attracted displaced authors even more than Tambimuttu, 'the young wartime poets: servicemen and women, civilians, nurses and land girls, conscientious objectors, those in reserved occupations or classified as unfit'. But in the *malaise* of the peace, Wrey Gardiner lured only the odd gang of the New Romantic poets, particularly Comfort and Nicholas Moore, Ruthven Todd and Fred Marnau, all of whom published books of poetry with Grey Walls. He continually mourned peacetime conditions in *The Flowering Moment*: 'Can one escape from the reading of proofs for which I seem destined, given to me by Tambi in the Burglar's Rest in the bad old Soho days, the proofs of Gascoyne's French poems, the Falcon Baudelaire, Patchen's poems, everything that comes my way is perhaps the wrong kind of life and leads to the hell of a strange business man's world for which I am not fitted.'

He took to himself a business partner, a demobilized officer called Captain Peter Baker, who was to be elected as the Conservative Member of Parliament for South Norfolk. He had bought the shell of a profitable publishing company, the Falcon Press, which was now merged with the Grey Walls Press to Wrey Gardiner's relief, although he should have seen in Baker more of a speculator than a financial saviour. As it was, Gardiner's chief hope now lay in his 'vigorous partner, suave and well-dressed and full of rather attractive laughter, dark-eyed and explosive, slipping from floor to floor like a flash of quick businesslike comedy ... Someday we shall both escape into the larger life to which our several geniuses have called us.' At the moment, Baker endeared himself to Gardiner by planting a bottle of brandy solidly among his unanswered letters.

Baker was, in fact, a man of a thousand schemes, which came to nothing after interminable discussions in the Gargoyle. He was neither as shrewd nor as wealthy as Peter Watson, who continued to support Connolly on *Horizon*. Tambimuttu continued to edit *Poetry London*; its tenth number was nicknamed 'Chums' Annual' because it included all the poems that Tambimuttu had promised to publish and had forgotten over the past five years. The most successful of the new publishers were the European *émigres* to London; André Deutsch, a refugee from Hungary along with his partner George Mikes; Walter Neurath of Thames & Hudson and Bela Horowitz of the Phaidon Press; the brother of Michael Hamburger, Paul Hamlyn, who began his publishing empire by selling books from a barrow in Oxford Street; Robert Maxwell, who had fought with distinction during the war and founded the Pergamon Press; and George Weidenfeld, an adviser to the BBC on life in all the cities of Europe, the publisher of *Contact* magazine, and the creator with Harold Nicolson's son Nigel of a publishing firm that would establish history and biography as international commodities. Immediately after the war, Weidenfeld was living with Peter Quennell near Regent's Park: Barbara Skelton, later Weidenfeld's wife, moved in and out to have an affair with the matinée idol Anthony Steele. Quennell had previously shared a Bedford Square apartment with Cyril Connolly, leading to a memorable dismissal from Evelyn Waugh, who asked 213

Quennell why they had left the place. '"For what reason?" he enquired. "Financial? Sexual?" "Neither, Evelyn," I replied. "Oh, then, for *sanitary* reasons, I suppose"; and, brusquely waving me aside, he turned his attention to a plate of oysters.'

Connolly's most valuable contribution in *Horizon* to the cause of the embattled English writer after the war was a questionnaire sent to leading authors, called 'The Cost of Letters'. Connolly had defined the disease of contemporary culture as 'Inflationary Decadence'; but the replies to his questionnaire made him view the problems of the author more practically. It was evident that writers wanted a fair wage, that their income was declining in a post-war world, that they were being forced into secondary occupations which were becoming primary, and that the decline of private incomes and private patrons meant 'the State must do more to help writers, preferably by indirect subsidy'. The replies to 'The Cost of Letters' were brave, jocular, contradictory and depressive.

No person requiring intoxicating drinks, cigarettes, visits to cinemas and theatres and food above British Restaurant standard can afford to live by writing prose if he is not 'established'. Not even a *popular* poet, if there is one, can live by his poetry.

JOHN BETJEMAN

I have no sympathy with the Chatterton–Rimbaud fairy stories which lead writers to starve in garrets, or, the more modern equivalent, sponge on non-literary friends, because they are poets and find work too mundane. Artists are not privileged people ... I don't think the artist should touch the State or its money with a barge-pole. The same applies to commercial patronage, increasingly, from day to day. In a period of barbarism one has to be able to cut oneself off from all patronage.

ALEX COMFORT

If he is to enjoy leisure and privacy, marry, buy books, travel and entertain his friends, a writer needs upwards of five pounds a day net. If he is prepared to die young of syphilis for the sake of an adjective he can make do on under ... The State, in so far as it supplants private enterprise, *must* supplant private patronage.

CYRIL CONNOLLY

Never write anything that you do not really want to write for its own sake, whatever the fee is. And if you have made no critical discovery about life or literature that you feel so important that you must write it down, putting everything else aside, in the most direct and careful language of which you are capable, then you are not a serious writer. Apply for a job with a newspaper, an advertising agency, or the B.B.C. But if you are a serious writer and have no money, then live on your friends, relations or wits, until you can collect a public large enough to support you.

ROBERT GRAVES

Look at the panting cross-country novelists. Look at the six-day-bicycle-riding script writers, struggling at poems while changing tyres. Their doom is in the pace and the payout; they are paid off by the number of milestones they cover, and not by their discoveries of the country in between. These are the things that break their hearts and wind ... What are the present alternatives? A he-man's job as wood cutter or crane-driver, with a couple of hours writing in the evenings? Romantic fallacy! The body's exhaustion is also the mind's. A State job, then – Ministry propagandist or B.B.C. hack? No; they fritter and stale like nobody's business.

LAURIE LEE

If I have advice to give to anyone who wants to write for a living, it is this:
a) Don't attempt it.
b) If you are crazy enough to try, be tough; get all you can. Price your work high and make them pay. Don't listen to your publisher's sob-stories about how little he can afford. He'll have a country house and polo ponies when you are still borrowing the price of a drink in Fitzrovia. Remember, *he* makes the money; make him give you as much as you can extort, short of using a gun or pincers. Art for art's sake is all cock, anyway.

JULIAN MACLAREN-ROSS

I do not think one can with justice expect a writer to do his best on a working-class income … If we are to have full Socialism, then clearly the writer must be State-supported, and ought to be placed among the better-paid groups. But so long as we have an economy like the present one, in which there is a great deal of State enterprise but also large areas of private capitalism, then the less truck a writer has with the State, or any other organized body, the better for him and his work. There are invariably strings tied to any kind of organized patronage … But if one wants to be primarily a *writer*, then, in our society, one is an animal that is tolerated but not encouraged – something rather like a house sparrow – and one gets on better if one realizes one's position from the start.

GEORGE ORWELL

Connolly's summing-up of 'The Cost of Letters' in the next issue of *Horizon* changed into a fear of state patronage. He realized the bourgeois attitude of most of his contributors and pointed out that the artist felt towards the state like the middle-class child asking the working-class window-cleaner to admire his toys. And by the end of 1947, Connolly wrote one of his better satires, 'In Jugular Vein', in which he foresaw a general offensive against Art by the government. 'The Cost of Letters' had shown the morale of authors to be sinking fast. The excessive cold of the previous winter had stopped all paper supplies and even closed the Third Programme on the wireless. Currency restrictions cut off artists from European travel and influences. Even the import of foreign films and books had been banned. The artist was an endangered species like the whale, which was now being wiped out and served as steaks to supplement the meat ration. People were reading less, literature was becoming as hard to sell as before the war. 'I hope we shall soon live to see the book and the periodical entirely superseded by the bulletin and communiqué.'

John Lehmann remained more optimistic than Cyril Connolly about prospects for publishers and writers. In 1945, he admitted that it was 'a most uncomfortable kind of peace'; some of the deep bruises inflicted on people's nerves and social life were coming to the surface. But by the next year, he himself had become a publisher under his own imprint, while improving Penguin *New Writing* with colour illustrations, and opening a superior literary magazine, *Orpheus*. He believed that   215 the wartime demand for books and the arts would not end in a peacetime 'Philistine Restoration'. There had been a true popular revolt against the material values and dogmas of British civilization. Cultural diffusion and cultural competition had come to stay, and they would be helped by the growth of the British Council and the Arts Council. There were many bodies now to encourage education and the arts where there had been few twenty years before, and through the plethora of initials, ABCA and CEMA, WEA and BBC, culture would be spread. He quoted with approval the series on the BBC, *The Challenge of Our Time*, which attracted up to five million listeners to hear the more distinguished thinkers of the day debate the eternal war between individual freedom and socialist planning. Only through Christopher Isherwood's eyes, when the absent poet at last returned to London after eight years in America, did Lehmann see what others saw in post-war society. The cruel winter and its fuel cuts were endured with misery and loathing. There was no longer a sense of shared danger in the face of a common enemy. 'We realised that we had become shabby and rather careless of appearances in our battered surroundings. That we had become crushed as civilians to accept the ordering about of officialdom. That we had become obsessively queue-forming, and were priggishly proud of it.'

For the demobilized writer, there was certainly a reaction from the subject-matter of his war experiences. Lehmann wished those with a war book in their pocket the best of luck with publishers and warned them to arrange for their work to be printed before the public refused to read anything more about what the world was like during the conflict. The literary critic, Daniel George, declared that no war novels would be worth reading for another ten years, when hindsight might correct vision: his advice was, 'Don't rush it.' And Stephen Spender now advised poets to ignore overwhelming public events and join the many who had refused during the war 'to put their distinguished client into metre and rhyme'. Of course, the war had been a deeply experienced emotion which affected all true poets at the time; in one sense, the poets were incapable of not being war poets; but the cataclysms of the peace did not demand a recognition of their significance by post-war poets. There was a reaction now. Most modern poets, finding themselves living in a world 'like a scene from Dante's Inferno' were appalled by its scale and looked inside themselves for something smaller. The inner or metaphysical journey of those who had tried to avoid or deny the fighting had become the universal direction and revulsion of the poets in the peace.

The sloth in building the New Jerusalem of the Welfare State in Britain because of the over-extension and near-bankruptcy of the country made the debate between individual choice and state control even more acute. A suspicion grew that the difficulties were due not to the problems of transition, but to a belief in warlike management. In an important article, 'The Surrender of Free Choice', Roy Harrod praised the greater equality of incomes after two years of peace, but blamed the all-pervading system of control. The British were now slaves in material matters and might be led on to mental servitude. Decisions were no longer made by the individual, but by the bureaucracy. Everybody was allocated a certain amount of meat or butter or petrol or travel, or none at all. This system of central decision was no longer a matter of 'national necessity'. The Labour government, which Harrod supported, had continued warlike central administration for too long after the war, and there would be a revolt from it. The Minister of Economic Affairs, Sir Stafford Cripps, with his innumerable working parties and committees and production targets and statistics was working himself to death in the rehabilitation of his country, but his means were cumbersome, his explanations too intellectual. He lacked the common touch to explain to the people why sacrifices were still necessary for so many years after victory. Technocracy was no substitute for advocacy.

John Lehmann had been correct in praising the BBC series of talks, *The Challenge of Our Time*. Its producer, Grace Wyndham-Goldie, was to become one of the more important cultural influences of her time through her increasing power in the BBC and devotion to quality on the air. She was, indeed, the best of the guardians, the one who needed no guard. In the agitated first spring of peace, she decided to hold a debate not on housing or prospects of work, but on values. What was the peace for? What society should be planned? Arthur Koestler led off with a swingeing attack on scientific socialism and collective action, accusing one of his respondents, Professor J. D. Bernal, a staunch supporter of the practice of Lenin and Stalin, of obeying party orders as the accused Nazis had in the Belsen trial. Bernal denied that planned scientific socialism was the 'new bible of Belsen'. Those who fostered the fear of using the power of the state were doing a grave disservice to humanity. E. M. Forster said that he could not answer the challenge because he could not interpret the questions. 'It is like shouting defiance at a big black cloud.' He admitted that the world of *laissez-faire* was bad and led to a black market and a capitalist jungle. 'We must have planning and ration books and controls, or millions of people will have nowhere to live and nothing to eat.' But equally, *laissez-faire* was the only system for the human spirit. 'If you plan and control men's minds you stunt them, you get the censorship, the secret police, the road to serfdom, the community of slaves.' He himself had to remain with the individual, because everybody was an individual. 'We want the New Economy with the Old Morality. We want planning for the body and not for the spirit.'

The scientists defended themselves against Forster. The proper use of science for good and not for ill was the challenge of the time. 'The scientist does not want to plan Forster's mind, but he does want Forster to use his own mind to help him with the plan and even to explain where planning is not in place.' Professor J. B. S. Haldane admitted that science had produced the flying bombs and the rocket and the atomic bombs, but this was all the fault of imperialist governments and the misuse of international relations. It was not enough to behave as morally as our forefathers did, we had to behave better than they did. Planning for world peace and a world economy according to the theories of Karl Marx was the challenge. So the economic argument was set against the spiritual one, the   217 dominant state against the individual choice, and no conclusion was reached except by the Canon of St Paul's, V. A. Dyment: 'Even apart from dangers of atomic destruction, there is a doom on our civilization.' The terrible paradox was that modern man was in great control over things and was also carried along by a process he could not control. Scientific planning was useless until men put down their roots in nature, in community and in eternity.

The debate on *The Challenge of Our Time* may have been inconclusive, but it showed that influential arguments were better aired on the wireless than in the pubs of Fitzrovia. To secure a living wage after the war, the writers and the poets were already making for Portland Place like drakes drawn to a duck. 'When the writers formed and clustered again,' Dan Davin noticed, 'it was about the knees of the BBC.' In August 1946, *Picture Post* ran an article about the poets already working for the broadcasting corporation, which was called 'A Nest of Singing Birds'. The antagonists, Louis MacNeice and Roy Campbell, were featured along with William Empson, now a news reader on the Eastern Service. Although George Orwell had left his position running 'Talks to India', Patric Dickinson was in charge of the poetry programmes. He held himself to be the best producer of verse for public performances in England and employed many of his peer group including Dylan Thomas, who was a regular reader and writer, although not on the staff, because of a certain prejudice against his occasional drunkenness while live on microphone. Another member of 'A Nest of Singing Birds' was James Monahan, one of the better new poets whose promise did not survive the peace: he had served in the Commandos and believed that his art had saved him from becoming a mental casualty of the war. The Yorkshireman Rayner Heppenstall also took to the BBC after demobilization as tripe to onions; his autobiography, *Portrait of the Artist as a Professional Man*, is a salutary lesson in how a Fitzrovian writer might be changed by a spell of army duty into a fit servant of a media corporation. He himself did not take to his colleague Roy Campbell, who seemed like a huge limping ram under his South African felt hat; Campbell repaid him in invective, once saying to him, 'Rayner, you look like a bald-headed gnome who has swallowed an acid-drop the wrong way.'

By virtue of the power of patronage, Heppenstall did much to shift the beer-holes of Fitzrovia from Charlotte and Dean Streets to the purlieus of Portland Place. He hymned the qualities of broadcasting pubs, the intimate Stag's Head with only a saloon and a public bar, the Windsor Castle and the Whore's Lament, the George or Gluepot and Shirreff's Wine Bar, and the between-hours Colony Room of north-west Fitzrovia, the 'M.L.' or Marie Lloyd, where afternoon drinkers forgot their microphones in a basement near the Gluepot. Heppenstall preferred the Stag's Head and brought there C. P. Snow and Pamela Hansford Johnson, now married to Snow after her odd engagement to Dylan Thomas. Rose Macaulay came and Norman Cameron, Sean O'Faolain and Angus Wilson, Laurie Lee and Henry Reed and Muriel Spark. George Orwell returned as an outside writer of feature scripts, forsaking the George for Heppenstall's chosen bar. But the other leading writers and poets, Wystan Auden and Theodore Roethke when in England, and George Barker and Dylan Thomas, usually drank with Louis MacNeice, while the poets from Cairo, Lawrence Durrell and Bernard Spencer, drank with Terence Tiller, another poet who had become a BBC producer: his third volume of poetry, *Unarm, Eros* of 1947, was his best, but as with so many of his fellow poets, working for the broadcasting corporation doused the fire of his creation. The ultimate Fitzrovian, Julian Maclaren-Ross, complained in the Wheatsheaf that everybody had gone, and tried to move crablike to the west and the Stag's Head. But as he entered, conversational groups ceased. He was considered 'a grinding, egoistical bore', and when Heppenstall tried to defend his merits as a writer and critic, he talked to deaf ears. Anthony Cronin saw him in the George 'like a scarecrow among seagulls'. In the new kingdom of the airwaves, the man with the monologue and the gold-topped cane was read out.

Just as military service was held to shackle the war poet, service for the broadcasting corporation was considered a creative death by a thousand programmes. The writer Jocelyn Brooke, who left the army to become a producer there, found the strain of the job could only be mitigated by alcohol, which caused a chronic hangover. His sense of guilt and his solitary nature could be assuaged only by a progressive increase in social activity: he was a fish out of water and soon resigned. In his five years of war duty in Portland Place, William Empson wrote only three short poems. He explained his inability to produce in one piece of six lines, entitled 'Let it go':

It is this deep blankness is the real thing strange.
   The more things happen to you the more you can't
     Tell or remember even what they were.

The contradictions cover such a range.
   The talk would talk and go so far aslant.
     You don't want madhouse and the whole thing there.

Patric Dickinson disagreed. He defended the regular employment of poets, declaring that fewer and better poems were needed. It was now a question of carrying round a poem like an unborn child until it had to be written. 'It will be written, in spite of everything,' he said, 'if I feel its body grow in the imagination with sufficient urgency.' In between producing five poetry programmes a month in *Time for Verse* before the Third Programme was instituted, he himself adopted the fashion of the time, certain of his own powers of patronage. He wrote *Theseus and the Minotaur*, a dramatic poem which was then broadcast. Many of the poets at the BBC turned their muse towards such siren songs. Henry Reed and W. R. Rodgers were also on the staff and wrote verse dramas, while Laurie Lee composed *The Voyage of Magellan* and Henry Treece, *The Tragedy of Tristan*. Louis MacNeice left more than one hundred and fifty scripts in the Play Library over twenty-two years of service. One of them was a masterpiece, a parable called *The Dark Tower*, 219 transmitted in January 1946; its hero Roland kept his date with destiny in spite of revelations about his fate. As MacNeice used to say in the bars to those who ran down the profundity of his talent, 'If you see through things, you never see into them.'

The Dark Tower did something to re-establish the reputation of one of the Marxist poets of the Spanish Civil War, whose general influence was now at its nadir. When it had been at its zenith in 1939, the belligerent Roy Campbell had been the only poet of significance to assault the Auden group in *Flowering Rifle*:

> As now in England the Triumphant Lie
> Is mesmerizing multitudes to die
> By radio, by newspaper, and, worse,
> In literature, in painting, and in verse,
> Where modern Southeys, to the mode who clown,
> For going Red, can bum the Laureate crown:
> While unbought men, who think and understand
> And indicate the actual with their hand,
> Like criminals are shunned throughout the land –
> As for myself I glory in my crime –
> Of English poets first in all my time
> To sock the bleary monster in my rhyme ...

Campbell went on socking the bleary monster in *Talking Bronco*, poems written by him during the war. This time his editor was T. S. Eliot himself, also a committed Roman Catholic and a reactionary. His publishing firm, Faber & Faber, printed many of the poets whom Campbell was attacking over their red beliefs, particularly Auden and Spender, Day Lewis and MacNeice. Eliot persuaded Campbell to drop a polemical preface which libelled them, although his verses sneering at the 'MacSpaunday' poets remained in *Talking Bronco*. Eliot cautiously seemed to agree with Campbell's low opinion of much modern poetry, but wrote that his sympathies had rather shifted to Auden's side as his friends, who had '(more or less) faced the terrors of London', were ready to cold-shoulder him. Eliot did not think that anyone who had not actually volunteered or fought was in a position to condemn Auden for sitting out the war in the United States of America, Eliot's own homeland.

When *Talking Bronco* appeared, Campbell was already a radio producer on the fledgeling Third Programme, while MacNeice had long been working for the BBC as a feature-writer and producer. Enraged at the 'MacSpaunday' satires, Cecil Day Lewis wrote to Stephen Spender suggesting that MacNeice should have Campbell 'chucked out of the BBC as a Fascist and an irresponsible calumniator and therefore a person not fitted to direct any civilized form of cultural expression'. Spender carried on the assault, accusing Campbell of being a gross slanderer and a coward and a bully as well as a fascist. Campbell replied by saying that he was a decorated non-commissioned officer who had fought against fascism, while Spender was a 'chairborne shock trooper of the Knife-and-Fork Brigade, one who dug himself in with his eating-irons in the rearguard of both wars'. MacNeice evaded the controversy, taking no direct action except to stop drinking with Campbell at the Stag's Head; but at the George, he finally did have to fight Campbell and bloodied the South African's nose. He became one of the many writers who stopped drinking with Campbell, who began to swing his fists in defence of his beliefs and his new literary friends.

He became the unlikely champion of Edith Sitwell, declaring to her, 'I will be your knight and fight your battles for you!' Actually, he threatened Geoffrey Grigson for criticizing somebody else, raising his knobbly walking-stick outside the BBC and reputedly knocking off Grigson's spectacles and sending him in flight into a nearby coffee-house. But Edith Sitwell was delighted at this attack on one of her detractors; she promoted Campbell from being a mere 'typhoon in a beer-bottle' to 'one of the very few great poets of our time'. It was in this role that Campbell had assaulted Stephen Spender at a poetry reading at the Ethical Church in Bayswater, limping on to the platform, cursing and aiming blows at his imagined enemy. This time he connected and drew blood from Spender's nose

John Pemberton

before he was hustled off by another bohemian drinker, John Gawsworth. Spender showed great dignity and mercy, refusing to call the police, and continuing with his reading. He even said of Campbell, 'He is a poet, and a very good one. We must try to understand.'

The wars of the poets added some gore to much bile. As Rayner Heppenstall noted, there was a lot of literary hitting at this time. Dylan Thomas, now subsidized by the BBC, went on being a boozer and a brawler in his new drinking-places, the George and the Stag's Head, which he left one evening to have a fight in Hallam Street. His subsequent bloodshot eye was said to have been caused by scratching the ball with the thorn of a rose, a romantic explanation that invited disbelief. He broke his chicken bones easily in accidents; he was never happy, his wife wrote, unless he was wandering around with his arm in a sling. Yet among the poets working for the BBC, his writing, which seemed to be penned to be read and heard, developed because of his employment into the finest English language ever broadcast by the medium across the world. As he declared of a Festival of Spoken Poetry, 'Known words grow wings; print springs and shoots; the voice discovers the poet's ear; it's found that a poem on a page is only half a poem.' Stephen Spender agreed that Thomas had gained more than any other poet from his war work, writing scripts and broadcasting, which had given him 'the sense of a theme, without taking away from the forcefulness of his imagery'.

The rest of Thomas's speaking was done in the broadcasting pubs of north-west Fitzrovia. There he was to be found in between his talking on the air waves. 'Ah,' a friend wrote, 'here is the green man at the height of his acclaim. He sits in a corner propped up by two walls, a smouldering, soggy firework sending up stars of singular lucidity. His admirers surround him. What will he do next? They wonder. Will he burst or explode? A long silence. Dylan moves his head. A dozen necks crane forward to gather crumbs of irreverence or, perhaps, to learn how to write a poem. "A pint, I say", he rumbles in that deep belly-voice that makes audiences shiver. The pint is quickly fetched.' The *enfant terrible* was becoming the morose and shocking celebrity. And yet he could still charm and excite the company in the George. On one night of drinking with Louis MacNeice and the young Richard Burton, the challenge was to declaim the greatest poem ever written. MacNeice intoned one of his own poems, Burton delivered a soliloquy from *Hamlet*, while Thomas concluded with the most exact and telling litany of them all.

> I am
> Thou art
> He, she and it is
> We are
> You are
> They are.

He was and is and will be in the spoken word the ultimate voice of the Fitzrovians
– sonorous, rich as Black Velvet, ultimate as a barman calling 'Time'. The last of

222

his plays for voices, *Under Milk Wood*, will remain the supreme orchestra of words for the discriminating ear. But *Return Journey*, first broadcast in June 1947, was Thomas's requiem for his lost innocence in the big city. Although it was set in Swansea, it took place among the blitz of the past, because Swansea itself had been bombed heavily for three nights and its centre was destroyed. In looking for his lost boyhood, Dylan Thomas ended on a roll-call of the dead like the long lists engraved on the memorials to those killed in the world wars, a chant of names. His account of the flaying of the seven skins of his young manhood by the seven sins in Fitzrovia had been left incomplete in 1941. His friend Vernon Watkins thought that Thomas had abandoned *Adventures in the Skin Trade* because the greater and crueller anarchy of the war, which distorted London beyond measure, took the place of a comic and imaginary metropolis. The black-out had made London even more of a pit than Thomas could dig for it. The Gayspot, where the Welsh innocent hero was taken, was like a coal cellar. 'This was a breath and scar of the London he had come to catch.' After a fracas in the Gayspot, the final plunge was into the ocean bed of the Cheerioh. 'There were deep green faces, dipped in a sea dye, with painted cockles for mouths and lichenous hair, sealed on the cheeks; red and purple, slate-grey, tide-marked, rat-brown ... the foul salt of the earth.' So *Adventures in the Skin Trade* came to its unfinished end, fathoms deep in the infernal tides of Fitzrovia, because Thomas himself could never deal fully with the problem of his disintegration through the drink and easy company of the bohemians of the cities.

Fitzrovia did not recognize its decadence in Dylan Thomas's descriptions nor did it accept the shift of its nucleus to the neighbourhood off Portland Place. Although the creation of the Third Programme would do much to make a minority of Britons a musical people with an appreciation of spoken verse, although the Arts Council and the British Council would increasingly subsidize authors and artists and actors, even granting a bursary to William Sansom for his writing, the role of the state as a patron hardly seemed yet to affect the life of London's central bohemia. Soho was still the workshop of the English film industry, which was given an extraordinary and lethal boost by the penal taxation of films not made at home, chiefly American, in order to save foreign currency. In spite of the departure of Tyrone Guthrie to the United States, the Old Vic company, led by Laurence Olivier and Ralph Richardson, was continuing to dazzle the theatre world with its repertory of classics at the New Theatre in St Martin's Lane. A National Theatre was surely being born in Soho. Opera and ballet were reviving at Covent Garden, even if both arts were being subsidized by the state. The BBC orchestras were being supplemented by the major London orchestras, which somehow had kept playing throughout the war, especially at that curious explosion of annual patriotism, the 'Proms', conducted by Sir Thomas Beecham in the Albert Hall. And the young British neo-Romantic artists still congregated in Soho, which became even more raffish and permissive in the post-war years. Where austerity and puritanism ruled all England, Fitzrovia remained a stewpot of possibilities, inviting by false 223 promises and real encounters. Its regulars had no idea that its wartime ferment was going flat, the kick leaving the beer, the brew tasting stale. State control and state aid hardly touched Charlotte and Dean Streets, where individual choice and postwar dislocation still created a turmoil in the pubs and clubs. Although nothing is further from progress than mere movement, Fitzrovia was still a swirling and lively place in its time of transition after the war. Alan Ross gave it an accolade as a question of its truth:

It was a time of search and of little money, when the price of a drink and a humanly welcoming bed was the most anyone could wish for. It seems to me now to have been enormously exciting and savagely happy, to have possessed a gaiety that seems never to have been repeated. Was any of it really as one imagined it, a sustaining hunting ground which writers and painters as young as one was then are today recreating in their own image?

SIXTEEN

The Good Old Time

The Café Royal – Osbert Lancaster

What panther stalks tonight as through these London
Groves of iron stalks the strawberry blonde?
Strung through the darkness each electric moon
Throbs like a wound ...

For now the inverted tombstone of a starched
And ghastly shirtfront shines like wax beneath
A lamp as something sidles to exchange
A blade for breath.

Where Swallow Street and Piccadilly join
It moves through half light with a slithering sound
And leaves a penknife in the seeded heart
Of the strawberry blonde.

So Mervyn Peake wrote of the central London of vice and crime that sprang up among the ruins in the post-war years. To the young demobilized Douglas Sutherland, it was the vice capital of Europe with prostitutes still lining the streets more frequently than lamp-posts and a red-light district of a square mile in the back-streets, crowded with the illegal drinking-clubs that were a hangover from the war. London was full of the bored and the lonely, looking for purpose or jobs, and they congregated in the basement clubs to bemoan the cut of their demob suits – 'a sort of never-never land of clipped moustaches, army-style overcoats and old school ties. They were suffering a post-war weariness from which many never recovered'.

New elements thronged the pubs of Fitzrovia, also looking for business opportunities. To the demobilized were added the black marketeers and the 'spivs', who shaded into the criminal class, always part of the Soho scene. The criminal boss of the lozenge between Piccadilly Circus, Shaftesbury Avenue, the Charing Cross Road, Oxford and Regent Streets, was Billy Hill, whose henchmen beat up any rivals like Jack Spot trespassing on their gambling and protection activities. Prostitution was more the preserve of the Maltese Messina brothers. Some of the street girls were murdered, and Soho became known as the 'Bloody Area', attracting more visitors looking for trouble because of its growing reputation for crime. The longest-serving of the club owners, Sammy Samuels, noticed that violence had increased in the drinking and illegal gambling-clubs during the war. 'The wartime player drifted, the here today and gone tomorrow stuff. Life was on a string, as we say, and if he did not drink, he gambled.' But the post-war Soho of protection rackets became still more rootless and malodorous, particularly with the flowering of the 'spivs' in their striped suits with padded shoulders, Brylcreemed hair under fedora hats, and yellow shoes as pointed as daggers. They lived in the inadequacy of the supply system. They could provide scarce goods at the right price from unknown sources, and they became the symbols, necessities and scapegoats of their age, just as a few notorious murders and murderers such as the con-man

Neville Heath seemed to represent the suppressed violence of the peace. A series of paintings commissioned by *Lilliput* illustrated the contemporary scene. Edgar Ainsworth, the art editor of *Picture Post* who lost an ear in a pub brawl, portrayed the gregarious underworld and vice 'In Darkest Soho', while James Fitton and Edward Burra painted bar scenes, where the public house was said to be 'a first-aid post, in which human beings receive treatment for injuries sustained in the battle with life'.

The real personalities of the post-war years, as Alan Ross knew, were those 'who in an age of rules, broke them'. Their names were a catalogue of deviance and crime: Max Intrator, Heath, Sidney Stanley, Haigh. They echoed 'the shabby world of forged cheques, travelling restrictions and export permits; of pathological sexual obsessions and murder. The Forties was lived largely "under the counter": economically, sexually and histrionically. Overt sexual exhibitionism gave way to isolated acts of great violence.' The figure of the larcenous 'spiv' spawned poetry, cartoons and literature, particularly caught in the restless and seedy novels of the alcoholic genius, Patrick Hamilton. And Virginia Graham admonished the type:

> Young man in a purple suit,
> balanced on pointed ginger feet
> at the corner of Denman Street,
> selling illicit silk stockings
> with fancy clockings
> in the furtive half-light
> of a dirty drunken Piccadilly night;
> young man in a purple suit
> doing a little business on the side,
> it was not for you my son died.

But A. S. J. Tessimond in *Voices in a Giant City* saw the 'Smart-boy' as an antidote to post-war restrictions:

> I'm your tall talker in the fug of bar-rooms,
> Quick at a deal, an old hand on the dog tracks,
> Knowing in clubs, stander at Soho corners.
>
> Go-between guy, I'm wiser than to work for
> What the world hands me on a shiny salver,
> Me the can't-catch-me-dozing razor-sharp-boy
>
> Ready to set my toe to Order's backside:
> Big-shot-to-be, big-city up-and-comer:
> Quickstepper, racer, ace among you sleepers.

While Bill Naughton summed up the raffish breed in the first number of *Pilot Papers*. 'Spivs are lary perishers. Anything goes wrong they'll never risk their own skins. They'll shove it on to you. But otherwise they'll help you. He'll be a lovely bloke to get along with. I mean they'll never make a guv'nor's man out of him. And he'll be game for anything, and he'll never split: providing he gets a share of the gravy, and he don't burn his fingers.'

The 'spiv', like the bootlegger during prohibition in the United States, saw himself as supplying a legitimate demand, which was curtailed by government restrictions. As the Osbert Lancaster cartoons showed, most people were prepared to use the 'spiv's' services if they had run out of coupons or sources. The problem was that his conspicuous presence and dubious morality added to the feverish and rootless expectations of the Fitzrovians, who were surrounded by shady practitioners and outright violence. It was not only a period of literary hitting, as Heppenstall noted, but of outright killing. Anthony Powell mentioned in his memoirs that two of his neighbours were murdered, one a young woman in Regent's Park, the other the used-car dealer Stanley Setty, who was severed with an SS knife by the false pilot Donald Hume, and his head in a baked beans carton and various pieces dropped from an aircraft into the Channel. Powell's acquaintanceship with murder ended with the death by violence of the young literary editor of *The Spectator*. It was enough for him, and he took to working for his fellow Etonian, Alan Pryce-Jones, on *The Times Literary Supplement*.

Osbert Lancaster, *Daily Express*. 24.6.47
"Don't be so stuffy, Henry! I'm sure that if you asked him nicely the young man would be only too pleased to give you the name of a really GOOD *tailor who doesn't worry about coupons!"*

The most sinister and inexplicable of the Soho murders was connected with the rise in vice and the beginning of the decline in the area. Freddie Mills had been a boxing champion and was found shot to death in his motor car outside the Chinese restaurant which he owned in Soho. He was a member of a ring of practising homosexuals, and blackmail was thought to be the motive. Homosexuality was still a crime in England. Even before the trial of Oscar Wilde, the area around Piccadilly had a long history of supplying youths for homosexuals, some of whom were wealthy or prominent in society. The law compelled gay artists and aristocrats to consort with criminals to satisfy sexual needs. Legislation to allow homosexual acts between consenting adults was still twenty years away, but already the Fitzroy Tavern was becoming a gay rendezvous, while the Golden Lion near the French pub was always of that persuasion, as was the Newman Arms. John Lehmann's *In the Purely Pagan Sense* disguised the names of the gay pubs and clubs, calling them the Broody Goose and the Alcibiades, but he attested to their prevalence after the war, filled with boxers, actors, businessmen and journalists. Eventually, the Fitzroy Tavern was to be raided in the nineteen-fifties, and its proprietor Charles Allchild accused of running a disorderly house. Incredibly, he was acquitted in spite of accusations by the counsel for the prosecution that the pub was a meeting-place for obvious male homosexuals and sailors, soldiers and marines. 'There can be very little doubt that this house was conducted in a most disorderly and disgusting fashion. These perverts were simply overrunning the place, behaving in a scandalous manner and attempting to seduce members of the forces.'

The transition of the Fitzroy Tavern, however, from the beacon of bohemia in the 'thirties to a sexual encounter parlour in the post-war years was a slow process. The regulars hardly noticed the changes over the years. Fitzrovia had always tolerated all sorts of behaviour. Prostitution and homosexuality were nothing new under the black-out or the lamp-light. What was new was their concentration in certain pubs and their overtness. In the war, open sexual behaviour had been permitted in the belief that the boys were having a good time before going back to camp or to die abroad. And there was the bombing. Danger allowed licence. But in what came to be called 'The Age of Austerity' after the war, the parade of sex in the pubs and the clubs and the streets seemed like flaunting it unnecessarily. Although London might have become the vice capital of Europe, performances were best left behind doors.

Expatriate Poles now dominated the scene of the West End clubs: Johnny Mills at the Milroy and Les Ambassadeurs, Erwin Schleyn at the Mirabelle, Siegi Sessler at Siegi's in Charles Street, and Rico Dajou beside Claridge's. They were no Warsaw Mafia: as they said of each other, they were Poles apart. They had learned the skills of survival and the means of obtaining luxuries without questioning their source. They moved the heart of clubland back to Mayfair although the Gargoyle persisted in its slow decline until sold by David Tennant to become a glorified strip club. It was there that Dylan Thomas winced when given a poem by a fellow Fitzrovian, 'On Seeing a Young Dog in the Gargoyle':

I saw him sitting in the Gargoyle,
Very drunk and very ill:
Fields of Fern Hill green and golden
Deep the shadows of Bunhill.
'Double whisky! Double brandy!
Double-dyed is hard to kill.
Where is Vernon? Where is Louis?
Have I slept with you before?

Sticks or paper, match or shovel
Cannot make an old flame roar.'
Pange lingua gloriosii ...
Pools of phlegm upon the floor.

As for the Café Royal, Wrey Gardiner noted its creeping dissolution after the war. 'The wines have gone as well as the poets and the artists. They all drink beer or cocoa. But time ticks and the clock hand moves into another world.'

In spite of the 'spivs' who had replaced the foreign soldiers as the colourful and lucrative elements in the pubs, the Fitzrovians could not see that the coming of the peace would prove to be a disaster for many of the writers and artists there. Dan Davin, who soon joined the migration from London to settle and work in Oxford, perceived that Soho's leading scribe, Julian Maclaren-Ross, was unaware of the loss of his public and his primacy. While the war went on, 'there was a captive mass audience, mad for any distraction from the shabby daylight and the dismal dark, starved of theatre and sport and the hundred diversions which in peacetime enable the English to dispense with art. Peace dissolved this audience.' For Maclaren-Ross, there was a further consequence, because he had been forced to serve in the army among other soldiers. 'The war had given him raw recruits for raw material, and rubbed his nose in the stuff of humanity. The war had made them conscripts of one another. Now his public had dispersed, leaving him a prisoner of his persona, an actor in an empty hall. And he had lost the wartime drama of the given.' The years of conflict had threatened those in uniform and civilians with sudden death, violence and change, while the years of peace provided only artificial drama for those who needed it for their image of themselves. Maclaren-Ross was now confined by his way of life and extravagant sense of self to the narrow ground of Fitzrovia. As the Soho writers began to disperse to the regions or migrate to the close embraces of the BBC, as the little magazines and wartime publishers began to fold, as new dealers and middlemen and chicaneries appeared, Maclaren-Ross became the unicorn on the bar-stool, the fabled beast that lived in a world of its own invention with no connection to the modern age. Even his old friend George Barker found him pathetic and absurd with 'a door-to-door salesman's eye for sharp evaluation ... faintly shameful because he had an eye for almost nothing else.' Seeing him in the same camel-hair coat in the corner of the same bar in 1950, flicking away from his long cigarette-holder the ash that had begun to smoulder five years before, G. S. Fraser wanted to creep up behind

Maclaren-Ross and whisper, 'It is later than you think!' But he did not, and Maclaren-Ross hardly heeded the nightly ritual pub reminder, 'Time, gentlemen, please. Time.'

Post-war Fitzrovia clung to its illusions of artistic confluence and importance. Its Homer during the end of the 'forties was John Heath-Stubbs. When he was still at Oxford University, the war had not affected him; in fact, there was a determined attempt to ignore it beside the Isis. But arriving in London during the time of the flying-bombs, he found life scary and unpredictable. After spending one night at the bottom of the garden in an air-raid shelter with two old ladies, he preferred the threat of the bombs and the company in the Fitzrovian pubs. Although pressure was put on him to write poetry about the war, he could not do so. 'It didn't impinge upon me with enough resolute force.' Of those who did write war poetry, he most admired Keith Douglas and Tambimuttu's editing of his work in *Alamein to Zem Zem*. Yet among the war poets, 'if you didn't die, you weren't recognised.' He lived on to become a bard of his age and also an acute recorder. It was a myth, for instance, that the Second World War destroyed the English class system. 'It is absolutely untrue. It did break it down. We have become less snobbish.' But Fitzrovia broke down Heath-Stubbs himself. 'One had to shed one's priggishness and one's pretentiousness and learn a great deal of social tolerance. That was one thing I learned of importance in that area ... It was Soho I think that finally got me out of my shell.' Yet if that was true, it left Heath-Stubbs with little of permanent value from his experiences, as he recorded in 'The Pearl':

> In my 'forties days, of Soho and Fitzrovia,
> The Bricklayers' Arms, affectionately known
> To all its regulars as the Burglars' Rest,
> Could serve a decent plate of fishcakes, or of shellfish.
> I found a pearl in a mussel once
> And showed it to the barman. He dropped it on the floor,
> And being no bigger than a small pin's head
> It was quite irrecoverable. This kind of thing
> Tends to occur with all the pearls I get.

Heath-Stubbs enjoyed the seedy element in Fitzrovia, preferring in the Wheatsheaf and in the Fitzroy Tavern the company of Sylvia Gough to her rival, Nina Hamnett. Sylvia came from a wealthy background and had drunk away a fortune. She was now reduced to begging for gins, which were not refused because she would then declare she would have to make a noise like a whore – and did so. She tended to upstage Hamnett's reminiscences, claiming that when she was in Paris, the graffiti in the lavatories were drawn by Toulouse-Lautrec. And when asked what she used to talk about with her friend Ronald Firbank, she would reply, 'Ourselves – mostly.'

The Coffee An', run by Boris Watson before he ran the Mandrake, and the Café Chez Alix in Rathbone Place attracted the 'characters' of Fitzrovia. Chief of them was the 'Countess', Eileen Devigne, who had married a South American 'Count',

231

cured herself of a heroin habit, lived on benzedrine and coffee and cream puffs, and dressed herself out of Mayfair dustbins. On one occasion, she stripped herself naked in the street to put on a discarded long bead gown and was arrested by the police for indecent exposure. When the magistrate asked her in court to explain her actions, she said that she had only been doing what every lady did in the evening, 'dressing for dinner'. John Heath-Stubbs lamented the passing of her like in 'Good Night, Ireen':

> I'm Ireen, the Sireen of Soho,
>   A marginal virgin of culture;
> From lunch-time to six in the caf *Chez Alix*
>   I brood like some gaily-plumed vulture;
> From six to eleven in a mild-bitter heaven
>   I gyrate through waste lands of Fitzrovia,
> While time's on the wing, like a doll on a string,
>   With strictly conditioned behaviour.

According to Dylan Thomas, Aleister Crowley, the Beast of Cefalu, used to haunt Chez Alix during the war, and afterwards, another mystic and fairground strong-man called Iron Foot Jack. To match 'Countess' Eileen, there was a self-styled 'Count' Potocki de Montalk, reputedly a New Zealander who served time for fraud and violence, but asserted he was the true King of Poland, and wore a long red robe with a silver paper star pinned to his breast and a tam-o'-shanter over his pigtail, which was tied with a bow. When he was met in the street by the other king in Fitzrovia, John Gawsworth, who claimed to be Juan I of the throne of a Caribbean island by virtue of inheritance from the mystery writer M. P. Shiel after his death in 1947, Potocki was greeted formally:

'Hallo, Poland,' Gawsworth said.

'Hallo, Redonda,' Potocki said.

'Remember me to Our Cousin of England,' Gawsworth said, referring to King George the Sixth.

John Gawsworth, alias Terence Armstrong, had a saturnine and Jacobite sense of humour and a determination to play the bohemian like his heroes Richard Middleton and Ernest Dowson, two romantic poets whose pockets had bulged with drafts of verses and whose lives had been eroded with drink. Gawsworth created a Fitzrovian pub aristocracy from Redonda of grand dukes and knights and admirals: titles were given to Dorothy L. Sayers and 'Ellery Queen', Dylan Thomas and Henry Miller. In *Who's Who*, Gawsworth listed his recreation as 'creating nobility'. The Colonial Office even granted him a form of legitimacy, informing him that perhaps he was entitled to call himself a king. 'If it makes him happy, why not?' But Gawsworth was still a serious, although facile poet: his *Collected Poems* of 1948 were praised by his traditional and neo-Georgian peers, and he took from Muriel Spark the important post of the editor of the *Poetry Review*. While he held the position, he could claim to be a Wrey Gardiner or a Tambimuttu, a poet of influence, one who preferred to live in bohemia, but who knew the difference between the quality of good writing and alcoholic dreams of superiority, fantasy and self-destruction. Unpublished verses of the period, 'Definitions of Drink', show how his poetic standards were slipping as his awareness grew:

> First he sips slowly from a sour glass
> And wonders why life is so sad for him.
> Then he repeats his dose; the hour glass
> Drips, and he hears faintly the cherubim.
>
> A third glass conquers, and the choir expands;
> He hears furore. Why should *he* not sing?
> Silence most dismal dreams on many lands,
> Such need a carnival. Is he no king?

Gawsworth was still a king of Fitzrovia in its decline, and he was still active in his field. 'Not all the people who frequented Soho were drunken layabouts, though a lot of them were,' John Heath-Stubbs said, 'and the number of fatalities, in terms of breakdowns and suicides, in these circles was high. But it was a place where one felt one was in touch with some of the main streams of modern literature.' He himself only survived in Fitzrovia on an inheritance from an aunt and was saved from bohemian penury in 1952 by the intervention of T. S. Eliot and Herbert Read, who recommended him for the Gregory Fellowship at Leeds University, which was followed by posts in Egypt and the United States of America. But he never regretted the 'university' of Soho in the 'forties nor his lack of recognition by the masters of his craft. A contemporary, W. Sydney Graham, paid a tribute to 'Heath-Stubbs the Poet as Hero':

> And who will ride with Heath-Stubbs now
> Upon the pages of the world.
> Sing me your out of fashion. Literature
> With courage is a thousand men.
> Shall I meet you with Artorius again?
>
> Another time I saw you tacking
> Across Oxford Street in a full
> Gale of traffic. You were crewed
> Adequately by David Wright
> And sailed into the Black Horse.
>
> I hardly see you nowadays.
> You hardly see me.
> Could I clasp your writing hand
> On this ridiculous, darkening stage?
> John, we are almost of an age.

Many of the demobilized writers did not view Fitzrovia as a university, but as an opportunity. The ethos of the place as the clearing-house of a democratic and innovative culture still lingered. After the blank relief of his escape from the armed services at the dispersal centre at Aldershot, G. S. Fraser went immediately to visit Tambimuttu, who had published some of his poems while in exile among the Salamanders in Cairo in their Fitzrovia by the Nile. Nicholas Moore was in the recognized office in Manchester Square and attempted to run an efficient poetry magazine from there: he was eventually to take over *Poetry London* from the erratic Tamil. But Tambimuttu would take Fraser drinking beer in the Hog and Pound in Oxford Street and later round his regular pubs in Fitzrovia, while carrying with him a fat file of manuscripts, which he lost and retrieved in taxis and from bars nightly. After his disastrous and voluminous 'Chums Annual' issue of *Poetry London* in 1946, Tambimuttu waited two years before reissuing his poetry magazine regularly, and this diffidence suited many of the war poets, who found the altered peacetime conditions an impediment to their muse. Fraser himself felt no urge to write. The spur of exile and loneliness had gone. He had married, settled down, gave weekly poetry readings in his Chelsea rooms, and even received a triennial literary award, which enabled him to exist. The first years of the peace were a fallow period for him and many other poets, who either matured or fell silent for ever. London seemed to have a strange effect on his sense of time. He was always meeting characters who had been going round the same bars saying the same things for twenty years. In spite of the fact that the peace was driving the Fitzrovians and their war friends apart, they clung to shared memories in nostalgic places. 'We had our different ways of life now, ranging from idleness to plodding, from dalliance to marriage; we had different political fancies and diverging tastes.' The way to keep together was to repeat the good old times. 'Our attitude towards the concept of the good time was, in fact, almost religious. There must have been a first good time, some time ... It was an idea, and an evening or a day spent drinking and gossiping was an attempt to make it real. Meanwhile, we had not written the books and poems our friends expected of us, and we were getting a little too old for the reviewers to go on talking genially about promise.'

Yet the attraction of the ambience stimulated and lingered, like mint after rain. Bohemia was its own instant nostalgia. By a process of osmosis, young artists still believed that they could infuse culture somewhere between Charlotte and Dean Streets. As a young poet who had castigated Cambridge and served with distinction in the Mediterranean, writing two of the more exact and laconic war poems, 'The Bofors Gun' and 'When a Beau Goes In', Gavin Ewart could not resist the lure of post-war Fitzrovia. With the remembrance and disbelief of hindsight, 'In the Old Days' recalled the time when he worked for Tambimuttu and *Poetry London*:

why, in those days, all these people were real!
Living and breathing and walking round London!
People in London were meeting in pubs and drinking,
they were falling in love and out of love again
and the black shiny taxis beetled through the streets!

But then, if memory was golden, it was also gauze.

> why then you will know that like the year 1946
> all the years before and all the years after
> are going to blur in the same way, and vanish!
> All those years – to remember – do we really want to?
> Perhaps we forget them as a kind of consolation.

The fact was that the publishing and reading boom of the war collapsed in 1947 or thereabouts. The severe winter of that year was the last judgement by ice. For two weeks, no magazines at all were allowed paper or publication: from *Horizon* to *Lilliput*, all periodicals noticed fewer subscribers and falling sales: the bookshops would no longer stock everything that came out, but only selected titles by established authors. And the reprinting of classic texts took up much of the limited wood pulp supplies, which might have been used to present new writers. Paper rationing, a change in public taste and the restocking of traditional works, these three factors reduced the opportunities for those who already found it difficult to write in the reaction of the peace. Sympathetic publishers such as Lovat Dickson might admit to putting old books back into print, but he also complained that fresh voices shouting from the war were slow to appear. 'A new age was dawning, but few were there to hymn it.' The writers and the great events were not coinciding. In the pubs of Fitzrovia, Dan Davin found that 'all the game was a funeral game', as he hunted for words and themes, and talked with others of the trade.

Although John Lehmann went against the trend by opening his own publishing house and printing up to twelve titles a year, commissioning illustrations from such artists as Keith Vaughan and John Minton and Edward Burra and Michael Ayrton and Lynton Lamb, and although he published Saul Bellow and Paul Bowles and Sartre and Malraux and Kazantzakis, he discovered no major English novelists, only the best-selling cookery books of Elizabeth David. The flair of Penguin *New Writing*, which had printed original and exciting stories and poetry, was not translated into the publishing venture, except for the issuing of the best poetry of the desert war, Hamish Henderson's *Elegies for the Dead in Cyrenaica*. Despite colour covers by John Minton, the Penguin magazine itself began to flag and fail. Lehmann had been lured into a reckless expansion because of the success of *New Writing*, but its standards did not persist in the peace.

There was the same falling-off of good writing among the poets who had clustered round *Twentieth Century Verse* and continued to support George Woodcock's *Now*. Among the central group, Julian Symons, H. B. Mallalieu, Keidrych Rhys, D. S. Savage and Woodcock himself all ceased to write poetry. Mallalieu's reason was that his admirable war verses had reflected a period rather than an individual talent; incidental things had mattered: 'one was trying to stop the bullet in its flight, trying to leave an imprint in the air.' Ruthven Todd and Gavin Ewart still produced a few poems; but only Roy Fuller continued to build a reputation as a major poet in the post-war world. Woodcock's explanation of the silence of the *Now* group was that they had come to the end of a movement and an epoch; they could not continue trying to work out the literary and political problems of the 'thirties. Julian Symons attributed the muteness of the poets he knew to the shattering of the ideals of reconstruction by the relative failure of the peace. Woodcock did not himself think that literary creativity was so closely linked to political hopes or despairs. Roy Fuller was as disillusioned as the rest at the end of the war, but he went on to write out of his pessimism and disappointment some of the better poetry of the peace. Mallalieu himself finally broke his silence to salute Fuller's achievements in whose work 'a shameless documentary' would survive.

> With laboratory skill
> You filter the trivia of the day until
> The alchemy of your words transmutes
> Residual meaning into lucid verse.

Fuller himself, trying to explain why an admired contemporary Kenneth Allott wrote little verse after 1943, merely stated that a proportion of every generation stopped when it was out of its youth. 'The War reinforced this fact of nature. The poet had two changed sets of conditions to try to grapple with – the different occupation (or even the same occupation) in wartime; the return to a different peace as an older and wiser man ... The premature termination of such a talent must have caused anguish to its possessor.'

Few asked the question, 'Where Are the Peace Poets?', because peace seemed so long a time in coming. Not until 1950 did International P.E.N. hold a publicized meeting to consider 'The Crisis in Poetry' and demand why the younger war poets had given up their craft, and why the heights of Parnassus were now occupied by the aged T. S. Eliot and Edith Sitwell and Edwin Muir, or by those who had not served in uniform, such as Dylan Thomas and Norman Nicholson. Religious and metaphysical and neo-Romantic poetry in England, nationalist and regional poetry in Scotland and Wales and Ireland, these characterized the aftermath of war. With his usual penetration, as early as 1946 Stephen Spender summarized the mood of the young poets in his important booklet for the new British Council, 'Poetry Since 1939'. They were involved with more than the ideology of British democracy, and although they supported left-wing policies on the whole, they were not enthusiastic. 'They have abandoned the hope of an integration of their own highest interests, their own humanity, their own personalities within any politically organized society. In this, they have reacted sharply from the writers of the 'thirties. They are concerned partly with trying to construct a vision of the time which accepts the fact of social disintegration, partly with trying to develop their own taste and talent within their own isolated conspiracy of intelligent and frustrated minds.' At its most extreme, Paul Dehn expressed the poet's reaction from urban life in the 'New Age':

> To-night the wind comes screaming up the road
> Like a train in the tube. Over my cringing head

Gas-lamps are ghosts of the still-marching dead
Whose butchered eyes, blown open,
Pity our cold condition.
Here, in this rotting air,
The traffic lights ripen
From green to yellow, from yellow to red;
And I, with a cobweb of rain in my hair,
Trudge between tram-lines, seeking a world's salvation.

Only the lost are with me, only the late
And the last, lonely stragglers in the street:
A drunkard in the lamplight, on whose coat
Something still glistens;
The frosted whore who marks
My footfall on the stone,
Sniffs in the wind and listens
Under the red lamp of the traffic light;
And a flash boy, adrift in the pin-stripe rain,
Edging towards the privacy of parks.

These, my cold company; whose nailed feet
Scrape on the pavements of eternal night ...

With the self-imposed or induced silence of many of the younger writers, the established publishers and authors recovered their nerve and control. Literature, as Alan Ross noticed, 'took a temporary turn to the Right. The days of social realism, of proletarian art and documentary reporting were gone forever ... The best writing was upper-middle class and upper-middle aged; and that too was a sign of the times.' T. S. Eliot had been sufficiently charitable and aware of the new romanticism in poetry to befriend Tambimuttu and even publish Henry Treece and other deserters from the cause of the Apocalypse. But now, in *Left Hand, Right Hand*, Osbert Sitwell began an autobiographical reconstruction of a past world of aristocratic excesses and eccentricities which showed that it was the privilege of the privileged, not of the bohemians, to shock in the arts. Edith Sitwell's literary parties had become the caravanserai of the established and the tamed rebels. Eliot and Spender and MacNeice would be joined by Dylan Thomas and Roy Campbell. There they would meet John Gielgud and Alec Guinness, and the luminaries of the ballet world, Robert Helpmann and Frederick Ashton and Constant Lambert. Critics and editors included John Lehmann and Alan Pryce-Jones, Maurice Bowra and Kenneth Clark as well as Osbert and Sacheverell Sitwell. It was almost a literary establishment reminiscent of the Bloomsbury circle, against which the Sitwells had once set themselves. Such people were the ones castigated by Edmund Wilson, when he saw English culture in decline after 1945 with its labouring and shopkeeping people made more equal by restrictions, but over-shadowed by 'a fading phantom of the English public school'.

The phantom still possessed a considerable body of influence. Although Cyril Connolly increasingly stated that there was a continuous decline in all the arts, and that the collapse of the wealthy world of the *haute bourgeoisie* had removed both the patronage and the true audience of great artists, the writers and poets who had made a name before the war re-established their pre-eminence through publishing companies such as Faber & Faber and Jonathan Cape, and through the rising state patronage organizations, the Arts and the British Councils as well as the British Broadcasting Corporation. The battle of the books in the war had led to a breakthrough into democratic publishing and opportunity for fresh writing; but now the old world revived in its power and values, while the new world aged and lost heart. There was a visible change in the relation of the artist to society. Bohemianism was going out of fashion. 'The best painters and writers preferred to be taken for stockbrokers or professional men of leisure,' Alan Ross wrote, 'rather than reveal their trade by their appearance. Since art and literature had the, at least nominal, support of the State, their practitioners were forced into the role of civil servants ... A reluctance to conform to accepted sartorial and social ethics denoted a lack of seriousness, an ostentation no longer coupled with nonsense about integrity and independence.'

As in post-war poetry, so in fiction. The war writers left the battlefield to the Americans, particularly to Norman Mailer in *The Naked and the Dead*. The most idiosyncratic and original use of war experience in the novel was made by Jocelyn Brooke in his autobiographical trilogy, *The Military Orchid*, *A Mine of Serpents* and *The Goose Cathedral*. Proust and Eliot were his ruling influences in interweaving time past and present and future; love of flowers was the theme, botany the quest, and orchids the *petites madeleines*. Brooke served as a 'pox-wallah' treating venereal diseases in the Royal Army Medical Corps and re-enlisted until he bought himself out to become a writer: his smart friends sneered that he was 'doing a little T. E. Shaw'. The 'Orchid' trilogy remains one of the best accounts of the aesthetic and gay world of some of the Oxford graduates, shocked into what Brooke called 'homocommunism' by the Depression and into realism by the war itself. Brooke himself preferred to wear uniform. A poem on 'Embarkation Leave' found him 'glad, on the whole, to be back in the bare and ordered world of War, where Death like Life is a routine, performed by numbers'. In 'Transit Camp', the soldier remembered 'without regret the dark and ruined vista of Civvy Street'. And even when Brooke finally left the army in 1948, he regretted it. 'Soldiering had become a habit with me – out of uniform I felt lost, uprooted, a kind of outlaw with no fixed place in the scheme of things. During the two years since my demobilization I had suffered from a growing sense of loss and betrayal: I had cast off my mistress – glad enough, at the time, to be free of her thraldom: yet I knew that, despite her tantrums, her cruelty and her possessiveness, I loved her still.'

Alone among the writers, Brooke bore true witness to the security of army life, the order imposed by routine, the anarchy of returning to civilian clothes and intolerable aimlessness. Other established novelists turned back to another ordered world of pre-war nostalgia, often a flight into childhood. A trilogy by L. P. Hartley expressed themes of innocence surprised or betrayed, while his sad and comic novel *The Boat* approved of a man of letters ignoring the war and trying to row his private craft upstream against local authority. With *Manservant and Maidservant* and *Two Worlds and their Ways*, the mannered, conversational and archaic milieu of Ivy Compton-Burnett continued to receive extravagant praise – another novelist P. H. Newby ranked her fiction with that of James Joyce as works which would be read in a hundred years' time. The most experimental of post-war novels, *Tea With Mrs Goodman* by Philip Toynbee, was clipped into mathematical arrangements of lines of consciousness. Joyce Cary's exuberance spilled over in two books about irresponsible women, *The Moonlight* and *A Fearful Joy*, but they failed to match the controlled invention of his masterly trilogy about Gulley Jimson. Only Graham Greene used his experience as an intelligence officer in West Africa to outdo even Cary's understanding of the declining colonial scene: his guilty romantic novel, *The Heart of the Matter*, established him with Elizabeth Bowen in *The Heat of the Day* as the inquisitioners of the tragic perplexities of passion and betrayal during a time of war. They were two of the few writers mentioned by V. S. Pritchett as unofficial historians of the crisis of civilization, responding to their private sensibility, taking 'possession of the novel as a mist takes possession of the streets and all who breathe it are transformed'.

Along with Joyce Cary, Henry Green seemed to find a certain failing in the cessation of hostilities. *Concluding* was set fifty years in the future; the subject was an aged scientist living out his last years as an unwanted guest in a girls' school; the impression was that of an author looking forward in pessimism to a futile past. Green's novel of 1950, *Nothing*, confirmed his revulsion from his wartime achievements in *Caught* and *Back*: a frivolous comedy of manners suggested a writer who was detached from his audience and from the significance of his times, and who used his craft to lull and entertain. In the words of the last lines of *Nothing*:

'And is there anything at all you want my own?'
'Nothing ... nothing' he replied in so low a voice she could barely have heard and then seemed to fall deep asleep at last.

THE END

The illuminating works of British fiction after 1945 were satires. Aldous Huxley was revived by Hiroshima into writing a bleak vision of a world destroyed by atomic explosions, *Ape and Essence*. Although the scene was set in Huxley's place of voluntary exile, California, the message was global: the atom bomb or the Thing had destroyed the world, where the Devil now ruled because of man's science and belief in progress. 'He created an entirely new race of men, with deformity in their blood, with squalor all around them, and ahead, in the future, no prospects but of more squalor, worse deformity and, finally, complete extinction.' Evelyn Waugh's assault on California was only on its modern cemeteries and mortuary parlours; 239

but *The Loved One* showed that his powers of sardonic observation and nice wit had been honed into bayonets. He confirmed the general feeling that the great war novels would not be written without the postscript of merciless revision. He was to write the disillusioned masterpiece of the war, *Sword of Honour*, throughout the next decade; but its tart cadences were not for immediate times.

George Orwell was the prickly intellect of the end of the war. His social fable, *Animal Farm*, was a damning indictment of socialist planning that shook the complacency of those who believed Utopias were practical constructs. One of four publishers to refuse it, T. S. Eliot, had rejected the novel at Faber & Faber, because he was not convinced this was the right criticism of the political situation at the present time. It went against the current of the moment: the pigs who ran *Animal Farm* might have been more public-spirited. Cyril Connolly, however, recognized at once the considerable achievement of his Old Etonian friend. He compared Orwell's feeling, penetration and verbal economy to those qualities in Jonathan Swift. Orwell, indeed, was the antithesis of Connolly – a man of self-discipline and courage, of passionate integrity and harsh honesty, of rare conviction and no pomposity, lacking all of Connolly's grace and style and accommodations with power. Yet the terms of Connolly's famous phrase, that imprisoned in every fat man a thin one was wildly signalling to be let out, suggest the thin man was the George Orwell, whom the self-indulgent editor of *Horizon* admired and could never be.

1984 was Orwell's last novel, although it might have been set in the wartime world of 1944. The grimy city, the façades of bombed buildings, the wooden and corrugated iron shelters on the rubble, the restrictions on food and drink and movement, even the occasional rocket falling almost at random, these were the evidence of recent and present times, not of the future, which was suggested by intrusive television and thought police and Orwell's invention of genius: Newspeak. Here was his reaction to his despair at the slogans of political ideology and at the war propaganda, which he had produced for the wireless. Newspeak was the negation of the language of truth. It was the Janus of all communication. In categorizing the two-faced false god of the media, Orwell left the people of the world in debt to his accurate, blunt prose.

John Craxton

A year after the publication of *1984*, George Orwell died. He did not live to see the equal and free society in Britain that he wanted. He complained to Stephen Spender that there were still too many Rolls-Royces in London under the Labour government. Visible signs of one class being better than another were bad for morale; but these were to become only more visible after his death. Paradoxically, his warnings in *Animal Farm* and *1984* of the vicious, semi-criminal autocracy which might grow in English society were used as a potent attack on the planning policies of the Labour government as well as on the new Stalinist dictatorships of Eastern Europe. Criticism, unlike charity, stopped at home. Orwell's criticism was true for all societies including his own. As Robert Conquest wrote of him:

> He shared with a great world, for greater ends,
> That honesty, a curious cunning virtue
> You share with just the few who don't desert you.
> A dozen writers, half-a-dozen friends.
>
> A moral genius ...
>
> – Than whom no writer could be less poetic
> He left this lesson for all verse, all art.

More conventional novelists, who had made their reputation by writing of the drabness of London in the 'forties, lost their audience and somewhat their talent, as if their pens had stuck in dried blood. This was particularly true of Gerald Kersh and to some degree of Nigel Balchin, after his success with *The Small Back Room*. One major talent, however, translated the violent and shabby-genteel *demi-monde* of wartime into the criminal sublife of pub and club in the peace. As a young writer, Patrick Hamilton had been heralded in the 'thirties for his major trilogy of London novels, *Twenty Thousand Streets Under the Sky*. They were followed by *Hangover Square*, the bar-room equivalent of Henry Green's *Party Going*; it showed the conniving and rootless society of saloons and drinking-clubs, boarding-houses and dingy hotels, the no man's land of the homeless and the opportunist. 'No English novelist', J. B. Priestley wrote, 'has had a better ear for the complacent platitudes, the banalities, the sheer idiocy of pub talk, than Hamilton.' Yet he saw the evil of the crack in the sherry-glass. Set in 1939, *Hangover Square* made of his shiftless hero, George Harvey Bone, a double murderer and a suicide, condemned by an aimless pub-crawling world that ignored the eve of war. Patrick Hamilton's other compelling piece of fiction, *The Slaves of Solitude*, saw the war through the eyes of the innocent Miss Roach in the setting of the Rosamund Tea Rooms on the Thames outside London; all the stratagems of survival and drunken superiorities of visiting foreign forces suggested the pressure of war conditions on the scale of a blitz in a saucer. Miss Roach, however, returned to London. 'You had to square up to the war. The horror and despondence of the Rosamund Tea Rooms resided in just the fact that it was not squaring up to it ... almost insensible of it, more absorbed in the local library. And this was not a war to be taken in a local-library way.' Before he died like Dylan Thomas of too many strangers buying him drinks in bars, Hamilton completed his final exposure of alcohol and criminality, the trilogy based on the murderous career of Ernest Ralph Gorse, who commenced his clever larcenies in *The West Pier*.

Moreover, Graham Greene had never wholly abandoned the company of the criminal and the violent of the city. From Pinky in *Brighton Rock* to Arthur Rowe in *The Ministry of Fear*, his protagonists suffered in the twilight between guilt and pain and reaction. Avoiding his pursuers in a tube station during an air raid, Rowe dreamed of talking to his dead mother and telling her that it all sounded like a thriller, 'but the thrillers are like life – more like life than you are'. Rose Macaulay took up the theme when she was asked about the future of post-war fiction: 'Life has flared for millions into a grim thriller; why, then, novels?' The answer was, as Alex Comfort pointed out in *The Novel and Our Time*, political and social and personal violence had become even more characteristic of big-city communities during and after the war. Atrocity propaganda against the Axis powers had degraded public taste. Literary sadism such as *No Orchids for Miss Blandish*, and pulp thrillers at a lower level than those of Hamilton or Greene, had become reflections of a true urban world.

All the same, street violence and the skullduggery of the 'spiv' did not offer to most writers the stimulus of the shared dangers of a bygone war. The loss of a common cause against an agreed enemy revived the emergence of a class system and an underclass. Even conscripts to the army under the terms of National Service found the barrack room a mere pub society of thieving and 'skiving', the army slang for shirking. The Labour government's attempts to institute a just and fair welfare state failed to unite the British people, and divided them more bitterly in society and in the arts. An establishment with state patronage was forming in London and forsaking the rebels and their bohemias. There was also a hardening of bourgeois values, which did not always approve of the causes or concerns of the planners of the new age. Even David Gascoyne made political statements, seeing in a false peacetime only a 'nightly black-out dream', and failing to find a commitment to future society in the average population passing along the great thoroughfare that divided Fitzrovia, 'Demos in Oxford Street':

> We have hardened our faces against each other's weariness
> Who walk this way; we are not bound to one another
> By bomb panic or famine and it is not Christmas Day.
> We are aware of Socialists in power at Westminster
> Who seem to be making a pretty mess of things ...
> Besides, we have our families to think of,
> And our families have not got too much to spare
> Of time or money, tears or trouble. Stare
> As boldly as you like into our faces, we'll not turn
> Aside out of your way. We're not the Working-Class.

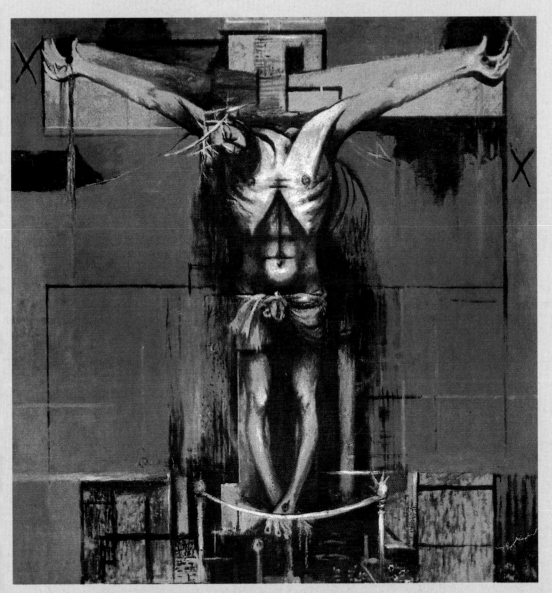

Graham Sutherland painted this *Crucifixion* for St. Matthew's Church, Northampton, where it hung near Henry Moore's *Madonna and Child*.

ABOVE: *Council Chamber, House of Commons, 1941* by John Piper showed the devastation after the German bombing.

OPPOSITE: *The Passage to the Control-Room at S.W. Regional Headquarters, Bristol,* a painting by John Piper.

The poster and a still
from Laurence Olivier's
film of *Henry V*.

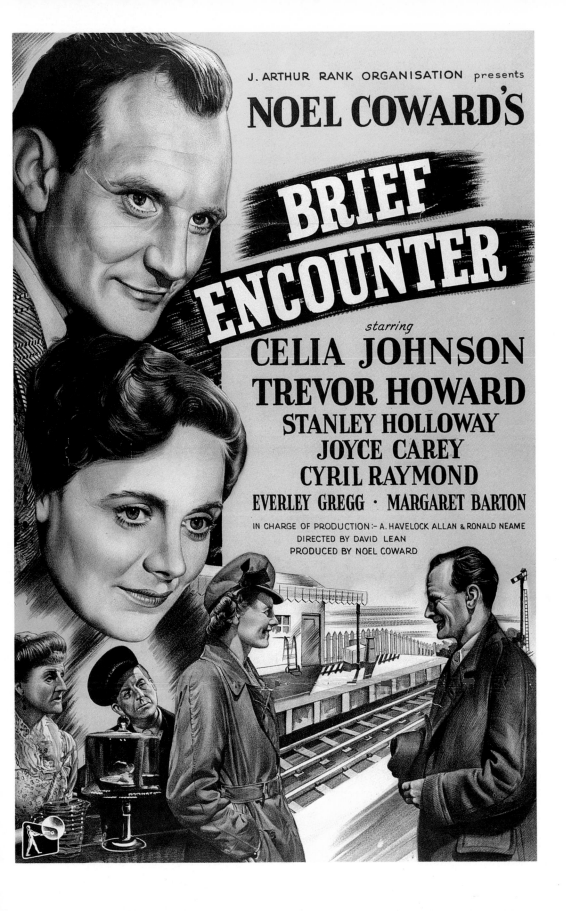

OPPOSITE: Keith Douglas painted this frontispiece for *Alamein to Zem Zem*.

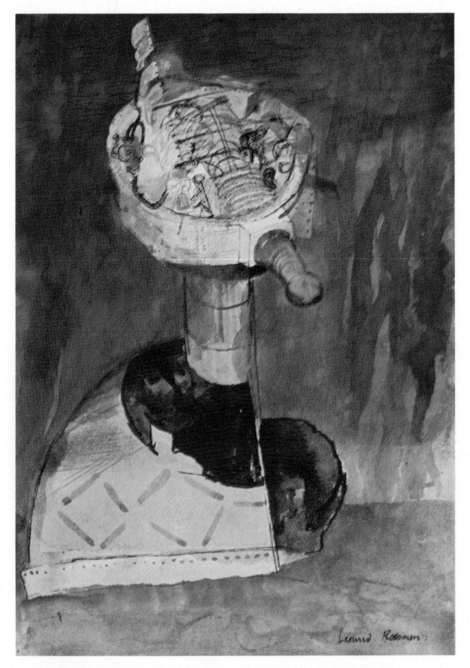

Radar Predictor by Leonard Rosoman showed his fascination with men and their war machines.

Leslie Hurry's cover for a book on Robert Helpmann.

John Piper's design for the backcloth for the last act of Ashton's ballet,
The Quest.

SEVENTEEN

State of the Art

Bank and turn, bank and turn,
Air-treading bull, my silver Alitalia!
Bank and turn, while the earth below
Swings like a dial on the wing-tip's axis,
Whirls and checks like a wheel of chance! ...
Over the Channel now, beneath the enchanting
Inane babble of a baby-blue sky,
We soar through cloudland, at the heights of nonsense.

So Cecil Day Lewis wrote of his 'Flight to Italy', part of a long poem, *An Italian Visit*, that Cyril Connolly used to front the last issue of *Horizon*, which had so long preached the escape to Europe and its superior culture. The artists of Fitzrovia certainly heeded the message. They led the diaspora after the war. It was a rush towards Mediterranean light. Francis Bacon, who was also to be featured in the final number of *Horizon*, returned to the France which he loved, fleeing from rationing into the hazards of the Riviera. He based himself in the Hotel de Ré near the casino in Monte Carlo, where he became obsessed by gambling. He would enter the casino at ten o'clock in the morning and spend sixteen hours there, coming out at dawn. At one point, he won £1,600, not subject to British foreign currency regulations, and took a villa and filled it with drink and food and 'an enormous number of friends'. He felt of gambling as he felt of painting: he wanted to win even if he always lost. He loved living 'in gilded squalor'. Graham Sutherland also liked gambling, 'the painter's vice', and followed Bacon to the South of France, after a lunch at the White Tower on one of Bacon's brief return journeys to London. Later, he took Lucian Freud out with him to the Riviera, and met Matisse once and Picasso often. He was commissioned by Somerset Maugham to paint a portrait, which pleased the sitter although it made him look to others like a Shanghai brothel-keeper. Sutherland now deserted his British and neo-Romantic influences for the more brilliant colours and definitions of the Mediterranean sun. He was liberated in a way that Bacon never had to be, remaining in the dark cages of the horrors of his time and screaming with the rest of mankind to be let out.

John Minton also left the ravaged docklands of London to travel south with Alan Ross. They went to Corsica to draw and write *Time Was Away* for John Lehmann. Ross returned to live for the best part of a year in the boiler room below the flat which Minton shared with Keith Vaughan, who himself travelled through France and Italy in 1948. Vaughan admired his companion's love of living, but not of destruction. Minton fled on other trips to Spain and Morocco and the West Indies. When he was to die a decade later of a mixture of drink and sleeping pills, his profligacy in everything was still envied by Vaughan. 'People never stopped laughing in his presence. "What does it all *mean*," he would repeat year after year, without really wanting to know the answer.'

For Minton, there was no flight into the Mediterranean light from himself. Nor was there for the two Roberts, Colquhoun and MacBryde. Colquhoun had finally escaped back to Scotland, where the War Artists' Advisory Committee eventually commissioned a Celtic subject from his brush; but he found that the Scots nationalist painters who lived north of the Tweed now considered him rather a Londoner. He and MacBryde burned their boats in England even with the Fitzrovians by wrecking the country house at Tilty Mill near Dunmow, which Ruthven Todd had taken over from the painter John Armstrong. Colquhoun and MacBryde sold Todd's collection of pictures and rare books and then dunned him for bottles of whisky across Fitzrovia. They were incorrigible to their own kind as well as to the other sort; to them, property was not only theft, but an opportunity for theft by themselves. Colquhoun had quality as a painter, MacBryde as an embellisher of other men's existences. But in 1949, their trip with George Barker round Italy for another aborted book to be published by John Lehmann removed Colquhoun from his British roots and directed him to painting puppets and masked figures and men confused with bulls and horses. His Mediterranean excursion led to the decline of his art and his luck into a terminal bohemianism, an extreme immediacy and an early death. As David Wright wrote in an epitaph on his Fitzrovian friend:

> Soho-wraiths bristle as I turn the square.
> Colquhoun's gone into his last coma,
> His ghost joins the throng on the pavements.
> Citizen, step aside, it is more alive than you are.

The escape of Michael Ayrton to Italy and on to Greece was a catharsis. He went to Italy with Constant Lambert in 1947, and then every following year until Greece and its ancient mythology became the dominating passions of his life. Light and monumental designs infused his works. Like Leonardo da Vinci or Dürer, he drew with grids across the anatomy or across the view. He might have been seeking the dead Roman state, so determined was he to find a discipline in art abroad. In 1950, he married the divorced wife of Nigel Balchin and moved with her three daughters from bohemian London to settle in the Essex countryside; the polymath of his generation now gave up the stimulus of Fitzrovia for classical myth and domestic life. He saw himself reborn as Daedalus, the primordial artist and engineer, the ultimate smith who had made the first wings for man to fly.

Unfortunately, the most British of the war artists, Paul Nash, had always known he would not soar except in death. Bronchial asthma had stopped him flying overmuch, when he was executing his supreme aerial paintings for the War Artists' Advisory Committee. His last two oils were of sunflowers, although he did not go to the South of France to emulate Van Gogh. His 'Eclipse ...' and 'Solstice of the Sunflower' were prophecies of the twilight of his creative power. His wings would never come from a modern Daedalus or from Aegean light, only from the dissolution of his body. As he wrote in 'Aerial Flowers' in his autobiography *Outline*: 'Death, I believe, is the only solution to this problem of how to be able to fly. Personally, I feel that if death can give us that, death will be good.'

John Craxton flew to Greece after the war and rarely returned. He had been happy in Fitzrovia, sharing a studio which was provided for him and Lucian Freud by Peter Watson. 'We were the same age,' Craxton remembered, 'at large in wartime London. We went nightclubbing because we were both enthusiastic dancers. We went jitterbugging at the clubs around Denman Street. Then, after a night of drinking and dancing, I would go home and paint to the sound of big bands on American Forces radio – is that how you imagined the neo-Romantic artist worked?' The two Roberts, Colquhoun and MacBryde, were also patronized by Peter Watson and served Craxton as protective guides round the pubs and bars of Soho, 'the London equivalent of a French bohemia, a whole group of artists, poets and writers like Dylan Thomas eking out a small existence – a marvellous atmosphere, rather fraught, dirty and seedy now I look back on it, but irresistible and wonderfully stimulating'. Craxton had met Graham Sutherland and was taken by him painting in Wales. He also met Britain's two leading composers, the warm and open Michael Tippett, and the tight and difficult Benjamin Britten – 'It was like talking to an oyster.' But such Fitzrovian stimuli could not keep Craxton there, especially as the childhood pleurisy which had kept him from military service sent him out to the sun for a cure. His escape to Greece was total, he felt a real person in real elements and a real sun. 'In a life of reality my imagination really works.' Soon he felt 'like an *émigré* in London and squashed flat'. He has lived on to old age in Crete, moulding the neo-Romantic vision of an earth force into a classical use of form. For him, the flight from Fitzrovia was finally his inspiration and salvation.

For some of those who did not get away, London would be their tomb. Jankel Adler died of a heart attack in 1949. He had been an inspiration from Europe to many of the young Fitzrovian painters. And the doyenne of them all, Nina Hamnett, suffered a slow decline into poverty and alcoholism. She made the transition to the new hang-out of the Fitzrovian painters, led by Francis Bacon and Lucian Freud. That was the Colony Room, a small upstairs drinking-club founded in 1948 by the formidable Muriel Belcher, whose language and partialities made her the Rosa Lewis of the Soho scene: the jazz singer George Melly says that the ancient Rosa gave her imprimatur personally to Muriel as her heir in repartee. Muriel referred to most men as 'Her' or 'Cunty' and to 'Miss' Hitler: her favourite 'daughter' Francis Bacon even painted a triptych of her. Nina Hamnett was tolerated with her Oxo tin of begged money, but not encouraged. One of her last refuges was the French pub, where her regular seat behind the door was scented with her incontinence. Her life ended in a similar manner to the gigantic poet Anna Wickham, who hanged herself out of her bedroom window – in Rayner Heppenstall's opinion, 'a curiously exhibitionistic proceeding (unless, of course, she had been unable to find a big enough drop elsewhere)'. Nina Hamnett also fell out of her bedroom window, but impaled herself on the spikes of the iron railings beneath her flat. The coroner's verdict was 'Accidental death'; indeed, death had resulted from a life lived as a series of drunken accidents. David Wright again mourned her in 'Verses at a Bohemian Funeral':

> Vanished unwasted hours of being
>   (Being not doing)
> In the religion of alcohol:
>   Be a memorial …
>
> Civilization, leering from its gin,
>   – A proper bad hat –
> Has left a high stool for the short way home.

The bohemian artist was becoming a member of a dying species because of the rise of state patronage. A defunct tradition of painting, Herbert Read noted, was being kept alive by the Arts Council and the provincial galleries 'like trying to keep the dodo alive in a zoo'. He joined with two wealthy patrons, Peter Watson and Ronald Penrose, in founding the Institute of Contemporary Arts in 1947 as a counterpoise to the growing influence of the Arts and British Councils, which were promoting internationally the works of certain British artists, who had been subsidized by the state during the war. Henry Moore was the chief beneficiary. His drawings of men working at the coal-face and his Shelter sketches of the sleepers during the blitz have come to be recognized as 'among the finest ever produced in Britain. Moore made use of both his acute perceptual observation, and his powers of intensive, imaginative transformation.' The same stimulus of war and the resurgence of English romanticism made Moore turn away from surrealism and modernism in sculpture. His *Madonna and Child* for St Matthew's Church in Northampton was a denial of the universal death-dealing of the time; it was a traditional monument to the sacredness of motherhood and life everlasting through the weight of the child. His reward in the post-war years was major national and international exhibitions subsidized by the state. Retiring from London to Hoglands in the country, this son of a Yorkshire miner became the universal symbol of the abiding qualities of British art.

Graham Sutherland was another painter to be helped by the increasing power and subsidy of the state. Sutherland was conscious of how official employment during the hostilities had given him security. 'I am far from unmindful of my good fortune during the war,' he told Kenneth Clark, who was one of those who saw that Sutherland's good fortune continued in the peace, both collecting his pictures personally and arranging for a retrospective of his work at the new Institute of Contemporary Arts. But Sutherland's international reputation was made in travelling group shows abroad, subsidized by the British Council, which also patronized Stanley Spencer, Edward Burra and the younger painters, Craxton and Minton, Freud and Vaughan. To be excluded from this patronage was to languish at home with little reputation.

British artists were no longer besieged within the shores of their islands. They did not have to contemplate their roots. The pervasive influences of modern

French painting, particularly of Picasso, thrust into the nostalgic underbelly of neo-Romanticism. Only John Piper, in spite of many visits to France and Italy, remained wholly under the spell of the romantic British tradition; when he designed the backcloths for the revival of the Sadler's Wells ballet of *Job* in 1948, he paid full tribute to William Blake. But already the fashion in art criticism was beginning to shift from praise of British painting for its forced ingrowth during the war to a denigration of any school of art that was not considered international in application. The echo of this war of the painters continues to reverberate louder than the anti-aircraft guns on the Home Front and on service overseas during the actual conflict.

The necessary commitment of British talent to working on British themes, which had made the wartime documentary and film the finest achievements of the island's cinema, were followed by a loss of concentration in the peace. Hollywood could again influence and entice. As the best of the producers and film-makers had noticed, the war had restored their faith in the national cinema. 'I have seen the British film industry at its best', Michael Balcon wrote in *Soho Centenary*, '– playing a useful role and playing it well – spreading the gospel of Britain and the British way of life throughout the free world – instructing our soldiers, sailors, airmen, war workers and civilians – educating our children.' What had been discovered was that films were really important, a power for good. And David Lean, whose wartime love story of 1945, *Brief Encounter*, was the critical success of its year, could explain its appeal by the fact that British audiences had come to love the 'real' film during the war, because of 'the life-and-death reality of the blitz. They knew what it was like to be frightened, and they knew that death came with a whistle and a roar, not with fifty violins and a heavenly choir.' Overdressed stars and a Hollywood dream world had nothing to do with the actuality of clothing coupons and black-out. That was the opportunity which the truthful wartime British cinema had taken, and might extend in the peace.

It did not, because the cinema audience was turning its eyes away from reality. David Lean had to admit that even *Brief Encounter* did not really succeed 'with this great new and enlightened British audience'. And large it was, with thirty million people going to four thousand five hundred cinemas every week. The problem was that they went to forget the rationing and austerity persisting in the peace: never had the fantasies of Hollywood proved more seductive. Although British film production doubled by 1948, when one hundred and seventy feature films were made, these were usually poor in resources although high in talent. The problem lay in the film strategy of the socialist government, which lurched from the inept to the inexpedient, and ended with the incompetent in pursuit of the ineffable.

The British cinema saw the failure of state aid for the arts. To staunch the outflow of seventy million dollars a year in rentals to America, the Chancellor of the Exchequer imposed a seventy-five per cent duty on imported films. Expecting this, Hollywood stopped sending films to Britain and relied on its stockpile of unreleased features already in the country to keep the dollars flowing back from

British cinema circuits. J. Arthur Rank was then encouraged by the Board of Trade to fill the gaps on the screen with features made at home: he announced a new programme of forty-seven films, including Laurence Olivier's *Hamlet*. But the distribution of British films in the United States was imperilled, and national audiences still wanted to see American movies. The government lifted the crippling duty, as long as the Americans exported only twenty-five per cent of their earnings in Britain and left the remainder here. This policy pulled the wooden horse inside the besieged walls of London. To spend their blocked currency, the American studios and distributors began to make co-productions in England, thus diluting and almost destroying the indigenous cinema created in the war. A rise in the British quota of features to be shown at home to forty-five per cent could not be sustained and had to be lowered again. Direct state funding of films through five million pounds given to the new National Film Finance Corporation and through the Eady Levy on box-office receipts was too little and too late, although some major British films were subsidized, including *The Third Man*, *The Wooden Horse* and *The Happiest Days of Your Life*. Within six years and with the best of intentions, the socialist government had wrecked the renascent British film industry, forged in the war. Meddle and muddle, delayed action and quick reneging, indecisive measures and inadequate funding, made the socialist dream of a people's cinema in Britain as tawdry as tinsel when the fair has moved on. Lenin had said, 'For us, the most important of all the arts is the cinema.' Harold Wilson, the President of the Board of Trade, reduced the wartime art of the British cinema to unimportance.

There were good films made in the post-war years, but, as in the novel, they were not concerned directly with the war. Charles Dickens proved what Sergei Eisenstein had said about him, that he was a natural screenwriter before his time: David Lean's *Great Expectations* and *Oliver Twist* along with Cavalcanti's *Nicholas Nickleby* managed to suggest a dramatized realism existing in the Victorian age. Alexander Korda, back from wartime Hollywood, produced and even directed himself one or two classic subjects, Oscar Wilde's *An Ideal Husband* with costumes by Cecil Beaton, and Tolstoy's *Anna Karenina*, with Ralph Richardson and Vivien Leigh, playing the role in which Garbo had drained tears from a million eyes. Carol Reed followed his F. L. Green story of the dying of an Irish gunman, *Odd Man Out*, with *The Third Man*, one of the few films to probe into the guilt of post-war corruption. Its troubling screenplay by Graham Greene, set 'in the classic period of the Black Market [when] we'd run anything, if people wanted it enough and had the money to pay', showed a microcosm of a Europe divided between the four victorious Allied powers; the story of the betrayal of friends and the death of one racketeer Harry Lime captured the disillusion of the contemporary urban scene. The great discovery of the war, the curative drug penicillin, had become an instrument of murder. As Lime commented in the film, 'Nobody thinks in terms of human beings. Governments don't, so why should we? They talk of the people and the proletariat, and I talk of the mugs. It's the same thing. They have their five year plans and so have I.'

Two film-makers, Michael Powell and Emeric Pressburger, were making the most interesting films in England. *A Canterbury Tale* was a surprising flight from the war into a romantic and mythological and pastoral England. Made in 1944, it confused Chaucer's pilgrims with contemporary warriors: a falconer was translated into a fire-watcher, a hawk dissolved into a Spitfire. A soldier from London, a woman in the Land Army, an arrival from America, put together ancient and modern, previous and present on their way across the downs to Canterbury Cathedral. Its epic weaving of history with mythology should have made *A Canterbury Tale* the wartime celebration of English tradition; instead, it found no audience and remained a lost commentary on a long-lasting culture. Its successor, *A Matter of Life and Death*, with its transcendental figure of an airman poet burned like Richard Hillary, but reborn into an Arcadian and actual England, succeeded in showing the skein of the heretofore and the now and the hereafter, and the need to defend the rich sensual past from the drab efficient future state. Powell and Pressburger then expanded their special vision and achieved international success with the ballet films, *The Red Shoes* and *Tales of Hoffmann*. They moved from expounding the sensibility of a country at war on to a European examination of the artist, who finds a dedication to art and life both ecstatic and destructive. The neo-Romantic mood of some of the better young poets and artists of the time seemed to inform the films of Powell and Pressburger in the 'forties.

The post-war British cinema was to be characterized by the Ealing comedies, the products of the small studio run by Michael Balcon. A socialist and an independent, Balcon assembled the better talents in the industry and supervised an extraordinary series of humorous films, ranging from the bright and breezy to the black and indigo. On the one side shone *Passport to Pimlico*, an amusing sniper's attack on government restrictions, and *Whisky Galore*, an escape from war in a tale of liquid treasure from a wrecked ship; on the other side lurked the dark genius of Robert Hamer, whose brooding study of the East End of London, *It Always Rains on Sunday*, was followed by his mordant elegy to murder, *Kind Hearts and Coronets*. Its mockery and justification of killing was the British answer to the expatriate Charles Chaplin's bitter masterpiece *Monsieur Verdoux*, the first film to denounce the whole world war as analogous to the killings of a succession of bigamous wives by a dismissed clerk, trying to look after his family. In Verdoux's world, society was destroying itself just as it had destroyed him. Robbery and murder were the true faces of such criminal times. 'Crime does not pay in a small way,' Verdoux said in his condemned cell. 'One murder makes a villain, millions a hero.'

Chaplin had refused to support the Allied cause during the conflict. He was consistent in his reaction to fighting and he was considered a subversive in the United States at the beginning of the Cold War against Russia. Many of the conscientious objectors in Fitzrovia shared his point of view. Alex Comfort wrote, in 'The End of a War', that in order to live, a man had to be the enemy of society. 'We have to learn the lesson of resistance, evasion, disappearance, which the occupation taught the people of France. Our own government, if it wants to make butchers or bomber pilots of our children, is as much our enemy as the Germans ever were.' Post-war disillusion led to a reaction both from the portrayal of war virtues, particularly in the most powerful medium of them all, the moving pictures, and from the faulty state planning that was destroying the film industry which it was meant to save. Fitzrovians such as Dylan Thomas no longer worked on purposeful documentaries, but horror scripts on the Edinburgh murderers and resurrectionists, Burke and Hare, or trivial comedies such as *Me and My Bike*. In a sardonic commentary on his own cinema work, Dylan Thomas made his Scots doctor declare that he would 'work *up* to the gutter'. He even begged Graham Greene to procure him more screenplays to pay his bills, saying that he could write 'other than horrible stories'. Indeed, he could, but the subjects would never be his own. The documentary film had aided many Fitzrovian writers during the war, but the feature film degraded their talents in the peace.

Laurence Olivier, however, was the one artist of stature, who seemed to bestride both cinema and theatre like a colossus. He was backed by Filippo del Giudice and J. Arthur Rank to produce, direct and play *Hamlet* as he had *Henry V*. His declared intent was 'to make a film of "Hamlet" as Shakespeare himself, were he living now, might make it'. Nothing suggested that Shakespeare himself enjoyed being 'cabin'd, cribb'd, confin'd' by the rudimentary conditions of the Elizabethan stage. In spite of eliminating the essential characters of Fortinbras and Rosencrantz and Guildenstern to keep the piece two hours long, Olivier directed and played a haunting Danish prince, brooding at Elsinore. His film did not seem like Claudius, a thing or 'a king of shreds and patches', but a complete translation from the stage to the screen that Shakespeare might have applauded in its expanse. Magnificently executed, *Hamlet* was poorly distributed. Filippo del Giudice fell out with Rank, accusing its chief executives of creating a madhouse in the British film industry and of accomplishing 'a work of destruction which cannot be compared to any war. This lively film art is, little by little, going into the drain.'

Except for Laurence Olivier and the Old Vic company, the theatre in London in 1945 appeared already in the drain. One in five of the theatres had been badly damaged or destroyed by the air raids, while a similar number were run down or closed. Entertainment tax at ten per cent of gross receipts made a profitable run difficult to achieve. The impresario Prince Littler had picked up for a song and a few pence many of the chief theatres and control over H. M. Tennant Limited, the leading producers and managers of plays in London. 'The Group' owned three out of seven of the West End theatres still in business and seven out of ten of the main provincial touring theatres. This empire of drama might be well advised by Tennant's through Hugh 'Binkie' Beaumont, who had John Gielgud and Ralph Richardson and George 'Dadie' Rylands on his board; but it held an undue power that bred resentment, particularly because of the dearth of exciting new British plays after the war and about it. There was nothing to compete against Anouilh's *Antigone* or the *Caligula* of Camus or the *Huis Clos* of Sartre. 'We are too   251 close to the war,' a survey of British drama said in 1947, 'and too fatigued by it to want to talk about it just now.'

The Old Vic at the New Theatre with Laurence Olivier and Ralph Richardson put on another triumphant repertory season of revivals of classic plays, Shakespeare and Sophocles and Sheridan. Olivier showed his extraordinary mastery and versatility by playing the dashing Hotspur in *Henry IV, Part One* and the ancient Justice Shallow in *Part Two*, then contrasting the tragic Oedipus with the comic Puff in *The Critic*. Richardson was content to play second fiddle to Olivier, although he was the first of the two to be knighted, beating Olivier to the honour by six months. The Old Vic finally linked with the National Theatre Committee, ensuring that it would eventually enshrine that long mirage; but it was too ambitious for its own good, expanding into two companies (one on tour and one in London), a repertory centre, an experimental studio, a drama school, and a children's theatre. Despite some backing from the Arts Council, the organization was underfunded and overstretched, and nearly collapsed when the two stars left for long periods to make films and tour abroad. Although Olivier played King Lear with Alec Guinness as the Fool and Richardson played Cyrano de Bergerac with Margaret Leighton as Roxanne in another splendid season during the terrible winter of 1947, they were summarily dismissed as directors of the Old Vic two years later in a boardroom plot worthy of the Restoration drama of Webster and Ford. The coup was said to be necessary to provide for changes which would establish a National Theatre – an enabling act had passed in parliament. Divine or poetic justice saw that the plotters failed, when Olivier was recalled to set up the National Theatre in the rebuilt Old Vic in Waterloo Road, which rose from its bombed debris to fulfil its destiny.

The replaying of classical verse drama encouraged the revival of modern verse drama. During the war, the Pilgrim Players had toured the country with three religious verse plays, Norman Nicholson's *The Old Man of the Mountains*, which retold the biblical story of Elijah in contemporary Cumbria; Ronald Duncan's *This Way to the Tomb* in the form of a masque and its antithesis with music by Benjamin Britten and dedicated to the Elizabethan Benjamin Jonson and the Director of Television; and Anne Ridler's *The Shadow Factory*, which used the roar of drills as well as the chant of verses and canteen backchat to present a nativity play. After the war, the plays were restaged at the small Mercury Theatre, along with T. S. Eliot's pre-war flop *The Family Reunion*, which now proved a success. Backed by the Arts Council, Christopher Fry's *A Phoenix Too Frequent* was also mounted in a poet's workshop. Fry followed it with *The Lady's Not For Burning* with John Gielgud in the leading role. Its success and that of T. S. Eliot's *The Cocktail Party* seemed to herald the renaissance of British dramas in modern verse with religious overtones: Olivier even commissioned Fry's *Venus Observed* for the St James's Theatre, where he was actor-manager in 1950. But all proved a false dawn, rated more highly than its worth by contemporary critics, who should have listened to Lavinia in *The Cocktail Party*: 'To say I always look my best can only mean the worst.' During the few years of its fashion, however, verse plays seemed the phoenix risen from the ashes of the war. As Christopher Hassall wrote in *The Masque*, both stage and broadcasting were reviving the original tradition of British drama, descended from the Miracle Plays. 'The Third Programme is providing the poet with a sort of Mercury Theatre of the air … Radio drama can affect the theatre. It has the power to convince its wide audience that poets can still write the *spoken* word, and what is worth hearing is probably worth seeing as well, whenever opportunity serves, and that the verse drama, on stage or air, is part of contemporary life.'

It was, but briefly so. The leading playwright of the post-war years was Terence Rattigan, while his chief rival, Noël Coward, was curiously muted. Both of them, however, did produce their commentaries on the war. Coward's *Peace in Our Time* beat the drums of melodramatic patriotism, a new *Cavalcade* about a resistance movement in a London bar, after the Germans had won the Battle of Britain and had occupied the island. Heroic publicans and regulars defied Nazi stormtroopers in the local, which was named 'The Shy Gazelle' and based on the Antelope in Knightsbridge. The Gestapo tortured the saloonkeeper's daughter to death and received their due bullets when the Free British invaded again. Of interest was Coward's chief quisling, Chorley Bannister, who was a villain because he was an intellectual and the editor of a literary magazine called *Forethought*. He had been a communist of the 'thirties who was happy to be a fascist in the 'forties: who ruled won his allegiance. He was denounced for running his little highbrow magazines and changing his politics with every wind that blew. He responded to the quotation of 'This blessed plot, this earth, this realm, this England' with the remark that 'Shakespeare was second to none in commercializing patriotism.'

It was a poor attempt by Coward to trim his sails to the winds of a socialist Britain and to denounce those who were his natural supporters. Terence Rattigan had more gall, attacking state patronage of the arts in *Harlequinade*. 'It means playing Shakespeare to audiences who'd rather go to the films; while audiences who'd rather go to Shakespeare are driven to films because they haven't got Shakespeare to go to. It's all got something to do with the new Britain … Good citizenship and good theatre don't go together.' But in the best of his post-war plays, *The Deep Blue Sea*, Rattigan commented only indirectly on the effects of the war and peacetime society. His heroine, who had left her husband, a judge, for an ex-fighter pilot, failed to commit suicide because she ran out of shillings for the gas meter. Her lover, who spoke in dated service jargon about blokes and bull and gongs, could not cope with the new Britain, 'because his life stopped in 1940. He loved 1940, you know. There were some like that. He's never been really happy since he left the R.A.F.' In the end, he left his mistress to go back to being a test pilot in South America, 'the old ace again – the old dicer with death'. He proceeded to a former world, while she might go on. There was no solution or adjustment, only endurance or return.

The bulk of state patronage was not channelled to the theatre or to art, but to ballet, opera and music. Among the arts, the ballet had flourished during the war. 253

When Tyrone Guthrie left the triad of Old Vic companies which he had helped to nurture and which were splitting apart, the ballet was already on its own and brilliantly successful, while the opera was rent with schism. It was the Sadler's Wells company which reopened the Covent Garden Theatre and turned it once again from a dance hall to a ballet and opera house. John Maynard Keynes had formed the Covent Garden Opera Trust and had persuaded the Sadler's Wells Ballet to migrate *en masse* with Ninette de Valois, Frederick Ashton and Constant Lambert. In February, 1946, Margot Fonteyn and Robert Helpmann danced *The Sleeping Beauty* in Covent Garden in the presence of the King and Queen. Ashton became such a friend of the Queen that he used to take tea with her weekly in Buckingham Palace: soon the ballet company was designated the Royal Ballet and became a jewel in England's crown. But although the war had stimulated ballet in England by forcing it to use native talent, it had destroyed opera. With the one shining exception of Benjamin Britten's *Peter Grimes*, followed by *The Rape of Lucretia* with sets by John Piper, English opera seemed stagnant. Bereft of the foreign *divas* who had excelled before the war, no comparable voices had been trained to fill the gap. 'We are suffering from six years of operatic isolation,' a leading critic complained: 'we have no standards, no models, not even a school of opera; our singers drift on to the stage with the minimum of general culture and musical taste.'

Opera, however, also returned to Covent Garden in December 1946, with a masque, Purcell's *The Fairy Queen*, conducted and arranged by Constant Lambert with superlative sets by Michael Ayrton, who based them on designs by Inigo Jones. Although it was a bold and insular statement of the worth of the British musical tradition, it showed a lack of confidence in the national ability to mount a pure opera, relying as it did heavily on Ashton's choreography for Fonteyn and Helpmann. Now an alcoholic dependent on the pubs as much as on the orchestra pit, Lambert was deposed as conductor in favour of the Austrian Carl Rankl, but he was reinstated after a revolt by the leading performers. *The Fairy Queen* was not a success, pleasing neither ballet- nor opera- nor theatre-goers. It was revived for the Festival of Britain in 1951 with new choreography by John Cranko, but it remained a testament to the failure of the musical heritage of British opera, unlike British painting, which had bloomed after its forced return to its roots.

Lambert's decline to an early death from drink and diabetes at the end of the decade showed that bohemianism and music mixed no dry Martini. He met the artist Isobel Nicholas, who had been married to the war correspondent Sefton Delmer; they agreed to marry and she steadied him enough to return to Covent Garden to conduct *The Three-Cornered Hat* and *Turandot* with sets by Leslie Hurry. His erratic behaviour and alcoholism forced his resignation, officially to write the score for the new version of the film of *Anna Karenina*. He and Isobel went on drinking: as Frederick Ashton said, 'People thought it might be better for them to drink together than alone.' Although he became artistic director at Sadler's Wells again, Lambert went on destroying himself and died at the age of forty-five. With him died one of the few links to Diaghilev in the English ballet. His passing seemed to confirm John Lehmann's opinion that, even with the talents at Sadler's Wells and the Ballet Rambert, the path from Diaghilev was still winding downhill.

Lambert had been considered one of England's most promising composers during the war, but his inspiration dried up with the peace and his reputation hardly survived his death. The war had bred the largest and keenest audiences for concerts ever known. 'In their breeding,' one critic wrote, 'Sir Henry Wood's "Proms" had the greatest and most influential effect, if not the most refining one. Things went well for orchestral concerts even during the most harrowing period of aerial attacks on London and the large provincial cities. They continued well enough for a period after the war. But then a freezing depression set in.' Although orchestral musicians made good money playing film scores, their salvation became more and more dependent on state and provincial and festival patronage. The Local Government Act of 1948 permitted local authorities to spend money on the arts, and most of this tax money was used to support orchestras such as the Hallé and the Liverpool Philharmonic and also music festivals. The Edinburgh and the Aldeburgh Festivals were founded; the new musical audiences of the war were now subsidized and encouraged by the Arts Council. And the biggest patron of them all, the British Broadcasting Corporation, used its Third Programme to provide good music for the ears of the nation, even contributing towards public performances by other orchestras than its own. Enlightened enough to aid all major orchestras from the London Philharmonic to the Hallé, the BBC added to its war reputation in the peace and became the great instructor of the nation in musical appreciation. It was the first institution to educate all of the people in one of the arts, until this time.

As in opera, so in architecture. In his pamphlet for the British Council, John Summerson set down the bleak truth. 'For five long years architecture in Britain has stopped. The newest buildings in London, Glasgow, Cardiff and Belfast belong to 1939 and many of them are shabby, patched and scarred from blast and fire.' The rebuilding of Britain in the peace was damned by inadequate planning, shortages of materials, lack of investment, and excessive controls. Architects were starved of means and shackled in invention. Public buildings were repaired economically, houses and flats built cheaply. The Nissen hut, the concrete block and the prefabricated home were still the characteristic structures of post-war London, as the government rushed to erect any new accommodation any old how. Until the Festival of Britain showed that imaginative ideas in design and building waited to be released, the bomb-site and nature appeared as the creators of a better environment. It had been five years since the last rocket had fallen, G. W. Stonier noted in 'The Flowering Wen'. But it was unanswerable that the bomb had often been a better designer than the builder, particularly in the perspectives now opened about St Paul's Cathedral. 'Yes, the war in London did a number of things besides killing people, imposing a curfew and encouraging the study of good books. It took the lid off poverty, the edge off reserve. It broke down the serried ugliness of

Leonard Rosoman

the view.' Accidental rock gardens grew among the rubble, catastrophe sprouted flowers. One hundred and twenty-six varieties of plants and ferns thrived in the bombed open spaces in the overbuilt metropolis. But next time, London would not be so lucky. 'Atom bombs will level and the radio-active particle will pursue: ruin absolute, death without flower or worm!'

The reconstruction of London would wait for another two decades, until private as well as state resources became available to misuse on new buildings without style, without reason, without sense or beauty. The enlightened patronage of the state in most of the arts never extended to architecture, which remained the orphan and Aunt Sally of the Welfare State, as neglected as it was miserable. The grand failure of the Labour government was the provision over the people's heads of decent roofs which did not offend the eye. The persistence of a shabby, dingy, patchwork city may have allowed seedy bohemias to last beyond their circum-stance, but a whole generation of Britons was also condemned to slum living in the name of austerity.

Wartime Fitzrovia was preserved artificially by the squalor of the peace, as a fly in decaying amber. It received only marginal benefits from the growing state patronage of the arts. Bohemians, above all, never, never, never shall be wage slaves. The musicians, however, did best, for their trade was still peripatetic, although their hiring was centralized in Soho. As Gerald Kersh wrote in 'The Musicians': 'Towards Piccadilly, in Archer Street, the musicians segregate them-selves. They also stand and wait in little groups. At the snap of a finger you may pick up a swing band, a washboard quartet, a phalanx of xylophonists, a couple of symphony orchestras, a whole encampment of tea-shop Tsiganes, complete with side-whiskers, or a hopeful and willing army of men who are ready to croon a Mammy song and play a tuba and douvle on an electric guitar, or do anything at all for the sake of a job. People in this locality move in unbreakable circles, like fish in a bowl. Archer Street – Charing Cross Road – which is the ante-room of Limbo and the waiting-place of the pallid damned.' To George Melly, Archer Street was 'a band cattle market' where musicians carried their instrument cases for hiring by the 'bookers' even when they could hardly play at all. Melly thought that Fitzrovia survived into the next decade because of its connection with the revival of jazz, at Humphrey Lyttelton's 100 Club in Oxford Street and at Ronnie Scott's Club 11 in the basement of Mac's Rehearsal Rooms in Windmill Street (later to be Cy Laurie's Jazz Club) and at Ken Colyer's off Cambridge Circus and at the Marquee, which began as a jazz place before switching to rhythm and blues, and at the Mandrake, where Melly himself and Mick Mulligan gave all-night jam sessions. Lack of development and low rents after the war allowed Soho to survive on cheap premises, a few banks and the absence of an otherwise intrusive state authority. At a time of punitive conventions and grey uniformity, Melly found Soho the only area in London where the rules did not apply. 'It was a Bohemian no-go area, tolerance its password, where bad behaviour was cherished – at any rate in retrospect. Only bores were made unwelcome. Above all, despite the ferocious drinking, the promiscuity, the bitchiness, it was an *innocent* time.'

Soho might be a place to be, but never to stay for too long. It was a slow death by ten thousand drinks except for those of the strongest constitutions, like Francis Bacon. And he was the antithesis of the Fitzrovian creed, a painter who survived success in a society which preferred failure. Even Melly agreed that flight was the only solution to Fitzrovian life. 'In the end there comes a time when you must fight free or go under.' Most of the Fitzrovians followed the artists and dispersed after the war or worked for the state. If they wanted to live long, they went away and returned only now and then.

EIGHTEEN

Dispersal and Survival

However dedicated to the Soho scene, many a Fitzrovian knew it was the long death of inspiration. Out of all his years of pub and club crawling, Michael Hamburger got only one poem, 'An Unnecessary Visit', in which he saw himself as a cold observer, an academic and an anthropologist. He never found it necessary 'to look for trouble or "suffering". Nor to inflict it deliberately on others, so as to set up an extreme situation conducive to the writing of poetry,' as some other Soho poets did. Hamburger's final rejection of the connection between bohemia and art began with a party at the Colony with Francis Bacon and John Minton and Lucian Freud. Bacon had ordered champagne and expounded on why 'artists have to become crooks'. Hamburger froze and became a wet blanket and was abandoned by the others. He was the observer of his own detachment, and he returned to Soho no more, while Bacon remained in it to develop into the ultimate artist of his age.

The emigration from Fitzrovia often went no further than a few London boroughs away. In the Wheatsheaf, Nina Hamnett saw a regular for the first time in three months. He said he had been away in Camden Town. 'It must be the gypsy blood in me.' With the increasing failure of the Grey Walls Press, Charles Wrey Gardiner moved to Paddington, where he rented rooms to other poets. The last of his five volumes of autobiography, *The Answer to Life is No*, was redolent with sadness for the lost places of no return. 'Old London is going. Life is reintegrating round the outer parts of Paddington and Kilburn, beyond the Walmer Castle, with the coloured throngs along the littered streets ... Soho is dead. It has been taken over by the boys from the East End. The juke boxes are in all the clubs. I suppose I am an old man in a harsh time, thinking of London as it was when beer was enough to make a night coruscate and flash like a thousand explosions at the time of the bomber's moon.'

Wrey Gardiner had suffered as a publisher because of his connection with the Falcon Press and Peter Baker, who had persuaded many leading financiers including the chairman of Marks and Spencer, the property tycoon Charles Clore and Sir Bernard Docker to provide bank guarantees for his business ventures. As these guarantees ran out, Baker forged their signatures on new guarantees. When these were called up by the bank, the forgeries were discovered and the alcoholic Baker was sent to gaol for seven years. Wrey Gardiner avoided following him to prison, but the days of his prosperity and publishing were over. 'Money is something that can be very frightening,' he wrote, 'when it disappears like a dying note at the end of a concerto. I used to "lend" John Gawsworth ten shillings to tide him over ... I miss the dark streets and the strange constricted corners of Soho, full of the most appalling people, and also some you can talk to for days at a time without getting bored, talk about women and brothels with impotent poets, property with the very poor, books with the ignorant.' When Wrey Gardiner died of drink and despair, his tenant and his mourner, John Heath-Stubbs, wrote his epitaph:

Now I remember him,
Myopic and spry as an old grey rat,

Penning his memoirs in a crumbling house
Eaten piecemeal by women and by drink.
'The answer to life is no,' he said, and sometimes
He really seemed to mean it. God help us all
If so indeed he did – that gate leads
Only into the 'nothing, nothing, nothing, *nothing;*'
Which he averred the sum of things.

John Gawsworth also began a terminal decline at the age of forty-two, when he was dismissed from his job at the *Poetry Review*. He drank himself slowly to death, selling titles as the King of Redonda to anyone who would buy him a glass at the bar. He lived on a houseboat on the Regent's Canal, flying the flag of his kingdom, and carrying round the ashes of the previous king, M. P. Shiel, in a bag until one day they were brewed as tea and sipped down. He existed for two more decades on memories, manuscripts and alcohol, until spirits and diabetes killed him. He regretted his wasted talents and even his use of his improbable kingdom, which he sold to various claimants. 'This is the ghastly age of the gimmick,' he admitted. 'I am a king. I've tried using that. Redonda, I regret to say, wasn't sufficient. All that happened to me is that in the boarding-house where the Queen and I live, I'm referred to as "that king upstairs".'

Tambimuttu also lost his grip on *Poetry London* and his little publishing empire. His publishers, Nicholson & Watson, went bankrupt, so Tambimuttu registered *Poetry London* under his own name. A new backer was found, who unfortunately became a Buddhist monk. 'For some time, apparently, he'd been brooding over Hiroshima,' Julian Maclaren-Ross declared, 'and not even Tambi could dissuade him from that course.' Another backer was found, a diplomat called Richard Marsh, who bought out Tambimuttu, and replaced him as editor with Nicholas Moore and himself. 'The climate of poetry too was changing,' Maclaren-Ross noted. 'Already from the academic desert of the Fifties a dry cold wind was blowing, the red brick Doctors were drumming in the distance and talk of Consolidation and the Critic as Poet could be heard.' Tambimuttu emigrated to New York, there to live on selling letters and manuscripts from his old supporters such as T. S. Eliot. He was the victim of Sohoitis, the disease which he had warned Maclaren-Ross to avoid, the state of staying in Soho always day and night and getting no work done ever.

One of the passing Fitzrovians tried to analyse the addiction to bars and booze that drained most of their talents away. Vernon Scannell, who had been there as a deserter, asked himself why heavy drinkers went on 'knocking themselves out with alcohol, wasting countless hours in bars, squandering money, energy and even, sometimes, wit and invention, and then, the next day or in the case of large-scale booze-ups over the next two or three days, suffering fairly intense physical and mental distress'. Scannell wondered whether the hangover was not unconsciously desired by the drinker, just as the gambler plunged heavily because he craved the punishment of losing. These were parallels or parodies of mystical states of consciousness, something like the 'dark night of the soul ... a sense of self-disgust, feelings of unfocused anxiety and terrible loneliness'. The escape was a return to the relaxing drug of alcohol, which led to 'a precarious and doomed state of euphoria'. But both the drinking and the aftermath were necessary in the cycle of the drinker's life, release followed by remorse. It was the only solution that Scannell could give for persisting in regular bouts of boozing, knowing they would be followed by the misery of hangovers which would murder the capacity for work and constructive thought. *In vino, vacuum.* As A. S. J. Tessimond wrote in his 'Song in a Saloon Bar':

> Somewhere yesterday-tomorrow's
>   Closing like two closing claws,
> But, in here, each mild-and-bitter
>   Makes the cunning clock-hands pause;
>
> Let us cluster and stand closer
>   Lest we've room to turn and run;
> Time for one more round, old man, for
>   Time for, time for ... one, for one ...
>
> We are here for fear we think of
>   Things that we would rather not;
> We are here lest we remember –
>   But we have forgotten what.

Why do writers and artists drink? is a question with too many answers. Drinking in pubs enables them to escape their lonely craft and sullen art. It provides them with the material of other people's lives. The hours are good, because they may choose their own time for their work. Drinking is expected of them as romantic figures – as Sinclair Lewis once asked, 'Can you name five American writers since Poe who did not die of alcoholism?' As with lechery, intoxication increases desire and inspiration while taking away performance. And finally, as a recent study on *Alcohol and the Writer* suggested, the rich fantasy lives of lone artists are released by drink into revelations that may be caught. All that is certain is that many writers and artist drink too much – and particularly did so in Fitzrovia in the 'forties.

The collapse of the Fitzrovian publishers was paralleled by the failure of the Old Etonian editors, John Lehmann and Cyril Connolly. Both Penguin *New Writing* and *Horizon* ceased publication by 1950. In that year, Penguin Books told Lehmann that they could only produce the magazine once or twice a year: its circulation had dropped from one hundred to forty thousand copies an issue. So the little magazine's career ended with the decade and its fortieth appearance, which prophesied the future in its swansong. It had reproductions of the work of John Minton and Barbara Hepworth; but it chiefly was devoted to photographs of its American contributors who were having an increasing influence on English letters, Nelson Algren and Saul Bellow, Paul Bowles and Lionel Trilling, Eudora Welty and Tennessee Williams. Most remarkable was an article by the young John Wain on the poetry of William Empson, which heralded the supremacy of the Movement poets of the 'fifties. Wain asked whether 'the landslide in English literary taste' had left a public capable of appreciating Empson's work. 'Many of the reputations which today occupy the poetic limelight are such as would crumble immediately if poetry such as Empson's, with its passion, logic, and formal beauty, were to become widely known ...'

The demise of Penguin *New Writing* followed that of *Horizon* and *Life and Letters*. 'Ten years for a little magazine,' Cyril Connolly commented, 'is about the same as for a dog, i.e., a lifetime.' It seemed that soon there would be no space for the aspiring poet or short story writer. 'It is the worst loss so far,' Stephen Spender wrote to Lehmann, 'and for the greatest number of people. Isn't there anything we could do? Isn't the failure of these magazines partly due not just to the public but to the failure of talent?' Cyril Connolly agreed. It was not *Horizon* which had declined, but there was a falling-off of material submitted to the magazine. Most of the major talents were unwilling to write except for dollars, or had become psychologically impotent or unproductive because of immersion in irrelevant jobs. Connolly himself was preoccupied with the sickness of the soul of contemporary literature, an obsession for which he later apologized. He feared he might be trying to externalize his own guilty sterility on to the world. 'The idea of decadence hugged and haunted me as if I were some Hebrew prophet,' he wrote; 'gangrene was spreading while I was powerless as a fly waving and buzzing among its silent companions on the poisoned paper.' Peter Watson was prepared to subsidize more issues of *Horizon*, but Connolly wanted the magazine to be judged as his elegy on the 'forties, when he had flown the flag of culture while all around him were draped in it in war. The offices were closed in Bedford Square, although contributions continued to be delivered inexorably 'like a suicide's milk'. And his final editorial continues to reverberate as the last judgement on the decade:

'Nothing dreadful is ever done with, no bad thing gets any better; you can't be too serious.' This is the message of the Forties from which, alas, there seems no escape, for it is closing time in the gardens of the West and from now on an artist will be judged only by the resonance of his solitude or the quality of his despair.

It was a wrong judgement. As the rising Irish playwright Brendan Behan declared in a Dublin pub to Anthony Cronin, 'Arrah sweet and holy Jesus, would you mind telling me what f—ing gardens of the West did you and I ever wander in?' Curiously enough, in the final issue of *Horizon*, Connolly reproduced paintings by Francis Bacon and an article recognizing his importance as the only painter of the time 'exclusively occupied with man, and his innate tendency to comment upon and expose the state of the human soul'. Connolly himself admired Bacon for his 'horror-fretted canvases' and linked his work with the despondence of *Horizon*'s finale, which also published an article on Dallapiccola's tragic Songs for Prisoners, 263

Paul Bowles's story of 'The Boy Who Wrote No' to all the institutions of society, and a commentary on the imprisoned Marquis de Sade saying 'No to God, No to Nature, No to Man.' Inadvertently, Connolly had published the painter who said yes to the revelation of the abominations of his time, and thus to their recognition and possible exorcism. His last *Horizon* saw the dawning of a future bleak image of civilization, bare, necessary, unaccommodating, true. But no critic heard the swansong of *Horizon*: in an obituary on the magazine, the *New Statesman* agreed with Connolly about the lack of good material. 'Five years after the war there is still no sign of any kind of literary revival; no movements are discernible: no trends.'

The close of the decade did seem the executioner's axe on the necks of the little magazines. Not only did the leading publications fold in the metropolis, *London Forum, Modern Reading, Our Time, Windmill, Now, Polemic, Transformation* and *Writing Today* along with *Horizon* and *Life and Letters* and Penguin *New Writing*, but also the leading provincial magazines went under, *Welsh Review* and *Wales*. The radical *Our Time* had believed that the 'cultural upsurge' of the war would last into the peace, but it joined the tumbrils on the way to the guillotine. Only one new quarterly, *Nine*, rose briefly from the massacre, beginning with a valedictory on the past from T. S. Eliot. 'The value of the "little reviews" for my generation was very great: literary history will have an impressive debt to acknowledge to their editors. They were issued always under difficulties; they were never adequately supported even by that public which professed a concern for the arts and for independent thought; they lived always under sentence of death: and they always died. Nevertheless, they helped to keep literature alive.... You are attempting the same thing in conditions still more difficult than ours; and the need is just as great.'

Species which foul their nests die out, and the despair which afflicted the cultural establishment at the end of the 'forties presaged its demise. On meeting James Pope-Hennessy and Alan Pryce-Jones at a party, Cyril Connolly said that all those people made him feel 'we were all part of a dead civilization'. T. S. Eliot was even more pessimistic than Connolly about the lowering of standards after the war. As the leading poet and publisher of poetry of his time, his *Notes Towards the Definition of Culture* of 1948 were striking in their pessimism:

We can assert with some confidence that our own period is one of decline; that the standards of culture are lower than they were fifty years ago; and that the evidences of this decline are visible in every department of human activity. I see no reason why the decay of culture should not proceed much further, and why we may not even anticipate a period, of some duration, of which it is possible to say that it will have *no* culture.

Although *no* culture was predicted by Eliot, London was still the centrifuge of the culture which remained. If members of the metropolitan establishment mourned the demise of civilization through their own lack of will-power, the provinces seemed to offer a rebirth of various cultures. On his deathbed, George Orwell changed his mind about preserving languages like Welsh and Gaelic; he thought them worth supporting. The word 'regionalism' rose in importance as a literary label almost as meaningless as 'modernism'. It was said to mean that a conscious artistic tradition could be forged outside the metropolis in areas that were grouped together by history or language – Wales, Scotland, Ulster, the North, Celtic Cornwall. Keidrych Rhys had put the ideology strongly as editor of the briefly revived magazine *Wales*. 'The war has made the Welsh realize that they are a nation with a country, a people, a culture and a tradition *different* from England's to fight for. There is a new wave of national feeling among our people.' Although the resurgent *Welsh Review* pointed out the obvious fact that Wales was a divided country with a cleavage of language and tradition and outlook and wealth, the disparate could be united in 'regionalism'. *Scottish Art and Letters* agreed. A region's art had to be locally directed, not from London. 'Most of the world's best artistic work proves on examination to be, not cosmopolitan, however international its appeal, but racial and national in the most uncompromising way.' The revival of Gaelic poetry and the hybrid poetry of the 'Lallans Makars', Hugh MacDiarmid and William Soutar and Robert Garioch and Sydney Goodsir Smith, seemed to herald a distinct language in an historical country. The appearance of the periodicals *Voice of Scotland*, *Poetry Scotland* and *Scots Writing* culminated in an anthology, *Modern Scottish Poetry* of 1946, which proved that there was a distinctive voice to a literary renaissance in Scotland. But the cleavage of language and poetic tradition was actually as pronounced as in Wales, with the Lallans radical lines confronting the contemplative Christian verses of Edwin Muir, considered by his London publisher T. S. Eliot as the leading Scots poet of his time. What 'regionalism' could encompass both Sydney Goodsir Smith's 'October, 1941' and Muir's 'Scotland 1941'?

> Tchaikovski man, I'm hearan yir Waltz o Flouers,
> A cry frae Russia fulls this autumn nicht;
> As gousty fell October's sabban in ma room
> As the frantic rammage Panzers brash on Moscow toun ...

So 'October, 1941' feared in Lallans the Nazi advance on the sympathetic Kremlin, while 'Scotland 1941' used another diction to mourn the rape of old Scotland by the new proletarianized cities.

> We were a tribe, a family, a people.
> Wallace and Bruce guard now a painted field,
> And all may read the folio of our fable,
> Peruse the sword, the sceptre and the shield ...
> We watch our cities burning in their pit,
> To salve our souls grinding dull lucre out,
> We, fanatics of the frustrate and the half,
> Who once set Purgatory Hill in doubt.
> Now smoke and dearth and money everywhere,
> Mean heirlooms of each fainter generation,

> And mummied housegods in their musty niches,
> Burns and Scott, sham bards of a sham nation ...

Even MacDiarmid had called Lallans 'synthetic Scots' and it was a created language, which was blended from the patois of past centuries, from modern dialect and from French and Latin roots that did not reflect any contemporary reality. The approving G. S. Fraser had to admit that Lallans had 'no vocabulary to express the interests of modern town life, or the complicated predicament of the modern intellectual'. The English language would have to serve and to unite a region, which believed it existed as one. Better to write in Gaelic and translate oneself into English, the poetry of two languages, than to try to coagulate different speeches. So Sorley Maclean believed in his poems published by George Bruce in his anthology, *The Scottish Literary Revival*:

> Knightsbridge, Libia
> (an Òg mhios 1942)

> Ged tha mi'n diugh ri uchd a' bhatail
> Chan ann an seo mo shac's mo dhiachainn:
> Cha ghunnachan's cha thancan Roimeil,
> Ach mo ghaol bhith coirbte briagach.

> Knightsbridge, Libya
> (June 1942)

> Though I am today against the breast of battle,
> not here my burden and extremity:
> not Rommel's guns and tanks,
> but that my darling is depraved and a liar.

'Regionalism' was also seen in the work of the Ulster poets, W. R. Rodgers and Robert Graecen, in two periodicals published there, *Lagan* and *Ulster Parade*, while in Eire *The Bell* and *The Dublin Magazine* and *Irish Writing* and *Irish Harvest* and *Circle* were established as magazines. They used the English language to communicate, as did the major epic poem of the decade, Patrick Kavanagh's *The Great Hunger*, which referred to the rural emptiness of Irish life rather than to the potato famine a century before. Although Kavanagh called the Irish Literary Movement of W. B. Yeats 'a thorough-going English-bred lie', his own vernacular was founded on the simplicity and rhythms of basic English. *Horizon* was wise enough to publish, in its Irish number of 1942, a part of *The Great Hunger* under the title of 'The Old Peasant', thus showing that the English metropolis could still appreciate the old sod and its servant Paddy Maguire:

> And he is not so sure now if his mother was right
> When she praised the man who made a field his bride.
> Watch him, watch him, that man on a hill whose spirit
> Is a wet sack flapping about the knees of time.

The regional short story, however, was the art of wartime. Before 1939, there were few takers for stories; but during the five years of the conflict with its incessant interruptions and brief attention spans, the country tale became widely popular. Welsh and Irish writers filled the magazines and the collections and the anthologies, *Modern Reading* and *Selected Writing*, *English Story* and *Argosy*, *New Short Stories* and *Writing Today* and the *Saturday Book*. From Ireland came Liam O'Flaherty and Frank O'Connor, Padraic Fallon and Bryan Macmahon, Jim Phelan and Frank Tuohy; from Wales were Gwyn Jones and Rhys Davies, Dylan Thomas and Alun Lewis, who managed to write enough for two collections of short stories, *The Last Inspection* and *In the Green Tree*, while serving in the army before his death in Burma. Among the English writers, William Sansom rose to literary recognition because of his short stories written from his fireman's experience in London, while Julian Maclaren-Ross, H. E. Bates and Gerald Kersh competed for space in the metropolitan magazines with their sketches about the armed services. Bates, indeed, pointed out that as Flying Officer X, he was 'the first state short story writer'. Unfortunately, most of the collections of tales collapsed with the other little magazines at the end of the 'forties, the only decade in which the art of the sketch and the story had flourished. London publishers now rejected short and rural pieces, which had provided for ten years a time out of war.

'Regionalism', as critics pointed out, should have involved the use of the actual *living language* of a region, just as war poetry in its narrowest sense meant using the slang and experience of the armed forces. But if Gaelic or even Lallans were used, the audience became confined to that part of the region which spoke the rare language, ever diminishing under the influence of the universal language of English spread by the wireless and the schools. Better words for local cultural influence were 'provincialism' or 'parochialism'. For Patrick Kavanagh, the provincial was still under the sway of the metropolis, while the parochial mentality was 'never in any doubt about the social and artistic validity of his parish'. All great civilizations were based on parochialism. Norman Nicholson used 'provincial' as Kavanagh used 'parochial' in a talk on being provincial. Living in the place where he was born gave the artist the strength of sharing from childhood in 'the culture of his native region' – in Nicholson's case, Cumbria and the North of England. But he was not sanguine that the apparent post-war dispersal from Fitzrovia and the rising influence of 'provincialism' would last. 'Civilization is becoming more and more centred on the metropolis,' he wrote in the broadcasting magazine *The Listener* in 1954. 'We must expect that literature and art will continue to be mainly metropolitan.'

Dylan Thomas, who was now living between rural Laugharne and lethal Fitzrovia, broadcast scathingly on metropolitan exiles and on 'regionalism' in 'Wales and the Artist'. Welsh artists who lived permanently in London corseted their voices and claimed Soho was good for their gouaches. 'They set up, in grey, whining London, a little mock Wales of their own, an exile government of dispossessed intellectuals dispossessed not of their country but of their intellects.' 267

Yet too many Welsh artists stayed at home too long, 'giants in the dark behind the parish pump, pygmies in the nationless sun, enviously sniping at the artists of other countries rather than attempting to raise the standard of art of their own country by working fervently at their own words, paint, or music.' Too many Welsh artists talked too much about their position in Wales. 'There is only one position for an artist anywhere: and that is, upright.'

This was the position of a Welsh poet writing in English who had earned an international reputation. Among the Fitzrovians, he shone, the luminary of his last decade. And the other leading Welsh poet of the 'forties, R. S. Thomas, was not considered 'regional', but universal in his appeal, although he always wrote about Welsh subjects. The provincials, indeed, could best take their revenge on the metropolis by improving its standards when they came there. The quality of the theatre company at Stratford-on-Avon under Barry Jackson and then Anthony Quayle was to develop into the Royal Shakespeare Theatre Company, which would transfer its productions to London and set new standards of excellence. And from Cambridge, the exact and stimulating magazine, *Scrutiny*, edited by F. R. Leavis and his wife, would finally dethrone the post-war London editors with university graduate students trained in provincial puritanism and rigorous analysis. Leavis unceasingly attacked 'the currency values of Metropolitan literary tradition', Stephen Spender as a member of 'the Auden Gang', and the Arts and British Councils as mere expressions of 'the coterie spirit' of their founder, John Maynard Keynes. What drove Leavis to fury in 1951 was an article on 'Literary Periodicals' by Alan Pryce-Jones in the British Council's *The Year's Work in Literature*, edited by John Lehmann. *Scrutiny* was said to 'read like the laboratory report of a small, but efficient laboratory'. Yet its analyses, applied by its disciples, would subject the old establishment to a new treatment.

Scrutiny itself was to die in 1953 soon after Connolly's *Horizon* and Lehmann's *New Writing*, which represented the effete and urban values despised by Leavis. But the message of the magazine had been passed on to its acolytes. Leavis did not despair of his achievements or of his generation as Connolly did. His young men would replace the older men, tired by the war and falling silent in the peace. The reasons for that silence were manifold. There was a sense of deflation, a disappointment that the millennium had not come, even if there was more social justice. Evil had not been destroyed by the war, but was still present in the individual. Alan Ross saw a premature literary middle age, V. S. Pritchett a post-war mental and physical exhaustion leading to a retreat into privacy:

There is nothing as dead as a dead war and, as the pace quickens, the latest war kills the one before it quickly. One is ridiculous to be still alive and the best thing is to keep one's mouth shut. Looking at the war egotistically from a writer's point of view, it was a feverish dispersal and waste of one's life. It is often said that this was a good time when all private defences gave way, especially the defence of class differences, and that we all came together for once; and one hears regrets that after the war this revolution spent itself and that we went back to our traditional privacy. We did; though not to the old

kind. I am not sure that to be so drowned in the mass was good for the act of writing ...
The unconscious benefits may be deep; the anarchy of war is a release for a time: the
ultimate effects are indirect.

V. S. Pritchett had staying power and remained an influential critic and writer, but
many voices were muted for many years or for good and ill. Things after the war
seemed to have no resonance or significance, particularly the political themes that
had informed the 'thirties. 'We had a lack of subject matter,' Roy Fuller has said. 'It
seemed a pointless repetition. I was diffident about writing about personal things.
During the war they had a social significance.' Fuller, indeed, thought of himself as
formed in the 'thirties and his naval service as an extension of the previous decade.
'I think of the 'forties as the dim period after the war.' He expressed his feelings in a
poem published in *Horizon*, 'The Divided Life Re-Lived':

> Once and only once we were in touch with brutal, bloody life
> When we got in or kept out of global strife;
> And in desert or in dockyard met our coarser fellow men,
> Wielding friendly gun or scrubber, not our pen.
>
> How we innocently thought that we should be alone no more,
> Linked in death or revolution as in war.
> How completely we have slipped into the same old world of cod,
> Our companions Henry James or cats or God.
>
> Waiting for the evening as the time of passion and of verse,
> Vainly hoping that at both we shan't get worse:
> While outside the demon scientists and rulers of the land
> Pile the bombs like busy crabs pile balls of sand.

Fuller's verdict on post-war writing was written for *Our Time*. He saw 'a refined
and not unskilful literature of academic respectability. There is a remarkable
consensus of opinion among influential literary figures that writers ought not to
touch politics, that social concern leads to bad writing. There is an equally
remarkable ability shared by many young writers to conform to the (not always
serious and genuine) standards set by the richer periodicals and the B.B.C.' His
friend Julian Symons concurred; although he continued to work as a critic, he
stopped writing poetry for 'lack of something to write about in a social sense'. Also
Symons found the 'neo-Romantic Wave' still dominating the richer periodicals
and the BBC in the post-war years, particularly the poetry of Edith Sitwell and
Dylan Thomas. Whether they had inspiration or not, social realist poets found it
difficult to be published and so gave up the craft. Without support or
subjects to write about, the poets fell silent from questioning their reasons to write,
which had been evident during the war. As J. C. Hall put the matter, asking
himself why he had hardly written a poem in 'Thirty Years':

... But nothing rests. Soon intellectual doubt,
Like sexual longing, troubled all my days.
Writing too often seemed a putting on
Of other garments, other thoughts, without
The real conviction of another's ways.
Better, I thought, to act than lose my tongue.

Now thirty years have gone I reckon up –
If such self-reckoning's true – the sum of all
Those words and words I've put upon the shelf.
Did they betoken life? Or did they grope
Blindly, like shadows leaping on a wall?
The days draw in. I turn to face myself.

The post-war years killed the subjects and inspiration of the writers of the 'thirties. The drab peace blunted the stimulus of the war. 'A diminishing bohemian spirit,' Philip O'Connor noted, 'met half-way an increasingly bohemianised conventionality.' The literary establishment included the rebels of yesteryear who were considered to have talent, and it bemoaned the general dearth of genius within a whole generation. The market for new writers and artists was diminishing along with the social and political issues which had previously inspired them. The retreat into privacy and even silence now began, and an actual dispersal from London into the country and the regions. The aftermath of the Second World War did not produce in Britain the literary explosions that had detonated at the end of the First. For despite its horrors and deprivations, it was less obdurate and bloody and murderous, and so it would sooner be read out of literary consciousness. 'Fewer people were killed,' Roy Fuller has said. 'There was a comparative lightness of suffering.' Only a quarter as many British troops died in battle in the second global conflict, while fewer civilians were killed by the blitz than by the influenza epidemic after the first struggle. Soon the culture of the Second World War would be ignored by those too young to suffer in it and by those too disillusioned about its results to wish to commemorate its worth at the time.

NINETEEN

Festival and Requiem

Constant Lambert
conducting Carmo
Anatrose

Kay Ambrose

'One mistake we should *not* make,' the director-general of the Festival of Britain wrote, 'we should not fall into the error of supposing we were going to produce anything conclusive. In this sceptical age, the glorious assurance of the mid-Victorians would find no echo.' The answer to the centenary of the Great Exhibition was not an expression of empire and might, but of experiment and humour. This is what Harold Nicolson discovered when he visited the festival on the South Bank, dominated by the largest dome in the world, the scalloped Dome of Discovery, and by the suspense of the elongated lozenge of the Skylon, which looked like Edward Lear's drawing of the Quangle-Wangle. Nicolson had expected the South Bank Exhibition to provide beauty and power, but not to be 'the very soul of wit ... conceived in a mood of high spirits'. It was full of a brave laughter, which might be gallows-humour. Yet it was not a memorial chapel or a monument to past greatness, but a testament to present resilience, 'a clamorous assertion of our infinite gifts of adaptability and resource ... resonant with the cries and gurgles of the world to be. I returned to the drab outside encouraged and entranced.'

It was the tribute of the old guard to the new planners of post-war Britain. The festival heralded the renaissance of British architecture and design and provided official confirmation of the state patronage of the arts. Some fifty architects and a hundred designers were commissioned to fabricate something for the festival: their energies were released from adapting Nissen huts and hangars and pillboxes and prefabs into making buildings bare and strange. If their gods were Gropius and Le Corbusier, if their 'thirties student realism would lead to the mistaken concrete towers and 'new brutalism' of the 'fifties, their festival work showed a sense of play as well as function. Moreover, the Arts Council was given the unprecedented sum of £400,000 to promote the festival: the government grant was spent widely, if not always well. Evelyn Waugh may have ended his autobiographical war trilogy of novels by damning the festival, but *Unconditional Surrender* did recognize the fact that the event was a watershed between two periods:

In 1951, to celebrate the opening of a happier decade, the government decreed a Festival. Monstrous constructions appeared on the south bank of the Thames, the foundation stone was solemnly laid for a National Theatre, but there was little popular exuberance among the straitened people and dollar-bearing tourists curtailed their visits and sped to the countries of the Continent where, however precarious their condition, they ordered things better.

Waugh's characters, however, held two private parties on the same June evening, where it was established that the hero, a surrogate for Waugh, had settled for good in the country, with things turning out very conveniently for him. As the playwright Michael Frayn declared, 'The Festival was a rainbow – a brilliant sign riding the tail of the storm and promising fairer weather. It marked the ending of the hungry 'forties, and the beginning of an altogether easier decade.' Restrictions were being lifted with the last gasp of the Labour government, ousted by Winston Churchill and the Conservatives in the election of 1951. As Joe Orton's agent was made to say in Alan Bennett's *Prick Up Your Ears*, the festival was 'when it all came off the ration ... food, sex, life, everything'.

So it seemed for the young. At last, austerity was ending, coupons could be jettisoned, even if there was not much to buy nor much money to spend, anyway. Stephen Spender thought that the festival symbolized the disappointment of the Labour Party's social revolution 'with its look of cut-rate cheerfulness cast in concrete and beflagged'. The catchword of the new decade would be 'Anti-'. He would become anti-communist in the Cold War and in 'a time of negation and reaction'. But at the half-cock apotheosis of the Festival of Britain, a cheap celebration that cost only eight million pounds and built the Royal Festival Hall to replace the bombed Queen's Hall as a concert centre, there was cause for a joyful requiem on the burial of the war decade. Orchestras and poetry readings, dramatic performances and art exhibitions, fireworks and sports days, radio shows and the first lengthy television programme on an artist, Henry Moore, broadcast the festivities to two thousand cities and towns and villages in Britain. The festival was, as its originator Herbert Morrison declared, 'the people giving themselves a pat on the back'.

One architect at the festival, Basil Spence, who designed the Sea and Ships Pavilion, was to carry with him the style of the event into the new cathedral at Coventry, which was to rise on the rubble of the old blitzed place of worship: Spence used the Sutherland motif of the Crown of Thorns, which the artist employed in his festival mural, *Origins of the Land*, unfortunately slashed by a vandal. Other festival architects, particularly Maxwell Fry and Jane Drew, would translate their construction of the New Schools Pavilion into the things themselves. But sculptors and artists proved the more apt designers of the festival, particularly John Piper and the cartoonist Osbert Lancaster in their bamboo Grand Vistas and Arcades and Rotundas and Tea Houses and other fantastical creations at downriver Battersea in the Festival Gardens, based on memories of the old London pleasure gardens of Cremorne and Ranelagh and Vauxhall. The Arts Council commissioned nearly fifty painters and half as many sculptors to grace the festival. Keith Vaughan did a nude Theseus mural for the Dome of Discovery, Michael Ayrton produced an exegesis on *The Elements as the Sources of Power*, Victor Pasmore wrought a ceramic mural for the Regatta Restaurant, and Feliks Topolski decorated a railway arch near the Transport Pavilion with a *Cavalcade of Commonwealth*. So short of funding was the Arts Council, and so short of material were the artists, that the council presented large canvases to sixty artists for their free festival contributions to an art competition: five winners were awarded five hundred pounds apiece, including Lucian Freud for his *Interior near Paddington*. Ayrton, Minton, Vaughan, Colquhoun and MacBryde all failed to win a prize for their pictures. Colquhoun was bitter about his exclusion from the festival, which seemed to mark his decline. And Francis Bacon never appeared there at all.

The sculptors were better represented, with Lynn Chadwick creating an abstract bronze for the courtyard of the Regatta Restaurant and a hanging 273 mobile at the summit of the viewing tower, Reg Butler a wrought-iron birdcage, Barbara Hepworth both an abstract sculpture and the monumental group on the podium of the Dome of Discovery, Frank Dobson his *London Pride* near the main entrance of the Royal Festival Hall, Jacob Epstein a gilded bronze by the Homes and Gardens Pavilion, and Henry Moore executing a bronze *Reclining Figure* for the South Bank Festival itself and a *Standing Figure* for the gardens at Battersea. The Arts Council chose to celebrate Moore as Britain's premier artist, opening London's first retrospective exhibition of his work at the Tate Gallery across the river on the north bank of the Thames. As Moore's biographer wrote, 'The Festival of Britain was in its way a Festival of Moore.'

The contribution of the British cinema to the festival was an accurate prediction of its own suicide. Although it had reached its apogee during the war decade, its achievement was hardly represented. One whole exhibition was devoted to the British invention of television, still unseen in most homes at the time, while the Telecinema was specially designed for the showing of films and television and the latest innovations of the trade, stereophonic sound called 'the borderless screen', cable television, three-dimensional stereoscopic films, and a tribute to the documentary tradition of the island. Television would destroy the cinema industry, and stereophonics and stereoscopics would not save it. The documentary would desert the big screen in the picture palace for the small box by the fireside; and so it would diminish a great tradition into a common denominator. A film to commemorate the architect of the movie camera, William Friese-Greene, was made, but it failed dismally. Already television was inheriting the invention of the moving pictures.

As usual, the Arts Council did little for literature at the festival, outside sponsoring eight touring exhibitions and one London show of books by a hundred contemporary authors. A few writers and poets lectured beside a rare book display at the Victoria and Albert Museum. One of them was Dylan Thomas, who packed the building for a reading of his verse. When asked if the flowers by the lectern would incommode his delivery, he replied, 'If they do, I'll pee on them.' As well as the small subsidies to the poetry readers, the Arts Council did announce an epic verse competition for poems of over 300 lines in length. The list of judges was doughty and worthy of the old establishment – Sir Kenneth Clark and Lord David Cecil, Professor C. M. Bowra and T. S. Eliot's companion, John Hayward, George 'Dadie' Rylands and Basil Willey. Fiercely attacked by *Scrutiny*, the judges, indeed, awarded the wrong prizes to the wrong poets. Of the eight who received awards, only one minor poet, the Cornishman Jack Clemo, and Robert Conquest ever achieved a later reputation. It was a swansong of the old literary guard, but a marker of the creation of state patronage for poetry. As John Hayward pointed out when he deplored the standard of the two thousand entries, this was practically the first public support for the art since the post of Poet Laureate had been created, and it coincided with the nadir of the publication of poetry by commercial firms. In principle, the festival competition set a precedent for subsidizing the muse, although only Laurie Lee was asked to contribute directly to the exhibition, writing all the captions for the enigmatic *Pavilion of the Lion and the Unicorn* including the wry statement, 'Democracy begins at home but doesn't stay there.'

For the drama, the festival provided promises without many performances. An Old Vic season with seven classic plays in repertory, and the husband-and-wife double act of Laurence Olivier and Vivien Leigh alternating *Antony and Cleopatra* with *Caesar and Cleopatra* at the St James's Theatre, were the major London attractions, while Salisbury commissioned Ronald Duncan to write *Our Lady's Tumbler* for performance in the cathedral there, and Christopher Fry's religious drama, *A Sleep of Prisoners*, progressed from one country church to another, turning crypts into internment camps, and signalling the end of modern poetic drama as well as showing a play about prisoners of war.

PETER Where are you going?
DAVID   If necessary
      To break our hearts. It's as well for the world.
PETER There's enough breaking, God knows. We die,
      And the great cities come down like avalanches.

The Arts Council report deplored the fact that so few plays of contemporary merit had emerged for the festival, but it gave the drama prize in its competition to John Whiting for his *Saint's Day* as a new play of contemporary significance. And so it proved to be, although the only step towards the establishment of the long-awaited National Theatre was the laying of a foundation stone on the South Bank site. It was a stone that was to be moved so often before the National Theatre was to be built that the Queen later suggested it should have been mounted on a trolley.

Music, opera and ballet were the chief beneficiaries of the festival. Orchestral and choral works were commissioned from Sir Arnold Bax and Sir Arthur Bliss and many other composers, the opera of *Billy Budd* from Benjamin Britten, and a new ballet from the ailing Constant Lambert for the Sadler's Wells at Covent Garden. Concerts and festivals of music were encouraged and subsidized across the nation. Alicia Markova and Anton Dolin's small ballet company was successful enough to establish itself as the Festival Ballet, providing a third major company for dance. The Arts Council also supported a Wagner season at Covent Garden and set the precedent for the lion's share of state funding to go to the opera, the ballet and the symphony orchestras. To the most expensive arts would it be given, even if their audiences were small and often privileged.

The importance of the Festival of Britain was that it happened at all, with its cut-rate cheerfulness. Correctly it celebrated a state of the arts that had flourished in the 'forties in spite of the conditions of war and the austerity of peace. It was also the signal of the end of the dreams of the planners of reconstruction as well as a last fanfare for an original age. King George VI should have been present at the closing ceremony of the festival when its flag was hauled down and the crowd sang 'Abide With Me' and 'Auld Lang Syne' and 'God Save the King', but he already 275 was beginning a process of dying. The new Conservative Minister of Works showed an indecent haste in having the Pavilions of the Festival dismantled, including the Dome of Discovery and the Skylon. Only the Royal Festival Hall, the Telecinema and a café below Waterloo Bridge and few high verandas survived demolition. A huge site of twenty-seven acres was cleared. It was to be the most enduring legacy of the festival, which had reclaimed the area from swampland and blitzed buildings. It would become in time, in a long time, the home of the South Bank complex, where at last various disciplines would be housed and subsidized and commingle, a *mélange* of concert halls and art galleries, theatres and film auditoria and museums, a conglomeration of the arts that had huddled together with such stimulation and cross-pollination in central London during the previous lost decade.

Another event in the June of 1951 took away the headlines from the festival and eroded the domination of the metropolis by a ruling intellectual group. The diplomats Guy Burgess and Donald Maclean defected to Russia at the point of the discovery of their treachery. Their flight to Moscow signalled a replacement of generations, a change of attitudes in London. Too long the open and self-indulgent conspiracy of the Oxbridge élite had been in power, too short now was the sanctuary of the old school tie. Malcolm Muggeridge, who had been the editor of the *New Statesman*, saw Burgess as an Etonian mudlark, the sick toast of a sick society. 'There was not so much a conspiracy gathered round him as just decay and dissolution. It was the end of a class, of a way of life; something that would be written about in history books.' Cyril Connolly, who quickly wrote a short book on his friend Burgess and on Maclean, agreed that the two traitors were distinct from the atomic spies, who were refugees or nonentities. The two defectors from London were members of the governing classes and high bureaucracy; Burgess and Connolly himself were also part of the Old Etonian network in the capital. Burgess had belonged 'to the febrile café-society of the temporary civil servant, while Maclean belonged to the secret citadel of the permanent'; but both were regular habitués of bohemia, where they met those of their background and persuasion. Burgess was prone to boasting of his Kremlin connections to incredulous friends, although his fellow Old Etonian Anthony Powell always considered him a man to steer clear of, 'a notorious scallywag, to whom no wholly baked person, among those set in authority, would ever have dreamt of entrusting the smallest responsibility, or access to secrets of even a low grade classification'.

The decade had begun terribly for Russian sympathizers with the betrayal of the Nazi-Soviet pact, which had seemed to negate their anti-fascist beliefs on the outbreak of the Second World War. Now the apparent treachery of Burgess and Maclean in 1951 ended the period, with past communists horrified at being associated with present treason during a Cold War which might lead to a Third World War. To John Lehmann, the defection 'acted like a small but violent earthquake in the fairly closely knit intellectual world of our generation'. It reminded his friends that the past could strike out at them. A subsidence of earth had taken place without anyone's realizing it. Lehmann himself had seen little of the defectors for some years, but he was told by the novelist Humphrey Slater that he had known Maclean was a communist agent for some time. His sister, the author Rosamond Lehmann, had also suspected that Burgess was a Soviet spy, trapped in the 'one-way lobster pot' of that conspiratorial role. John Lehmann wrote to Stephen Spender about these informants, and Spender gave the letter to a journalist. The result was a rift between old literary friends, who felt betrayed by each other as well as by the defectors. The dragon's teeth of time past had sprouted suspicion, fear and investigation. When Connolly also wrote on *The Missing Diplomats*, the betrayal of the ruling intellectual class by itself appeared self-evident. Each member would inform on the other for profit and exculpation. The necessary coherence of an élite was eroded by its adherents washing their hands quicker than Pontius Pilate in a hurry.

The betrayal of the 'Auden Gang' by its own members escalated. The Federal Bureau of Investigation approached Christopher Isherwood in America and threatened to have him deported unless he named names of communists, whom he had known at university and in Germany before the war: Isherwood gave away a dozen of the intellectuals of his generation, including Spender and Auden. Auden himself lived in America and took pains to disavow his past, suppressing two poems of the 'thirties, 'A Communist to Others' and 'To a Writer on his Birthday'. The first poem appealed to an unhappy poet to defect and serve the communist cause.

> You need us more than you suppose
> And you could help us if you chose.

The second poem was even more explicit, confessing that 'Our hopes were still set on the spies' career [where] all the secrets we discovered were Extraordinary and false.'

Philip Toynbee was another of Lehmann's group who was implicated by association with the two traitors. In a review of Goronwy Rees's autobiography, *A Chapter of Accidents*, he declared that Burgess was 'a bore of gigantic proportions; a figure to elude, if I possibly could, on the many occasions our paths crossed in the Bohemian rabbit-warrens of London in the 'forties'. Goronwy Rees had already written self-serving and profitable articles on his friend Burgess for the *People*, calling down on himself the enduring hatred of the Oxford and Lehmann world of intellectuals. But Rees had served in military intelligence for six years and claimed that he had not shown Burgess and Blunt the plans for Operation Overlord, the invasion of France, at their notorious flat in Bentinck Street, although Rees often visited there in the spring of 1944. Rees noted that Burgess was always bringing back a series of boys and soldiers and sailors and airmen, whom he picked up from the thousands who thronged the streets of London; 'for war, as Proust noted, provokes an almost tropical flowering of sexual activity behind the lines which is the counterpart of the work of carnage which takes place at the front'. In his witty play about Burgess in Moscow, *An Englishman Abroad*, Alan Bennett makes

277

the defector say, 'One got so spoiled during the war. The joys of the black-out. London awash with rude soldiery.' Knowing Burgess at that time, Goronwy Rees never thought that the spy was more than an eccentric member of the British intellectual ruling class, who was using the war to advance his own career. Only shortly before the defection of the two traitors did Rees suspect Burgess of being a spy, when the drunk Maclean lurched over to his table at the Gargoyle and said aggressively, 'I know all about you. You used to be one of us, but you ratted.' Burgess had once tried to recruit Rees to work for the Comintern, but Rees always asserted that he never believed Burgess to be a spy after the Nazi-Soviet pact, when so many communist sympathizers like himself had left the party.

The Cold War against Russia confirmed the disillusion of those radicals, who might oppose the ruling cultural élite, but who had believed in the Marxist dream of revolution in the 'thirties. Roy Fuller voiced his disappointment for a world

> Where there's no neat solution
> For melting wills or gold,
> And hope is revolution
> And revolution's sold.

He admitted to his friend Alan Ross in a dedicatory epistle to his *Epitaphs and Occasions* of 1949, which was published by John Lehmann:

> We disagree in much, I know:
> I'm over-fond of Uncle Joe:
> You find in Auden not an era –
> Simply a poet who grows queerer;
> The working-class for you's a fact,
> No statue in the final act ...
> Dear friends, I wish this book bore out
> More than the bourgeois' fear and doubt.
> Alas, my talent and my way
> Of life are useless for today.
> I might have cut a better figure
> When peace was longer, incomes bigger ...
> But now, I feel, the 'thirties gone,
> The dim light's out that could have shone.
> My richest ambiguity
> Is nightmares now, not poetry ...

In estimating the poetry of the latter half of the 'forties for the British Council, Alan Ross agreed that there was cultural stagnation by 1951. The ruling élite may have felt despondent and betrayed from within and waiting to be dislodged; but the poets also felt the same. The political role of poetry had grown obsolete, so the art had lost its spine and a reference outside itself, while writers were still uncertain of their individual roles. 'The present period is one in which impulses have tended to dry up and movements to come to a natural end, without, as yet, being replaced by new ones. The war must be held largely responsible for this; a

278

curious numbness, a detachment from the contemporary scene, has taken poetry into individual, less social forms.'

Ross was as disenchanted as Connolly when he closed *Horizon* or Louis MacNeice lamenting on the wireless that the times were 'against major poetry proper'. He found that Marxism had degenerated into a cliché, while religions and political and psychoanalytical formulas had lost novelty and effectiveness. Western civilization was mere dead ground between the United States and the totalitarian state. There was no single major influence on modern poetry nor any movement in the offing. The outlets for serious verse were now restricted to *The Listener, Tribune* and the *New Statesman*. It was the doldrums of British culture.

The shape of the Forties was, in the end, the shape of a tent – a slow climb of the emotional chart to the great watershed of 1945 and the parallel drop to the unimaginative ground, the dead terrain before a new election. A time of earnest characteristics and unrecognisable features; of worthiness and respectable achievement and mediocrity. A time of social experiment and sober behaviour; of artistic and literary conventionality; of theatrical sluggishness with frequent insulin stabs from foreign importations ... The modern world had become a great big Oxford Street with neither distinctions nor distinction. Social life, religion, the Arts, had dropped slowly below the horizon. It was an Augustan age of austerity pleasures; a new social period painfully coming to terms with itself.

The general agreement that the Festival of Britain marked the apogee and requiem of the radical planning of the doomed Labour government, that the defection of the two diplomats exposed the rottenness of the ruling élite, and that literature and theatre and cinema were stalled in their expression of modern concerns, created a convenient hiatus in British culture on the cusp of the 'fifties. It also provided for a later misjudgement of the whole previous decade. In an acute analysis of the period, G. S. Fraser noted that the reputation of a decade was often an agreed fiction. Every generation of young men ran down its immediate predecessors. And indeed, the war children and youths, once they arrived at their arrogant maturity, were particularly keen to savage the combat heroes of their adolescence and extend the deprivations of rationing to a dearth of contemporary culture. The sweets and the meat they had never had were also seen as a parsimony in the arts. The minimal school of the Apocalyptics in poetry was held to represent the verse of the whole decade. Although the New Romantic mode of Dylan Thomas and George Barker and David Gascoyne derived from the 'thirties, it was considered characteristic of the poetry of the 'forties. This was signally false. War poetry was generally laconic, unsentimental, and suspicious of glory or commitment. It was hardly romantic. Some post-war poetry did find appropriate expression for an austere and dingy world; Roy Fuller was its most successful translator, along with Charles Causley and Norman Nicholson and R. S. Thomas. Although T. S. Eliot and the New Romantics appeared to rule the roost at the end of the 'forties, particularly Edith Sitwell and Dylan Thomas, whose *Deaths and Entrances* of 1946 made him appear to be the supreme poet of his time, there had been much good ironical and 279 detached writing in the war, and less good visionary and religious writing in the peace. The poetry of the period was sometimes experimental and often illuminating. As the silenced poet Kenneth Allott said of the war period in 1950: 'It is impossible to indict a whole poetic decade.'

Curiously enough, the poet whose style was to inform the decades to come, Philip Larkin, was making his name as an author after the war. He published two novels with Faber & Faber, *Jill* and *A Girl in Winter*, both anatomical with the petty details and nuances of everyday life. His early book of poetry, *The North Ship*, was Yeatsian, an affliction wished on him by Vernon Watkins, then stationed at an air force camp near Oxford. Larkin joined in the widespread taciturnity of poetry after the war, and only the recent publication of his poems of the late 'forties shows him groping toward the precise, sceptical and throwaway fashion of the 'fifties, that war poets such as Keith Foottit and David Bourne and Gavin Ewart had always practised, and that Roy Fuller had developed. Truth and brevity came to Larkin in 'Neurotics' of 1949:

> ... The mind, it's said, is free:
> But not your minds. They, rusted stiff, admit
> Only what will accuse or horrify,
> Like slot-machines only bent pennies fit.

And Larkin's awareness of his limitations reached him that same year in 'Modesties':

> Thoughts that shuffle round like pence
> Through each reign,
> Wear down to their simplest sense,
> Yet remain.
>
> Weeds are not supposed to grow,
> But by degrees
> Some achieve a flower, although
> No one sees.

A sudden sense of reality and its brief dismissal, the putting into place of the awful fact, these were characteristics of war poetry – and now they struck Larkin. He had pleaded that the war years were a bad time to start writing poetry, although he recognized that the principal poets of the day in his opinion – Eliot, Auden, Dylan Thomas, Betjeman – were all speaking out loud and clear. He dismissed as 'a failure of judgement' those Romantic poets who allowed themselves 'to become entangled in the undergrowth of *Poetry Quarterly* and *Poetry London*', edited by Charles Wrey Gardiner and Tambimuttu. He was to associate with the Oxford group of poets from St John's College, himself and John Wain and Kingsley Amis, who were to dismiss the poets of the 'forties, particularly those who came from the rival Queen's College, Sidney Keyes and Drummond Allison and John Heath-Stubbs. The Queen's group had, indeed, called themselves *Romantic* writers in

Eight Oxford Poets in 1941, distinguishing themselves from the Auden group; but their work did not characterize their whole decade, it merely embellished the time. A riposte to a minor crisis by the Isis should not have misrepresented the poetic achievement of the 'forties, most of which was understated to the pitch of human survival in war, but only some of which was unashamedly romantic. After the funeral of the unconsidered Charles Wrey Gardiner, John Heath-Stubbs answered the disinformation of a later and ungenerous age:

> Burying him, we bury part of ourselves
> And the poetic forties, – we, the mourners,
> Ageing survivors of an abused
> Unfashionable decade. Bohemians, drunks,
> Undisciplined and self-indulgent – so, perhaps, we were.
> And yet I think we still believed in poetry,
> More than some who now possess the scene:
> Dot-and-carry Long John Silvers with small dried-up
> Professors perched upon their shoulders.
> At least our parrots had real and gaudy feathers.

Power abhors a vacuum. And culture abhors a loss of direction absolutely. As the ageing élite feared for its influence and doubted its coherence, a new breed of self-centred artists was on the make. The writers of the 'thirties had spoken for the masses. The writers of the 'fifties would speak for themselves and demand their place among the patrons and the privileged, who were still clinging on to their positions of power. The general imitation of upper-class standards before 1939 and the uniformity of the war decade would be followed by a reaction from aristocratic habits in the 'fifties, a stress on working-class origins as badges of merit. Chips on the shoulder would be worn like epaulettes, a provincial accent exaggerated like a drill sergeant barking orders to squaddies. He who had followed in the past would command in the future after the interim was over.

The salons were closing down with the loss of Connolly's and Lehmann's magazines and with the gradual eclipse in reputation of Edith Sitwell. The *ersatz* courts of the Ladies Cunard and Colefax were irrelevant in post-war Britain under a Labour government, and Mrs Keppel moved out of the Ritz to die in Italy two years after the end of the war. The social and Oxbridge and Old Etonian connections met more rarely, because of mild impoverishment and the need to live more cheaply away from central London, which was falling under the cultural influence of the state bodies, the British and the Arts Councils. Private patronage was giving way to official subsidy. Symptomatic of the times was the rise in esteem of the poets of suburbia, John Betjeman and William Plomer, who both satirized and admired decency and gentility. Alan Ross went so far as to say that Betjeman's poems accomplished a minor aesthetic revolution, forcing the reader to look more charitably at Victorian romanticism and Anglican bric-à-brac and stained glass fanlights in mock-Tudor, semi-detached *Dunroamins*. William Plomer was both sardonic and affectionate, as in 'The Bungalows':

Between the vast insanities
That men so cleverly invent
It may be here, it may be here,
A simulacrum of content ...

The denizens of each hermitage,
Of 'Nellibert' and 'Mirzapore',
Bird-watchers all, in love with dogs,
Are primed with useful garden-lore ...

The commonplace needs no defence,
Dullness is in the critic's eyes,
Without a licence life evolves
From some dim phase its own surprise:

Under these yellow-twinkling elms,
Behind these hedges trimly shorn,
As in a stable once, so here
It may be born, it may be born.

While the poets of suburbia flourished, those of metropolis declined. T. S. Eliot
had long gone away from mourning London in *The Waste Land* to writing verse
plays for the theatre: his heirs were lesser poets, Paul Dehn and David Wright and
A. S. J. Tessimond, whose *Voices in a Giant City* suggested the tawdry truth and
dingy glitter of the post-war capital with his gallery of copywriters and journalists,
prostitutes and wide-boys, minor artists and musicians. He recognized that no war
condition or government intervention had changed the fundamental divisions of
his 'London' where 'tears fall inward':

I am the city of two divided cities
Where the eyes of rich and poor collide and wonder;
Where the beggar's voice is low and unexpectant,
And in clubs the feet of the servants are soft on the carpet
And the world's wind scarcely stirs the leaves of *The Times* ...

I am the city whose fog will fall like a finger gently
Erasing the anger of angles, the strident indecorous gesture,
Whose dusk will come like tact, like a change in the conversation,
Violet and indigo, with strings of lemon streetlamps
Casting their pools into the pools of rain
As the notes of the piano are cast from the top-floor window
Into the square that is always Sunday afternoon.

Fitzrovia received no bonus from the Festival of Britain, no aid from the state, no
benefit from the decline of private patronage or the increase of bureaucracy. It
had been the temporary refuge of the drifting and the dissident, and so it remained,
an area of pubs and clubs and cafés where some artists and writers still congregated

LONDON-SEASON-OF-THE-ARTS

FESTIVAL OF BRITAIN

May — June

1951

ENQUIRIES for all stage productions, concerts and exhibitions, Festival of Britain Information Centre, Swan & Edgar Building, Piccadilly, S.W.1
BOOKINGS—All Box Offices and Ticket Agents

FESTIVAL — SEASON

1951

ST. JAMES's THEATRE
KING STREET, S.W.1
Lessees: S. J. & L. Ltd.
Joint Managing Directors: GILBERT MILLER and PRINCE LITTLER
Licensed by the Lord Chamberlain to PRINCE LITTLER
Under the direction of SIR LAURENCE OLIVIER

A FESTIVAL OF BRITAIN PRODUCTION
by arrangement with the Arts Council of Great Britain
on behalf of ST. JAMES's PLAYERS, LTD.

LAURENCE OLIVIER

6D

presents

CAESAR and CLEOPATRA

by

BERNARD SHAW

First Performance Thursday, 10th May, 1951

to live out their wartime habits. Over from Dublin to become literary editor of the staid *Time and Tide*, Anthony Cronin found himself avoiding the fading élite in Bloomsbury and Holborn and Mayfair, and he spent his drinking time in the pubs west of the Charing Cross Road. His vision of literary success was closer to the aspirations of the ruined men of Soho than to his safe English poetic contemporaries. He sought the archetypal patterns which had created the great art of his time. 'In Soho the standards which had made the true *avant-garde* art of the century were represented, even if only by the casualties of the assault.'

The surviving Fitzrovians had to live on something, and except for the few lucky ones like Francis Bacon, who was receiving much recognition, times were getting harder, particularly for poets and writers. Bohemianism was out of fashion as well as pocket. Respectability cured many of the fraternity; Gavin Ewart gave up working for Tambimuttu for a job with the British Council, which began to suck into its ranks as many poets as the BBC; John Heath-Stubbs deserted Fitzrovia for a succession of teaching jobs. The yellow brick road from Charlotte and Dean Streets now led to universities and councils rather than to war ministries, to broadcasting rather than to the armed services. But body and soul had to be kept together even by the most determined scroungers and bohemians like Colquhoun and MacBryde. As David Wright acknowledged in 'A Ballad for Hard Times', which was printed in the final issue of *Poetry London* in the winter of 1951, a poet could no longer live by verse and friends at the bar of his free choice:

> Why don't I get a job that's cultural?
>   The British Council, or the B.B.C.?
> Or lecture blockheads in a county hall?
>   Or write reviews or novels? T.S.E.
>   Worked in a bank or something, didn't he?
> I'll get a job, and find the time to spare
> For words the public does not want to hear.
>
> Sir, after office-hours I, like the clerk
>   Who builds a fretwork model railway-station
> Out of bus-tickets and old bits of cork,
>   Hope to create a first-class piece of work,
> And give it buckshee to the bloody nation.

TWENTY

Discovery of a Lost Decade

Kay Ambrose

'The mania for decades', as Charles Wrey Gardiner had pointed out, 'is no more stupid than the passion of sailors for the exactitude of latitudes which only exist in the minds of makers of maps.' Ten year periods are a literary convenience, and although the lost decade of the 'forties properly begins in September 1939, with the declaration of the Second World War, and ends twelve years later in 1951 with the Festival of Britain and the loss of power by the Labour Party, it passes as a war and post-war decade with a brief prologue and a longer postscript of summary judgement. Certainly, it replaced the ethos of the fading Bloomsbury and the rising Auden groups of the 'thirties, which Auden himself called 'a low dishonest decade' and F. R. Leavis 'the Marxist decade'. The Second World War, if anything, was expected too much; as Gavin Ewart said, everyone knew 'something would fall like rain and it wouldn't be flowers'. When the declaration of war came, it was rather a relief as well as the termination of the false years of the peace. Later, the war and post-war period of the 'forties was dismissed as a neo-Romantic hiatus in culture by the literary critics and Movement poets of the 'fifties. Both in its denial of pre-war British attitudes and its denigration by future generations, the lost decade of the 'forties has a textual existence in the minds of readers. The time span is recognized as a distinct period, if rather thin on art. 'A book on the war culture of the 'forties?' is the habitual query about this text. 'Was there one?'

There was a culture then. Just before the war and during the fighting and in the post-war years, artistic London coalesced round the pubs and drinking-clubs of Fitzrovia, Soho and Chelsea. Owing to shortages of alcohol, the pub and the club became the centres of social life. In them met most of the creative talent of its day. This transient series of London groups suffered from bombing and black-out and call-up, yet managed to produce extraordinary poetry and painting and writing that displaced the Bloomsbury and Auden ambience. Although this metropolitan rootlessness of culture was later condemned for its excess, it produced a feverish body of work that characterized its time.

The Fitzrovians have not been considered as a series of groups because they did not keep together. War conditions and drink restrictions forced them to meet in the pubs and the clubs; but when drink became readily available in the home and prices rose in London, they split apart in the early 'fifties. They were a loose coterie for a dozen years, without stamina like the Bloomsberries. Their chief editors also undervalued them – a fault not committed by the Hogarth Press or the *Burlington Magazine*. To be able to secure a supply of rationed paper during the war was to be an editor. Cyril Connolly for *Horizon*, John Lehmann for Penguin *New Writing*, Tambimuttu for *Poetry London*, Charles Wrey Gardiner for *Poetry Quarterly* and the Grey Walls Press, and Tom Hopkinson for *Picture Post* and *Lilliput* managed to secure the paper. Relative failures themselves as writers and poets, many of the wartime editors put something of their own failure on to their generation and decried the contribution of the authors they had published. They ended by rejecting the stimulus of the conflict, which stung most people like a wasp. Cyril Connolly even suggested in 1944 a universal shout of 'Phooey to the war.' Actually, in painting and poetry and the arts, war conditions led to a new realism and simplicity in the reporting of great events as well as to neo-Romanticism, an escape to an emotional past from the intolerable monotony of army life and civilian deprivation. Only those who avoided the war and mourned the passing of 'civilization' like Connolly failed to recognize the importance of the altered British culture of the time. But Connolly was not a great artist. 'Being so nearly one was the cause of his distress,' as Michael Wishart wrote of him. His unfulfilment encouraged the growth of defensive weapons. 'People feared Cyril which made him lonely. Perhaps scorpions are sad too. Cyril's tail was ever poised to swing over and stab himself.' As Connolly wrote finally and ruefully of his own failings, 'I work best in scraps and, besides, a little of me goes a long way'.

Artistic life in London, centred in Fitzrovia, was also enriched by contact with European *émigrés* such as Arthur Koestler and Jankel Adler, and Americans such as Ernest Hemingway and Randall Jarrell. The millions of soldiers and sailors and airmen of all the Allied nations who flowed through the West End during the air raids and the black-out, gave the period an intense and vagabond quality that was reflected in its art. There were multitudinous poems and short stories and sketches because there was little time to read and write them. There were few serious novels and large paintings because materials and attention were short. The nation was at war and intermittently engaged. The Fitzrovians were willy-nilly part of it and made use of it. Most of them supported the war, if not always the war effort. The right-wing and pacifist intellectuals of the 'thirties such as T. S. Eliot became largely irrelevant, while after Hitler's invasion of Russia in 1941 and the end of the Nazi pact with the Soviet Union, the British Marxists gave up their anti-war propaganda and embraced patriotism as well as the international revolution. In fact, the Second World War seemed the last Just War: the fascists were obviously villains. The fashionable anti-militarism of the Depression appeared outdated. The Fitzrovians were ready to fight to the end of the bitter in the Swiss pub – and many of them did serve in the armed forces, although they tended to get out before their full time of engagement.

There is no question but that their experience of war did influence their art and sullen craft, as Dylan Thomas called the writing of poetry. Although it was difficult to find the privacy to compose in barrack rooms or fo'c's'les or messes, it was possible. H. B. Mallalieu found himself writing about the incidental: that was what mattered. 'We were being called upon to fight against something we regarded as wrong without, at the same time, having the conviction that we were defending a way of life that was right.' Julian Symons found comradeship in the ranks as his subject-matter along with a bitterness for the bureaucracy and class distinctions of the British army. For Herbert Corby, the war years in the Royal Air Force provided a ready-made subject for his spare and observant verse, also the immediate years following his demobilization, when the impetus of the war poems kept him writing in the peace. And even for those serving poets who would not write about their military life, their experience was a nudge for their inspiration. As Vernon Watkins 287 commented, 'The truest statements about war are made under one's breath, and the most false on public platforms.'

There was no sudden translation into peace. The slow demobilization and continuing demoralization, squatting and rent and food restrictions made the conditions of the conflict last for the whole of the lost decade. The victory of the Labour Party in 1945 may have pleased the social reformers, but not many of the Fitzrovians. They still suffered from the deprivations of the time without the prick of possible action or even death. The flowering of the arts, in films and music as well as in poetry and painting, had to do with the fear of parting and sudden ending. The blitz had concentrated the mind wonderfully. Like Athens in the Peloponnesian War or like Renaissance Florence, the Fitzrovians felt themselves to be in a threatened city state, beleaguered into giving their best. 'I would rather have been in London under siege between 1940 and 1945 than anywhere else,' John Lehmann said before he began to weary of the literature of the period, 'except perhaps Troy in the time that Homer celebrated.' The post-war years eroded the pressure on the Fitzrovians; endurance was needed rather than bursts of inspiration; a terrible listlessness ensued. The Fitzrovians fell apart, retired to the country and accepted the verdict of their famous editors and critics – T. S. Eliot and Connolly and the visiting American pundit Edmund Wilson, who decided that nothing had succeeded 'the Bloomsbury circle' and that English culture was almost completely dead.

Although the metropolitan cultural élite of the 'forties finally concluded that the decade was pretty well worthless in its achievement, G. S. Fraser, editing *Poetry Now* in 1951, not only included in his anthology most of the interesting young poets forged by the war, but recognized the break of poetic tradition from the pre-war years. The eight Arts Council pamphlets named *Since 1939* and written by Stephen Spender and other leading critics also acknowledged the originality and importance of the 'forties in the cinema, music, painting, the ballet and the drama as well as in the novel, prose literature and poetry. The culture of the period was not entirely neo-Romantic, but also sceptical and experimental in many of the arts; it renewed the older creators and stimulated the younger. The decade saw major work not only from the Romantic poets, George Barker and David Gascoyne and Dylan Thomas, but also from T. S. Eliot and Edith Sitwell and Edwin Muir, from Louis MacNeice and Cecil Day Lewis and Stephen Spender; from Roy Fuller and Julian Symons and Alan Ross; from H. B. Mallalieu, A. S. J. Tessimond, Hamish Henderson, Charles Causley, Keith Douglas, Sidney Keyes, Alun Lewis and many other war poets cut off in their prime. It also saw the initial poetry of Kingsley Amis, Robert Conquest, Donald Davie, William Empson, D. J. Enright, Philip Larkin, Norman Nicholson, W. R. Rodgers, W. Sydney Graham, G. S. Fraser, R. S. Thomas, and Vernon Watkins as well as that of John Heath-Stubbs and David Wright. It also provoked good occasional poems from a host of minor poets, who were remembered by Louis MacNeice in his elegy for them, those 'who knew all the words but failed to achieve the Word':

Who were the world's best talkers, in tone and rhythm
Superb, yet as writers lacked a sense of touch,
So either gave up or just went on and on –
Let us salute them now their chance is gone.

It was the guilt of those who did not serve in war, but ran the magazines in London, which led them to devalue the war prose and poetry which they printed. It was the disillusion of the post-war years which did not achieve the social reconstruction of Britain, but led to a Cold War with Russia, that also made the writers and artists of the time underrate their own significant contributions. In his wry way, Roy Fuller wrote his own 'Obituary for R. Fuller' for *Horizon* in 1949, as though he were already dead along with his pre-war ideals. He found 'no spiritual worth / In guided missiles, torture, dearth':

If any bit of him survives
It will be that verse which contrives
To speak in private symbols for
The peaceful caught in public war.
For there his wavering faith in man
Wavers around some sort of plan,
And though foreseeing years of trouble
Denies a universal rubble,
Discovering in wog and sailor
The presages of bourgeois failure.
Whether at this we weep or laugh
It makes a generous epitaph.

The later poetry of the 'fifties, indeed, did not even dare to deal with the major problems of the lost decade. As Donald Davie admitted in his 'Rejoinder to a Critic', recent history, particularly the atomic bombing of Japan, had shown the risk of feeling, of the Romantic idea of sensibility and self-fulfilment. 'How dare we now be anything but numb?' Many of the poets of the 'forties had tried to feel and describe the horrors of their time. 'There was an enthusiasm for poetry then,' John Heath-Stubbs has said. 'One feels that people really did love it, and were exploring imagery, exploring themes, exploring worlds – interested in metaphysics, in religion, in dream imagery ... There is a hostile myth about our generation. I hate that modern poetry has become academic.' At least, during the war, the poets had believed that the winning of it would allow for a reconstruction of society. They could have faith as the earlier Romantic poets had, that a new dawn was possible. But how credit that a world order of peace and social justice would emerge, as Spender asked, when the terrible rain after Hiroshima fell on East and West, both of which merely piled up atomic weapons 'in a meaningless struggle between potential ashes to gain a world of ashes?' Losing the faith of the 'forties in influencing public events, the poets of the 'fifties felt obliged to condemn such Romantic naïvety and search for a private and limited vocabulary of no great significance.

289

The war itself was condemned to cultural oblivion. As one serving poet had observed among the debris of the Egyptian front, 'There's nothing that's so rustily antique as yesterday's battlefield.' The critics and the writers of the 'fifties thought so, forgetting that the war had also provoked a matter-of-fact style that might inform the work of the next generation. Alan Ross pointed out that, in the war poetry he liked, 'the more serious issues were rarely raised because there was so little to be said about them. The war was a fact.' The economy and astringency of the best writing on politics and mass murder were expressed in a poem by Norman Cameron published in Penguin *New Writing*, 'The Verdict':

> It was taken a long time ago,
> The first pressure on the trigger.
> Why complain that the verdict is so?
> It was taken a long time ago.
> And our grave will have many a digger,
> The Mongol, the Yank and the nigger.
> It was taken a long time ago,
> The first pressure on the trigger.

While the most significant change in the arts in Britain was the coming of state aid during the war, Fitzrovia was a pullulating souk where the last private patrons such as Peter Watson kept alive artists and editors and poets in the absence of government. Watson's own suspicious death by drowning in his bath in 1956 would end his glorious generosity. Although a national ballet and opera and theatre would rise from the ashes of the blitz, the 'forties was the last period of the essential individual Maecenas. The cinema industry, centred on Soho, also remained dependent on private finance and bloomed during the lost decade. The cinema of the 'forties produced many excellent war films, the Shakespearean epics of Laurence Olivier, the classics of the end of the decade, *Odd Man Out* and *The Third Man*, and the Ealing comedies. These were the best years for Carol Reed and David Lean, Michael Powell and Emeric Pressburger. A new school of acting led by Olivier and Gielgud and Richardson was changing the style of performance of the Cowards and Novellos of the 'thirties towards a greater naturalism and realism. The actual language of film also affected the writing of the scenarists, especially of Dylan Thomas and Graham Greene. And during the war, the subsidized, but independent BBC became the voice of the nation, particularly in music and poetry reading and verse drama. The needs of talking on the wireless altered the modes of its contributors such as Thomas and Louis MacNeice, who both began setting down plays for voices; the rise of verse drama presaged a fresh, although traditional form after the war. The Fitzrovians were pioneers in the recovery of the cinema and the spoken theatre, designed for the ear.

As if to prove its significance, there emerged from Fitzrovia in the 'forties one radical genius, whose images have changed the perception of our time. Now eighty years old, Francis Bacon has survived the last fifty years of a bohemian way of life in London. It helps him to achieve the 'reality' which he seeks in his art. For Bacon, the message of the artist is necessarily subversive, also his way of life. 'Artists are always disruptive,' he says, 'by their sense of reality they undermine the whole structure around them. It's the look of reality – they break the chain.' In his caged Velázquez popes screaming dumbly like the bloodied nurse in *The Battleship Potemkin*, in his flayed carcasses of men and meat of flesh, he has shown the face of our time, its torture and its violence, its horror and its waste of being. An admirer of Ezra Pound, Bacon has supplied what the poet asked, 'The age demands an image, / Of its accelerated grimace.' So radical, disruptive, seminal and real are Bacon's images that he has achieved what the Auden group of the 'thirties dreamed of, a major exhibition of pictures in Moscow, seen there as revolutionary protests against religious authority and the destruction of humankind. 'I was very much helped towards painting,' Bacon wrote to the Soviet government, 'after I saw Eisenstein's films "Strike" and "The Battleship Potemkin" by their remarkable visual imagery.' Eisenstein's pictures gave Bacon a form for his 'reality', which had nothing to do with the dialectical materialism of scientific Marxism. He also quoted to the Soviets a definition of painting by Vincent Van Gogh: 'How to achieve such anomalies, such alterations and refashionings of reality that what comes out of it are lies if you like but lies that are more true than literal truth.'

'Reality' to Bacon is created by technique and by the capture of chance. He searches for concentration on certain human situations. 'Somewhere there's a very hard rock, an instinct. You can't go beyond that.' He admires Homer and the classical Greek tragedians for their unsparing view of life, and he quotes a translation of a line from Aeschylus, 'The reek of human blood spills out of me.' Reality is 'the tough roughness of being. The painter's job is to make the images which return to reality more violently, if you're lucky.'

Bacon refuses to recognize that his paintings have achieved a Greek 'reality' that is the essence of the spirit of our age, although he knows that he has achieved a communication to all the people of his era. This cannot result only from technique and caught luck and the violence of Bacon's own experience in Berlin in the 'twenties, in Paris in the 'thirties, and in bohemian London during the war and thereafter. His brutal way of living, amoral and disruptive, makes him an unlikely recipient for the gift of conveying a universal message. But Rimbaud and, indeed, Shakespeare also received that improbable gift, when neither had the vocabulary nor the background to compose their imperishable verses, which are still resonant for any age or country. Although Francis Bacon thinks that the old society of Soho is now moribund, he still believes that his best works lie ahead of him, and that, without the stimulus of bohemia, he will record the 'reality' of the 'nineties. He demonstrates that a Fitzrovian life may provoke an artist into fifty years of supreme creativity, while Dylan Thomas remains the testimony to its morose fatality.

Just as there are horses for courses, there are drinkers for Soho, which was, after all, originally a call to the hunting dogs pursuing a hare to the kill. Many of the 291

Fitzrovian painters and composers and poets were hounded to their deaths, the victims of alcoholic excesses in the decades after the 'forties – Nina Hamnett and John Minton, Roberts Colquhoun and MacBryde, Constant Lambert and Dylan Thomas, who had already foreseen his end, calling himself 'an old ramrod dying of strangers'. His actual death in 1953 after a drinking bout in New York signalled the destructive powers of too many pints and chasers in too many pubs full of artists and their acolytes. The life that Fitzrovia gave also took away. In his poem, 'At the Wake of Dylan Thomas', George Barker told of the example of his fellow poet's burial:

> ... Simply by dying we add to the manic chorus
> And put the fear of God up all surviving.
>
> And now he's gotten, first of all and foremost,
> You, Dylan, too, the one undoubting Thomas,
> The whistler in the dark he's taken from us.

Thomas's death confirmed that the decade of the Romantic poets, old and new, was over. The last *New Romantic Anthology*, edited by Stefan Schimanski and Henry Treece, was published by Charles Wrey Gardiner in 1949: Schimanski himself also died in 1953 during the Korean War in an aeroplane crash and was remembered in an elegy by his friend, G. S. Fraser:

> Not like the hawk, nor like the hooded airman
> But a mild seeker for a lost kind God,
> A literary scout, a sort of chairman
> For groups of bothered notions! And how odd
> He should end so ...

Fraser now recognized that the 'New Romantics' among the poets had finished their ten years' innings. In spite of producing some fine poems, they had left their craft in a state of confusion. The next generation would have to be more relevant and restrained, as much of the war poetry had already been. His own poetry would be so, changing from the early apocalyptic to the late laconic.

Moreover, the conditions for writing experimental poetry in Fitzrovia were in decline. George Barker saw that young poets could no longer create and eat at the same time. 'It is already impossible for them to drink and write as they wish: the beer is no longer singing beer.' For economic and social reasons, artists were moving from Soho by the early 'fifties, because of the rise of crime and rents, which could be afforded only by strip-tease shows and pornographic bookshops. The Fitzrovians who stayed in the area had to be able to pay for it, and even, as Lucian Freud did, seek the company 'of the criminal as well as the posh' – or so George Melly found when Freud took him on the occasional binge to the Stork Club where the hostesses served whisky in teapots outside licensing hours. In an acerbic poem, Robert Conquest spoke of the replacement of the little publishers and good bookshops by the new 'Literature in Soho':

Gamboge neon BOOKS AND MAGAZINES
   Is a convention which means
      You'd be lucky to find

Eliot here, or Waugh or Amis – Lawrence
   Yes, but as reassurance
      Only, a kind of a kind

Gesture to the bourgeois, the genteel
   Who otherwise might feel
      Ill at ease, out of sorts ...

Lady Chatterley's Lover in a brown paper wrapper was hardly a substitute for the literary and artistic Fitzrovia that was dying or dead, even if some of its luminaries such as Bacon or Freud would live on to an advanced age and the recognition and success which they deserved and despised. The sting of war and bohemia was blunted in the 'forties. The future of writing and the arts would be less concentrated, yet more restricted and overly cautious in the middle 'fifties, the suburban celebrations of John Betjeman, the provincial pastorals of Philip Larkin. State patronage would increasingly make for safe production for subsidy. Some noble and unfashionable Romantics would continue to laud the lost decade and intermittently try to live as they had then; but even they were aware that their peers had departed and that modern times were replacing the beery universities of their fledgeling days. Knowing that a favourite pub was being pulled down, John Heath-Stubbs wrote the requiem of his sort and his young age:

                Enough bad poets
Have romanticized beer and pubs,
And those for whom the gimcrack enchantments
Of engraved glass, mahogany, plants in pots,
Were all laid out to please, were fugitives, doubtless
Nightly self-immersed in a fake splendour.

Yet a Public House perhaps makes manifest also
The hidden City; implies its laws
Of tolerance, hierarchy, exchange.
Friends I remember there, enemies, acquaintances,
Some drabs and drunks, some bores and boors, and many
Indifferent and decent people. They will drink elsewhere.

ROLL-CALL

At the end of *Return Journey*, Dylan Thomas finds himself in his old school and makes a roll-call of the names of his fellow schoolboys, dead or forgotten. In my schools, at my universities, I remember the long metal lists of those who died in the war. Now I would wish to list some of those innovative and modern writers and poets and artists, who died on active service. These are the lost creators of their time, so talented and so falsely judged.

Drummond Allison (East Surreys)
Brian Allwood (RAF)
J. P. Angold (RAF)
Cameron Bailey (KRRC)
A. D. Bass (RAMC)
J. R. Blythe (Merchant Navy)
J. F. Boughey (Coldstream Guards)
David Bourne (RAF)
Clive Branson (RAC)
O. O. Breakwell (Coldstream Guards)
O. C. Chave (RAF)
M. Chevenix Trench (RE)
Timothy Corsellis (RAF)
Keith Douglas (Sherwood Rangers)
F. R. Dunton (RAF)
James Farrar (RAF)
David Graves (R. Welch Fusiliers)
Stephen Haggard (Intelligence Corps)
Thomas Hennell (War Artist)
Richard Hillary (RAF)
T. R. Hodgson (RAF)
John Jarmain (RA)
Robert Joly (Grenadier Guards)
D. R. Geraint Jones (RAC)

Sidney Keyes (Queen's Own R. West Kents)
Alun Lewis (South Wales Borderers)
John MacLeish (King's Own R. Regt)
J. D. Maclure (Royal Scots)
M. MacNaughton-Smith (RAF)
H. N. T. Medrington (RAF)
I. O. Meikle (RA)
T. A. Mellows (7th Lancers)
David Raikes (RAF)
Eric Ravilious (War Artist)
Albert Richards (War Artist)
William Rose (Royal Navy)
R. Brian Scott (Army)
Richard Spender (Parachute Regt)
Gervase Stewart (Fleet Air Arm)
R. D. D. Thomas (Grenadier Guards)
Frank Thompson (RA)
Andrew Tod (R. Scots Fusiliers)
Bertram Warr (RAF)
Nigel Weir (RAF)
Jonathan Wilson (Scots Guards)
Rollo Woolley (RAF)

NOTES

THE PROLOGUE

T. S. Eliot was writing in a preface to *A Little Book of Modern Verse* (selected by Anne Ridler, London, 1941). Herbert Read, 'Art in an Electric Atmosphere', was published in *Horizon*, Vol. III, No. 17, May 1941. Malcolm Bradbury has written on modernism in his essays 'An Age of Parody' and 'Closing Time in the Gardens' in *No, Not Bloomsbury* (London, 1987): he describes the 'forties as 'a vacancy in recent cultural history'. For the context of this book, Valentine Cunningham's masterly *British Writers of the Thirties* (Oxford, 1988) is seminal in its creation of the atmosphere of British writing at the coming of the Second World War. He rightly places a literature in a history and a society. He looks for a set of sign-systems and fictions that are themselves histories. He understands that writers and artists have a very co-operative subconsciousness, and that people and events, fictions and facts have a way of fitting together, of moulding each other. He stresses the relationships of writers of the period through their schools and families. But his writers of the nineteen-thirties are concerned with foreign wars and frontiers, not with the Second World War at home and its conditions in the nineteen-forties.

CHAPTER ONE

Arthur Ransome, *Bohemia in London* (London, 1907) locates his bohemia in Fleet Street as well as in Bloomsbury, Soho and Chelsea. The quotation from George Sterling, the intimate friend of Jack London and a *habitué* of the bohemias of San Francisco and Greenwich Village in New York, is taken from Allen Churchill, *The Improper Bohemians* (London, 1959), p. 26. The story about Augustus John paying the bill at the Eiffel Tower comes from Ruthven Todd's *Fitzrovia and the Road to the York Minster, or Down Dean Street* (London, 1973). John Gawsworth's diary entry comes from his Verse Notebook VIII, 5–18 December 1940, MS in possession of Jon Wynne-Tyson, his executor and the present King of Redondo. Philip O'Connor, *Memoirs of a Public Baby* (intro. Stephen Spender, London, 1958) is a classic of the period, while Nina Hamnett's comments derive from her second autobiographical work, *Is She a Lady?* (London, 1953), p. 78. A. F. Tschiffely, *Bohemia Junction*, was published in London in 1950. John Pearson's biography of Edith, Osbert and Sacheverell Sitwell, *Façades* (London, 1978) remains definitive, and the quotation comes from Edith Sitwell's letter to Richard Jennings, 3 March 1937. Harold Nicolson claimed that Sibyl Colefax knew that people hated her parties. Anthony Powell's remark on

Etonian novelists was made at the St John's College, Cambridge, Literary Society in 1961, and surprised the author of this book. The quotation from Virginia Woolf comes from her essay 'The Leaning Tower', published by John Lehmann in *Folios of New Writing* in 1940. Evelyn Waugh wrote to Cyril Connolly on 21 September 1952: *The Letters of Evelyn Waugh* (London, 1980) have been edited well by Mark Amory.

The remark on the Cavendish Hotel was said to the author by Michael Harrison, who has also written a biography of Rosa Lewis. Theodora Fitzgibbon's entertaining period reminiscences, *With Love* (London, 1982) provide Rosa Lewis's comment on modern girls, while Anthony Powell's observation on the Cavendish comes from the second volume of his autobiography, *Messengers of Day* (London, 1978). Anna Wickham's poems were edited by John Gawsworth for the Richards' Shilling Selections from Edwardian Poets, undated. Geoffrey Grigson writes about the Café Royal in his *Recollections* (London, 1984). The description of the Café Royal in wartime comes from Lovat Dickson, *The House of Words* (London, 1963). Daniel Farson writes of John Minton in the Gargoyle in *Soho in the Fifties* (London, 1988). Peter Quennell tells of the Nut-house in his second volume of autobiography, *The Wanton Chase* (New York, 1980). Joseph Vecci has put down his memoirs in *The Tavern Is My Drum* (London, 1948), and the story of the lift at the Milroy comes from an interview with Lord Ampthill.

Julian Maclaren-Ross's *Memoirs of the Forties* (London, 1965) is the indispensable Baedeker of the place and period. I have quoted from his piece on 'Tambimuttu and the Progress of *Poetry London*'. Tambimuttu's editorial was printed in its first issue, February 1938. The opinions on Charles Wrey Gardiner are those of the poets G. S. Fraser and Derek Stanford, whose literary memoirs, *Inside the Forties* (London, 1977), are another vital guide to the period. Gardiner himself wrote five volumes of autobiography and *pensées*: the quotation about the mania of decades is taken from his last book, which was published anonymously under the title *The Answer to Life is No* (London, 1951). The other little magazines to close were *Purpose*, *Wales*, *Welsh Review* and the *Voice of Scotland*. Stephen Spender's comment on Barker, Gascoyne and Thomas comes from 'Some Observations on English Poetry between Two World Wars', *Transformation*, 3, 1945, while Nicolas Bentley's squib comes from *Second Thoughts* (London, 1939). Cyril Connolly's definitive broadcast on 'Literature in the Nineteen-Thirties' was printed in *Talking to India* (ed. George Orwell, London, 1943).

Thomas Driberg's poem 'Party Line' was printed in *Horizon*, Vol. I, No. 6, June 1940. John Lehmann's comments on September 1939 come from the opening of his second volume of autobiography, *I Am My Brother* (London, 1960). His *In the Purely Pagan Sense* was published under his name in London in 1976. George Orwell was writing for Lehmann's Penguin *Folios of New Writing* in a piece called 'My Country Right or Left'. Stephen Spender's journal of the beginning of the war is printed in *Horizon*, Vol. 1, Nos 2, 3 and 5, February–May 1940. Cyril Connolly wrote to his wife Jean in September 1939, quoted in David Pryce-Jones, *Cyril Connolly: Journal and Memoir* (London, 1983), p. 287.

Both Patric Dickinson and Roy Fuller have written autobiographies: the quotation is from Fuller's poem, 'Autumn 1939'. Phyllis Castle's comment comes from 'A Week in the W.A.A.F.'s'. *William Medium* by Edward Hyams was published in London in 1947, while David Gascoyne's *Paris Journal 1937–1939* was published in London in 1978. The excellent and neglected poet James Monahan published 'The Feckless Years' in *Far from the Land* (London, 1944). Anne Ridler's 'Now as Then: September 1939' is taken from *The Nine Bright Shiners* (London, 1943), while the quotation from Roy Fuller is from 'Poem', published in *The Middle of a War* (London, 1943). Lawrence Durrell's 'Journal to David Gascoyne' comes from the *New English Weekly*, 7 September 1939. Christopher Hassall's lines come from his Sonnet XXVII, *Crisis* (London, 1939). The public school poet is Drummond Allison, whose poem 'For Karl Marx' is printed in *For Your Tomorrow: An Anthology Written by Young Men from English Public Schools Who Fell in the World War 1939–1945* (Oxford, 1950). The quotations from Ruthven Todd are taken from 'In September 1939' and 'Elegy' in *Garland for the Winter Solstice* (London, 1961). Henry Green's self-portrait, *Pack My Bag*, was published in London in 1940.

George Barker's verse comes from *The True Confessions of George Barker* (New York, 1962), p. 31. Douglas Fairbanks Jr reminisces about Laurence Olivier's behaviour on 3 September 1939. Osbert Lancaster tells his reminiscences in *With an Eye to the Future* (London, 1967), while the episode of the guardsmen in the shelter at St James's Palace was told to the author by Hugh O'Shaughnessy. Mollie Panter-Downes wrote her admirable 'London War Notes' for the *New Yorker* from 1939 to 1945; this entry is for 10 September 1939. Lovat Dickson's remark is in his autobiography, *The House of Words* (see above), p. 219. The poem is by Ruthven Todd and is called 'It Was Easier' (London, 1942). George Woodcock's article 'Failures of Promise' on editing *Now* is in the important issue of *Aquarius*, 17/18, published in 1986/7, and dealing with the poetry of the 'forties. Michael Hamburger is one of the more discerning analysts of Fitzrovia

in his autobiography, *A Mug's Game* (London, 1980): the young Pole who was killed was Stefan Schimanski, secretary to various Members of Parliament and editor of *Transformation* with its creed of 'Personalism'. Jon Wynne-Tyson talked to the author in 1988. George Orwell's complaint comes from his 'As You Please' column in the *Tribune*, 3 December 1943. The extract is taken from David Wright's poem 'On a Friend Dying', addressed to the war poet Julian Orde and printed in *To the Gods the Shades* (Manchester, 1976).

CHAPTER TWO

The quotation is from Malcolm Muggeridge, 'The Beginning of the 'Forties', *The Windmill*, 1946. Joan Wyndham's two war diaries, *Love Lessons* and *Love Is Blue* (London, 1986), are enlightening accounts of the effects of the war on young women of artistic temperament. *Fire and Water: An Anthology by Members of the NFS* (London, 1942) is prefaced by Stephen Spender's poem, 'Destruction and Resurrection: England Burning'. Spender also wrote an illustrated account of civil defence, *Citizens In War – And After* (London, 1945), praising an extremely active citizen army 'performing a violently energetic and dangerous duty misnamed passive defence'. Woodrow Wyatt, who has talked to me, has written entertaining memoirs, *Confessions of an Optimist* (London, 1985) as has Sir Alec Guinness, whose memoirs are *Blessings in Disguise* (London, 1985). James Pope-Hennessy wrote to Clarissa Churchill on 20 June 1940; the letter is published in *A Lonely Business: A Self-Portrait of James Pope-Hennessy* (ed. Peter Quennell, London, 1981). John Strachey and Osbert Sitwell contributed to symposia in *The Author* in the spring and summer of 1940. *War Begins At Home* by Mass-Observation, edited by Tom Harrisson and Charles Madge, was published in London, 1940. Peter Watson is quoted by Stephen Spender in his illuminating *The Thirties and After: Poetry, Politics, People (1933–75)* (London, 1978). Goronwy Rees's letter and Cyril Connolly's reply were printed in *Horizon*, Vol. I, No. 7, July 1940. Connolly wrote 'The Ivory Tower' for the *New Statesman*, 7 October, 1939: his letter to his mother is mentioned in Michael Shelden's important study, *Friends of Promise: Cyril Connolly and the World of Horizon* (London, 1989). Lionel Birch wrote the piece on 'Leave, 1940', printed in *Lilliput*, April 1941, in which Lesley Osmond also described 'September at the Windmill'.

Robert Speaight on 'Drama since 1939' in *Since 1939* (London, 1946–7) (see below) and Peter Noble, *British Theatre* (London, 1946) are essential reading. The quotation about the Pilgrim Players comes from Henzie and E. Martin Browne's moving *Pilgrim Story* (London, 1945).

The creator of *Balletomania*, Arnold L. Haskell is definitive on Sadler's Wells Ballet. I have used his wartime book, *The National Ballet: A History and a Manifesto* (London, 1943). Leslie Hurry did the cover for Caryl Brahms, *Robert Helpmann: Choreographer* (London, 1943), from which the supporter's words to Helpmann are taken, while Edward J. Dent reported the comment on Sadler's Wells during the blitz in *A Theatre for Everybody* (London, 1945). Desmond Shawe-Taylor's *Covent Garden* (London, 1948) is interesting on opera.

Robert Hewison refers to John Piper's comment on the Royal Academy show in his indispensable *Under Siege: Literary Life in London 1939–1945* (London, 1977). Herbert Read denounces the Forces Exhibition in 'Vulgarity and Impotence', *Horizon*, Vol. V, No. 28, April 1942. The letter from Peter Watson is quoted in the catalogue to the important neo-Romantic painting exhibition at the Barbican Art Gallery, *A Paradise Lost* (ed. David Mellor, London, 1986).

Graham Sutherland's comments are quoted in Alan Ross's excellent study, *Colours of War: War Art 1939–54* (London, 1987), pp. 37, 44. Paul Nash's remarks are taken from 'A Painter's Preoccupations', *Little Reviews Anthology*, 1946.

The comment on British war films comes from Dilys Powell's contribution to *Since 1939* (see above), the British Council's indispensable contribution to an evaluation of the 1940s with articles by Robert Speaight on drama, Henry Reed on the novel, Stephen Spender on poetry, John Hayward on prose literature, Arnold L. Haskell on ballet, Rollo Myers on music, and Robin Ironside on painting. For Maclaren-Ross's film experience, see his *Memoirs of the Forties* (cited, Chapter 1), pp. 109–34, while the story about Robert Herring is quoted in *Leaves in the Storm* (London, 1945). Louis MacNeice's comments on making propaganda are contained in R. D. Smith, 'Castle on the Air', *Time Was Away: The World of Louis MacNeice* (ed. T. Brown and A. Reid, Dublin, 1974). 'Bar-Room Matins', written in July 1940, comes from Louis MacNeice, *Plant and Phantom* (London, 1941). For Priestley's BBC career, see John Braine's downright biography, *J. B. Priestley* (London, 1978), pp. 105–10. Victor Bonham-Carter writes with authority on efforts to put writers in harness during the war in *Authors by Profession* (2 vols, London, 1984).

Douglas Reed made the comment on the sloth of the call-up in *A Prophet at Home* (London, 1941). Angus Calder, *The People's War: Britain 1939–45* is the seminal work on conditions and defence on the Home Front. Stephen Spender's comments come from his *The Thirties and After* (cited above), p. 85. The leader is from *The Times*, 25 March 1941, and David Gascoyne's verse from 'Farewell Chorus', included in his *Collected Poems* (Oxford, 1965).

CHAPTER THREE

E. S. Turner quotes the conscientious objector at the tribunal in his excellent study, *The Phoney War* (London, 1961). Julian Symons's poem on 'Conscript' comes from *More Poems from the Forces* (ed. Keidrych Rhys, London, 1943) as does 'Khaki Soul' by J. B. Sidgwick, then serving as a lieutenant in the Royal Artillery. The article by the private, 'Ours Not To Reason Why', was printed in *Horizon*, Vol. III, No. 15, March 1941. Keidrych Rhys defends the war poets and attacks the editors of *Horizon* and Penguin *New Writing* in his introduction to *Poems from the Forces* (London, 1941). Joan Wyndham's friend in *Love Is Blue* (cited in Chapter 2) is Leonard Purvis, defending himself from the verbal assaults of a recently enlisted rear-gunner. 'Can We Be Educated up to Art?', Michael Rothenstein's note on lecturing to the army, was printed in *Horizon*, Vol. VII, No. 40, April 1943: he found that obvious symbolism had a marked appeal, particularly Paul Nash's smashed Nazi bomber with white cliffs towering in the background. Keith Henderson, 'Notes of a Peaceful Artist in War Time', was printed in *The Listener*, November 1941. Francis Scarfe's poems '25-Pounder' and 'Grenade' were printed in *More Poems from the Forces* (cited above), as were R. N. Currey's 'Boy with a Rifle' and 'At the Range' by H. B. Mallalieu. Andrew Young's 'Field-Glasses' was published in two versions, in *Horizon*, Vol. III, No. 13, January 1941, and in *Orion*, Vol. I, 1945. John Manifold's superb sonnet 'Camouflage' comes from *Poems from the Forces* (cited above), while John Gawsworth's 'Bayonet Instruction' is taken from his poetry notebook, dated 15 August 1941. Robert A. Chaloner was a lieutenant in the Royal Artillery and knew the subject of his poem, 'Home Front – 1942', also printed in *More Poems from the Forces*.

The anonymous article, 'The Creation of a Class', is taken from *Horizon*, Vol. IV, No. 21, September 1941. Maclaren-Ross's *The Stuff To Give The Troops* was printed in London, 1944, although most of the stories had previously appeared in *Horizon*, *Tribune*, *Lilliput*, *Modern Reading*, Penguin *New Writing*, *Bugle Blast*, *First Eighteen*, *Writing Today*, the *Strand Magazine*, *Printers' Pie* and the *Saturday Book*: at the time, Ross seemed to be the new Kipling in his command of soldiers' vernacular and thought. His 'Second Lieutenant Lewis: A Memoir' appears in *Memoirs of the Forties*, first published by Alan Ross, who had it reprinted in 1984 with an introduction by himself, commemorating its author.

The comment on the black-out is taken from *War Begins at Home* (cited in Chapter 2). Kenneth Allott's opening lines from 'Blackout' come from *The Ventriloquist's Doll* (London, 1943). The poem 'People in Safe Areas' was written by Richard B. Wright and was printed in *More Poems from the Forces*.

Keith Vaughan's 'Exiles in Khaki' was printed in the 297

Little Reviews Anthology of 1943. Two of the best of Alan Ross's poems are his 'Night-train Images' and 'Leave Train', published in his *Poems, 1942–67* (London, 1968). Henry Green's admirable war novel *Caught* appeared in 1942. Timothy Corsellis's complaint about training was published in *Poems of This War by Younger Poets* (Oxford, 1945): his poem to Spender was included in *More Poems from the Forces. In the Purely Pagan Sense* by John Lehmann has already been acknowledged in Chapter 1, while Quentin Crisp's autobiography *The Naked Civil Servant* (London, 1968) gives special insight into Fitzrovia during the 'forties from his own idiosyncratic point of view. Francis Scarfe's 'Ballad of the Safe Area' appeared in Tambimuttu's anthology for Faber & Faber, *Poetry in Wartime* (London, 1942). Alfred Perles, 'Soldiers and Civilians', derives from the *Fortune Anthology* (London, 1942).

CHAPTER FOUR

John Bayliss dedicated his 'Epilogue: Testament and Prophecy' to the conscripted poet Derek Stanford: the poem was printed in Geoffrey Grigson's *Poetry of the Present* (London, 1949). Seán Jennett's 'Autumn 1940' comes from his *Always Adam* (London, 1943). William Sansom wrote a brilliant account of *Westminster in War*, published in London, 1947. The verse comes from Christopher Hassall's 'Tube Shelter: Leicester Square, 1941', printed in *The Slow Night and Other Poems, 1940–48* (London, 1949). Tambimuttu's talk on 'The Man in the Street' comes from *Talking to India* (cited in Chapter 1). The description of the East End shelter is by Ritchie Calder, *The Lesson of London* (London, 1941). The American journalist who described the shelters at the Isle of Dogs and at the Dorchester was Ralph Ingersoll, quoted in *The Home Front: An Anthology of Personal Experience, 1938–1945*, excellently edited by Norman Longmate and published in London, 1981. Cecil Beaton's comments come from *The Years Between: Diaries 1939–1944* (London, 1965). Charles Ritchie, *The Siren Years: Undiplomatic Diaries 1937–1945* was published in London in 1974 and is quoted twice in this chapter. 'Blitz Dinner' was written by Fred Smewin and printed in *More Poems from the Forces* (cited in Chapter 3). Julian Symons's opinions of London under the blitz come from *Notes From Another Country* (London, 1972).

John Braine's biography of J. B. Priestley has been cited (Chapter 2), as has William Sansom's *Westminster in War* (see above). George Orwell's comment comes from his 'Wartime Diary', 17 September 1940, later published in the four volumes of his collected shorter works, edited by Sonia Orwell. Peter Quennell's *The Wanton Chase* has already been cited (Chapter 1). Stephen Spender wrote a factual account of civil defence, *Citizens In War – And After* (cited in Chapter 2). His further comments on the blitz come from *The*

Thirties and After (cited in Chapter 2) and from *World Within World* (London, 1951).

J. C. Hall's poem 'Journey to London' is printed in *The Summer Dance and Other Poems* (London, 1960). The verses from 'Cities are People' are by John Singer and were reprinted in the *Little Reviews Anthology* of 1946. The verse from Sagittarius (Olga Katyin) comes from 'London Burning', reprinted in *Quiver's Choice* (London, 1945). A. P. Herbert's 'Ode on the Schedule of Reserved Occupations' and 'Domestic Hollow-ware, etc.' are also reprinted in *Leave My Old Morale Alone* (New York, 1948). Cyril Connolly's editorial comes from *Horizon*, Vol. III, No. 17, May 1941. David Wright wrote a poem deliberately entitled 'Waste Land' about a walk through the bombed city of London. Graham Greene's essay 'At Home' was written about October 1940, and printed in *The Lost Childhood and Other Essays* (London, 1951). Graham Sutherland is quoted in Roger Berthoud, *Graham Sutherland* (London, 1982). The verse from Stephen Spender is taken from 'Air Raid Across The Bay At Plymouth' and the description of the colours of the blitz from *Westminster in War*. 'Punishment Enough' by Norman Cameron was reprinted in *The Poetry of War 1939–45* (ed. Ian Hamilton, London, 1965). The poem by Bertram Warr on 'Stepney 1941' was printed in *Poems from the Forces* (cited in Chapter 3). Mervyn Peake's poem, 'The Shapes', was published in his *Shapes & Sounds* (London, 1941). James Monahan's remarkable poem 'Ludgate Hill – December Night', written in March 1941, comes from *Far from the Land* (cited in Chapter 1). Spender's view of the revival of the arts under the blitz comes from his *World Within World* and *The Thirties and After* (see above). Alan Ross's illustrated reminiscence, *The Forties: A Period Piece* (London, 1950) is underrated because of its admirable brevity.

Peter Quennell described 'The Lost Girls' in *The Wanton Chase* (cited in Chapter 1). John Gawsworth wrote to Olga Adair on 26 April 1941. Alan Ross's 'Variety Girls' comes from his *Poems, 1942–67* (cited in Chapter 3). Francis Scarfe's 'Lines Written in an Air Raid' was published in the anthology *Lyra* (Billericay, 1942). 'Two Pairs of Shoes' by Keith Foottit appeared in *For Your Tomorrow*, the anthology of young writers from the public schools cited in Chapter 1. Francis Gelder was the author of 'A Ballad of 1941', which was printed in *Poems of This War by Younger Poets* (cited in Chapter 3). *Caught* by Henry Green was cited in Chapter 3. *No Directions* by James Hanley was published in 1943, while Nigel Balchin's *Darkness Falls From The Air* was published in London in 1942. Roy Fuller's lines come from his 'Soliloquy in an Air Raid', published in *The Middle of a War* (cited in Chapter 1). Basil Woon, *Hell Came to London*, was published in 1941. 'But time is a firework …' comes from 'And At Dawn Are Shot', a poem by Peter Hellings, printed in *Firework Music* (London, 1946), while Tambimuttu's lines end 'The Spreading Cross', also printed in *Lyra*.

CHAPTER FIVE

George Orwell's 'As One Non-Combatant to Another' was subtitled 'A Letter to "Obadiah Hornbrook"', the pseudonym taken by Alex Comfort in his previous satirical poem, printed in *Tribune*, 4 June 1943. Orwell's counterblast was printed in *Tribune*, 18 June 1943. John Lehmann's testimony appears in his autobiography, *I Am My Brother* (cited in Chapter 1). *The White Horseman* (ed. J. F. Hendry and Henry Treece) was published by Herbert Read at Routledge in 1941, while G. S. Fraser in 'The Autobiography of an Intellectual', *A Stranger and Afraid* (Manchester, 1983) commented wisely on his participation in and disillusion from the New Apocalypse. Mulk Raj Anand commented on writers returning via mental homes to Soho in 'Notes for an Unbuttoned Survey of the Contemporary English Novel', *Transformation*, 3, 1945, while Paul Potts's 'Inside' was printed in the second edition of *Poetry London*, April 1939. Julian Symons's comment on *Now* appeared in George Woodcock's article 'Failures of Promise' in *Aquarius*, 17/18, 1986/7.

Theodora Fitzgibbon's memoirs *With Love* have already been cited in Chapter 1. In *Dead as Doornails* (Dublin, 1970), Anthony Cronin proves himself to be one of the more lively and illuminating guides to Fitzrovia. John Heath-Stubbs made his remarks to me. Peter Vansittart's entertaining writer's memoir is called *Paths from a White Horse* (London, 1985). David Wright's account of meeting Dylan Thomas on 17 March 1943 comes from a letter home, printed in *Aquarius*, 17/18, 1986/7. Graham Greene's account of the 'great blitz' of 16 April 1941, comes from his diary, included in his memoir, *Ways of Escape* (London, 1980). George Orwell's account of the raid on the docks comes from his 'Wartime Diary', 8 April 1941. I am indebted to Constantine Fitzgibbon's stirring book, *The Blitz* (London, 1957) for details on the Café de Paris and its bombing, also for the remarks of the young women on the excitement and stimulus of wartime. This one of Mollie Panter-Downes's 'London War Notes' for the *New Yorker* was dated 22 March 1941. Nicolas Bentley's squib comes from *Second Thoughts* (cited in Chapter 1). Philip O'Connor's *Memoirs of a Public Baby* has already been cited in Chapter 1. Bertram Warr's 'Working Class' was printed in *Poems from the Forces*, David Bourne's 'Night Club' in *More Poems from the Forces* (both cited in Chapter 3).

Louis MacNeice's poem on 'Alcohol' was printed in *Horizon*, Vol. VII, No. 37, January 1943. The verses from Sagittarius come from 'Strange Bedfellows', written in June 1941, and reprinted in *Quiver's Choice* (cited

in Chapter 4). The general level of her satirical poems and those of A. P. Herbert makes the author believe that light verse distinguished English culture in the war years as well as light music. Cyril Connolly wrote about Burgess and Maclean after their defection in *The Missing Diplomats* (London, 1952). Julian Symons's 'Pub' was printed in *Poetry in Wartime* (cited in Chapter 3). John Arlott's poem 'Music Hall' was printed in *Modern Reading*, No. 9, 1944. Theodora Fitzgibbon gives Constantine his accolade in his autobiography, *Through the Minefield* (London, 1967).

George Orwell tells of his remarkable meeting with Stafford Cripps and Guy Burgess in his 'Wartime Diary', 7 June 1942. Martin Green tells the anecdote of Brian Howard in the Ritz Bar in his *Children of the Sun* (London, 1976). Denis Brogan told me of his wartime experiences in the Free French club off St James's.

Peter Quennell's *The Wanton Chase* has been cited (Chapter 1); the 'Lost Girl' of the fire raid introduced Quennell to Barbara Skelton; the first volume of her autobiography, *Tears Before Bedtime*, was published in London in 1987. The witness to Joyce Cary's meeting with Gerald Wilde at Oxford in February 1949, was Dan Davin, to whom I am deeply indebted for his extraordinary reminiscences of Cary, Julian Maclaren-Ross, W. R. Rodgers, Louis MacNeice and Dylan Thomas, contained in his *Closing Times* (Oxford, 1975). I am also indebted to Denise Hooker's biography, *Nina Hamnett* (London, 1986), for the exceptional descriptions of the wartime *vie-de-bohème* with her written by Julius Horwitz, then serving with the US Eighth Air Force. Joan Wyndham's riveting *Love Is Blue* and Theodora Fitzgibbon's *With Love* have already been cited (Chapters 2 and 1 respectively). For the early days of Colquhoun and MacBryde, I am grateful for the essay on Colquhoun printed in *A Paradise Lost* (cited in Chapter 2). The autobiography of Paul Potts, *Dante Called You Beatrice* (London, 1960), is a series of remarkable essays by the wisest fool in Fitzrovia, while 'The World of George Barker' was printed in *Poetry Quarterly*, Summer 1948. Henry Reed wrote about the rebels and the Auden group in *New Writing and Daylight*, June 1943. Alan Ross wrote on Fitzrovian pubs in the *London Magazine*, December 1962. I am again indebted to John Lehmann, *I Am My Brother*, the indispensable testament of the leading editor of the 'forties (cited in Chapter 1), while Charles Ritchie, *The Siren Years*, has been quoted in Chapter 4: Elizabeth Bowen made her remark on people's personalities to him.

Sir Alec Guinness tells of the encounter with Edith Sitwell in his entertaining autobiography, *Blessings in Disguise* (cited in Chapter 2). For the description of Mrs Keppel's war at the Ritz, I am obliged to Theo Aronson, *The King in Love* (London, 1987); her friend who made the remark about her escape from France was Mrs

Ronald Greville. Michael Wishart tells of Edomie at the Ritz in *High Diver* (London, 1983). The description of the Hulton dinner in the Dorchester comes from the entertaining memoirs of the editor of *Picture Post* and *Lilliput*, Tom Hopkinson, *Of This Our Time: A Journalist's Story, 1905–50* (London, 1982).

J. B. Priestley's piece, 'Labour Leaders at the Ivy', was printed in *Horizon*, Vol. I, No. 6, June 1940. Desmond Hawkins, 'Night Raid', was printed in *Poetry in Wartime* (cited in Chapter 3).

CHAPTER SIX

A. P. Herbert's account of the river on the day of the fall of France comes from *The Home Front: 1938–1945* (cited in Chapter 4); he spent the war commanding a Royal Navy Auxiliary Patrol boat with a beat of sixty miles to the mouth of the Thames. W. R. Rodgers's 'Escape' was printed in *Horizon*, Vol. II, No. 9, September 1940.

George Orwell's description of Italian shops in Soho comes from his 'Wartime Diary', 12 June 1940. 'Nothing Alien is Human' comes from the works of Sagittarius (see Chapter 5). Geoffrey Grigson's lacerating and revealing *Recollections* have been mentioned in Chapter 1. Joseph Brodsky gave a speech at a conference on exiles in Vienna in December 1987, published in the *New York Review of Books*, 21 January 1988.

The quotation about military uniforms in London is taken from William Sansom's evocative *Westminster in War* (cited in Chapter 4). Paul Tabori, *They Came to London*, was published in London in 1942. 'Letter to Henry Miller' by 13802023 Private Alfred Perles was printed in *Horizon*, Vol. II, No. 12, December 1940. Lincoln Kirstein's *Rhymes of a PFC* was the best sustained poetry of the war in Auden's opinion, although he may have been influenced in his view by his admiration for Kirstein as an ex-communist from Harvard who founded the New York City Ballet with Balanchine. Randall Jarrell, 'The Death of the Ball Turret Gunner', is taken from his *Selected Poems* (London, 1956). Alice Duer Miller, *The White Cliffs*, was published with a foreword by Sir Walter Layton in London, 1940.

'The Murder of the Prostitutes' was written by Philip O'Connor and published in his *Selected Poems 1936/1966* (London, 1967). Jack Beeching, 'Spring Offensive', and Vita Sackville-West, 'The Wines of France', appear in Nancy Cunard's *Poems for France* (London, 1944). An account of Norman Holmes Pearson's life in London as an operative for American intelligence is contained in Robin Winks, *Cloak and Gown* (London, 1987). Denise Hooker's admirable biography of Nina Hamnett has already been cited in Chapter 5; but the author is also responsible for discovering Julius Horwitz's letters to Clement Greenberg from wartime London, presently housed in the Mugar Memorial Library, Boston University, Massachusetts, to whom I am indebted for permission to quote from them. Quentin Crisp's extraordinary autobiography, *The Naked Civil Servant*, has already been acknowledged in Chapter 3, while his story on posing during the bombing, 'The Declining Nude', appeared in the *Little Reviews Anthology*, 1949.

Peter Quennell's description of London as a vast caravanserai comes from *The Wanton Chase* (cited in Chapter 1). Dan Davin's *Closing Times* (cited in Chapter 5) contains an illuminating essay on Maclaren-Ross. William Sansom's journal appeared as a reprint in *Leaves in the Storm* (cited in Chapter 2). 'London Welsh' is taken from the *Selected Poems of Idris Davies* (London, 1953). Alun Lewis's extraordinary analysis of the feeling of alienation as a soldier, 'Lance Jack', suggests that he might have become one of the finer writers as well as poets of his time, had he not died on the Burmese front: 'Lance Jack' was also reprinted in *Leaves in the Storm*.

John Pudney's wartime log was published as *Who Only England Know* (London, 1943). Edwin Muir, 'The Refugees', is published in his *Collected Poems* (London, 1963).

CHAPTER SEVEN

Cyril Connolly's 'Comment on the War Poets' is to be found in *Horizon*, Vol. III, No. 13, January 1941. Keidrych Rhys's introduction to the cited anthology *Poems from the Forces* and its preface by Colonel Walter Elliott are important commentaries on the nature of poetry written by servicemen (cited in Chapter 3). Patric Dickinson's comment is from his introduction to *Soldiers' Verse* (London, 1945).

Stephen Spender, 'The Year's Poetry, 1940', appeared in *Horizon*, Vol. III, No. 14, February 1941. Sir Hugh Walpole's attack on the Auden group appeared in the *Daily Sketch*, when he was reviewing John Lehmann's *New Writing in Europe*: Lehmann records his sole meeting with Walpole in *I Am My Brother* (cited in Chapter 1). Louis MacNeice defended Auden's exit to America in 'Traveller's Return'; because Cyril Connolly had written in *Horizon*, Vol. III, No. 12, December 1940, 'From America no traveller returns', MacNeice, who had returned, entitled his piece 'Traveller's Return' and it appeared in *Horizon*, Vol. III, No. 14, February 1941, printed with Spender's criticism of Auden's verse. Sir Stephen Spender reported the remark of Auden's pupil to me. Christopher Lee, 'Trahison des Clercs', was published in *Under the Sun* (London, 1948). Spender's review of 'Poetry in 1941' appeared in *Horizon*, Vol. V, No. 27, March 1942. Alex Comfort's answer to Spender's review appeared in the correspondence of *Horizon*, Vol. V, No. 29, May 1942, and was answered by Spender in the following issue of the magazine. Cecil Day Lewis, 'Dedicatory Stanzas' to

Stephen Spender, appear in his translation of Virgil's *Georgics* (London, 1940). Robert Graves and Stephen Spender both wrote articles for the *Listener*, 'War Poetry in this War', 16 and 23 October 1941, which provoked fierce responses from Herbert Read and Keidrich Rhys and Geoffrey Grigson, among others. Roy Fuller's remark comes from the second volume of his autobiography, *Vamp Till Ready*, as does Alan Ross's from *The Forties* (cited in Chapter 4). Cecil Day Lewis, 'Where are the War Poets?', appears in *Word Over All* (London, 1943). Roy Fuller, 'A Wry Smile', appeared in *The Middle of a War* (cited in Chapter 1). Julian Symons's poem on 'Conscript' has already been mentioned (Chapter 3). The poet trying to fiddle a poem on the march is W. W. Gibson, whose 'Soldier Poet' appeared in *The Best Poems of 1943* (ed. Thomas Moult, London, 1944). Sidney Keyes, 'War Poet', comes from his *Selected Poems*, which were edited by Michael Meyer and published in London in 1945. Donald Bain's 'War Poet' from his *Selected Poems* was reprinted in *The Poetry of War 1939–45* (cited in Chapter 4). Keith Douglas, 'Poets in this War', is an undated manuscript published in the *Times Literary Supplement*, 23 April 1971. Julian Symons compiled *An Anthology of War Poetry* for Penguin Books in 1942. Tambimuttu, *Poetry in Wartime* (cited in Chapter 3) included work by forty-nine poets ranging from W. H. Auden and Dylan Thomas and Stephen Spender to the very different J. F. Hendry and Henry Treece and Lawrence Durrell and Fred Marnau and Lynette Roberts: it is the subject of an excellent analysis by H. M. Klein published in *The Second World War in Literature* (Edinburgh, 1988): Klein also discusses the influence of *Poetry in Wartime* on later war anthologies. For an understanding of the New Apocalypse, there is an important interview with J. F. Hendry by A. T. Tolley in *Aquarius*, 17/18, published in 1986/7, and a description of the movement in Tolley's own book, *The Poetry of the Forties in Britain* (Ottawa, 1985): also essential is Henry Treece's *How I See Apocalypse* (London, 1946).

The Bombed Happiness was published by Herbert Read at Routledge in 1942: Read sympathized with the Apocalyptic as well as the Romantic poets: his introduction to the anthology *Lyra* (cited in Chapter 4) emphasized insurrection rather than romanticism. Stephen Spender's criticism of *Lyra* comes from *Horizon*, Vol. V, No. 29, May 1942. Peter Baker was an officer in the Royal Artillery and general editor of Resurgam Books, which produced pamphlets of romantic poetry: after the war, he became Wrey Gardiner's partner in the Grey Walls Press, and was one of the few Members of Parliament to be convicted for fraud. John Lehmann's remarks on reviewing war writing came from *I Am My Brother* (cited in Chapter 1). Stephen Spender's 'Lessons of Poetry 1943' appeared in *Horizon*, Vol. IX, No. 39, March 1943.

'Why Not War Writers?' appeared in *Horizon*, Vol. IV, No. 22, October 1941, and a combatant's answer to it in *Horizon* two months later. The extract from Cecil Day Lewis's school lecture comes from the understanding biography of him by his son Séan Day Lewis, *C. Day Lewis: an English Literary Life* (London, 1980). Denys Val Baker edited *The Little Reviews Anthology* between 1943 and 1949. Canetti's thought comes from his *The Human Province* (London, 1985). Tom Harrisson, 'War Books', was printed in *Horizon*, Vol. IV, No. 24, December 1941. Henry Reed, 'The Novel Since 1939', in *Since 1939* (cited in Chapter 2) is an invaluable view of the contemporary vision of the novelists at the time: *Prose Literature Since 1939* by T. S. Eliot's companion John Hayward is also useful, as is G. S. Fraser, *The Modern Writer and His World* (London, 1953; rev. edn 1964). Henry Green's four novels were published in London as follows: *Party Going* (1939), *Caught* (1943), *Loving* (1945), *Back* (1946). Pamela Hansford Johnson wrote well on 'Joyce Cary' in the *Little Reviews Anthology*, 1949, while V. S. Pritchett is definitive on 'Rex Warner', also reprinted in the *Little Reviews Anthology*, 1946. Evelyn Waugh, *Put Out More Flags*, was published in London in 1942, *Work Suspended* in 1943 and *Brideshead Revisited* in 1945 with a new preface by the author for the later edition of 1960. The criticism of Elizabeth Bowen's *The Demon Lover* comes from Henry Reed's article in *Since 1939* (see above). Cecil Day Lewis, 'Word Over All', was printed in the book of poems of that same title (see above). Richard Hillary, *The Last Enemy*, was published in the first of many editions in London, 1943. Arthur Koestler, 'The Birth of a Myth', was published in *Horizon*, Vol. IX, No. 40, May 1943. There has been an adequate biography of Hillary by Lovat Dickson, published in London in 1950, and a collection of his letters to Mary Booker edited by her later husband, Michael Burn, *Mary and Richard*, published in London in 1988. Cyril Connolly, *The Unquiet Grave: A Word Cycle by Palinurus* was published in London in 1945.

'From Many a Mangled Truth a War Is Won' by Clifford Dyment is taken from his *Collected Poems* (London, 1970). W. R. Rodgers, 'Censorship' was printed in *Horizon*, Vol. II, No. 12, December 1940. Cyril Connolly's comment on artist-administrators is in *Horizon*, Vol. V, No. 29, May 1942. John Waller, 'Hell Is Where One Starts From' was printed in *Wartime Harvest* (ed. Stefan Schimanski and Henry Treece, London 1943). Alan Ross's definition of the experience of war comes from the first volume of his autobiography, *Blindfold Games* (London, 1985). John Lehmann's speech in defence of the poetry of wartime is printed in part in *I Am My Brother* (cited in Chapter 1); it is a seminal document for an understanding of the time. T. S. Eliot's reference to *Four Quartets* as 'patriotic poems' is mentioned in Peter Ackroyd's admirable biography, *T. S.*

Eliot (London, 1984), while his talk about war conditions leading to *Four Quartets* is in the third volume of John Lehmann's autobiography, *The Ample Proposition* (London, 1966). Edith Sitwell's 'Lullaby' comes from her *The Canticle of the Rose* (London, 1949). Stephen Spender spoke about 'modernism' to me. Brian Gardner edited the admirable *The Terrible Rain: The War Poets 1939–1945* (London, 1966) and disproved in his selection the strange myth that little good poetry was written by those serving in the air force. David Wright's reflection on the Oxford dead in the air force comes from *Deafness: A Personal Account* (London, 1969). John Pudney, 'For Johnny', was printed in *Dispersal Point and Other Air Poems* (London, 1942), the first of a trilogy of moving collections of air force poetry by Pudney. The other two books were *Beyond This Disregard* (London, 1943) and *South of Forty* (London, 1943). Pudney began the war as a journalist, became a poet, and ended working for the RAF Public Relations Branch.

CHAPTER EIGHT

Henry Reed's 'Lives' and his 'Lessons of War' were printed in *A Map of Verona* (London, 1946): a contemporary reviewer in *Time and Tide* stated correctly, 'No better first book of poetry has appeared for many years and it would be foolish to expect another comparable for as long.' 'The Land Girl' by Diana Gardner was reprinted in the *Little Reviews Anthology* of 1943. Phyllis Castle, 'A Land Army Gardener', was published in *Leaves in the Storm* (cited in Chapter 2). Anne Ridler, 'For this Time' was published in *The Nine Bright Shiners* (cited in Chapter 1). Cecil Day Lewis, 'Watching Post' and 'The Stand-To', appear in *Word Over All* (London, 1943). 'They Come' by Alun Lewis was published in *English Story*, No. II, 1941. Keidrych Rhys published his own poem 'Cinque Ports' in his *Poems from the Forces* (cited in Chapter 3).

C. E. M. Joad's blast against England being devastated by the war machine, 'The Face of England: How it is ravaged and how it may be preserved', appeared in *Horizon*, Vol. V, No. 29, May 1942. Norman Nicholson wrote on 'The Regional Poets of the Forties' in *Aquarius*, 17/18 (cited in Chapter 5). Edwin Muir's poem was called 'Reading in Wartime', Clive Sansom's 'September Holiday', Laurie Lee's 'The Armoured Valley', J. C. Hall's 'The Spring Offensive', Clifford Dyment's 'Flying Words: The Fleet Air Arm', Ruthven Todd's 'Combat Report', while Herbert Corby's 'Missing' was published in *New Lyrical Ballads* (London, 1945). Frank Thompson's poem was called 'Allotrias Diai Gynaikos' and was published in *For Your Tomorrow* (cited in Chapter 1). Charles Hamblett, 'Bombs On My Town', was published in *Poems from the Forces* (see above).

George Orwell comments on the difference between the middle-class intellectual and the proletarian in *The Road to Wigan Pier* (London, 1937). Henry Green was commenting on C. M. Doughty's *Arabia Deserta* in *Folios of New Writing*, IV, Autumn 1941, when he praised the war for making writers voyage to factories. V. S. Pritchett comments on his factory visits in his autobiography, *Midnight Oil* (London, 1971). James Pope-Hennessy comments on the Scots working class in a letter to Clarissa Churchill, 6 November 1940, quoted in *A Lonely Business* (cited in Chapter 2). J. B. Priestley wrote an interesting appreciation, *British Women Go To War* (London, 1943). The phrase about the woman munitions worker comes from Wilfred Gibson's 'Shells', while the rhyme 'She's the girl ...' is quoted in the excellent anthology for the young, *In Time of War* (ed. Anne Harvey, London, 1987). Inez Holden, 'Fellow Travellers in Factory', was printed in *Horizon*, Vol. III, No. 14, February 1941. John Lehmann's letter to B. L. Coombes is published in A. T. Tolley's fine *John Lehmann: A Tribute* (Ottawa, Canada, 1987). *New Lyrical Ballads* was published in London in 1945: it contained Maurice Carpenter's poems, '1941 – Bombers in May' and 'Machine Shop: Nightshift'. Norman Nicholson's 'Cleator Moor' is taken from his *Five Rivers* (London, 1944). For an appreciation of the war artists, I am indebted to *War Through Artists' Eyes* (sel. and intro. by Eric Newton, London, 1945) and Alan Ross, *Colours of War: War Art 1939–45* (intro. Kenneth Clark, London, 1983). *Picture Post* featured Stanley Spencer on 2 October 1943. Laurie Lee, 'Look into Wombs and Factories and Behold', was published in Tambimuttu's *Poetry in Wartime* (cited in Chapter 3).

CHAPTER NINE

Liam O'Flaherty's views of air domination come from *Shame the Devil* (London, 1934). Stephen Spender's 'To Poets and Airmen' was published in *New Poems 1940* (ed. Oscar Williams, New York, 1941). John Sommerfeld's letter to John Lehmann was quoted in his diary entry for 12 August 1940, and reprinted in *I Am My Brother* (cited in Chapter 1), while Sommerfeld's evocative description of aerodromes was printed in Penguin *New Writing*, No. 4, 1941. John Pudney's 'Combat Report' and 'The Bomb Dump' come from *Dispersal Point and Other Air Poems* (cited in Chapter 7); David Bourne's 'Parachute Descent' was printed in *Air Force Poetry* (ed. J. Pudney and H. Treece, London, 1944), his 'Fighter By Night' in *For Your Tomorrow* (cited in Chapter 1) and Brian Allwood's 'Airmen' in *More Poems from the Forces* (cited in Chapter 3). Olivia Fitzroy's 'Fleet Fighter' was reprinted in *In Time of War* (cited in Chapter 8). R. N. Currey's poem, 'Disintegration of Springtime', was printed in *This Other Planet* (London, 1945). Randall Jarrell's 'Losses' was printed in his *Selected Poems* (cited in Chapter 6). Elias Canetti's diaries, *The Human Province*, have been cited in Chapter 7. Michael MacNaughton-Smith's 'Raiders Over Troy' was also printed in *For Your Tomorrow* (see above). Patric Dickinson, 'Bombers: Evening' comes from *Theseus and the Minotaur* (London, 1946).

'S.S. City of Benares' is published in *Poems of G. S. Fraser* (Leicester, 1981), while Roy Campbell's 'One Transport Lost' comes from his *Selected Poetry* (London, 1968). Alan Ross has reprinted his epic poem 'J.W.51B' in the first volume of his autobiography, *Blindfold Games* (cited in Chapter 7); the second volume, *Coastwise Lights* (London, 1988) confirms the fact that Ross could have become a major writer of prose as well as a poet and a selfless recorder of the many artists he met in London and in Sussex during the nineteen-forties and fifties. His 'Arctic Convoy' was published in *Leaves in the Storm* (cited in Chapter 2). Charles Causley spoke to Ian Hamilton of his naval poetry in *The Poetry of War: 1939–45* (cited in Chapter 4). Norman Hampson's 'Corvette' and 'Convoy' were published in *More Poems from the Forces* (cited in Chapter 3). 'The Gregale' by F. J. Salfeld was printed in Penguin *New Writing*, No. 24, 1945, and 'The Hours of Darkness' by Roger Anscombe in No. 25, 1945, while 'How Is It with the Happy Dead' by Eric Joysmith was published in *English Story*, No. IV, 1943. Denis Saunders, 'Almendro' and J. G. Meddemmen, 'War's Dullard', about legal murder, were included in *Return to Oasis* (see below). John Bayliss, 'Home Thoughts from Abroad', was republished in the *Little Reviews Anthology*, 1945. The story of the death of the Signals Officer, 'All This Is Ended', by Norman Swallow appeared in Penguin *New Writing*, No. 27, 1946. David Raikes wrote about sorting out the kits of the dead in 'Let It Be Hushed', printed in *For Your Tomorrow* (cited in Chapter 1). Bruce Bain's important 'Departure and Arrival' was published in *The Windmill*, 1946, and 'De Gustibus' in *Writing Today*, October 1943.

Dan Davin's novel, *For the Rest of Our Lives* (London, 1947) describes the desert campaigns and life in Alexandria and Cairo, as does Olivia Manning's *The Levant Trilogy* (London, 1977–1980). She also wrote 'Poets in Exile' for *Horizon*, Vol. X, No. 58, October 1944, and 'Middle East Letter' for *Modern Reading*, No. 9, 1944, from which the quotation about the hyperconsciousness of death is taken. Seminal to an understanding of literary activity in the Middle East and to its works are *Return to Oasis: War Poems and Recollections from the Middle East 1940–1946* (London, 1980), in which Lawrence Durrell wrote an introduction and G. S. Fraser made his comment on the value of the poetry from there. Also essential is its sequel, *From Oasis Into Italy: War Poems and Diaries from Africa and Italy 1940–1946* (London, 1983). *Poems from the Desert* with a foreword by General Montgomery hoping that the greatness of mind and spirit of the Eighth Army was reproduced in its poems

was published in London in 1944. Cecil Beaton was loaned by the Ministry of Information to the Air Ministry to collect material for reports and to photograph the theatre of war in the Middle East: the result was his absorbing *Near East* (London, 1943), which describes Egypt before the disaster of Tobruk and retreat to El Alamein. The comment on the poets' defensive reply to stagnation is taken from Robin Fedden's introduction to *Personal Landscape: An Anthology of Exile*, published by Editions Poetry London in 1945. G. S. Fraser's 'Recent Verse: London and Cairo', and Tambimuttu's answer were published in *Poetry London*, X (London, 1944), as was Lawrence Durrell's 'Airgraph on Refugee Poets in Africa'.

Lawrence Durrell wrote of John Gawsworth in *Spirit of Place* (London, 1969). 'The Salamanders' by John Gawsworth was privately printed in *Some Poems* (Sussex, undated). 'Monologue to a Cairo Evening' was reprinted in *The Poems of G. S. Fraser* (see above); his other comments on the Cairo circle come from his excellent autobiography, *A Stranger and Afraid* (cited in Chapter 5). Keith Douglas, 'Cairo Jag' was first printed in *Alamein to Zem Zem* (London, 1945), and Terence Tiller, 'Lecturing to Troops', in *Unarm, Eros* (London, 1947). Hamish Henderson wrote an introduction to his *Elegies for the Dead in Cyrenaica*, published by John Lehmann in 1948: the extracts are from his First and Sixth Elegies. Henderson wrote on 'The Poetry of War in the Middle East, 1939–1945' in *Aquarius*, 17/18, published in 1986/7; he published Sorley Maclean's 'Going Westwards' (*Dol and Iar*) in the article. Tambimuttu wrote an appreciation 'In Memory of Keith Douglas' in *Poetry London*, X, while Keith Douglas was writing to J. C. Hall on 10 August 1943, on the subject of Bullshit: it is reproduced in *Keith Douglas: A Prose Miscellany* (ed. Douglas Graham, London, 1985): Graham has also written an excellent biography of Douglas. Edmund Blunden's poem 'To Wilfred Owen' was published in *Augury: An Oxford Miscellany of Verse and Prose* (Oxford, 1940).

Eight Oxford Poets (London, 1941) was turned down for publication by T. S. Eliot and John Lehmann before it was accepted by Herbert Read at Routledge. In the most recent edition of *The Collected Poems of Sidney Keyes* (London, 1988), Michael Meyer has included a memoir of how Keyes really died as well as 'To Keep Off Fears'. The description of Drummond Allison at Oxford is given by David Wright in *Deafness* (cited in Chapter 7). Drummond Allison's poem, 'Come Let Us Pity Death' as well as his 'For Karl Marx' appeared in *For Your Tomorrow* (cited in Chapter 1). Michael Meyer spoke to me of *Eight Oxford Poets* and of being a survivor. *Poems from India by Members of the Forces* was edited by R. N. Currey and R. V. Gibson (Oxford, 1946), while *Poems from Italy: Verses Written by Members of the Eighth Army in*

WAR LIKE A WASP

Sicily and Italy, July 1943–March 1944 was published with an introduction by Siegfried Sassoon in London, 1945. Alun Lewis's 'The Earth Is A Syllable' was published in *English Story*, Vol. IV, 1943. His collected works should be republished, including his two volumes of poetry, *Raider's Dawn* (London, 1942) and *Ha! Ha! Among the Trumpets* (London, 1945), and two works of prose, *The Last Inspection* (London, 1942) and *In the Green Tree* (London, 1948). Dylan Thomas's radio talk on 'Welsh Poets' was published in *Quite Early One Morning* (London, 1954). Richard Hoggart wrote on the Three Arts Club in Naples in *From Oasis into Italy* (see above). John Lehmann wrote on writers in exile during the war in *I Am My Brother* (cited in Chapter 1). John Heath-Stubbs's poem in memory of Sidney Keyes was the title of his book, *The Divided Ways* (London, 1946). Patricia Ledward was one of the two editors of *Poems of This War by Younger Poets* (cited in Chapter 3); she printed the best of Timothy Corsellis's work. George Barker's tributes to Stephen Spender and T. S. Eliot come from his 'Eros in Dogma', printed in his *Collected Poems* (London, 1988). David Wright's tribute to Tambimuttu appears in *Deafness* (see above).

CHAPTER TEN

As always, I am indebted to John Lehmann for his opinions in *I Am My Brother* (cited in Chapter 1) and to Stephen Spender for his corroboration of popular interest in the arts in wartime in *World Within World* (cited in Chapter 4). Malcolm Yorke's *The Spirit of Place: Neo-Romantic Artists and Their Times* (London, 1988) has some interesting things to say about Fitzrovia and its painters. The story on John Minton's army career comes from Alan Ross's second volume of biography, *Coastwise Lights* (cited in Chapter 9); he and Minton were commissioned by John Lehmann to create a travel book on Corsica, *Time Was Away* (London, 1948). Keith Vaughan spoke on London life in the 1940s to Noël Barber, *Conversations with Painters* (London, 1964). The letter of Constant Lambert to Michael Ayrton was quoted in Andrew Motion's *The Lamberts* (London, 1986). *Poems of Death*, edited by Phoebe Pool, was published in London in 1945. Michael Ayrton's attack on Picasso, 'A Master of Pastiche', appeared in *New Writing and Daylight* (cited in Chapter 5), while his important statement 'The Heritage of British Painting IV' was published in *Studio*, November 1946, and derived from his articles in *The Spectator* during the previous two years. I am again indebted to Anthony Cronin in his *Dead As Doornails* (cited in Chapter 5) for his comments on 'The English Romantics' in Fitzrovia, and also to Theodora Fitzgibbon's memoirs for her account of Francis Bacon, who has also talked personally to me. John Craxton talked to Virginia Button

about his wartime life in London in the indispensable *A Paradise Lost: The Neo-Romantic Imagination in Britain 1935–55* (cited in Chapter 2). Stephen Spender talked to me about Peter Watson, while Michael Wishart talks of Peter Watson and of Francis Bacon in his autobiography *High Diver* (cited in Chapter 5). Michael Shelden makes the only important study of Peter Watson in his *Friends of Promise* (cited in Chapter 2). Meryle Secrest has written *Kenneth Clark: A Biography* (London, 1984), to which I am indebted. Harold Nicolson's comment on Clark is dated 8 November 1940, and is printed in his *Diaries and Letters 1939–1945* (London, 1967); he quoted a telling phrase from Winston Churchill during the blitz: 'At this time we saw no end but a demolition of the whole Metropolis.'

I am again indebted to Julian Maclaren-Ross in his *Memoirs of the Forties* (cited in Chapter 1) for his descriptions of John Minton and the two Roberts Colquhoun and MacBryde fighting in the Soho club and for Tambimuttu's mollifying of John Banting. Alan Ross is sympathetic and illuminating on the characters of Minton and Keith Vaughan, both of whom he knew well, in *Coastwise Lights* (see above). Ruthven Todd reported Spender's remark to him about Lucian Freud's grandfather in his *Fitzrovia and the Road to the York Minster* (cited in Chapter 1). Graham Sutherland's costumes for *The Wanderer* were not successful, one critic calling them 'the most unfortunate in modern ballet', suggesting the Boy Scout Movement and Hitler Youth. Humphrey Jennings's remarkable *Pandaemonium* was finally published in London in 1985. Michael Balcon's important observations on 'The British Film During the War' were printed in the Penguin *Film Review* of 1946. For Ralph Richardson's story about drinking with Laurence Olivier, I am grateful to Garry O'Connor's *Ralph Richardson: An Actor's Life* (London, 1982) and for Olivier's comments on the mess of wartime life to Felix Barker, *The Oliviers* (London, 1953). Cecil Day Lewis, 'Newsreel', comes from *Overtures to Death* (London, 1938). Dylan Thomas's contribution to 'The Cost of Letters' was printed in *Horizon*, Vol. XIV, No. 81, September 1946. John Minton's remark on George Barker was told to Derek Stanford and printed in his memoirs, *Inside the Forties* (cited in Chapter 1). The comment on Gielgud's performance of Hamlet in 1939 is that of the drama critic Audrey Williamson. Laurence Olivier wrote a preface to the publicity brochure of *Henry V*, printed in 1944. Gabriel Pascal's account of filming *Caesar and Cleopatra* was published in London in 1945 and contains G. B. Shaw's remark on himself and Shakespeare as putative screenwriters.

Tyrone Guthrie's remarks on the Old Vic appear in his autobiography, *Life in the Theatre* (London, 1961). Tschiffely's *Bohemia Junction* has been cited in Chapter 1, while the quotation from Henry Moore comes from

304

the introduction to the British Museum publication of *A Shelter Sketchbook* in 1988.

CHAPTER ELEVEN

I am again indebted to Elias Canetti's *The Human Province* (cited in Chapter 7) for his wise comments on the security which war gave. Elizabeth Bowen, *The Heat of the Day* (London, 1949) is the seminal novel on the latter years of the war. The description of the MPs is from Mrs Robert Henrey, *The Incredible City* (London, 1944). Charles Ritchie, *The Siren Years* was cited in Chapter 4. John Lehmann, *I Am My Brother* (cited in Chapter 1), remains an invaluable guide to wartime London, both the pubs and the Sitwells' Royal Poetry Reading. Joan Wyndham, *Love Is Blue* (cited in Chapter 2), is full of Fitzrovian war encounters, while Alan Ross, *The Forties* (cited in Chapter 4), is the best quick Baedeker of the area and period. Mollie Panter-Downes reported the war from London for the *New Yorker*. James Pope-Hennessy was writing to Dorothy Colston-Baynes on 1 January 1943, quoted in *A Lonely Business* (cited in Chapter 2). Julian Symons talks of the division between writers in his autobiography, while Maclaren-Ross confirms the wars of the poets in his *Memoirs of the Forties* (cited in Chapter 1). *The Collected Poems of A. S. J. Tessimond* contains his poem on 'The Lesser Artists': it was published in Reading in 1985.

For accounts of the Royal Poetry Reading of 1943, I am indebted to John Pearson's *Façades* (cited in Chapter 1), and to Barbara Guest, *Herself Defined: The Poet H.D. and her World* (London, 1985). Neuro's 'Notes on War Guilt' appear in *Horizon*, Vol. V, No. 27, March 1942, and Connolly's editorial in *Horizon*, Vol. IX, No. 50, February 1944. *The Unquiet Grave* by 'Palinurus', the Trojan steersman on Aeneas's voyage to Italy, was first published in 1944 (cited in Chapter 7). Peter Quennell's autobiography has already been cited in Chapter 1, and he confirmed his wartime experience to me. Connolly's churning guilt about the war was expressed in his 'Letter from a Civilian', published in *Horizon*, Vol. X, No. 57, September 1944. See also Ian Hamilton's article on Connolly at *Horizon* in *The Little Magazines: A Study of Six Editors* (London, 1976). Ernest Hemingway's letter to Cyril Connolly is dated 15 March, 1948. The original is at the McFarlin Library, University of Tulsa, Oklahoma, and is quoted in Michael Shelden, *Friends of Promise* (cited in Chapter 2). Michael Barsley's *Ritzkrieg* was published in London in 1940. David Jones, *Dai Greatcoat* (ed. René Hague, London, 1980) contains his letter of 14 September 1940, written during the blitz on Chelsea and describing the difference of the war for rich and poor. Sir Stephen Spender has talked to me. The anonymous 'A Letter from Another London' by someone who lived in the East End was printed in *Orion*, I, 1945. Sagittarius, 'The Passionate Profiteer to his

Love', comes from her collected poems, *Quiver's Choice* (cited in Chapter 4). Daphne Nixon's poems, *In These Five Years*, were printed in London in 1946, and Joyce Rowe's 'Dieppe' in *New Lyrical Ballads* (cited in Chapter 8) and *Poems for France* (cited in Chapter 6).

J. B. Priestley wrote his 'Prologue to Planning' for *Horizon*, Vol. III, No. 15, March 1941. C. E. M. Joad, *The Adventures of the Young Soldier in Search of the Better World* was published in London in 1943. Cyril Connolly warned of the dangers of state control of the arts and cultural diffusion in 'Writers and Society', *The Condemned Playground: Essays, 1927–1944* (London, 1945). Koestler's essay on 'The Intelligentsia' appeared in *Horizon*, Vol. IX, No. 51, March 1944. Sir Stephen Spender's remark about pay as pocket-money was made to me, while his comments on the difference between warriors and planners come from his *World Within World* (cited in Chapter 4). Angus Calder is excellent on the BBC in *The People's War: Britain 1939–45* (cited in Chapter 2). The producer of the Goons and Tony Hancock is Dennis Main Wilson, and his comments on the effects of Hitler's war appeared in the *Observer*, 26 June 1988.

CHAPTER TWELVE

The *New Yorker* correspondent was Mollie Panter-Downes, whose 'London War Notes, 1939–1945' have already been highly recommended. Arnold Rattenbury, 'Calendar Song', was printed in *New Lyrical Ballads* (cited in Chapter 8). Denis Glover, 'It Was D-Day', appeared in Penguin *New Writing*, No. 23, 1945. William Golding has talked to me about his experience on D-Day: see also Andrew Sinclair, 'William Golding's *The Sea, The Sea*', *Twentieth Century Literature*, Vol. 28, No. 2, Summer 1982. Elizabeth Bowen wrote an article, 'Calico Windows', for *Soho Centenary 1844–1944* (London, 1945). John Lehmann's comments on the flying bomb raids and the Sitwell reading at the Churchill Club come from *I Am My Brother* (cited in Chapter 1). Cyril Connolly's complaint about the flying bombs comes from his 'Letter from a Civilian' (cited in Chapter 11). George Stonier wrote 'Shaving Through the Blitz' under the name of 'Fanfarlo'. William Sansom, *Westminster in War*, has already been cited (in Chapter 4), as has Theodora Fitzgibbon, *With Love* (in Chapter 1). Ruthven Todd's phrase about the flying bombs comes from his 'Love Poem to Accompaniment of Rockets'. Canetti, *The Human Province*, has already been cited (in Chapter 7), while Inez Holden's diary of the rocket raids appears in *Leaves in the Storm* (cited in Chapter 2). Philip O'Connor, *Memoirs of a Public Baby*, has already been cited in Chapter 1.

The lines from T. S. Eliot come from 'Little Gidding' in *Four Quartets* (London, 1944). David Wright's lines come from his poem 'On a Friend Dying'; it is addressed to Julian Orde, whose lines are taken from 'The Changing World', reprinted in *Aquarius*, No. 17/18, 1986/7. Michael Wishart, *High Diver*, has already been cited in Chapter 5. Augustus John's model was Constance Graham and she spoke to Michael Holroyd about the artist's unconcern. Roy Fuller wrote a poem about the frightening little noises of the house called 'During a Bombardment by V-Weapons'. Edith Sitwell, 'Still Falls the Rain', is published in *The Canticle of the Rose* (Selected Poems 1920–1947) (London, 1949), and her poetry was reviewed by Stephen Spender in *Horizon*, Vol. X, No. 58, October 1944, while her complaint about Julian Symons was quoted in John Pearson's excellent biography of the Sitwells, *Façades* (cited in Chapter 1). Tyrone Guthrie, *A Life in the Theatre*, was published in London in 1961. Woodrow Wyatt tells the story of his drunken evening with J. B. Priestley in his autobiography, *Confessions of an Optimist* (cited in Chapter 2). Connolly's editorial about the state and the arts was printed in *Horizon*, Vol. X, No. 60, December 1944. 'The Guinea Pigs' Song' was published in *Airman's Song Book* (ed. C. H. Ward-Jackson, London, 1945), while Hugo Manning's 'So They Went Back to Blighty' was printed in *The Windmill*, 1944.

Dylan Thomas's accounts of the New Quay incident and his failure to come to Vernon Watkins's wedding are contained in two letters to Watkins, dated 28 October 1944, and 28 March 1945, printed in *The Collected Letters of Dylan Thomas* (London, 1983). David Niven spoke to me about the murders in bars at the end of the war. Julian Symons's fine poem, 'Hospital Observation', is in *The Second Man* (London, 1943). As always, Alan Ross in *Blindfold Games* (cited in Chapter 7) is a superb guide around Fitzrovia. John Heath-Stubbs, 'Letter to David Wright', also captures the attraction of Soho in the 'forties. It is printed in his *Collected Poems, 1943–1987* (Manchester, 1988).

CHAPTER THIRTEEN

Once more I have relied on Canetti's thoughts, *The Human Province* (cited in Chapter 7), for the most illuminating commentary on the war from a European refugee living in London. Edmund Wilson's remarks on London in 1945 are printed in Edmund Wilson, *The Forties: From Notebooks and Diaries of the Period* (ed. Leon Edel, New York, 1983). John Lehmann talks of W. H. Auden's visit to London in 1945 in *I Am My Brother* (cited in Chapter 1). G. S. Fraser tells the story of the temporary reconciliation in Cairo on VE Day in his autobiography, *A Stranger and Afraid* (cited in Chapter 5). Quentin Crisp tells of becoming the lost landmark of Fitzrovia in *The Naked Civil Servant* (cited in Chapter 3). Henry Treece's comments on the VE Day celebrations in London were printed in *Leaves in the Storm*, already cited in Chapter 2; see also Theodora Fitzgibbon's *With*

Love (cited in Chapter 1). Virginia Graham's poem 'The Tumbrils' comes from *Consider The Years 1938–1946* (London, 1947). Cyril Connolly's contradictory remarks about the Labour government before and after the election of 1945 were made in *Horizon*, Vol. XI, No. 66, June 1945 and Vol. XII, No. 69, September 1945. John Heath-Stubbs told me the story of the encounter in the Wheatsheaf after the election. Woodrow Wyatt's question about revolution in the House of Commons is quoted in Anthony Howard, 'We Are the Masters Now', included in *Age of Austerity* (ed. M. Sissons and P. French, London, 1963). C. P. Snow, 'The Moral Un-Neutrality of Science' (1960), is included in his *Public Affairs* (London, 1971).

Roy Campbell, 'The Beveridge Plan', is printed in his *Selected Poetry* (cited in Chapter 9). The epigram on 'Fear' was written by John Rimington and printed in *Return to Oasis* (cited in Chapter 9); Joan Wyndham's *Love Is Blue* was cited in Chapter 2. John Heath-Stubbs, 'For George Barker at Seventy', is published in his *Collected Poems* (cited in Chapter 12), while Stephen Spender's conversation with David Gascoyne is printed in *World Within World* (cited in Chapter 4). William Golding's remarks on Hiroshima come from his review of Paul Fussell's *The Great War and Modern Memory*, in the *Guardian*, 20 November 1975. Mervyn Peake's drawings for 'The Rime of the Ancient Mariner' were reproduced in *Poetry London*, X, December, 1944, while the *Drawings of Mervyn Peake* was published by the Grey Walls Press in 1949. His poem on drawing the dying girl in Belsen was reproduced in the excellent introduction by John Watney to *Peake's Progress* (ed. Maeve Gilmore, Woodstock, NY, 1981). Graham Sutherland's account of the flying-bomb site and painters as the blotting paper of their time and the crucified holocaust victims, comes from Roger Berthoud's fine biography of him, already cited in Chapter 4, also from Alan Ross's excellent *Colours of War*, cited in Chapter 8. The painter Patrick Procktor informed me of Francis Bacon's concentration camp paintings. Robert Melville criticized Bacon's paintings and was quoted in John Rothenstein and Ronald Alley, *Francis Bacon* (London, 1964). Francis Bacon has talked of his life and art to David Sylvester, whose *The Brutality of Fact: Interviews with Francis Bacon* (3rd enlarged edition, London, 1987) is invaluable. Graham Sutherland's illustrations to David Gascoyne's *Poems 1937–42* were published by Editions Poetry London in 1943: Sutherland referred to them as having the 'knockabout quality of William Blake's original *Songs of Innocence*: they could also be read and carried about in the pocket'. Sutherland did three more lithographs for *Poetry London*, IX, and a lyre-bird design for its cover. Geoffrey Grigson's views of Graham Sutherland's art are described in 'Authentic and False in the New "Romanticism"', *Horizon*, Vol. XVII, No. 99, March

1948. Edith Sitwell's 'Three Poems of the Atomic Bomb' end her volume, *The Canticle of the Rose: Selected Poems 1920–1947* (see Chapter 12). Alan Ross's appreciation of her qualities appears in his important contemporary monograph for the British Council, *Poetry 1945–1950* (London, 1951). Robert Conquest's 'Poem in 1944' was reprinted in his *New and Collected Poems* (London, 1988). Wrey Gardiner's comments were printed in his editorials in *Poetry Quarterly*, Winter 1944 and Spring 1946. Orwell was writing his London letter to *Partisan Review*, 24 July 1944. Cyril Connolly's remark on the war poets was published in *The Unquiet Grave* (cited in Chapter 7). Robert Herring dismissed war poetry in 'Reflections on Poetry prompted by the Poets of 1939–1944', *Transformation*, 3, 1945. Constantine Fitzgibbon's gloom about the Fitzrovians in 1945 derives from his biography, *The Life of Dylan Thomas* (London, 1965). James Pope-Hennessy wrote to Bill Vinson on 30 November 1945, to express his pleasure in not going to Germany. Cyril Connolly's editorial and Alan Moorehead's 'Glimpses of Germany: II – Belsen' were printed in *Horizon*, Vol. XI, No. 67, July 1945. The poem of I. F. Porter, 'The Jew', was dated 30 April 1944 and was published in the *New English Review*, April 1946. Randall Jarrell, 'A Camp in the Prussian Forest', was published in his *Selected Poems* (cited in Chapter 6). Patric Dickinson, 'A Warning to Politicians', was printed in his *Theseus and the Minotaur* (cited in Chapter 9).

CHAPTER FOURTEEN

Randall Swingler, 'Sixty Cubic Feet', was published in *New Lyrical Ballads* (cited in Chapter 8). Bruce Bain, 'Troopship', was published in *Leaves in the Storm* (cited in Chapter 2). Roy Fuller, 'Saturday Night in a Sailor's Home', appears in *The Middle of a War* (cited in Chapter 1). Thomas Skelton, 'Inside the A.F.V.', and Jack Partridge's memories of El Alamein, appear in *From Oasis Into Italy: War Poems and Diaries from Africa and Italy 1940–1946* (cited in Chapter 9). Louis Challoner, 'Alternative', Victor West, 'La Belle Indifference' and John Jarmain, 'Prisoners of War', appear in *Return to Oasis: War Poems and Recollections from the Middle East 1940–1946* (cited in Chapter 9). Robert Joly's two poems, 'To Lazarus' and 'Hospital: October 1944', appear in the public schools anthology, *For Your Tomorrow* (cited in Chapter 1). Captain Robin Campbell, DSO, wrote his article 'Prisoner of War' for *Horizon*, Vol. IX, No. 51, March 1944. Robert Garioch, 'The Presoner's Dream' appeared in *From Oasis Into Italy* (see above). Mel Calman's illuminating memoir on being evacuated appears in B. S. Johnson's indispensable *The Evacuees* (London, 1968): Johnson is the only evacuee to record that his evacuation to the country made him aware of class distinction and the class war at the age of

seven. The poet Vernon Scannell wrote his autobiography, *The Tiger and the Rose* (London, 1971). John Manifold's 'The Deserter' was printed in *New Lyrical Ballads* (cited in Chapter 8). Christopher Hassall's sonnet, 'Hats, Demob. Depot, York', is printed in *The Slow Night and Other Poems 1940–1948* (London, 1949). For details of demobilization, I am grateful to Harry Hopkins, *The New Look: A Social History of the Forties and Fifties* (London, 1964). Henry Green's *Back* was cited in Chapter 7. Jon Wynne-Tyson was the witness to the post-war fragmentation of Fitzrovia.

Dirk Bogarde has written an illuminating biography, *Snakes & Ladders* (London, 1978): his poem 'Steel Cathedrals' was published in *Poetry Review* and later in many anthologies of war poetry. Allan Davis has talked to this author. Alan Ross made his usual shrewd observations about the demobilized in *The Forties* (cited in Chapter 4), while *Portrait of a Decade: London Life 1945–1955* (London, 1988) was written by Douglas Sutherland. Bryher wrote her interesting article 'Genteel Nissen' for *Life and Letters To-Day*, Vol. 43, No. 86, October 1944. Henry Treece's letter to G. S. Fraser is printed in Fraser's *A Stranger and Afraid* (cited in Chapter 5). Roy Fuller's analysis of his life on the lower deck was a contribution to *The Poetry of War: 1939–1945* (cited in Chapter 4). David Kendall published 'mediterranean convoy: homeward bound' in his *Poems of an Ordinary Seaman* (London, 1946).

CHAPTER FIFTEEN

Cecil Day Lewis's poem, 'Will It Be So Again?', comes from his *Word Over All* (cited in Chapter 7). Henry Pelling, *The Labour Governments, 1945–51* (London, 1984) is excellent on the problems of the post-war years. The Conservative who denounced the American loan was Robert Boothby. As late as the 1960s, Hugh Gaitskell told me that the reason he did not support Britain's joining the Common Market was that he and the Labour Party felt a responsibility for overseeing the remnants of the British Empire to independence. Cyril Connolly's approval of the bombing of parts of London appears in *The Condemned Playground* (cited in Chapter 11). Stephen Spender's caveat appears in *World Within World* (cited in Chapter 4). Alan Ross in *The Forties* (cited in Chapter 4) remains an essential guide to the period, while Anthony Powell's second volume of autobiography, *Faces in My Time*, was published in London in 1980. G. S. Fraser's comments on post-war London come from his important *The Modern Writer and His World* (cited in Chapter 7); it was the first post-war attempt to assess fully the importance of modern British writing and it emphasized the contribution of those who wrote during the war. Peter Watson's letter to Waldemar Hansen is quoted in Michael Shelden, *Friends of Promise* (cited in Chapter 2).

Gilbert Frankau's views on post-war Britain come from Donald Brook, *Writers' Gallery: Biographical Sketches of Britain's Greatest Writers, and their Views on Reconstruction* (London, 1944). J. B. Priestley wrote on the disappearance of class in favour of the people in *Out of the People* (London, 1941): it was the unique herald of a planned series of Vigilant Books, which would deal with the problems of reconstruction after the war. Jack Lindsay's poem 'The Two Pulls' was printed in *New Lyrical Ballads* (cited in Chapter 8), as was Paul Potts, 'My Work'. Sid Chaplin's complaint about Bevin was written to Woodrow Wyatt on 30 March 1946: Wyatt was then a Labour MP and Chaplin hoped he could do something about Labour foreign policy. Donald Bishop, 'Colour Bar', was reprinted in the *Little Reviews Anthology*, 1945. Alan Ross, 'A Lament for the "Thirties" Poets' appeared in *Poetry Quarterly*, Summer 1948. While Lehmann's riposte to Toynbee is in *Horizon*, Vol. XI, No. 62, February 1945. Charles Wrey Gardiner's musings of 1945 and 1946 were published by his Grey Walls Press in 1949 under the title of *The Flowering Moment*; they share in Connolly's depression, but their insights are romantic rather than classical in tone: in them is Gardiner's impression of his partner, Peter Baker.

I have again used Cyril Connolly's thoughts on regionalism from *The Condemned Playground* (see above), while Maurice Bowra wrote on 'The Next Stage in Poetry' in *Horizon*, Vol. XIV, No. 79, July 1946. G. S. Fraser's comment on young writers after the war comes again from his *The Modern Writer and His World* (see above). The important pamphlet, *The Battle of the Books*, with contributions from Stanley Unwin as well as Osbert Sitwell and Henry Green and Rupert Hart-Davis, was published in London in June 1947. Two excellent articles have been written about R. A. Caton: one by Timothy D'Arch Smith in *The Books of the Beast* (London, 1987), the other by A. T. Tolley, the indispensable source on poetry and publishing in the 1940s, 'The Fortune Press and the Poetry of the Forties', *Aquarius*, 17/18, 1986/7, to which I am indebted for Nicholas Moore's description of Caton and also Julian Symons's memories. Douglas Sutherland in *Portrait of a Decade: London Life 1945–55* (cited in Chapter 14) gives a good account of Peter Baker, while Peter Quennell tells the Evelyn Waugh story against himself in his autobiography (cited in Chapter 1). 'The Cost of Letters' was published in *Horizon*, Vol. XIV, No. 81, September 1946, and 'In Jugular Vein' in *Horizon*, Vol. XVI, No. 95, November 1947.

John Lehmann's comment on the uncomfortable peace is in Penguin *New Writing*, No. 25, 1945; his disbelief in a 'Philistine Restoration' in *New Writing and Daylight*, II, May 1946; his self-realization through Isherwood's eyes in the third volume of his autobiogra-

phy, *The Ample Proposition* (cited in Chapter 7); and his advice to war novelists in Penguin *New Writing*, No. 28, 1946. Daniel George's advice to war novelists comes in his 'An Alphabet of Literary Prejudice', *Little Reviews Anthology*, 1949. Stephen Spender, 'Poetry for Poetry's Sake and Poetry Beyond Poetry', was printed in *Horizon*, Vol. XIII, No. 76, April 1946: he was reviewing Robert Graves, T. S. Eliot, W. H. Auden, Edith Sitwell, Dylan Thomas ('who has gained more than any other from having to do war work'), Walter de la Mare, Edmund Blunden, John Betjeman, Vernon Watkins, and *The War Poets*, edited by Oscar Williams, on which Geoffrey Grigson commented that no good war poems were written that were 'thumps on the tub, the morale poems'. Roy Harrod, 'The Surrender of Free Choice', appears in *Horizon*, Vol. XIV, No. 96, December 1947. *The Challenge of Our Time* was published in London in 1948: its contributors were Arthur Koestler, E. L. Woodward, J. D. Bernal, E. M. Forster, Benjamin Farrington (who chided Forster's distrust of scientists), Michael Polanyi, J. B. S. Haldane, V. A. Dyment, C. H. Waddington, A. D. Ritchie and Lord Lindsay.

Picture Post published 'A Nest of Singing Birds' on 10 August 1946. Rayner Heppenstall's autobiography *Portrait of the Artist as a Professional Man* was published in London, 1969. John Heath-Stubbs told me of Roy Campbell's attack on Heppenstall. Jocelyn Brooke wrote of his experiences in the BBC in *Coming to London* (ed. John Lehmann, London, 1957). William Empson, 'Let it go', is published in his *Collected Poems* (London, 1955). Patric Dickinson spoke on poetry to *Picture Post*. R. D. Smith wrote an excellent memoir of MacNeice's broadcasting career, 'Castle on the Air', in *Time Was Away: The World of Louis MacNeice* (ed. T. Brown and A. Reid, Dublin, 1974). Roy Campbell, *Flowering Rifle*, was published in London, 1939. There is an understanding work, *Roy Campbell: A Critical Biography* (Oxford, 1982) by Peter Alexander, but of the many versions of Campbell's literary fisticuffs I have also relied on Derek Stanford and John Heath-Stubbs and Jon Wynne-Tyson. Dylan Thomas, 'The English Festival of Spoken Poetry', is printed in *Quite Early One Morning* (cited in Chapter 9). Charles Fisher, a friend of Dylan Thomas, described his London drinking habits: he is recorded in Andrew Sinclair, *Dylan Thomas: Poet of the People* (London, 1975). Richard Burton told me the story of Thomas's greatest poem. Dylan Thomas's unfinished novel *Adventures in the Skin Trade*, was first published in London in 1955. Alan Ross's accolade to Fitzrovia was published in the *London Magazine*, December 1962.

CHAPTER SIXTEEN

Mervyn Peake's 'Poem' on the strawberry blonde is printed in *The Glassblowers* (London, 1950). Douglas Sutherland, *Portrait of a Decade: London Life 1945–1955* (cited in Chapter 14) gives a brilliant picture of the ex-officers trying to come to terms with a journalistic, commercial and semi-criminal London life. Sammy Samuels (with Leonard Davis), *Among the Soho Sinners* (London, 1970) is a unique account of Soho club life in the 'forties. Edgar Ainsworth's paintings for *Lilliput* were printed in the issue of December, 1947; James Fitton's paintings in June, 1947, and Edward Burra's in November, 1947, while James Minton painted London River in July, 1947. Virginia Graham, '1946: A Thought for Denman Street', comes from her *Consider the Years* (cited in Chapter 13); already cited in Chapter 11 are *The Collected Poems of A. S. J. Tessimond*, which include 'Smart-boy'. Bill Naughton's essay on the 'spiv' was published in *Pilot Papers* (London, 1946). Anthony Powell's third volume of memoirs, *Faces in My Time*, was cited in Chapter 15. *Portrait of a Decade* (see above) is again my source on the killing of Freddie Mills. Daniel Farson's engaging *Soho in the Fifties* (cited in Chapter 1) quotes the counsel for the prosecution's indictment at the trial of the owner of the Fitzroy Tavern. The poem to Dylan Thomas in the Gargoyle was written to him in 1950 by Robert Pocock in imitation of John Betjeman's 'On Seeing an Old Poet in the Café Royal': it is quoted in Ruthven Todd, *Fitzrovia and the Road to the York Minster* (cited in Chapter 1). Wrey Gardiner wrote of the Café Royal in *The Flowering Moment* (cited in Chapter 15). Dan Davin in *Closing Times* (cited in Chapter 5) gives the best analysis of Julian Maclaren-Ross yet recorded.

The first edition of *Memoirs of the Forties* (cited in Chapter 1), published by Alan Ross in 1965, does contain facsimile pages of Maclaren-Ross's intentions for a completed memoir, including a comprehensive list of Fitzrovians, whom he knew and intended to include in 'Portraits from Memory'. They seem to prove the reality of the Fitzrovian pubs as a meeting-place for artists during the 1940s. Listed or mentioned in the fragments of the *Memoirs* are Michael Ayrton, Francis Bacon, John Banting, Roberts Colquhoun and MacBryde, Lucian Freud, Nina Hamnett, Augustus John, John Minton, Picasso (because of one visit), Matthew Smith, Feliks Topolski, Keith Vaughan and Gerald Wilde. Writers include James Agate, Walter Allen, Eric Ambler, George Barker, Arthur Calder-Marshall, Roy Campbell, Anthony Carson, Joyce Cary, John Davenport, Dan Davin, Kay Dick, Norman Douglas, Willi Frischauer, John Gawsworth, W. S. Graham, Henry Green, Graham Greene, Rayner Heppenstall, Gerald Kersh, Alun Lewis, Hugh MacDiarmid, Nicholas Moore, Bill Naughton, Liam O'Flaherty, George Orwell, Alun Owen, Peter de Polnay, Paul Potts, Anthony Powell, Alan Ross, William Sansom, William Saroyan, Humphrey Slater, Stevie Smith, C. P. Snow, Stephen Spender, Julian Symons, Dylan Thomas,

Ruthven Todd, Philip Toynbee and John Waller. Literati and publishers and others included David Archer, Anthony Asquith, Sonia Brownell, Jonathan Cape, David Cecil, Claud Cockburn, Cyril Connolly, Nancy Cunard, André Deutsch, Wrey Gardiner, Val Gielgud, Sylvia Gough, Gerald Hamilton, Brian Howard, John Lehmann, Ivan Moffatt, Malcolm Muggeridge, Beverley Nichols, Raymond Postgate, Alan Pryce-Jones, Goronwy Rees, Keidrych Rhys, Maurice Richardson, J. Meary Tambimuttu and Woodrow Wyatt.

G. S. Fraser's descriptions of London post-war life are in his autobiography, *A Stranger and Afraid* (cited in Chapter 5). John Heath-Stubbs talked to me, and to G. H. B. Wightman in *Aquarius*, 10: *In Honour of John Heath-Stubbs* (London, 1978): 'The Pearl' and 'Good Night, Ireen' are printed in his *Collected Poems* (cited in Chapter 12). Potocki de Montalk wrote two intriguing but rather libellous pamphlets, *Social Climbers in Bloomsbury* and *Driven Mad*, which are interesting comments on the places and the times. For more information on John Gawsworth, I am much indebted to Steve Eng, 'Profile: John Gawsworth', *Night Cry*, March 1987. W. S. Graham, 'Heath-Stubbs the Poet as Hero', appears in *Aquarius*, 10, work cited, while John Gawsworth's own poem, 'Definitions of Drink', appears in his unpublished 'Notebook Thirty-One', 1949. Gavin Ewart, 'In the Old Days', appears in *Aquarius*, 17/18, 1986/7. Lovat Dickson's autobiography, *The House of Words*, has already been mentioned in Chapter 1. There is a good article by Alan Smith, 'John Lehmann Ltd.', in *John Lehmann: A Tribute* (cited in Chapter 8). I am indebted to George Woodcock for his memoir on *Now*, 'Failures of Promise', *Aquarius*, 17/18, 1986/7, and also to Julian Symons, who sent me the recent posthumous limited edition of H. B. Mallalieu's *On The Berlin Lakes and Other Poems* (Dover, 1988), which contains his 'Lines to Roy Fuller': a larger volume of his longer poems is in preparation and should confirm the reputation of one of the finer poets of his time, silent for too long. Fuller's comments on the post-war silence of Kenneth Allott appear in his introduction to Allott's *Collected Poems* (London, 1975). Mallalieu's declaration about his war poetry, appears in *The Poetry of War 1939–45* (cited in Chapter 4), while Paul Dehn, another poet of the period who deserves a higher reputation, published 'New Age' in *The Fern on the Rock: Collected Poems 1935/65* (London, 1965). Alan Ross again contributes to the understanding of the period in *The Forties* (cited in Chapter 4). Edmund Wilson's comment on England in 1945 comes from *Europe Without Baedeker* (London, 1948). Cyril Connolly's lament on the decline of English culture came from his editorial in *Horizon*, Vol. XVII, No. 100, April 1948: he ended with the correct prophecy that *Horizon* would continue to exist for only another two years, which would enable it to cover the whole of the 'forties and, like a skilled anaesthetist, put the arts into final oblivion. Jocelyn Brooke, *The Orchid Trilogy*, was republished with an introduction by Anthony Powell in 1981 in London: its three parts were originally published in 1948, 1949 and 1950. Brooke's poems were published in *December Spring* (London, 1946). The comparison of James Joyce and Ivy Compton-Burnett appears in P. H. Newby's booklet for the British Council, *The Novel 1945–1950*, which also highly praised L. P. Hartley's trilogy, *The Shrimp and the Anemone* (1944), *The Sixth Heaven* (1946) and *Eustace and Hilda* (1947). Graham Greene, *The Heart of the Matter*, was published in 1948, while Henry Green's novels *Concluding* and *Nothing* were published in 1948 and 1950. V. S. Pritchett's comments on Greene and Bowen were in his contribution to an interesting symposium on 'The Future of Fiction' in *New Writing and Daylight*, 1946. Aldous Huxley, *Ape and Essence*, was published in London in 1949. Bernard Crick refers to T. S. Eliot's letter of rejection of *Animal Farm* in his admirable biography, *George Orwell* (London, 1980). Cyril Connolly reviewed *Animal Farm* in *Horizon*, Vol. XII, No. 69, September 1945. Spender wrote of his last meeting with Orwell before his death in 1949 in *The Thirties and After* (cited in Chapter 2). Robert Conquest, 'George Orwell', comes from his *New and Collected Poems* (cited in Chapter 13). J. B. Priestley wrote of Patrick Hamilton in an introduction to a new edition of *The Slaves of Solitude*, republished in 1972, after its first publication in London in 1947: *Hangover Square* was published in 1941. Rose Macaulay also contributed to 'The Future of Fiction' in *New Writing and Daylight*, 1946. Alex Comfort, *The Novel and Our Time*, was published in London, 1948. The anonymous 'Letter from an Ex-conscript' about 'skiving' in the army was published in *Horizon*, Vol. XX, No. 115, July 1949. David Gascoyne's 'Demos in Oxford Street' comes from his *Collected Poems* (cited in Chapter 2).

CHAPTER SEVENTEEN
Cecil Day Lewis, 'Flight to Italy' from *An Italian Visit* was published in *Horizon*, Vol. XX, Nos 120–1, December 1949 and January 1950. For Francis Bacon's evidence on his own life, I am again indebted to David Sylvester, *The Brutality of Fact* (cited in Chapter 13). Alan Ross quoted Keith Vaughan's opinion of John Minton in *Coastwise Lights* (cited in Chapter 9). David Wright, 'A Stroll in Soho: I. M. Robert Colquhoun – 1914–62' was printed in his *To the Gods the Shades* (cited in Chapter 1); his 'Verses at a Bohemian Funeral' were printed in *New Poems*, a P.E.N. anthology (London, 1957). Paul Nash wrote on 'Aerial Flowers' in *Outline: An Autobiography and Other Writings* (London, 1949). John Craxton is quoted from an interview with Anne

Campbell Dixon in *The Times*, 22 October 1988, and from the catalogue to the Barbican exhibition of neo-Romantic painting, *A Paradise Lost* (cited in Chapter 2). Rayner Heppenstall commented on Anna Wickham's death in his *Four Absentees* (London, 1960). Herbert Read wrote on 'The Fate of Modern Painting', *Little Reviews Anthology*, 1949, while the tribute to Henry Moore's Shelter drawings is by Peter Fuller, 'Henry Moore: An English Romantic' in the catalogue of Moore's definitive exhibition at the Royal Academy of Arts, London, 1988. Michael Balcon, 'A Glance Backwards, With No Lament', appeared in *Soho Centenary 1844–1944* (cited in Chapter 12). David Lean wrote on 'Brief Encounter' in the Penguin *Film Review*, 4, 1947. The screenplay of Graham Greene's *The Third Man* was published in London in 1973. Charles Chaplin's *Monsieur Verdoux* was released in 1947. Alex Comfort, 'The End of a War, October, 1944' appeared in his *Art and Social Responsibility* (London, 1946). The screenplay of Dylan Thomas about Burke and Hare was called *The Doctor and the Devils*; it was published in London in 1953. Laurence Olivier wrote an introduction to *Hamlet: The Film and the Play* (London, 1948). Filippo del Giudice wrote to Woodrow Wyatt on 18 August 1949, complaining about Rank. Robert Speaight, *Drama Since 1939* (London, 1947) made the remark about the absence of war plays in England. T. S. Eliot, *The Cocktail Party*, was published in London in 1950: his first verse play, *Murder in the Cathedral*, was the *fons et origo* of the revival of modern verse drama in Britain. Christopher Hassall, 'Notes on the Verse Drama', filled the whole issue of *The Masque*, No. 6, 1948. Noël Coward, *Peace in Our Time*, was presented in 1947; Terence Rattigan's *Harlequinade* in 1948 in a double bill with *The Browning Version*, and his *The Deep Blue Sea* in 1952. Tyrone Guthrie made his comments on the Old Vic in 1945 in his autobiography, *A Life in the Theatre* (cited in Chapter 12). Desmond Shawe-Taylor criticized British opera in the *New Statesman*, 18 October 1947, but he wrote more hopefully of its prospects in *Covent Garden* (cited in Chapter 2). I am indebted to Andrew Motion, *The Lamberts* (cited in Chapter 10) for Frederick Ashton's comment on Constant Lambert's last marriage. John Lehmann wrote dismissively of post-war ballet in *New Writing and Daylight*, 1946. Eric Blom was the critic who wrote on 'The Future of Music' in *The Prospect Before Us* (London, 1948). John Summerson, 'Architecture in England', was published by the British Council in 1946. G. W. Stonier, *Round London with the Unicorn*, was printed in London in 1951. Gerald Kersh's story, 'The Musicians', appears in *The Horrible Dummy and Other Stories* (London, 1944). George Melly's remarks on Soho appear in his introduction to Daniel Farson, *Soho in the Fifties* (cited in Chapter 1). He has also talked to me.

CHAPTER EIGHTEEN

Michael Hamburger's autobiography, *A Mug's Game*, has already been cited, as has Nina Hamnett, *Is She A Lady?*, both in Chapter 1. Charles Wrey Gardiner's *The Answer to Life is No* was also cited in Chapter 1. John Heath-Stubbs, 'Funeral Music for Charles Wrey Gardiner', was published in his *Collected Poems* (cited in Chapter 12), Steve Eng's 'Profile: John Gawsworth' was cited in Chapter 16, Julian Maclaren-Ross, *Memoirs of the Forties* in Chapter 1, and Vernon Scannell, *The Tiger and the Rose* in Chapter 14. A. S. J. Tessimond, 'Song in a Saloon Bar' was printed in his *Collected Poems* (cited in Chapter 11). Donald W. Goodwin wrote *Alcohol and the Writer* (New York, 1988). Connolly's remark on the dog's life of little magazines comes from his collection of essays, *The Evening Colonnade* (London, 1973). Stephen Spender's letter to John Lehmann on the demise of Penguin *New Writing* is quoted in the third volume of Lehmann's memoirs, *The Ample Proposition* (cited in Chapter 7). Cyril Connolly's reappraisal of his editorials in *Horizon* comes from his introduction to a collection of his writing, *Ideas and Places* (London, 1951), while his final editorial was printed in *Horizon*, Vol. XX, Nos 120–1, December 1949 and January 1950. Brendan Behan talked on the 'Gardens of the West' to Anthony Cronin in *Dead as Doornails* (cited in Chapter 5). Robert Melville was the critic who wrote on Francis Bacon in the final issue of *Horizon*. T. S. Eliot's letter to the editors is printed in *Nine*, No. 1, Autumn 1949. Barbara Skelton, now married to Cyril Connolly, heard his remark about belonging to a dead civilization: her memoirs *Tears Before Bedtime* have been mentioned in Chapter 5. T. S. Eliot's *Notes Towards the Definition of Culture* were published in London in 1948. George Orwell spoke on preserving Welsh and Gaelic to Rayner Heppenstall, who recorded it in *Four Absentees* (cited in Chapter 17).

Sydney Goodsir Smith, 'October, 1941' was published in *The Wanderer* (Edinburgh, 1943). Edwin Muir, 'Scotland 1941', was published in his *Collected Poems* (cited in Chapter 6). G. S. Fraser wrote on Lallans in *Vision of Scotland* (London, 1948). Sorley Maclean's versions of 'Knightsbridge, Libya' in Gaelic and English are reproduced in George Bruce's excellent anthology, *The Scottish Literary Revival* (London, 1968). Patrick Kavanagh's lines from *The Great Hunger* were printed as 'The Old Peasant' in *Horizon*, Vol. V, No. 25, January 1942. I am much indebted to A. T. Tolley's *The Poetry of the Forties in Britain* (cited in Chapter 7) for reference to the discussion about 'provincial' and 'parochial' between Patrick Kavanagh and Norman Nicholson, who wrote 'On Being Provincial' for *The Listener*, 12 August 1954, while Kavanagh, 'The Parish and the Universe', appears in his *Collected Prose* (London, 1967).

Dylan Thomas's broadcast, 'Wales and the Artist', was printed in *Quite Early One Morning* (cited in Chapter 9). For the attacks of F. R. Leavis on the metropolitan establishment, see his 'Mr Pryce-Jones, The British Council and British Culture (1951)', collected in *A Selection from* Scrutiny *Compiled by F. R. Leavis* (Vol. I, Cambridge, 1968). V. S. Pritchett's comments on the influence of the war on writers come from *Midnight Oil* (cited in Chapter 8). Roy Fuller spoke to me about this book: his poem, 'The Divided Life Re-Lived' was first printed in *Horizon*, Vol. XIX, No. 109, January 1949: his article on post-war writing appeared in *Our Time* in 1947. Julian Symons also talked to me. J. C. Hall, 'Thirty Years', appeared in *The Summer Dance* (cited in Chapter 4). Philip O'Connor's remarks on post-war bohemianism come from his *Memoirs of a Public Baby*, already mentioned in Chapter 1.

CHAPTER NINETEEN

The director-general of the Festival of Britain was Gerald Barry, the editor of the *News Chronicle*, who declared that the festival was a way of showing 'what the Land has made of the People, and what the People have made of themselves'. Harold Nicolson, 'Visit to the South Bank', appeared in *The Spectator* and was reprinted in *Spectator Harvest* (London, 1952), along with Gerald Hodgkin, 'Festival Preview', which compared the Skylon to the Quangle-Wangle. The final novel of Evelyn Waugh's war trilogy, *Unconditional Surrender*, was published in London in 1961. Michael Frayn has written the definitive article 'Festival' on the event of 1951 for *Age of Austerity* (cited in Chapter 13). Vanessa Redgrave, playing the part of Joe Orton's agent Peggy Ramsey, spoke the lines about the festival in Alan Bennett's screenplay for *Prick Up Your Ears*. Stephen Spender condemned the festival and the post-war social revolution in *The Thirties and After* (cited in Chapter 2). Herbert Morrison was Lord President of the Council and the Labour minister ultimately responsible for the festival. Valuable descriptions of the achievements of the festival appear in Michael Yorke's *Spirit of Place* (cited in Chapter 10), and in Robert Hewison, *In Anger: Culture in the Cold War 1945–60* (London, 1981). Wyndham Lewis tells of Colquhoun's disappointment over the festival in *Rotting Hill* (London, 1961). Roger Berthoud's *Life of Henry Moore* was published in London in 1987. The excellent guidebook, *The South Bank Exhibition*, by Ian Cox (London, 1951) tells of cinematic and art contributions to the festival. The veteran bookseller Eric Norris told me about Dylan Thomas reading at the Victoria and Albert Museum. John Hayward voiced his complaint in his introduction to the Penguin collection of the festival verse entrants, *Poems, 1951* (London, 1951). The extract from Christopher Fry's *A Sleep of* **311**

Prisoners comes from its text, published in Oxford in 1951.

Malcolm Muggeridge wrote on Guy Burgess in *The Infernal Grove* (London, 1973), while Cyril Connolly, *The Missing Diplomats*, has been cited in Chapter 5. Anthony Powell's volume of autobiography, *Messengers of Day*, has already been mentioned in Chapter 1, as have John Lehmann's second and third volumes of autobiography (Chapters 1 and 7). John Costello secured a copy of the Isherwood denunciation of British communist intellectuals under the terms of the Freedom of Information Act in the United States: the document is quoted in *The Mask of Treachery* (London, 1988): Costello has also talked to me. I am indebted to Stan Smith, *Inviolable Voice: History and Twentieth-Century Poetry* (Dublin, 1982) for pointing out Auden's two suppressed poems, 'A Communist to Others' and 'To a Writer on his Birthday'. Philip Toynbee reviewed Goronwy Rees, *A Chapter of Accidents* (London, 1972) in the *Observer*, 13 February 1972. Roy Fuller's lines come from his *Epitaphs and Occasions* (London, 1949), while Alan Ross wrote his pamphlet on *Poetry 1945–1950* for the British Council (cited in Chapter 15). His work, *The Forties*, with its comment on culture as a great big Oxford Street, has already been mentioned in Chapter 4. G. S. Fraser, *The Modern Writer and His World* (cited in Chapter 7) is essential reading on the literature of the period. Kenneth Allott said in his introductory note to *The Penguin Book of Contemporary Verse* (London, 1950) that it was impossible to indict a whole poetic decade. Philip Larkin's *Collected Poems* were admirably edited by Anthony Thwaite and published in London in 1988. Philip Larkin made his comments on wartime Oxford in his introduction to a new edition of *The North Ship* (London, 1965). Although he was excluded from *Eight Oxford Poets* in 1941, he was published together with Drummond Allison, John Heath-Stubbs and David Wright in 1944 in *Poetry from Oxford in Wartime*, thus finding himself in Romantic and bohemian company. John Heath-Stubbs, 'Funeral Music for Charles Wrey Gardiner', has already been quoted in Chapter 18. William Plomer, 'The Bungalows', was published in his *Collected Poems* (London, 1960). 'London' by A. S. J. Tessimond is printed in his *Collected Poems* (cited in Chapter 11). Anthony Cronin again commented on the lonely and suffering geniuses of Soho in *Dead as Doornails* (cited in Chapter 5). David Wright, 'A Ballad for Hard Times', was printed in the final issue of *Poetry London*, Vol. 6, No. 23, Winter 1951.

CHAPTER TWENTY

Charles Wrey Gardiner, *The Answer to Life Is No*, has already been cited in Chapter 1. Auden's remark on the 'thirties comes from his '1 September 1939' and F. R. Leavis's from 'Retrospect of a Decade', *Scrutiny*, 1940.

Gavin Ewart made his remark on the war to this author. A. T. Tolley condemns the metropolitan rootlessness of culture in his important *The Poetry of the Forties in Britain* (cited in Chapter 7), as has been Michael Wishart's *High Diver* (in Chapter 5), which contains interesting passages on Cyril Connolly and Francis Bacon and Lucian Freud. Connolly's remark about working best in scraps is from the foreword to a special revised American edition of *Enemies of Promise* (New York, 1948). The comments of the poets who contributed to *The Poetry of War 1939–45*, edited by Ian Hamilton and published by Alan Ross in 1965 (cited in Chapter 4), remain essential reading for an understanding of the war experience. Vernon Watkins's sentence on the truest statements about war was made in *A Little Treasury of Modern Poetry* (ed. O. Williams, New York, 1952). Louis MacNeice, 'Elegy for Minor Poets', is printed in his *Collected Poems, 1925–1948* (London, 1949). Roy Fuller, 'Obituary of R. Fuller', was first printed in *Horizon*, Vol. XIX, No. 109, January 1949, and reprinted in his *Epitaphs and Occasions* (cited in Chapter 19). Donald Davie, 'Rejoinder to a Critic', is quoted in Stan Smith, *Inviolable Voice: History and Twentieth-Century Poetry* (cited in Chapter 19). John Heath-Stubbs talked to me, and to A. T. Tolley in *Aquarius*, 10. Stephen Spender's *World Within World* has already been cited in Chapter 4. C. H. Bevan wrote the verse about the antiquity of yesterday's battlefield in 'Medjez-el-bab', printed in *From Oasis Into Italy* (cited in Chapter 9). Alan Ross comments on war poetry in his British Council pamphlet, *Poetry 1945–1950*: he reprints Norman Cameron's poem 'The Verdict': the poem was composed at Mola, 1945.

Francis Bacon talked to me about this book in Fitzrovia for four hours and drank me under the table. He discussed fully his vision of 'reality' and how his experience of his time related to his painting. Michael Wishart visited Bacon at his studio, once that of Millais, in Cromwell Place; among Bacon's few books were works by Pound and Eliot. Bacon's letter to the Soviet government of 4 June 1988, is reproduced in the catalogue of his Moscow exhibition. He quoted to me the line from Aeschylus, also a favourite line from Valéry about technique, 'Modern man wants a sensation without the boredom of its conveyance.'

George Barker, 'At the Wake of Dylan Thomas', is published in his *Collected Poems* (cited in Chapter 9), while G. S. Fraser's elegy to Stefan Schimanski was first published in *Leaves without a Tree* (Tokyo, 1953) and republished in the *Poems of G. S. Fraser* (cited in Chapter 9). Robert Hewison in his *In Anger: Culture in the Cold War 1945–1960* (cited in Chapter 19) refers to G. S. Fraser's opinion that the innings of the 'New Romantics' was over and to George Barker's comments on the bad prospects of young experimental poets. George Melly told me about Lucian Freud's liking of criminals as well as aristocrats as the subjects of his art and life. Robert Conquest, 'Literature in Soho', is printed in his *New and Collected Poems*, already mentioned in Chapter 16. John

Heath-Stubbs has talked to me: his poem, 'Lament for the "Old Swan"', is printed in his important *Collected Poems, 1943–1987* (cited in Chapter 12).

ACKNOWLEDGEMENTS

ILLUSTRATIONS
The author and publishers would like to thank all those who have given permission to reproduce the illustrations in this book. While every effort has been made to trace copyright holders, this has not been possible in all cases; any omissions brought to our attention will of course be remedied in future editions.

Colour and black and white illustration sections
Grateful acknowledgements are due to the following:
The Royal College of Art for illustration on Penguin *New Writing* cover and painting of *St. Paul's from the River* by John Minton; Daniel Farson for photographs of the regulars drinking with the Navy in the Fitzroy Tavern and of Cyril Connolly and Lady Caroline Blackwood; The Hulton Deutsch Collection for photograph of 'forties stars drinking in the Coach and Horses; The Hulton Picture Company for photograph of W. H. Auden, C. Day Lewis and Stephen Spender, by permission of Lady Natasha Spender; Mr Jon Wynne-Tyson, literary executor of the estate of John Gawsworth for two photographs of John Gawsworth; Mrs Noya Brandt for photographs of Henry Moore, Dylan Thomas, Stephen Spender, Alun Lewis, Cecil Day Lewis, Laurie Lee, Louis MacNeice, Theodora Fitzgibbon and Windmill girls, by Bill Brandt; Mrs Kaye Webb for covers for December 1942 and March 1944 issues and other material from *Lilliput*; The Trustees of the British Museum for *Shelter* drawing by Henry Moore; Mrs Elisabeth Ayrton for illustrations from *Poems of Death* and E. A. Poe's *Tales of Mystery and Imagination* by Michael Ayrton; The Trustees of the Imperial War Museum for *A Black Aeroplane on a Red Deck* and *Radar Predictor* by Leonard Rosoman, *Crashed Gliders, at the Landing Zone at Ranville* by Albert Richards, *Shipbuilding On the Clyde – Burners* by Stanley Spencer and *Battle of Britain* by Paul Nash; Thomas Gibson Fine Art Ltd for drawings *Barrage Balloon* and *Two Nuns and a Peasant Family* by Edward Seago; The Lefevre Gallery for *Snack Counter* by Edward Burra; Mr T. Fitton for *West End – Two Doubles* by James Fitton; Mrs Sheila Wilson for *Two Sisters* by Robert Colquhoun: the vicar of St Matthew's, Northampton, for *Crucifixion* by Graham Sutherland;

The Tate Gallery, London, for *Three Studies* by Francis Bacon; John Piper for *The Passage to the Control-Room at S.W. Regional Headquarters, Bristol, Council Chamber, House of Commons, 1941* and backcloth for the last act of Ashton's ballet, *The Quest*; stills from the films *Henry V* and *Brief Encounter* by courtesy of the Rank Organisation Plc; Mr J. C. Hall, literary executor of the Keith Douglas estate for frontispiece from *Alamein to Zem Zem* (Editions Poetry London, 1946).

Line drawings in the body of the text
The illustrations on pages 13 and 65 are by Leonard Rosoman for William Sansom's article on Soho in *Flower of Cities: A Book of London* (Max Parrish, London 1949). The illustrations on pages 34, 139, 152 and 256 are also by Leonard Rosoman for 'What do you mean, DIVERSION?' for *Diversion* (John Sutro ed., Max Parrish, London 1950). The cartoon on page 42 is from Michael Barsley's *Ritzkrieg* (The Pilot Press, 1940). The drawings of the blitz on pages 53, 83, 93, 113, 123 and 155 are by Leonard Rosoman; they were printed in *Fire and Water: An Anthology by Members of the NFS* (Lindsay Drummond, 1942). The illustrations on page 165 are by Mervyn Peake for C. E. M. Joad, *The Adventures of the Young Soldier in Search of the Better World* (London, 1943) and are reprinted by permission of the estate of Mervyn Peake. The illustration on page 168 is from Mervyn Peake, *The Rhyme of the Flying Bomb* (Colin Smythe, 1973), as is the illustration on page 169. Keith Douglas drew the picture on page 179: it was printed in *Alamein to Zem Zem* (Editions Poetry London, 1946) and is reprinted by permission of the estate of Keith Douglas. On page 193, Tom Purvis illustrates Negley Farson's *Bomber's Moon* (Harcourt Brace, 1942). The illustration on page 200 is from Osbert Lancaster, *Further Pocket Cartoons* (John Murray, 1942). The illustration on page 203 is by Lynton Lamb for G. W. Stonier, *Round London with the Unicorn* (Turnstile Press, 1951). The drawings on page 221 by John Pemberton is for Patric Dickinson's 'The BBC', printed in *Flower of Cities* (cited above). The Osbert Lancaster cartoon of Fitzrovia on page 12 of the Café Royal on page 225 were both printed in *Horizon* magazine by Cyril Connolly, who is depicted in the

checked overcoat (centre left) in the Café Royal. The illustrations on page 240 are by John Craxton for *Poetry London*. Katerina Wilczynski illustrates Robert Helpmann's article, 'The Orchestration of Movement', on pages 243 and 258: both were printed in *Diversion* (cited above).

QUOTATIONS IN TEXT

The author and publishers would like to thank all the writers, publishers and literary representatives, who have given permission for quoted material. In some instances it has been difficult to track down copyright holders and the publishers will be glad to make good any omissions in future editions. Writers whose work has been quoted from are listed in alphabetical order below. Drummond Allison: extract from 'Come Let Us Pity Death' from *For Your Tomorrow*, OUP, 1950. Kenneth Allott: extract from 'Black Out' from *Collected Poems*, 1975, reprinted by permission of Martin Secker & Warburg Ltd. Brian Allwood: extract from 'Pilot' from *More Poems from the Forces* ed. K. Rhys, Routledge, 1943. Nigel Balchin: extract from *Darkness Falls from the Air*, Collins, 1942, reprinted by permission of Blanche Marvin. Michael Balcon: extract from 'The British Film During the War' from *The Penguin Film Review*. Felix Barker: extract from *The Oliviers*, Hamish Hamilton, 1953. George Barker: extract from 'The True Confessions of George Barker' and 'At the Wake of Dylan Thomas' reprinted by permission of Faber & Faber Ltd from *Collected Poems* by George Barker. John Bayliss: extract from 'Epilogue: Testament and Prophecy' from *Poetry of the Present* ed. A. Grigson, Phoenix House, 1949; from 'Home Thoughts from Abroad' from *Little Review Anthology*, Eyre & Spottiswoode, 1945. Cecil Beaton: extract from *The Years Between: Diaries 1939–1944*, Weidenfeld & Nicolson, 1945. Donald Bishop: extract from 'Colour Bar' from *Little Review Anthology*, Eyre & Spottiswoode, 1945. Edmund Blunden: extract from 'To Wilfred Owen and His Kind' from *Anyway*, Blackwells, 1940. David Bourne: extract from 'Fighter by Night' from *For Your Tomorrow*, Oxford University Press; from 'Night Club' from *Poems*, The Bodley Head; from 'Parachute Descent' from *Airforce Poetry*, reprinted by permission of The Bodley Head and the estate of David Bourne. Elizabeth Bowen: extracts from *The Heat of the Day*, reprinted by permission of Jonathan Cape Ltd and the estate of Elizabeth Bowen. John Braine: extract from *J. B. Priestley*, Weidenfeld & Nicolson, 1978. Ritchie Calder: extract from *The Lesson of London*, Martin Secker & Warburg, 1942. Mel Calman: extracts from 'Memoirs of an Evacuee' from *The Evacuees*, ed. G. S. Johnson, Gollancz, 1968; reprinted by permission of Mel Calman. Norman Cameron: extracts from 'Punishment Enough' and 'The Verdict' from *Collected Poems*, 1957, reprinted by permission of The Hogarth Press and the Executor of the Norman Cameron Estate. Roy

Campbell: 'One Transport Lost' and 'Flowering Rifle' from *Collected Works*, reprinted by permission of Francisco Campbell Custodio and Ad. Donker (Pty) Ltd. Elias Canetti: *The Human Province*, Andre Deutsch Ltd, 1985. Maurice Carpenter: '1941 – Bomber in May' and 'Machine Shop: Nightshift'. Charles Causley: from *The Poetry of War: 1939–1945* ed. Ian Hamilton, Alan Ross Ltd, 1968. Louis Challoner: extract from 'Alternatives' © The Salamander Oasis Trust, from *Return to Oasis*, Shepherd-Walwyn Ltd. Robert A. Chaloner: extract from 'Home Front – 1942' from *More Poems from the Forces* ed. K. Rhys, Routledge, 1943. Alex Comfort: *Art and Social Responsibility*, © Books and Broadcasts Inc. Cyril Connolly: *The Missing Diplomats*, Weidenfeld & Nicolson, 1952; *The Unquiet Grave*, Hamish Hamilton 1945; *Horizon* No 17; 'The Condemned Playground' from *Essays: 1927–1944*, Routledge 1944; *Ideas and Places* (intro), Weidenfeld & Nicolson 1953. Robert Conquest: extracts from 'Poem in 1944', 'George Orwell' and 'Literature in Soho' (?) from *New and Collected Poems*, © 1988 Robert Conquest; Century Hutchinson, 1988; reprinted by permission of Curtis Brown, London. Herbert Corby: extract from 'Missing', Fortune Press. Timothy Corsellis: 'What I Never Saw' from *Poems of this War by Younger Poets*, eds P. Ledward and C. Strang, Cambridge University Press 1942. Quentin Crisp: *The Naked Civil Servant*, Gerald Duckworth & Co. Anthony Cronin: extract from *Dead as Doornails*, Anthony Cronin copyright 1976, reprinted by permission of John Calder (Publishers) Ltd. R. N. Currey: extracts from 'Boy With A Rifle' and 'Unseen Fire' from *This Other Planet*, Routledge, 1945; extracts from 'Troops Cinema' and 'Unconsidered Bodies' from *Poems From India*, OUP, 1946. Idries Davies: extract from 'London Welsh' from *Collected Poems*, Faber & Faber Ltd, reprinted by permission of E. Morris. Dan Davin: extract from *Closing Times*, OUP, 1975. Cecil Day Lewis: extract from 'Dedicatory Stanzas' from *The Georgics of Virgil*, and extracts from 'An Italian Visit', 'Newsreel', 'Will It Be So Again?', 'Where are the War Poets?', 'Word Over All', 'The Stand-To' from *Collected Poems*, 1954, reprinted by permission of The Hogarth Press and Jonathan Cape Ltd and the executors of the estate of C. Day Lewis; extract from 'In the Shelter' included in *Cecil Day Lewis: An English Literary Life* by Sean Day Lewis, Weidenfeld & Nicolson Ltd, 1980. Patric Dickinson: extracts from 'Introduction' from *Soldier's Verse*, Frederick Muller Ltd (part of the Century Hutchinson publishing group), 1945; extracts from 'Bombers: Evening' and 'A Warning to Politicians' from *Theseus and the Minotaur*, Cape, 1946; by permission of the author. Keith Douglas: extract from 'Cairo Jag' © Marie J. Douglas 1978; reprinted from *The Complete Poems of Keith Douglas* edited by Desmond Graham (1978) by permission of the Oxford University Press; extract from letter to J. C. Hall from *A Prose*

Miscellany, Carcanet Press Ltd. Tom Driberg: extract from 'Party Line', originally published in *Horizon*. Lawrence Durrell: extracts from 'Airgraph on Refugee Poets in Africa' from *Poetry London X*, copyright Lawrence Durrell 1944, and 'Journal to David Gascoyne' from *New English Weekly*, copyright Lawrence Durrell 1939, reprinted by permission of Curtis Brown Ltd. Clifford Dyment: extract from 'From Many a Mangled Truth a War is Won' from *Collected Poems*, Dent & Sons, 1970. T. S. Eliot: extract from *Notes Towards a Definitor of Culture*, 'Little Gidding' from *Collected Poems* and from preface of *A Little Book of Modern Verse* ed. Anne Ridler, reprinted by permission of Faber & Faber Ltd. William Empsom: extract from 'Let It Go' from *Collected Poems*, 1955, reprinted by permission of Lady Empson and The Hogarth Press. Gavin Ewart: extract from 'In the Old Days' reprinted by permission of the author. Constantine Fitzgibbon: extracts from *Through the Minefield*, The Bodley Head Ltd, *The Life of Dylan Thomas*, J. M. Dent & Sons Ltd, 1965, and *The Blitz*, Macdonald & Co Ltd, 1970. Theodora Fitzgibbon, extracts from *With Love*, Century Hutchinson Ltd, 1982. Olivia Fitzroy: extracts from 'Fleet Fighter' by permission of Viscount Daventry reprinted from *In Time of War*, edited by Anne Harvey, Blackie & Sons Ltd. Keith Footit: extract from 'Two Pairs of Shoes' from *For Your Tomorrow*, OUP, 1950. G. S. Fraser: extracts from 'Monologue to a Cairo Evening' and 'An Elegy for Stefan Schimanski' from *Poems of G. S. Fraser*, edited by Ian Fletcher and John Lucas, University of Leicester Press; extracts from *A Stranger and Afraid*, Carcanet Press, 1983; extracts from *The Modern Writer and His World* reprinted by permission of Mrs G. S. Fraser. Christopher Fry: extract from *A Sleep of Prisoners* (1951) reprinted by permission of Oxford University Press. Roy Fuller: extracts from 'Soliloquy in an Air Raid', 'November 1939', 'A Wry Smile', 'Saturday Night in a Sailor's House', from *New and Collected Poems 1934–84*, Martin Secker & Warburg; extracts from 'The Divided Life Re-lived' from *Epitaphs and Occasions*, John Lehmann Ltd, 1949; extract from introduction to *The Poetry of War* edited by I. Hamilton, Alan Ross Ltd, 1965; extract from introduction to *Kenneth Allott: Collected Poems*, Secker & Warburg Ltd, 1975. Robert Garioch: extract from 'The Prisoner's Dream' © South Side, Edinburgh, reprinted in *From Oasis Into Italy*, Shepheard-Walwyn Ltd. David Gascoyne: extract from *Paris Journal 1937–39*, Enitharmon Press, 1978 (to be reprinted by Skoob Books); extracts from 'Farewell Chorus' and 'Dreams in Oxford Street' from *Collected Poems*, OUP, 1988. John Gawsworth: extracts from *Diary (1)* and *Notebook 31. 1949*, reprinted by permission of the Estate of T. I. F. Armstrong ('John Gawsworth'). Francis Gelder: extract from 'A Ballad of 1941' from *Poems of the War by Younger Poets* eds. P. Ledward & C. Strang, Cambridge University Press,

1942. William Golding: extract from a review of Paul Fussell's *The Great War and Modern Memory*, *The Guardian*, 20 November, 1975, reprinted by permission of Faber & Faber Ltd. Virginia Graham: extracts from 'The Tumbrils' and 'A Thought for Denman Street' from *Consider the Years, 1938–1946*, Jonathan Cape Ltd. Henry Green: extracts from *Caught, Nothing, Party Going*, reprinted by permission of The Hogarth Press and the Estate of Henry Green. Graham Greene: extract from 'At Home' from *Collected Essays*, The Bodley Head. Geoffrey Grigson: from editorial comment in *New Verse* ed. Geoffrey Grigson, Macmillan. Barbara Guest: from *Herself Defined: The Poet H.D. and Her World*, William Collins, Sons & Co Ltd, 1985. Alec Guinness: extract from *Blessings in Disguise*, Hamish Hamilton, 1985. J. C. Hall: extract from 'Thirty Years' from *The Summer Dance and Other Poems*, John Lehmann Ltd, 1951; reprinted by permission of the author. Michael Hamburger: extract from *A Mug's Game* reprinted by permission of the author. Charles Hamblett: extract from 'Bombs on My Town' from *The Cactus Harvest and Other Poems*, Fortune Press, 1946. Patrick Hamilton: extract from *The Slaves of Solitude*, Constable & Co Ltd, 1947. Christopher Hassall: extract from 'Hats, Demob Depot, York' from *The Slow Night*, Arthur Barker, 1949; extracts from 'Sonnet XXVII' and 'Tube Shelter: Leicester Square, 1941' from *Crisis*, Heinemann. Desmond Hawkins: extract from 'Night Raid' from *Poetry in Wartime*, Faber & Faber Ltd. John Heath-Stubbs: extracts from 'Letter to David Wright', 'For George Barker at Seventy', 'The Divided Ways', 'The Pearl', 'Goodnight, Trees', 'Funeral Music' from *Collected Poems* Carcanet Press Ltd. Hamish Henderson: extracts from 'End of a Campaign' from *First Elegy* and 'Acroma' from *Sixth Elegy*, John Lehmann, 1948, reprinted by permission of Hamish Henderson. Mrs Robert Henrey: extract from *The Incredible City*, J. M. Dent & Sons, 1944. Julius Horowitz: extract from *Can I Get There by Candlelight?*, André Deutsch Ltd, 1964; extract from letter to Clement Greenberg reprinted by permission of Special Collections Department, Mugar Memorial Library, Boston University, and Mr Jonathan Horwitz. Aldous Huxley: extract from *Ape and Essence*, reprinted by permission of Mrs Laura Huxley and The Hogarth Press. Edward Hyams: extract from *William Medium*, The Bodley Head Ltd, 1947. John Jarmain: extract from 'Prisoners of War' from *Poems by John Jarmain*, William Collins, Sons & Co Ltd. Randall Jarrell: extracts from The Death of the Ball Turret Gunner', 'Losses' and 'A Camp in the Russian Forest' reprinted by permission of Faber & Faber Ltd from *The Complete Poems*. Sean Jennett: extract from 'Autumn, 1940' from *Always Adam*, Faber & Faber Ltd, 1943. C. E. M. Joad, extract from 'The Face of England', *Horizon*, 29. David Jones: extract from *Dai Greatcoat* reprinted by permission of Faber & Faber Ltd. Patrick

Kavanagh: extract from 'The Great Hunger' from *Collected Poems* reprinted by kind permission of Katherine B. Kavanagh, c/o Peter Fallon, Loughcrew, Oldcastle, County Meath, Ireland. David Kendall: extract from 'mediterranean convoy: homeward bound', Fortune Press, 1946. Gerald Kersh: extract from 'The Musicians' from *The Horrible Dummy and Other Stories* by Gerald Kersh, William Heinemann Ltd, 1944. Philip Larkin: extracts from 'Neurotics' and 'Modesties' reprinted by permission of Faber and Faber Ltd from *Collected Poems* by Philip Larkin. Christopher Lee: extract from 'Trahison des Clercs' from *Under the Sun*, The Bodley Head, 1948. Laurie Lee: extract from 'Look into Wombs and Factories and Behold' from *The Sun My Monument*, The Hogarth Press. John Lehmann: extracts from *In the Purely Pagan Sense* (G.M.P.), *I Am My Brother* (Longmans) and *The Ample Proposition* (Eyre & Spottiswoode). Alun Lewis: extracts from 'Lance Jack' from *Leaves in the Storm* (poetry collection published by Lindsay Drummond) and 'The Earth is a Syllable' from *In the Green Tree*, George Allen & Unwin Ltd, 1948. Jack Lindsay: extract from 'The Two Pulls' from *New Lyrical Ballads*, Nicholson & Watson, 1945. Julian Maclaren-Ross: extracts from *Memoirs of the Forties*, Alan Ross Ltd, 1965. Sorely Maclean: extract from 'Going Westwards' from *Aquarius, 17/18*, and extract from 'Knightsbridge, Libya' reprinted by permission of Sorely Maclean. Louis MacNeice: extracts from 'Alcohol' and 'Elegy for Minor Poets' reprinted by permission of Faber and Faber Ltd from *The Collected Poems of Louis MacNeice*. John Manifold: extracts from 'Camouflage' and 'The Deserter' from *Poems from the Forces* ed. K. Rhys, Routledge, 1943. George Melly: extract from introduction to *Soho in the Fifties* by Daniel Farson: © Daniel Farson 1987, introduction by George Melly, published by Michael Joseph Ltd. Alice Duer Miller: extract from 'The White Cliffs' from *The White Cliffs*, Methuen, 1940. James Monahan: extracts from 'The Feckless Years' and 'Ludgate Hill 1941' from *Far From the Land*, Macmillan. Henry Moore: from introduction to *A Shelter Notebook*, The Henry Moore Foundation/British Museum Publications Ltd, 1988. Nicholas Moore: extract from 'The Flag' from *The White Horseman*, Routledge, 1941. Malcolm Muggeridge: extract from 'The Beginning of the Forties' from *The Windmill* reprinted by permission of the author. Edwin Muir: extracts from 'The Refugees' and 'Scotland 1941' reprinted by permission of Faber & Faber Ltd from *Collected Poems* by Edwin Muir. Norman Nicholson: extract from 'Cleator Moor' from *Five Rivers* reprinted by permission of Faber and Faber Ltd. Daphne Nixon: extract from 'In These Five Years', Fortune Press, 1946. George Orwell: extracts from *Tribune* entry and from 'As One Non-Combatant to Another' from *Collected Essays: Journalism and Letters*, reprinted by permission of the estate of the late Sonia Brownwell Orwell and Secker & Warburg Ltd. Philip O'Connor: extracts from *Memoirs of a Public Baby*, Fourth Estate, 1988. Mervyn Peake: extract from 'Poem' from *The Glass Blower*, Eyre & Spottiswoode, 1940; extract from 'The Consumptive, Belsen' from *Poems*, Faber & Faber, reprinted by permission of the estate of Mervyn Peake; extract from 'Palais de Danse' from *Shapes and Sounds*, The Bodley Head, reprinted by permission of Mrs Maeve Peake. William Plomer: extract from 'The Bungalows' from *Collected Poems*, 1960, reprinted by permission of Jonathan Cape Ltd and the estate of William Plomer. James Pope-Hennessey: extract from *A Lonely Business: A Self-Portrait of James Pope-Hennessey* ed. P. Quennell, George Weidenfeld & Nicolson Ltd, 1981. Paul Potts: extracts from 'Inside', published in *Poetry London*, 1939, and *Dante Called You Beatrice*. Anthony Powell: extract from *Messengers of Day*, Heinemann, 1978. J. B. Priestley: extracts from *Out of the People*, Collins-Heinemann, 1941, and 'From the War – And After' from *Horizon*, 1, 1940, reprinted by permission of the Peters Fraser & Dunlop Group Ltd. V. S. Pritchett: extract from *Midnight Oil*, 1972, reprinted by permission of the author and Chatto & Windus. John Pudney: extracts from 'For Johnny' and 'Combat Report' from *Ten Summers*, The Bodley Head, 1942. Peter Quennell: extract from *The Wanton Chase*, Athenaeum, 1980. David Raikes: extract from 'Let It Be Hushed' from *For Your Tomorrow*, OUP, 1950. Herbert Read: extract from 'Vulgarity and Impotence', *Horizon*. Henry Reed: *A Map of Verona*, Jonathan Cape Ltd, 1946. Keidrych Rhys: extract from introduction to *Poems from the Forces* ed. K. Rhys, Routledge, 1943. Anne Ridler: extract from 'For This Time' from *The Nine Bright Shiners* reprinted by permission of Faber & Faber Ltd. W. R. Rodgers: extracts from 'Escape' and 'Censorship' reprinted by permission of the Estate of W. R. Rodgers. Alan Ross: extracts from 'J W 51 B', 'Arctic Convoy', 'Night-Train Images' from *Poems 1942–67*, Eyre & Spottiswoode, 1967; also from *Poetry 1945–1950* (British Council); from *Colours of War*, Jonthan Cape; from 'A Lament for the 'Thirties Poets', *Poetry Quarterly*, 1948; from *The Forties*, Weidenfeld & Nicolson, 1950; from 'Fitzrovia', *London Magazine*, December 1962; from introduction to J. Maclaren-Ross, *Memoirs of the Forties*, Alan Ross Ltd, 1965; all reprinted by permission of the author. Extracts from *Coastline Lights* (1988) and *Blindfold Games* (1984) are reprinted by permission of Collins Harvill. Joyce Rowe: extract from 'Dieppe' from *New Lyrical Ballads*, Nicholson & Watson, 1945; Sagittarius (Olga Katyin): extracts from 'Nothing Alien is Human', 'Paternoster Row', 'Strange Bedfellows', and 'The Passionate Profiteer to His Love' from *Quiver's Choice*, Jonathan Cape Ltd, 1945. William Sansom: extracts from Westminster at War, Faber & Faber, 1947, and 'The Wall' from *The Stories of William Sansom*, Hogarth Press, 1963. Francis Scarfe: extract from 'Grenade' from *More Poems from the Forces* ed. K. Rhys, Routledge, 1943; also from 'Lines Written in an Air Raid'. J. B. Sedgwick: extract from 'Khaki Soul' from *More Poems from the Forces* ed. K. Rhys, Routledge, 1943. John Burns Singer: extract from 'Cities are People' from *Little Review Anthology*, Eyre & Spottiswoode, 1946. Edith Sitwell: extracts from 'Lullaby', 'Still Falls The Rain', and 'The Shadow of Cain' from *Collected Poems*, Macmillan, 1957. Thomas Skelton: extract from 'Inside the A.F.V.', © The Salamander Oasis Trust, from *From Oasis into Italy*, Shepheard-Walwyn Ltd. Fred Smewin: 'Blitz Dinner' from *More Poems from the Forces* ed. K. Rhys, Routledge, 1943. Sidney Goodsir Smith: extract from 'October 1941' from *Collected Poems*, John Calder Ltd, 1975. Stephen Spender: extracts from 'Destruction and Resurrection', 'Air Raid Across the Bay at Plymouth', from *The Thirties and After* (Macmillan), *World Within World* (Hamish Hamilton), and 'To Poets and Airmen'. G. W. Stonier: extract from *Round London With a Unicorn*, Turnstile Press, 1951. Douglas Sutherland: extracts from *Portrait of a Decade*, Harrap Ltd, 1988. Randall Swingler: extract from 'Sixty Cubic Feet' from *New Lyrical Ballads*, Chatto & Windus. Julian Symons: extracts from selection in *Aquarius* 17/18, 'Conscript' and 'Hospital Observations' © Julian Symons, 1943. Tambimuttu: extract from 'The Spreading Cross' from *Out of This War: A Poem by Tambimuttu*, Fortune Press. A. S. J. Tessimond: extracts from 'The Lesser Artists', 'Smart-Boy', 'Song in a Saloon Bar' and 'London' from *Collected Poems of A. S. J. Tessimond*, Whitenights Press, reprinted by permission of H. Nicholson, editor and literary executor. Dylan Thomas: extracts from *The Collected Letters*, 'A Festival of Spoken Poetry' from *Adventures in the Skin Trade*, and 'Wales and the Artist' from *Quite Early One Morning*, all published by J. M. Dent & Sons Ltd. Terence Tiller: extract from 'Lecturing to Troops' from *Unarm, Eros*, The Hogarth Press, 1947. Ruthven Todd: extracts from 'In September 1939' and 'Garland for the Winter Solstice' from *Garland for the Winter Solstice*, J. M. Dent & Sons Ltd. A. T. Tolley: extract quoting Nicholas Moore on Caton from *Aquarius*, 17/18. Bertram Warr: extract from *Poems from the Forces* ed. K. Rhys, Routledge. Evelyn Waugh: extract from *Unconditional Surrender*, Chapman & Hall. Victor West: extract from 'La Belle Indifference' © Victor West from *Return to Oasis*, reprinted by permission of The Salamander Oasis Trust and Shepheard-Walwyn Ltd. Anna Wickham: extracts from 'The Sick Assailant' and 'Pugilist' from *Richard's Shilling Collection* (1936) from *The Writings of Anna Wickham: Free Woman and Poet*, Virago Press, 1984; copyright © James and George Hepburn. Edmund Wilson: extract from *The Forties* copyright © 1983 by Helen Miranda Wilson; reprinted by permission of Farrar, Strauss & Giroux, Inc. David Wright: extract from 'Verses on a Bohemian Funeral' from *New Poems, P. E. N. Anthology*, eds. Nott, Lewis & Blackburn, 1957; extract from *Deafness* reprinted by permission of A. D. Peters; extracts from 'On a Friend Dying' and 'A Stroll in Soho' from *To The Gods The Shades*, Carcanet Press Ltd, 1976. Richard B. Wright: extract from 'People in Safe Areas' from *More Poems from the Forces* ed. K. Rhys, Routledge, 1943. Joan Wyndham: extract from *Love is Blue*, William Heinemann Ltd, 1986.

INDEX